Jenni Currie Santamaría
ABC Adult School
Los Angeles Unified School District
Cerritos, CA

Mary Myers-Hall
ABC Adult School
Los Angeles Unified School District
Cerritos, CA

New Readers Press

English—No Problem!®
English—No Problem! Level 3 Teacher's Edition
ISBN 1-56420-353-0

New Readers Press
Division of ProLiteracy Worldwide
1320 Jamesville Avenue, Syracuse, New York 13210
www.newreaderspress.com

Printed in the United States of America
9 8 7 6 5 4 3 2

All proceeds from the sale of New Readers Press materials support literacy programs in the United States and worldwide.

Acquisitions Editor: Paula L. Schlusberg
Developer: Mendoza and Associates
Project Director: Roseanne Mendoza
Project Editor: Pat Harrington-Wydell
Content Editor: Rose DeNeve
Production Director: Heather Witt-Badoud
Designer: Kimbrly Koennecke
Cover Design: Kimbrly Koennecke
Cover Photography: Robert Mescavage Photography

Authors

Jenni Currie Santamaría
ABC Adult School
Los Angeles Unified School District
Cerritos, CA

Mary Myers-Hall
ABC Adult School
Los Angeles Unified School District
Cerritos, CA

Contributors

National Council Members
Audrey Abed, *San Marcos Even Start Program, San Marcos, TX*
Myra K. Baum, *New York City Board of Education (retired), New York, NY*
Kathryn Hamilton, *Elk Grove Adult and Community Education, Sacramento, CA*
Brigitte Marshall, *Oakland Adult Education Programs, Oakland, CA*
Teri McLean, *Florida Human Resources Development Center, Gainesville, FL*
Alan Seaman, *Wheaton College, Wheaton, IL*

Reviewers
Sabrina Budasi-Martin, *William Rainey Harper College, Palatine, IL*
Linda Davis-Pluta, *Oakton Community College, Des Plaines, IL*
Patricia DeHesus-Lopez, *Center for Continuing Education, Texas A&M University, Kingsville, TX*
Gail Feinstein Forman, *San Diego City College, San Diego, CA*
Carolyn Harding, *Marshall High School Adult Program, Falls Church, VA*
Trish Kerns, *Old Marshall Adult Education Center, Sacramento City Unified School District, Sacramento, CA*
Lydia Omori, *William Rainey Harper College, Palatine, IL*
Debe Pack-Garcia, *Manteca Adult School, Humbolt, CA*
Pamela Patterson, *Seminole Community College, Sanford, FL*
Catherine Porter, *Adult Learning Resource Center, Des Plaines, IL*
Jean Rose, *ABC Adult School, Cerritos, CA*
Eric Rosenbaum, *Bronx Community College Adult Program, Bronx, NY*
Laurie Shapero, *Miami-Dade Community College, Miami, FL*
Terry Shearer, *North Harris College Community Education, Houston, TX*
Abigail Tom, *Durham Technical Community College, Chapel Hill, NC*
Darla Wickard, *North Harris College Community Education, Houston, TX*

Pilot Teachers
Connie Bateman, *Gerber Adult Education Center, Sacramento, CA*
Jennifer Bell, *William Rainey Harper College, Palatine, IL*
Marguerite Bock, *Chula Vista Adult School, Chula Vista, CA*
Giza Braun, *National City Adult School, National City, CA*
Sabrina Budasi-Martin, *William Rainey Harper College, Palatine, IL*
Wong-Ling Chew, *Citizens Advice Bureau, Bronx, NY*
Renee Collins, *Elk Grove Adult and Community Education, Sacramento, CA*
Rosette Dawson, *North Harris College Community Education, Houston, TX*
Kathleen Edel, *Elk Grove Adult and Community Education, Sacramento, CA*
Margaret Erwin, *Elk Grove Adult and Community Education, Sacramento, CA*
Teresa L. Gonzalez, *North Harris College Community Education, Houston, TX*
Fernando L. Herbert, *Bronx Adult School, Bronx, NY*
Carolyn Killean, *North Harris College Community Education, Houston, TX*

Elizabeth Minicz, *William Rainey Harper College, Palatine, IL*
Larry Moore, *Long Beach Adult School, Long Beach, CA*
Lydia Omori, *William Rainey Harper College, Palatine, IL*
Valsa Panikulam, *William Rainey Harper College, Palatine, IL*
Kathryn Powell, *William Rainey Harper College, Palatine, IL*
Alan Reiff, *NYC Board of Education, Adult and Continuing Education, Bronx, NY*
Brenda M. Rodriguez, *San Marcos Even Start, San Marcos, TX*
Juan Carlos Rodriguez, *San Marcos Even Start, San Marcos, TX*
Joan Siff, *NYC Board of Education, Adult and Continuing Education, Bronx, NY*
Susie Simon, *Long Beach Adult School, Long Beach, CA*
Gina Tauber, *North Harris College, Houston, TX*
Diane Villanueva, *Elk Grove Adult and Community Education, Sacramento, CA*
Dona Wayment, *Elk Grove Adult and Community Education, Sacramento, CA*
Weihua Wen, *NYC Board of Education, Adult and Continuing Education, Bronx, NY*
Darla Wickard, *North Harris College Community Education, Houston, TX*
Judy Wurtz, *Sweetwater Union High School District, Chula Vista, CA*

Focus Group Participants
Leslie Jo Adams, *Laguna Niguel, CA*
Fiona Armstrong, *New York City Board of Education, New York, NY*
Myra K. Baum, *New York City Board of Education (retired), New York, NY*
Gretchen Bitterlin, *San Diego Unified School District, San Diego, CA*
Diana Della Costa, *Worksite ESOL Programs, Kissimmee, FL*
Patricia DeHesus-Lopez, *Center for Continuing Education, Texas A&M University, Kingsville, TX*
Frankie Dovel, *Orange County Public Schools, VESOL Program, Orlando, FL*
Marianne Dryden, *Region 1 Education Service Center, Edinburgh, TX*
Richard Firsten, *Lindsay Hopkins Technical Center, Miami, FL*
Pamela S. Forbes, *Bartlett High School, Elgin, IL*
Kathryn Hamilton, *Elk Grove Adult and Community Education, Sacramento, CA*
Trish Kerns, *Old Marshall Adult Education Center, Sacramento City Unified School District, Sacramento, CA*
Suzanne Leibman, *The College of Lake County, Grayslake, IL*
Patty Long, *Old Marshall Adult Education Center, Sacramento City Unified School District, Sacramento, CA*
Brigitte Marshall, *Oakland Adult Education Programs, Oakland, CA*
Bet Messmer, *Santa Clara Adult School, Santa Clara, CA*
Patricia Mooney, *New York State Board of Education, Albany, NY*
Lee Ann Moore, *Salinas Adult School, Salinas, CA*
Lynne Nicodemus, *San Juan Adult School, Carmichael, CA*
Pamela Patterson, *Seminole Community College, Sanford, FL*
Eric Rosenbaum, *Bronx Community College, Bronx, NY*
Federico Salas, *North Harris College Community Education, Houston, TX*
Linda Sasser, *Alhambra District Office, Alhambra, CA*
Alan Seaman, *Wheaton College, Wheaton, IL*
Kathleen Slattery, *Salinas Adult School, Salinas, CA*
Carol Speigl, *Center for Continuing Education, Texas A&M University, Kingsville, TX*
Edie Uber, *Santa Clara Adult School, Santa Clara, CA*
Lise Wanage, *CASAS, Phoenix, AZ*

Contents

Scope and Sequence

Unit Number and Title	Global Unit Theme (across all levels)	Unit Topic/Skill	Lesson-Specific Life Skills	Vocabulary	Language
Unit 1 Closing the Gap	Life stages: Personal growth and goal-setting	Opportunities for all ages	L1: Get information about local activities L2: Express agreement and disagreement L3: Decide which physical activities are best for you	Words that describe people and activities	Present-tense questions and statements Compound sentences
Unit 2 Smoothing Things Over	Making connections	Dealing with miscommunication	L1: Understand how body language can cause miscommunication L2: Make apologies and give explanations L3: Learn about American public behavior	Conflicts and resolutions	Past continuous and simple past Direct speech
Unit 3 Better Safe Than Sorry	Taking care of yourself	Making our lives safe	L1: Be able to report workplace accidents L2: Learn ways to make your home safer L3: Learn how to make your neighborhood safer	Safety words	Past-tense questions and answers Sentences with *when, before,* and *after*
Unit 4 Planning Ahead	Personal finance	Planning for financial security	L1: Understand how to interpret and choose health insurance L2: Interpret property insurance policies L3: Learn about different kinds of savings plans	Financial planning words	Sentences with *because* *Have to, must,* and *have got to*
Unit 5 Making Ends Meet	Consumer awareness	Different ways to shop	L1: Identify and describe product features L2: Learn about second-hand shopping L3: Find bargains in the newspaper	Shopping words	Superlative adjectives *Used to*

Culture	Pronunciation	Tasks and Unit Project	EFF Skill/Common Activity (The basic communication skills—read with understanding, convey ideas in writing, speak so others can understand, listen actively, and observe critically—are taught in every unit.)	SCANS Skills (The basic skills of reading, writing, listening, and speaking are taught in every unit.)	Technology
Women in sports	Contrasting sounds Linking	T1: Role-play a phone conversation T2: Write a conversation T3: Give a presentation UP: Presentation of community classes	Resolve conflict and negotiate	Exercise leadership Negotiate to arrive at a decision	Type, print, laminate, and bind the unit project information
Personal space and public behavior	Stress in negative vs. affirmative statements Syllable stress	T1: Write a letter T2: Write a conversation T3: Write a story UP: Write a skit	Observe critically	Work with cultural diversity Sociability	Search the Internet for information on cultural diversity and body language
Neighborhood safety	Past-tense endings Stress on important words	T1: Complete an accident report form T2: Design an escape route T3: Make a crime-prevention flyer UP: Make a safety poster	Solve problems and make decisions	Understand systems Improve and design systems	Use a computer to make a small version of the unit project poster and print copies
Saving for the future	Choice intonation Schwa in unstressed syllables	T1: Compare medical insurance plans T2: Analyze an insurance policy T3: Choose a savings account UP: Do a survey	Plan	Manage money Decision making	Search the Internet for information on affordable insurance
Second-hand shopping	Stress on superlative adjectives Reductions	T1: Find the best deal T2: Describe items for sale T3: Ask for information about items for sale UP: Classroom "garage sale"	Learn through research	Manage money Understand systems Decision making	Search a web site that sells second-hand items

Scope and Sequence

Unit Number and Title	Global Unit Theme (across all levels)	Unit Topic/Skill	Lesson-Specific Life Skills	Vocabulary	Language
Unit 6 Facing Problems Head On	Protecting your legal rights	Dealing with abuse	L1: Learn about drug and alcohol laws L2: Understand laws about child abuse L3: Learn about getting support	Words about abuse and support	Gerunds as subjects and objects Present perfect
Unit 7 Pitching In	Participating in your new country and community	Getting involved in your community	L1: Learn how to organize events L2: Learn about processes for change in the US L3: Describe positive personal qualities	Community involvement words	Verbs followed by gerunds Present perfect with *for* and *since*
Unit 8 Into Your Own Hands	Lifelong learning	Becoming a lifelong learner	L1: Learn ways to improve study habits L2: Use library resources L3: Understand enrollment procedures	Words for learning and planning	Future with *will* and *be going to* Polite requests with modals
Unit 9 Keeping Up with the Times	Celebrating success	Dealing with change	L1: Describe pros and cons L2: Learn about changing technology in the US L3: Describe the benefits of technology	Words about dealing with change	Present perfect continuous Present/future sentences with *if*

Culture	Pronunciation	Tasks and Unit Project	EFF Skill/Common Activity (The basic communication skills—read with understanding, convey ideas in writing, speak so others can understand, listen actively, and observe critically—are taught in every unit.)	SCANS Skills (The basic skills of reading, writing, listening, and speaking are taught in every unit.)	Technology
Disciplining children	Reduction of *-ing* Disappearing initial *h*	T1: Write a convincing argument T2: Write a handout about discipline T3: Write and practice a call to a hotline UP: Make a booklet	Take responsibility for learning Solve problems and make decisions	Understand systems Decision making Problem solving	Use the Internet to research hotlines and support groups
Processes for change	Diphthongs Stress on adjectives	T1: Plan a project T2: Write a petition T3:Make a personal qualities idea map UP: Make a poster for a community project	Cooperate with others Advocate and influence	Participate as a member of a team Exercise leadership Self-management	Use a computer to make a flyer announcing a community project
Opportunities for lifelong learning	Reduction of *be* and *will* Reduction of *would you* and *could you*	T1: Make a study plan T2: Narrow down a topic T3: Write about a topic of interest UP: Make a research action plan	Take responsibility for learning	Acquire and evaluate information Responsibility	Search the Internet for books about a research topic
Changing workplaces	Primary and secondary stress List intonation	T1: Weigh pros and cons T2: Rank the effects of technology in the community T3: Find someone who can help you learn to use technology UP: Teach how to use something	Use information and communications technology Learn through research	Select technology Apply technology to task Decision making	Use a computer to write directions for using an item of technology; illustrate them with art found on the Internet

About This Series

Meeting Adult Learners' Needs with *English—No Problem!*

English—No Problem! is a theme-based, performance-based series focused on developing critical thinking and cultural awareness and on building language and life skills. Designed for adult and young adult English language learners, the series addresses themes and issues meaningful to adults in the United States.

English—No Problem! is appropriate for and respectful of adult learners. These are some key features:

- interactive, communicative, participatory approach
- rich, authentic language
- problem-posing methodology
- project-based units and task-based lessons
- goal setting embedded in each unit and lesson
- units organized around themes of adult relevance
- contextualized, inductive grammar
- student materials designed to fit into lesson plans
- performance assessment, including tools for learner self-evaluation

Series Themes

Across the series, units have the following themes:

- Life Stages: Personal Growth and Goal Setting
- Making Connections
- Taking Care of Yourself
- Personal Finance
- Consumer Awareness
- Protecting Your Legal Rights
- Participating in Your New Country and Community
- Lifelong Learning
- Celebrating Success

At each level, these themes are narrowed to subthemes that are level-appropriate in content and language.

English—No Problem! Series Components

Five levels make up the series:

- literacy
- level 1 (low beginning)
- level 2 (high beginning)
- level 3 (low intermediate)
- level 4 (high intermediate)

The series includes the following components.

Student Book

A full-color student book is the core of each level of *English—No Problem!* Literacy skills, vocabulary, grammar, reading, writing, listening, speaking, and SCANS-type skills are taught and practiced.

Teacher's Edition

Each teacher's edition includes these tools:

- general suggestions for using the series
- scope and sequence charts for the level
- lesson-specific teacher notes with reduced student book pages
- complete scripts for all listening activities and Pronunciation Targets in the student book

Workbook

A workbook provides contextualized practice in the skills taught at each level. Activities relate to the student book stories. Workbook activities are especially useful for learners working individually.

 This icon in the teacher's edition indicates where workbook activities can be assigned.

Reproducible Masters

The reproducible masters include photocopiable materials for the level. Some masters are unit-specific, such as contextualized vocabulary and grammar activities, games, and activities focusing on higher-level thinking skills. Others are generic graphic organizers. Still other masters can be used by teachers, peers, and learners themselves to assess the work done in each unit.

Each masters book also includes scripts for all listening activities in the masters. (Note: These activities are not included on the *English—No Problem!* audio recordings.)

 This icon in the teacher's edition indicates where reproducible masters can be used.

Audio Recording

Available on CD and cassette, each level's audio component includes listening passages, listening activities, and Pronunciation Targets from the student book.

 This icon in the student book and teacher's edition indicates that the audio recording includes material for that activity.

Lesson-Plan Builder

This free, web-based *Lesson-Plan Builder* allows teachers to create and save customized lesson plans, related graphic organizers, and selected assessment masters. Goals, vocabulary lists, and other elements are already in the template for each lesson. Teachers then add their own notes to customize their plans.

They can also create original graphic organizers using generic templates.

When a lesson plan is finished, the customized materials can be printed and stored in PDF form.

This icon in the teacher's edition refers teachers to the *Lesson-Plan Builder,* found at www.enp.newreaderspress.com.

Vocabulary Cards

For literacy, level 1, and level 2, all vocabulary from the Picture Dictionaries and Vocabulary boxes in the student books is also presented on reproducible flash cards. At the literacy level, the cards also include capital letters, lowercase letters, and numerals.

Placement Tool

The Placement Test student booklet includes items that measure exit skills for each level of the series so that learners can start work in the appropriate student book. The teacher's guide includes a listening script, as well as guidelines for administering the test to a group, for giving an optional oral test, and for interpreting scores.

Hot Topics in ESL

These online professional development articles by adult ESL experts focus on key issues and instructional techniques embodied in *English—No Problem!,* providing background information to enhance effective use of the materials. They are available online at www.enp.newreaderspress.com.

Addressing the Standards

English—No Problem! has been correlated from the earliest stages of development with national standards for adult education and ESL, including the NRS (National Reporting System), EFF (Equipped for the Future), SCANS (Secretary's Commission on Achieving Necessary Skills), CASAS (Comprehensive Adult Student Assessment System) competencies, BEST (Basic English Skills Test), and SPLs (Student Performance Levels). The series also reflects state standards from New York, California, and Florida.

About the Student Books

Each unit in the student books includes a two-page unit opener followed by three lessons (two at the literacy level). A cumulative unit project concludes each unit. Every unit addresses all four language skills—listening, speaking, reading, and writing. Each lesson focuses on characters operating in one of the three EFF-defined adult roles—parent/family member at home, worker at school or work, or citizen/community member in the larger community.

Unit Opener Pages

Unit Goals The vocabulary, language, pronunciation, and culture goals set forth in the unit opener correlate to a variety of state and national standards.

Opening Question and Photo The opening question, photo, and caption introduce the unit protagonists and engage learners affectively in issues the unit explores.

Think and Talk This feature of levels 1–4 presents questions based on classic steps in problem-posing methodology, adjusted and simplified as needed.

What's Your Opinion? In levels 1–4, this deliberately controversial question often appears after Think and Talk or on the first page of a lesson. It is designed to encourage lively teacher-directed discussion, even among learners with limited vocabulary.

Picture Dictionary or Vocabulary Box This feature introduces important unit vocabulary and concepts.

Gather Your Thoughts In levels 1–4, this activity helps learners relate the unit theme to their own lives. They record their thoughts in a graphic organizer, following a model provided.

What's the Problem? This activity, which follows Gather Your Thoughts, encourages learners to practice another step in problem posing. They identify a possible problem and apply the issue to their own lives.

Setting Goals This feature of levels 1–4 is the first step of a unit's self-evaluation strand. Learners choose from a list of language and life goals and add their own goal to the list. The goals are related to the lesson activities and tasks and to the unit project. After completing a unit, learners revisit these goals in Check Your Progress, the last page of each workbook unit.

First Lesson Page

While the unit opener sets up an issue or problem, the lessons involve learners in seeking solutions while simultaneously developing language competencies.

Lesson Goals and EFF Role The lesson opener lists language, culture, and life-skill goals and identifies the EFF role depicted in that lesson.

Pre-Reading or Pre-Listening Question This question prepares learners to seek solutions to the issues presented in the reading or listening passage or lesson graphic that follows.

Reading or Listening Tip At levels 1–4, this feature presents comprehension and analysis strategies used by good listeners and readers.

Lesson Stimulus Each lesson starts with a reading passage (a picture story at the literacy level), a listening passage, or a lesson graphic. A photo on the page sets the situation for a listening passage. Each listening passage is included in the audio recording, and scripts are provided at the end of the student book and the teacher's edition. A lesson graphic may be a schedule, chart, diagram, graph, time line, or similar item. The questions that follow each lesson stimulus focus on comprehension and analysis.

Remaining Lesson Pages

Picture Dictionary, Vocabulary Box, and Idiom Watch These features present the active lesson vocabulary. At lower levels, pictures often help convey meaning. Vocabulary boxes for the literacy level also include letters and numbers. At levels 3 and 4, idioms are included in every unit.

Class, Group, or Partner Chat This interactive feature provides a model miniconversation. The model sets up a real-life exchange that encourages use of the lesson vocabulary and grammatical structures. Learners ask highly structured and controlled questions and record classmates' responses in a graphic organizer.

Grammar Talk At levels 1–4, the target grammatical structure is presented in several examples. Following the examples is a short explanation or question that guides learners to come up with a rule on their own. At the literacy level, language boxes highlight basic grammatical structures without formal teaching.

Pronunciation Target In this feature of levels 1–4, learners answer questions that lead them to discover pronunciation rules for themselves.

Chat Follow-Ups Learners use information they recorded during the Chat activity. They write patterned sentences, using lesson vocabulary and structures.

In the US This feature is a short cultural reading or brief explanation of some aspect of US culture.

Compare Cultures At levels 1–4, this follow-up to In the US asks learners to compare the custom or situation in the US to similar ones in their home countries.

Activities A, B, C, etc. These practice activities, most of them interactive, apply what has been learned in the lesson so far.

Lesson Tasks Each lesson concludes with a task that encourages learners to apply the skills taught and practiced earlier. Many tasks involve pair or group work, as well as follow-up presentations to the class.

Challenge Reading

At level 4, a two-page reading follows the lessons. This feature helps learners develop skills that prepare them for longer readings they will encounter in future study or higher-level jobs.

Unit Project

Each unit concludes with a final project in which learners apply all or many of the skills they acquired in the unit. The project consists of carefully structured and sequenced individual, pair, and group activities. These projects also help develop important higher-level skills such as planning, organizing, collaborating, and presenting.

Additional Features

The following minifeatures appear as needed at different levels:

One Step Up These extensions of an activity, task, or unit project allow learners to work at a slightly higher skill level. This feature is especially useful when classes include learners at multiple levels.

Attention Boxes These unlabeled boxes highlight words and structures that are not taught explicitly in the lesson, but that learners may need. Teachers are encouraged to point out these words and structures and to offer any explanations that learners require.

Remember? These boxes present, in abbreviated form, previously introduced vocabulary and language structures.

Writing Extension This feature encourages learners to do additional writing. It is usually a practical rather than an academic activity.

Technology Extra This extension gives learners guidelines for doing part of an activity, task, or project using such technology as computers, photocopiers, and audio and video recorders.

Assessment

Assessment is completely integrated into *English—No Problem!* This arrangement facilitates evaluation of class progress and provides a systematic way to set up learner portfolios. The pieces used for assessment are listed below. You may use all of them or select those that suit your needs.

Check Your Progress

Found on the last page of each workbook unit, this self-check is tied to the goals learners set for themselves in the student book unit opener. Learners rate their progress in life and language skills.

Unit Checkup/Review

For each unit, the reproducible masters include a two-page Unit Checkup/Review. You can use this instrument before each unit as a pretest or after each unit to assess mastery. If it is used both before and after, the score differential indicates a learner's progress.

Rubrics for Oral and Written Communication

The reproducible masters include a general rubric for speaking and one for writing (Masters 8 and 9). You can use these forms to score and track learner performance on the unit tasks and projects. Copy the rubric for each learner, circle performance scores, and include the results in the learner's portfolio.

Forms for Evaluating Projects or Tasks

For several tasks or projects, the reproducible masters include a form on which you can evaluate learner performance. Make a copy for each learner, record your assessment, and add the form to the learner's portfolio.

Peer Assessment

Peer assessment helps learners focus on the purpose of an activity. Encourage learners to be positive in their assessments of each other. For example, ask them to say one thing they liked about a presentation and one thing they did not understand. Use the Peer Assessment Form (Master 12 in the reproducible masters) when learners are practicing for a performance. Peer assessment is best used to evaluate groups rather than individuals and rehearsals rather than performances.

Self-Assessment

Self-assessment is a way for learners to measure their progress. Use the self-check masters (Masters 10 and 11 in the reproducible masters) at the beginning of Unit 1 and at the end of Units 3, 6, and 9. Then save them in learners' portfolios.

Ongoing Assessment

These minirubrics and guidelines for evaluating specific activities in the student book are integrated into the teacher notes. They often focus on assessing one particular language or life-skill function. You can include the pieces you evaluate in learners' portfolios. After using these resources, you will probably develop similar ways of assessing learners' progress on other activities.

Teaching Effectively with *English—No Problem!* Level 3

The following general suggestions for using level 3 of *English—No Problem!* can enhance your teaching.

Before beginning a unit, prepare yourself in this way:

- Read the entire set of unit notes.
- Gather the materials needed for the unit.
- Familiarize yourself with the student book and workbook pages.
- Prepare copies of masters needed for the unit.

Materials

The notes for each unit include a list of specific materials. These lists may not include the following, which are recommended for all or most units:

- large sheets of paper (butcher or flip-chart)
- magazines, newspapers, catalogs (to cut up)
- art supplies (scissors, glue, tape, colored pencils, markers, colored and plain paper, etc.)
- a "Treasure Chest" box or other container of prizes (new pencils, pens, erasers, rulers, stickers, hard candy, small candy bars, key chains, and things collected at conferences or found at dollar stores)

Grouping

Working in groups increases learner participation and builds teamwork skills, which are important in the workplace.

Learners can be grouped randomly. Four or five on a team allows for a good level of participation. For increased individual accountability, assign roles to group members. These commonly include

- group leader, who directs the group's activities
- recorder, who writes group responses
- reporter, who reports the group's responses to the whole class
- timekeeper, who lets everyone know how much time is left for an activity

Groups and roles within groups can be changed as needed.

Talking about the Photos

Contextualized color photos are used as starting points for many unit activities. Talking about the photos with learners is a good way to assess prior knowledge and productive vocabulary. For every photo, follow one or more of these suggestions:

- Ask general questions about what learners see: Who are the people in the photo? What is their relationship? Can you say anything about their ages, jobs, or nationalities? Where are they? What's happening? What do you think is going to happen next? Encourage learners to explain their answers.
- As learners name items in the photos, write new vocabulary on the board or an overhead transparency.

- If a photo has a lot of detail, groups can compete to list the most items or to write the most sentences about it. Make this more challenging by showing the photo for 30 seconds and asking the groups to work from memory.

Reading Titles and Captions

Focusing on titles and captions helps learners create a context for the unit or lesson.

Idiomatic Unit and Lesson Titles Level 3 of *English—No Problem!* emphasizes idioms. Many unit and lesson titles are idiomatic. Discuss the vocabulary in these titles, and talk about the literal meaning of the words. Definitions are suggested in the teacher notes. Ask learners if they know the idioms or can guess what they mean. Provide examples of when you might use the idioms, and ask learners to think of more examples.

Other Titles Discuss vocabulary appearing in titles. Ask learners to talk about how the titles relate to the lessons. In some cases, you can ask learners to predict what will happen in the story.

Captions Use the captions to discuss the characters and the story. Ask questions like these: Do you know anyone like this or in this situation? What do you think the character will do?

Identifying and Analyzing Problems

The questions in What's the Problem? set up the central issue for the unit. Directions in the student book are purposely open-ended ("Think or talk with a partner."). Learners may think about the questions individually or discuss them with a partner or group. If they discuss the questions, ask volunteers to share ideas from their small groups. Then follow up with a class discussion.

Setting Goals

Write the goals listed in the student book on large strips of paper. Then follow these steps:

- Post the goals around the room.
- Have each learner stand next to his or her number one goal.
- Count the number of people in each group and rank the goals for your class.
- Ask the group standing next to each goal to discuss why they chose that goal as most important for them.
- Ask one learner from each group to share the group's reasons with the class.

You can use this activity to discuss the concepts of majority, fractions, and proportion.

Listening Comprehension

One lesson in each unit is driven by a listening passage, such as a recorded phone message, conversation, speech, or commercial announcement. There are also other listening activities, including dictations.

Ideally, you will have access to a cassette or CD player and will be able to use the *English—No Problem!* audio recording. The recording allows learners to hear a variety of native-speaker and non-native-speaker voices. For teachers who need or prefer to read the audio portions, scripts for listening passages and selected activities are printed on pages 118–120 of the student book. Complete scripts for the passages and for all student book listening activities are on pages 118–124 of this book.

In doing listening activities, the following sequence is recommended:

- Review the directions.
- Play the audio or read the listening script as often as learners want.
- If the passage is long, play a short section and ask learners questions about what they heard.
- Have learners exchange papers or books to correct their answers.
- Have volunteers write answers on the board or an overhead transparency.

Reading Comprehension

The readings in *English—No Problem!* are designed to be as useful as possible to adult English language learners. They are modeled on practical documents that adults want and need to read in everyday life. The reading lessons present the strategies and skills needed to successfully navigate such documents.

Attention Boxes The words in these unlabeled boxes are not active vocabulary, but learners will need them to understand the passage. When possible, demonstrate each word by pointing or miming. Pronounce each word and elicit a definition from the class. Write the words and definitions on the board or an overhead transparency. Then write a sample sentence for each word.

Reading Tips Each tip focuses on a reading strategy, for example, scanning for specific information or predicting content. Help learners apply these strategies to other student book and workbook readings.

In-Class Reading Follow some or all of these suggestions when learners read in class:

- Ask learners to read the passage silently first. They can mark any problem words, but they should not open their dictionaries at this point.

- Read the passage aloud so that learners can hear correct pronunciation of the words.
- Encourage learners to answer comprehension questions before dealing with new vocabulary. Have learners discuss questions in pairs or write answers individually before they answer.
- Review problem vocabulary and ask learners to read the passage aloud in pairs or in groups.

Introducing Vocabulary

Read the words aloud and have learners repeat them after you. Elicit definitions or sample sentences for vocabulary words that learners already know, and write them on the board or an overhead transparency. Then ask learners to write sentences in pairs. Collect the sentences, or ask volunteers to write one of their sentences on the board or transparency. Focus on the meaning of the vocabulary word rather than on grammar.

One Step Up After learners have discussed their sentences, do the following:

- Write headings such as *Noun, Verb,* and *Adjective* on the board or an overhead transparency. Refer learners to the list on page 126 of the student book for definitions of grammatical terms. Ask learners to categorize the vocabulary words. Some words will fall into more than one category.
- Elicit alternate forms of the words (e.g., *enthusiasm, enthusiastic*). Some alternate forms are introduced in the student book.

Reinforcing Vocabulary

The words in the Vocabulary boxes are used often in the student book and the workbook. These activities can provide further reinforcement:

- Put each word on a large vocabulary card. Use the cards throughout the unit to review meaning, pronunciation, and form.
- Distribute vocabulary cards to small groups of learners. Ask each group to pronounce the word, give its alternate forms, and create a sentence using the word.
- Use story writing to reinforce both meaning and use of vocabulary. First create a sample story that uses your own set of five words. Write the words on the board or an overhead transparency. Tell learners the story, or write it on the board too. Then give each group a set of five words and a large piece of paper. Some words may appear in more than one set, or you can include words from previous units. Ask each group to create a story using all of its words. Emphasize that although the story can be silly, it should make sense. It is not necessary to put a vocabulary word in every sentence.

Writing Skills

At this level, learners are moving from writing single sentences to writing short paragraphs. The writing activities in the student book emphasize supporting main ideas with related details and using correct paragraph form. Do not try to correct every mistake in learners' writing. Learners need to be aware of the *focus* of the writing activity, and your corrections should help them focus.

Writing well involves both fluency and accuracy. To help learners develop fluency, have them write often, but do not always collect and correct their writing. Rather, ask them sometimes to share their writing in groups and to respond to the content. This helps them learn to communicate ideas effectively.

Partner/Group Chats

While learners are conversing in pairs or groups, circulate; join as many conversations as possible. Pair fluent learners with learners who have more difficulty.

Role-Plays

When learners role-play, encourage them to think about the beginning and end of the conversation. How will the people greet each other? How will they say good-bye? Put commonly used phrases on the board so that learners can use them for greeting, introducing, thanking, and saying good-bye. Discuss the level of formality appropriate for the situation. After learners finish, ask volunteers to perform role-plays for the class.

For telephone role-plays, position learners back-to-back to better simulate phone use.

Grammar

The student book deliberately uses only essential grammatical terminology. Each Grammar Talk includes example sentences and questions to help learners arrive at the grammar concept deductively. Follow these steps to introduce a grammar point:

- Read the sentences to learners.
- Ask learners to repeat.
- Discuss the questions as a class. (Suggested answers are included in the teacher notes.)
- Elicit more example sentences and write them on the board or an overhead transparency.
- Discuss any specific issues related to the grammar point, and answer learners' questions.

A list of grammatical terms appears on page 126 in the student book.

Pronunciation

Many adult ESL series give scant attention to pronunciation, but *English—No Problem!* gives it proper emphasis within an array of integrated skills.

Stress Word and sentence stress, which are so important for good English pronunciation, are often overlooked by learners themselves, who tend to focus on challenging sounds.

When teaching a new word, elicit the stress and number of syllables from learners. Use chants or songs to practice stress and rhythm. When learners are preparing to role-play, have them exaggerate syllable length and intonation. (Hiiiiii! How've you beeeen lately?) Demonstrate how drawn-out syllables and question intonation can signal friendliness as well as providing important clues to meaning.

Reductions Closely tied to sentence and word stress is the issue of reduced vowel sounds. Most unstressed vowels in English have the schwa ("uh") sound. When learners stress an unstressed vowel, it interferes with the rhythm of their speech. When teaching a new word, point out which vowels have reduced pronunciation.

Voiced and Voiceless Sounds The words *voiced* and *voiceless* are not used in the student book, but the issue comes up in Unit 1 (contrasting sounds) and Unit 3 (past-tense endings). *Voiced* sounds produce a vibration in the voice box. They include all vowel sounds as well as most consonant sounds. Ask learners to touch their throats while pronouncing *go, run,* or *name.* They should feel a vibration in the throat. *Voiceless* sounds are softer and do not cause the voice box to vibrate. There are eight voiceless sounds in English: /f/, /s/, /th/ (as in *think*), /sh/, /ch/, /p/, /t/, and /k/.

The voiced/voiceless distinction is tied to several important issues in English pronunciation:

- Voiceless sounds followed by *s* produce an /s/ rather than a /z/ sound: *bets* vs. *beds.*
- Adding a regular past-tense ending to a verb that ends in a voiceless sound other than /t/ produces a /t/ rather than a /d/ sound: *tapped* (tap<u>t</u>) vs. *tagged* (tag<u>d</u>).
- Vowels are shortened before voiceless consonants: *rope* is shorter than *robe.*

Unit Project

Prepare learners for the unit project at the beginning of each unit. During the introduction, tell them what they will be doing at the end of the unit. Highlight information and materials that may be needed for the project as they come up in the unit.

Customizable Graphic Organizers

The teacher notes indicate when to use one of the Customizable Graphic Organizers in the reproducible masters. Gather Your Thoughts in each unit opener and the Class/Group/Partner Chats almost always can be done using one of these forms. Follow these steps to customize one of these masters:

- Make one copy of the Customizable Graphic Organizer (chart, idea map, etc.) appropriate for the activity you are doing.
- Fill in the heads as shown in the student book.
- Duplicate enough copies for each learner or group and distribute them.

After learners complete their graphic organizers, conduct a chat debriefing:

- Draw a large chart on the board or an overhead transparency.
- Fill in the appropriate headings.
- Ask learners to read the answers they recorded on their individual charts.
- Write the answers on the large chart.

Tried-and-True Techniques and Games for Low Intermediate Learners

Use these lively activities as needed to reinforce previous instruction and to create a dynamic learning environment.

Listening and Writing Activity

This writing activity also helps learners listen for main ideas:

- Tell learners that you are going to read a story or paragraph. Explain that they will need to remember the content without taking notes.
- Use a simple story or paragraph with familiar vocabulary. Read it aloud at a normal speed twice.
- Ask groups to discuss what they remember.
- Read the story or paragraph a third time.
- Give each group a large piece of paper and ask them to re-create the story. Stress that it is not important to use the exact words you did. The purpose is to capture the content.

Use pictures with this activity to help learners remember the content.

Jigsaw Reading

Jigsaws help learners practice all language skills and require real communication. This type of activity can be done with any piece of text that can be divided into four sections. Choose text with previously learned vocabulary. You may also want to use an illustration or photo for each section of text. Jigsaws work best when completed in one session. You may also find that they work best when used at the end of a unit.

Follow these steps:

- Prepare questions or a task that requires learners to synthesize information from all sections of the text (e.g., read about four people and decide which you would hire, read about four apartments and decide which you would rent, read about someone's life and identify the most important, happiest, and saddest events).
- Model a jigsaw for learners and walk them through each step. First, divide the text into four sections and put one section in each corner of the room. Then put learners in groups of four. Each person from a group goes to a different corner of the room to read and learn the information there. (If your class does not divide evenly into groups of four, put five learners in some groups. Have two learners look at the same information in those groups.)
- Have learners return to their original groups to share the information they have learned. Learners should not take notes until they are back in their groups.
- Once learners return to their groups, they can complete the task or answer the questions together. Allow them time to read the task or questions and to practice telling their part of the story to one another.

Password

Make vocabulary cards for the unit vocabulary words. Divide the class into teams. Hold a card over the head of a learner on the first team so that the rest of the team can read the card. Team members then describe the word using definitions or examples; if anyone uses native language, the team loses its turn.

If the learner guesses the word within 30 seconds, the team gets a point and the word card is removed from play. If the learner cannot guess the word in the allotted time, the card is put back in the middle of the deck and the second team takes a turn. The game is over when all the cards are gone; the team with the most points wins.

Concentration

Make flash cards for the unit vocabulary words with the definition on one card and the word another. Then walk learners through a few rounds of the game:

- Keeping words and definitions separate, learners arrange the cards in rows, facedown on the table.
- Each learner takes a turn turning over one word card and one definition card and reading them aloud.
- If the cards do not match, the learner turns them facedown again in the same place. Play then passes to another learner.
- A learner who finds a matching pair keeps the cards.
- The game ends when all the cards are gone; the learner with the most matches wins.

You can model this game using an overhead projector. Make a transparency of the words and definitions and cover each with a small piece of card stock. Remove and replace the pieces until you make a match.

If the class is large, learners can play this game in smaller groups. Monitor learners to make sure they read the cards aloud as they turn them over.

Bingo

Playing bingo is another good way to review vocabulary. Prepare sets of definition cards for the words to be reviewed—one definition on each card. You will need at least 16 words. Learners play this game in groups of four; make a set of cards for each group.

Ask learners to make their own 16-square bingo cards by folding a piece of paper in half twice horizontally and twice vertically. Write the vocabulary words on the board or an overhead transparency. Ask learners to choose words randomly and write a word in each square on their bingo cards. Circulate to be sure that they are writing the words in random order.

First play one game as a class. Give each learner a pile of markers—dried beans, paper clips, pennies, or small squares of card stock. Shuffle a set of definition cards. Read the first definition and have learners place a marker on the word on their bingo cards that matches the definition. The first learner to mark a row of four words down, across, or diagonally calls "Bingo!" and wins. Ask winners to read out the words they have marked and tell you the meanings.

Once learners understand the game, divide the class into groups of four and give a set of definition cards to each group. Each group should choose one member to be the caller who will read the definitions. After someone reaches bingo, the group should play again with a new caller.

Flyswatter

This game can be played in front of the class with two flyswatters.

Write unit vocabulary words on an overhead transparency, spreading them out so they are spaced around the glass. Divide the class into two teams. One member of each team holds a flyswatter and stands near the projector screen.

Read a definition. The first learner to hit the correct word on the screen earns a point for the team. Then the flyswatter is passed to another team member. Team members can help by yelling answers, but learners may hit the screen only once. They are not allowed to change their minds and try a new word.

Flyswatter can also be played to reinforce spelling (you read a word, and learners hit the correct spelling) or grammar (you read a sentence with a missing word, and learners hit the correct word).

Question Exchange

Use this activity to practice a particular grammar point.

Write questions using the grammar point. The questions should be ones learners can answer from their own experience (e.g., "Where did you go last weekend?" to practice the past tense). Write each question on an index card, and give a card to each learner. (It is all right for some learners to have the same questions.)

Learners stand up and find a partner. Partners then ask each other the questions they are holding. When they finish talking, they exchange questions; then each finds a new partner to answer the new question. Encourage learners to talk about their experiences, not to just give one-word answers.

For a follow-up activity, ask each learner to write on the board or an overhead transparency one memorable thing he or she discovered about another learner. Then have all learners together correct the sentences.

Unit 1: Closing the Gap

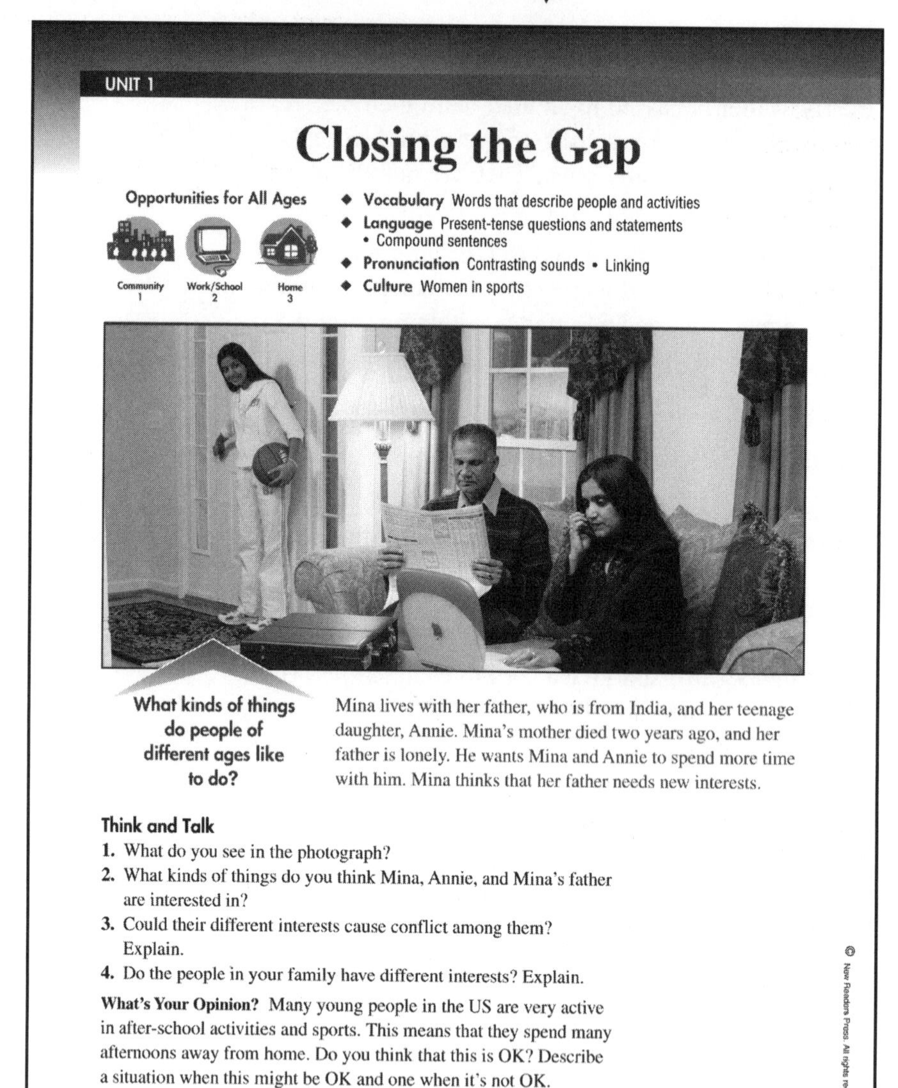

UNIT 1

Closing the Gap

Opportunities for All Ages

Community 1 · Work/School 2 · Home 3

- **Vocabulary** Words that describe people and activities
- **Language** Present-tense questions and statements • Compound sentences
- **Pronunciation** Contrasting sounds • Linking
- **Culture** Women in sports

What kinds of things do people of different ages like to do?

Mina lives with her father, who is from India, and her teenage daughter, Annie. Mina's mother died two years ago, and her father is lonely. He wants Mina and Annie to spend more time with him. Mina thinks that her father needs new interests.

Think and Talk

1. What do you see in the photograph?
2. What kinds of things do you think Mina, Annie, and Mina's father are interested in?
3. Could their different interests cause conflict among them? Explain.
4. Do the people in your family have different interests? Explain.

What's Your Opinion? Many young people in the US are very active in after-school activities and sports. This means that they spend many afternoons away from home. Do you think that this is OK? Describe a situation when this might be OK and one when it's not OK.

10 *Unit 1*

Materials for the Unit

- Telephones (if available) for telephone role-play
- Clothing catalogs or magazines with pictures of people
- Brochures and class schedules from community organizations offering recreational activities
- Customizable Masters 2–4, 7
- Generic Assessment Masters 8, 10–12
- Unit Masters 13–19

Self-Assessment

Before starting Unit 1, give each learner a copy of the Speaking and Listening Self-Checks and the Writing and Reading Self-Checks (Generic Assessment Masters 10–11). Go over the assessments together. The completed forms will become part of each learner's portfolio.

Closing the Gap

Follow the suggestions on p. 5 for talking about the title.

Discuss the meaning of the word *gap* (a space between two things; an unfilled period of time):

- To provide a simple visual example, draw two squares with a space between them. The space represents the gap.
- Draw arrows connecting the squares to illustrate the idiom *closing the gap,* which can be used to describe catching up in a race or coming closer together.

Photo

Follow the suggestions on p. 4 for talking about the photo; then read the question below the arrow.

Caption

Follow the suggestions on p. 5 for talking about captions.

Think and Talk

Read the questions aloud. As learners generate answers, write them on the board or an overhead transparency.

What's Your Opinion?

Have learners consider the issue presented and then discuss their opinions.

Some examples of situations when spending afternoons away from home might be OK include these:

- The parents encourage their children to be active.
- The parents enjoy being involved with their children's activities.
- The children's activities don't interfere with homework time.

Some examples of situations when this might not be OK include these:

- A child is doing poorly in school.
- Teammates are a bad influence.
- Teams spend the night away from home.
- Overly competitive activities produce undue stress.

Vocabulary

Follow the suggestions on p. 6 for introducing and reinforcing vocabulary words.

Extension

Point out the different stress patterns in the verb *conflict* and the noun *conflict.*

One Step Up

Follow the suggestions on p. 6 for categorizing vocabulary words as nouns, verbs, and adjectives.

- Nouns: *confidence, conflict, generation, opportunity*
- Verbs: *conflict, fulfill, join, participate*
- Adjectives: *confident*

Gather Your Thoughts

Use Customizable Master 4 (Idea Map). Follow the directions on p. 7 for customizing and duplicating the master and distributing the copies.

- Divide learners into small groups.
- Ask them to think about and discuss what activities people they know like to do.
- Have learners complete their idea maps.

If the groups have difficulty generating ideas on their own, brainstorm activities as a class and then have the groups categorize them.

What's the Problem?

Follow the suggestions on p. 5 for identifying and analyzing problems.

Setting Goals

Follow the suggestions on p. 5 for setting goals.

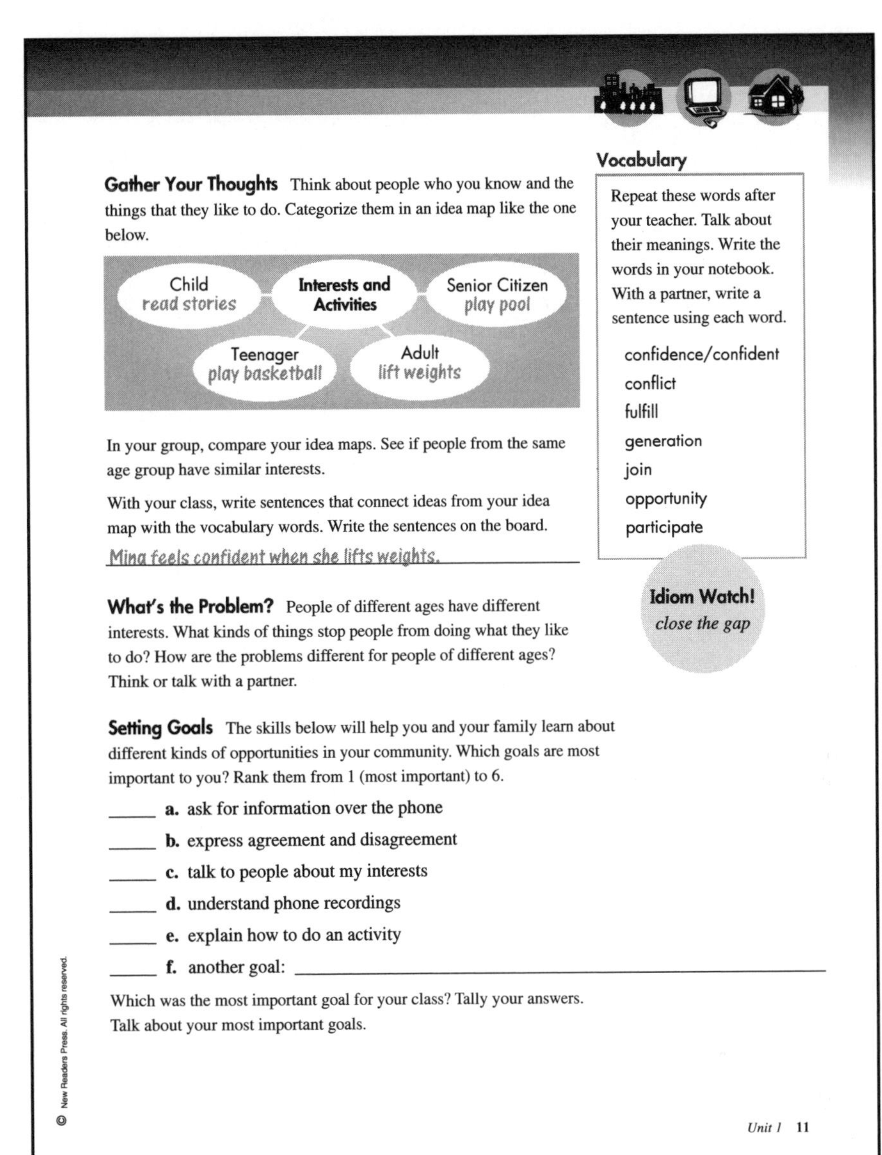

Gather Your Thoughts Think about people who you know and the things that they like to do. Categorize them in an idea map like the one below.

In your group, compare your idea maps. See if people from the same age group have similar interests.

With your class, write sentences that connect ideas from your idea map with the vocabulary words. Write the sentences on the board.

Mina feels confident when she lifts weights.

What's the Problem? People of different ages have different interests. What kinds of things stop people from doing what they like to do? How are the problems different for people of different ages? Think or talk with a partner.

Setting Goals The skills below will help you and your family learn about different kinds of opportunities in your community. Which goals are most important to you? Rank them from 1 (most important) to 6.

_____ **a.** ask for information over the phone

_____ **b.** express agreement and disagreement

_____ **c.** talk to people about my interests

_____ **d.** understand phone recordings

_____ **e.** explain how to do an activity

_____ **f.** another goal: ______________________________

Which was the most important goal for your class? Tally your answers.
Talk about your most important goals.

Vocabulary

Repeat these words after your teacher. Talk about their meanings. Write the words in your notebook. With a partner, write a sentence using each word.

confidence/confident
conflict
fulfill
generation
join
opportunity
participate

Idiom Watch!
close the gap

Lesson 1: Activities for Young and Old

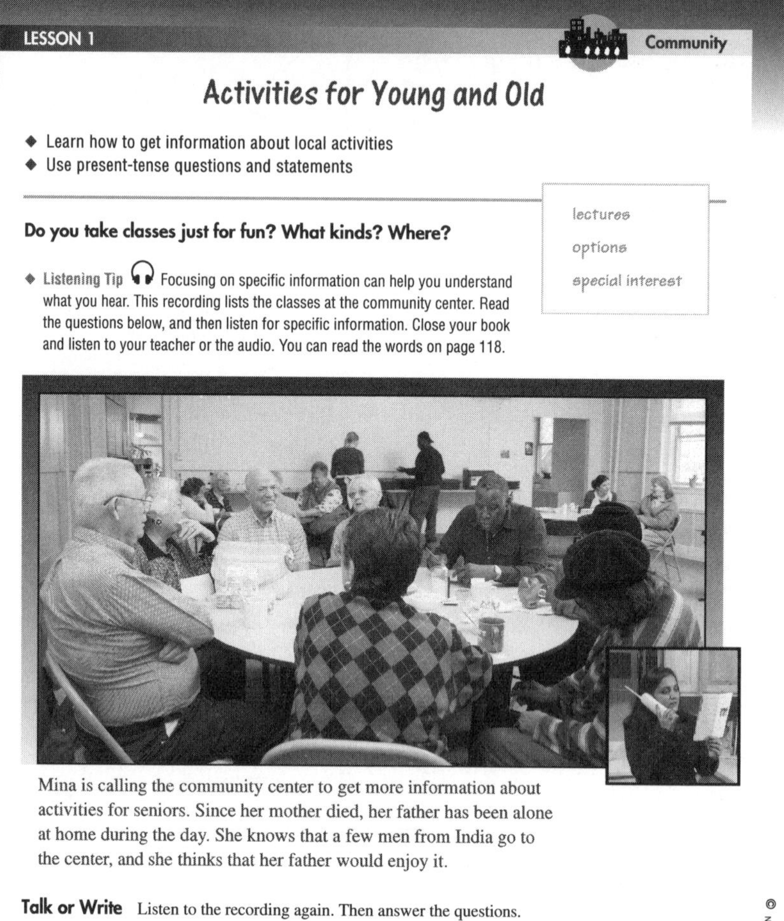

LESSON 1 — Community

Activities for Young and Old

- Learn how to get information about local activities
- Use present-tense questions and statements

lectures
options
special interest

Do you take classes just for fun? What kinds? Where?

- **Listening Tip** Focusing on specific information can help you understand what you hear. This recording lists the classes at the community center. Read the questions below, and then listen for specific information. Close your book and listen to your teacher or the audio. You can read the words on page 118.

Mina is calling the community center to get more information about activities for seniors. Since her mother died, her father has been alone at home during the day. She knows that a few men from India go to the center, and she thinks that her father would enjoy it.

Talk or Write Listen to the recording again. Then answer the questions.

1. Which number do you press for information about teen basketball?
2. What age group can participate in senior activities?
3. How many days a week is the community center open?
4. What does Mina ask for? Why does she spell her last name?

12 *Unit 1 Lesson 1*

Follow the suggestions on p. 5 for talking about the lesson title.

Questions

Read the questions above the photo. Encourage good listening skills by asking more questions about learners' responses (e.g., What class did Maria take? Where did she take the class?).

Attention Box

This vocabulary should be understood, but learners should not be expected to produce the words at this point.

Listening Tip

Before beginning this exercise, have learners read the questions at the bottom of the page. Then play the audio or read the listening script on p. 118.

One Step Down

Divide the exercise into three parts.

Part 1

Before playing or reading the first part of the listening passage, write the following questions on the board or an overhead transparency:

- What number do you press for location and hours? *(1)*
- What number do you press for a youth activities schedule? *(2)*
- What number do you press for adult special-interest classes? *(3)*
- What number do you press for activities for seniors? *(4)*
- Who answers when you press zero? *(operator)*

After the direction "To hear these options again, press *five,*" stop and play the audio again. Have learners answer the questions on the board.

Part 2

Before playing or reading the second part of the listening passage, ask learners to listen for activities offered for seniors.

- Stop after the direction "Please leave your name and address after the tone." Play or read Part 2 again.
- Have learners tell you which activities are for seniors and write them on the board or an overhead transparency.

Answers

exercise, craft classes, sports and games, travel opportunities, special-interest clubs, movies, health lectures

Part 3

Ask learners to write Mina's last name and address as they listen to the third part of the listening passage.

Replay the audio or read the listening script as often as necessary.

Talk or Write

Play the audio or read the listening script again. This time, ask learners to listen for details. Then have them answer the questions.

Answers

1. two
2. 50 and older
3. six (Monday through Saturday)
4. a brochure; so her name will appear correctly on the envelope

Group Chat

Use Customizable Master 2 (3-Column Chart). Follow the suggestions on p. 7 for customizing and duplicating the master and distributing the copies.

- After the Group Chat, discuss which activities are most popular.
- If learners are of different ages, discuss whether their interests are the same or different.

Vocabulary

Follow the suggestions on p. 6 for introducing and reinforcing vocabulary words.

To check comprehension, ask volunteers to act out or mime vocabulary words, and have other learners guess what each word is.

Grammar Talk

Follow the suggestions on p. 6 for introducing the grammar point.

Suggested Answers

- The second, third, and fourth questions have *do* or *does* because the main verb is not *be* and requires the helping verb *do/does.*
- The first, second, and third statements have verbs that end in *s* because they are third person singular verbs with no helping verb.
- Present-tense questions with *be* begin with *Is* or *Are,* followed by the subject. Present-tense answers with *be* begin with the subject, followed by *is* or *are.* In present-tense questions that require *do* or *does,* the main verb stays in the base (simple) form.

Pronunciation Target

Play the audio or read the sentences in the student book.

- Point out that the Vocabulary box contains many plural nouns. Learners often drop the final *s* when they are speaking. Model and practice final *s* sounds to help learners focus on this sound.

Group Chat Talk to your group about activities that you like and don't like. Ask each other these questions. Take notes in a chart like this one.

What's your name?	What do you like?	What don't you like?
Sonya	swimming	cheerleading

Vocabulary

Repeat these words after your teacher. Talk about their meanings. Write the words in your notebook. With a partner, write a sentence using each word.

aerobics
ceramics
cheerleading
chess
crafts
gymnastics
lectures
martial arts

Grammar Talk: Present-Tense Questions and Statements

Is the Senior Center open on Sundays?	The Senior Center **isn't** open on Sundays.
Does the Senior Center **offer** aerobics?	The Senior Center **offers** aerobics.
When **does** the Senior Center **open**?	The Senior Center **opens** at 7:30 A.M.
Where **do** we **go** for lectures?	We **go** to room 23 for lectures.

Which questions have do *or* does*? Why? Which statements have verbs that end in* s*? Why do they end in* s*? With your class, write rules for present-tense questions and answers with* be *and with other verbs.*

Pronunciation Target • Linking

Listen to your teacher or the audio.

What time does the park open? Do you have activities for seniors?
When does this class end? The center offers aerobics.

A consonant sound at the end of a word links, or connects, *to the beginning vowel of the next word. Practice linking the underlined sounds from the sentences above.*

Activity A Listen to your teacher or the audio. Write the sentences that you hear. Listen again and check your writing for correct punctuation. Can you find the linking sounds? Underline the linking sounds. Practice the sounds by reading the sentences to your partner.

- The pronunciation of final *s* is affected by voiced and voiceless sounds. (See p. 7 for an explanation of final voiced and voiceless sounds.) All of these words are pronounced with a final /s/ sound except for *lectures,* which is pronounced with a /z/ sound.

Activity A

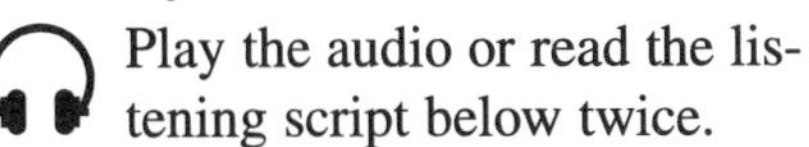

Play the audio or read the listening script below twice.

Listening Script/Answers

Listen. Write the sentences that you hear.

1. Is the pool open today?
2. The ceramics class meets in room 30.
3. When does the guitar class end?
4. The gymnastics class starts at 10 A.M.
5. They offer aerobics.

Listen again and check your writing for correct punctuation. Then underline the linking sounds.

Ask volunteers to write the sentences on the board. Correct the sentences together.

Assign Workbook pp. 4–5.

Activity C

Play the audio or read the listening script below twice. The first time, ask learners to just listen; then have them listen and fill in the blanks.

Listening Script/Answers

1. Do you <u>think</u> that aerobics is fun?
2. <u>Does</u> the community college offer aquatics?
3. <u>Is</u> cheerleading popular in your home country?
4. <u>What</u> do people make in a ceramics class?
5. Do you <u>know</u> how to play chess?
6. Do you like to <u>do</u> crafts?
7. What kinds of lectures <u>are</u> interesting to you?
8. <u>Where</u> can children learn gymnastics?
9. <u>Do</u> many people practice martial arts in your home country?

Listen again and fill in the missing words.

Task 1

Before learners role-play, review language for clarifying information over the telephone:

Could you repeat that, please?
Could you spell that, please?
Did you say 8:00?

Some learners may benefit from practicing letter/word correspondences for spelling (e.g., *A* as in *apple*, *B* as in *boy*).

Ongoing Assessment

- Circulate to listen to at least four or five pair conversations.
- Take notes on how well learners do on the following criteria:
  a. General quality of question
     0 = lack of questions or incomprehensible
     1 = partially formed/partially understood
     2 = clear and appropriate but not perfect
  b. Features of language functions (asking for information, giving information)
     0 = many problems/not understandable
     1 = some problems with clarity
     2 = clear and appropriate but not perfect
- Discuss and model appropriate communication before continuing.

Extension

Have learners create their own charts showing letter/word correspondences for the entire alphabet.

One Step Down

- Guide learners in brainstorming a sample conversation together.
- Write the conversation on the board for learners to practice together. See suggestions on p. 6 for partner chats.

One Step Up

Review language for extending and accepting or rejecting invitations. Then follow the suggestions for role-playing on p. 6.

- Inviting
  Would you like to . . . ?
  Do you want to . . . ?
  Would you be interested in . . . ?
- Accepting
  I'd love to.
  That would be great.
- Rejecting
  I'm sorry, I can't because . . .

Use Unit Master 13 (Grammar: Information Gap) now or at any time during the rest of this unit.

Activity B **Group Chat Follow-Up** Look at the chart from your Group Chat on page 13. In your notebook, write sentences about your group members.

Sonya likes swimming. She doesn't like cheerleading.

Activity C Listen to your teacher or the audio. You will hear questions about activities. Listen again and fill in the missing words.

1. Do you ______________ that aerobics is fun?
2. ______________ the community college offer aquatics?
3. ______________ cheerleading popular in your home country?
4. ______________ do people make in a ceramics class?
5. Do you ______________ how to play chess?
6. Do you like to ______________ crafts?
7. What kinds of lectures ______________ interesting to you?
8. ______________ can children learn gymnastics?
9. ______________ many people practice martial arts in your home country?

Correct your answers with your class. When you finish, ask your partner the questions.

TASK 1: Role-Play a Phone Conversation

In pairs, choose an activity that you are interested in. Write questions to ask an organization that offers the activity. Leave space between the questions to write the answers.

Role-play a phone call with your partner. Your partner should answer the phone with the name of the place you are calling. You can say

- "I'm calling for information about _____."
- "I'd like some information about _____."
- "I'd like to know about _____."

Ask your partner the questions you wrote. When your partner gives you an answer, repeat the information before you write it down. You can end your conversation like this: "Thank you for your help."

One Step Up

a. Role-play a phone call to one of your friends. Ask if your friend would like to go to a class with you.
b. Call a community organization and ask questions about activities that they offer. Report back to the class.

Lesson 2: Conflict at the Office

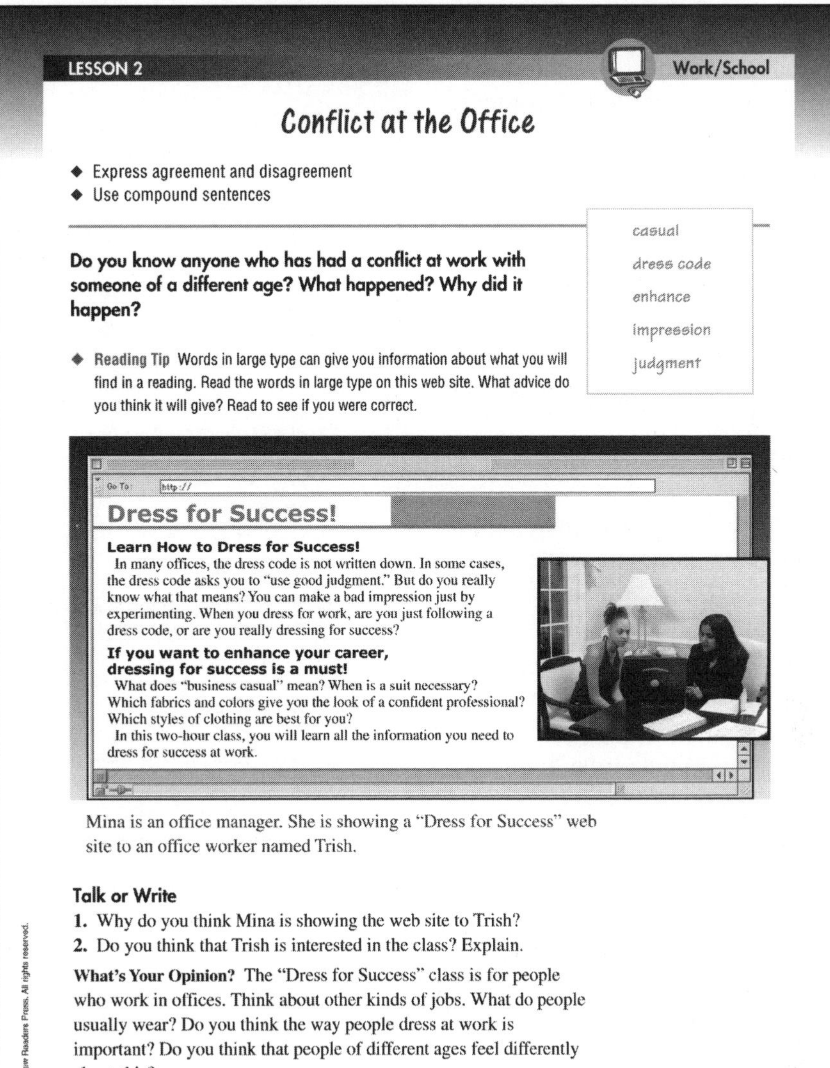

LESSON 2 Work/School

Conflict at the Office

- Express agreement and disagreement
- Use compound sentences

casual
dress code
enhance
impression
judgment

Do you know anyone who has had a conflict at work with someone of a different age? What happened? Why did it happen?

◆ **Reading Tip** Words in large type can give you information about what you will find in a reading. Read the words in large type on this web site. What advice do you think it will give? Read to see if you were correct.

Go To: http://

Dress for Success!

Learn How to Dress for Success!
In many offices, the dress code is not written down. In some cases, the dress code asks you to "use good judgment." But do you really know what that means? You can make a bad impression just by experimenting. When you dress for work, are you just following a dress code, or are you really dressing for success?

If you want to enhance your career, dressing for success is a must!
What does "business casual" mean? When is a suit necessary? Which fabrics and colors give you the look of a confident professional? Which styles of clothing are best for you?
In this two-hour class, you will learn all the information you need to dress for success at work.

Mina is an office manager. She is showing a "Dress for Success" web site to an office worker named Trish.

Talk or Write

1. Why do you think Mina is showing the web site to Trish?
2. Do you think that Trish is interested in the class? Explain.

What's Your Opinion? The "Dress for Success" class is for people who work in offices. Think about other kinds of jobs. What do people usually wear? Do you think the way people dress at work is important? Do you think that people of different ages feel differently about this?

Follow the suggestions on p. 5 for talking about the lesson title.

Questions

Read the questions above the photo. Ask learners what kinds of conflicts they think might occur at an office.

Reading Tip

Follow these steps to introduce the reading:

- Tell learners that when they read information on a web site, they should read the titles first to preview the content.
- Read the tip aloud. Ask for volunteers to answer the lead-in question.

Attention Box

This vocabulary should be understood, but learners should not be expected to produce the words at this point.

Extension

Have small groups of learners look through clothing catalogs and magazines and do the following:

- Cut out and categorize pictures of clothing as either appropriate or inappropriate for most office jobs.
- Select items from each of these categories and have learners justify their choices to the class.
- Use the magazine pictures to review clothing vocabulary.

Talk or Write

This exercise helps learners locate the main idea in what they read. Have learners discuss the questions with a partner or write their answers individually. Then discuss their answers as a group.

Possible Answers

1. The web site's purpose is to advertise a class on dressing for success.
2. Answers will vary.

What's Your Opinion?

Have learners call out different kinds of jobs, and write them on the board or an overhead transparency. Discuss the relative importance of clothing or uniforms in the various jobs.

Vocabulary

Follow the suggestions on p. 6 for introducing and reinforcing vocabulary words.

- Write the prefixes *in-, un-, dis-,* and *ir-* on the board or an overhead transparency.
- Explain that each is a different way to make a word negative.
- Find out if learners already know some words that begin with these prefixes (e.g., *unhappy*).

One Step Up

Hold a contest:

- Divide learners into small groups.
- Have each group generate a list of words they know that begin with any of the four prefixes.
- Assign a recorder in each group to record the words that group members know.
- Set a two-minute time limit.
- Give one point for each correct word.

Class Chat

Use Customizable Master 7 (Johari Window). Follow the suggestions on p. 7 for customizing and duplicating the master and distributing copies.

- Follow the directions in the student book.
- Have pairs add more statements to their organizers.
- After learners finish, elicit answers from the *Both A and B* and *Neither A nor B* boxes to find out which opinions were most popular and most unpopular.

Grammar Talk

Follow the suggestions on p. 6 for introducing the grammar point.

Point out that *I do too* and *so do I* have the same meaning, and that *neither do I* and *I don't either* mean the same.

Suggested Answers

- *Too* means *also.* Used together with *and,* it shows agreement.

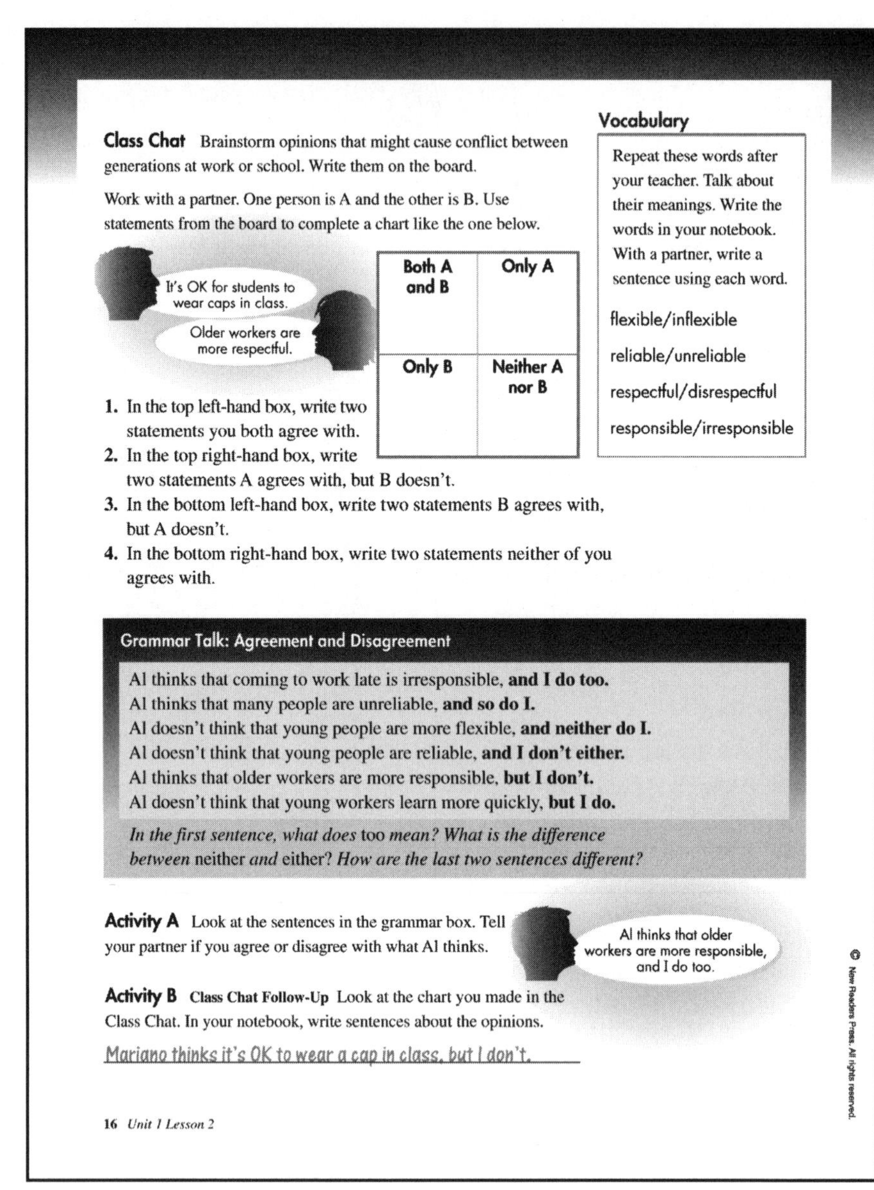

Class Chat Brainstorm opinions that might cause conflict between generations at work or school. Write them on the board.

Work with a partner. One person is A and the other is B. Use statements from the board to complete a chart like the one below.

Both A and B	Only A
Only B	Neither A nor B

1. In the top left-hand box, write two statements you both agree with.
2. In the top right-hand box, write two statements A agrees with, but B doesn't.
3. In the bottom left-hand box, write two statements B agrees with, but A doesn't.
4. In the bottom right-hand box, write two statements neither of you agrees with.

Vocabulary

Repeat these words after your teacher. Talk about their meanings. Write the words in your notebook. With a partner, write a sentence using each word.

flexible/inflexible

reliable/unreliable

respectful/disrespectful

responsible/irresponsible

Grammar Talk: Agreement and Disagreement

Al thinks that coming to work late is irresponsible, **and I do too.**
Al thinks that many people are unreliable, **and so do I.**
Al doesn't think that young people are more flexible, **and neither do I.**
Al doesn't think that young people are reliable, **and I don't either.**
Al thinks that older workers are more responsible, **but I don't.**
Al doesn't think that young workers learn more quickly, **but I do.**

In the first sentence, what does too *mean? What is the difference between* neither *and* either? *How are the last two sentences different?*

Activity A Look at the sentences in the grammar box. Tell your partner if you agree or disagree with what Al thinks.

Activity B **Class Chat Follow-Up** Look at the chart you made in the Class Chat. In your notebook, write sentences about the opinions.

Mariano thinks it's OK to wear a cap in class, but I don't.

16 *Unit 1 Lesson 2*

- *Either* and *neither* have the same meaning. *Either* is used with a negative verb; *neither* is used with a positive verb.
- The last two sentences contain the word *but,* which indicates disagreement.

Activity B

Before learners begin, write the sentences below on the board or an overhead transparency. Explain how the grammar rule applies in each case:

Taylor is blonde, but I'm not.

Mauricio is short, and I am too.
Mauricio is short, and so am I.

Hayat isn't tired, and neither am I.
Hayat isn't tired, and I'm not either.

Alex can swim, but I can't.

Haley can dance, and I can too.
Haley can dance, and so can I.

Jordi can't type, and neither can I.
Jordi can't type, and I can't either.

Have partners discuss the opinions from the Class Chat. Then have them write sentences about their similarities and differences.

Extension

Explain that *me neither* is often used as a short response to a negative statement (e.g., "I don't like liver." "Me neither.").

 Assign Workbook pp. 6–7.

Pronunciation Target

Follow the suggestions on p. 7 for explaining voiced and voiceless sounds.

- Pronounce *think* and *that* slowly.
- Point out that the mouth and tongue position is the same for both sounds. The difference between them is the voicing.
- Demonstrate that both the /ch/ sound in *chess* and the /sh/ sound in *should* are voiceless.

Ask learners to follow the directions in the student book for making and using the chart in their notebooks. Then play the audio or read the listening script below.

Listening Script

Listen for the contrasting sounds.

those, thin, thick, breathe, brother, tenth

chair, share, she's, cheese, teacher, T-shirt, watch, wash

After the listening exercise, do the following:

- Ask learners to put their hands in front of their mouths and say *think.* They should feel a puff of air on the hand when /th/ is produced. When they pronounce *that,* they should not feel a puff of air.
- Ask learners to practice all of the *th* words in their charts with their hands in front of their mouths.

Activity C

As learners discuss the conflicts outlined in their book, encourage them to be specific in describing what might have led to the conflict. For example, in explaining conflict 2, rather than saying, "The young worker is disrespectful," they should say, "The young worker uses slang" or "The young worker speaks rudely."

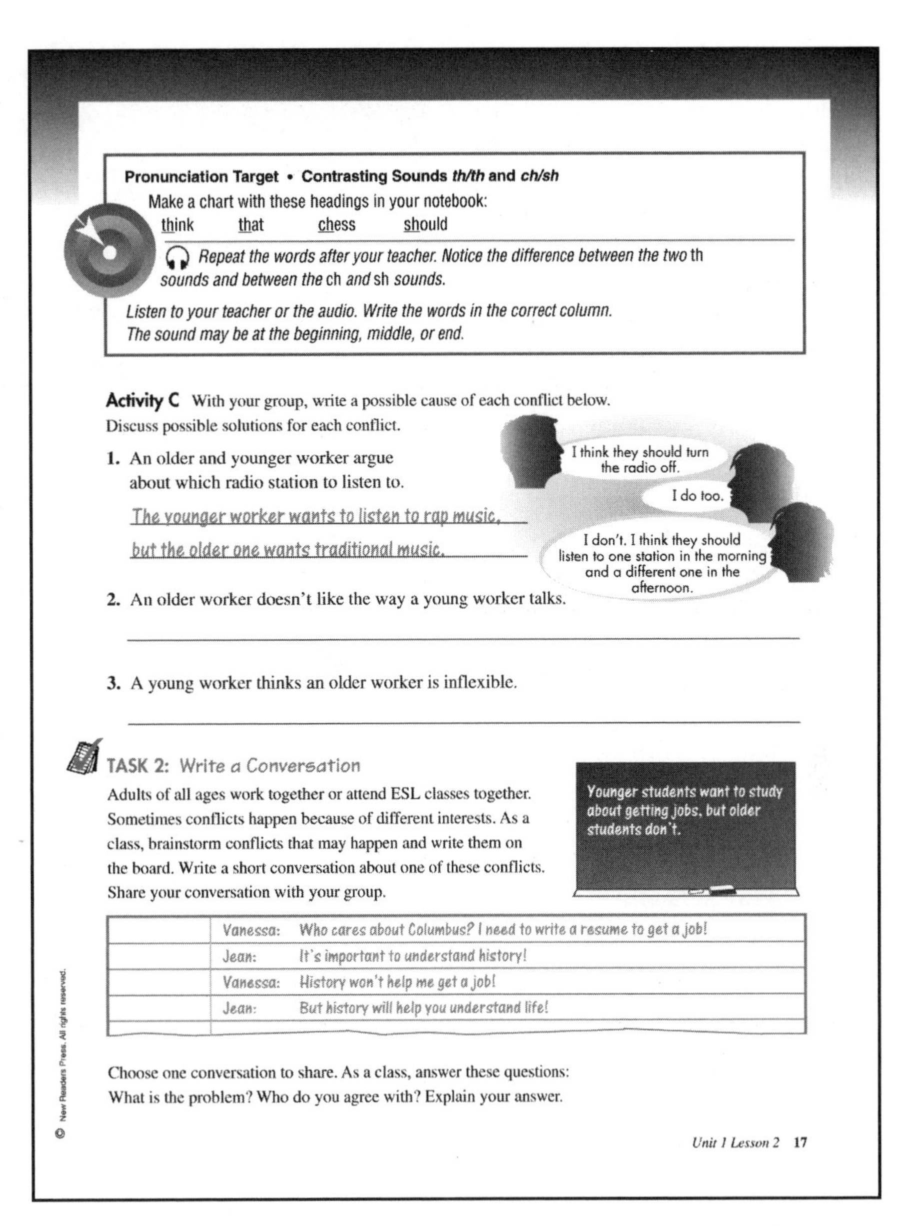

Pronunciation Target • Contrasting Sounds *th/th* and *ch/sh*

Make a chart with these headings in your notebook:

think that chess should

Repeat the words after your teacher. Notice the difference between the two th *sounds and between the* ch *and* sh *sounds.*

Listen to your teacher or the audio. Write the words in the correct column. The sound may be at the beginning, middle, or end.

Activity C With your group, write a possible cause of each conflict below. Discuss possible solutions for each conflict.

1. An older and younger worker argue about which radio station to listen to.
   The younger worker wants to listen to rap music, but the older one wants traditional music.

2. An older worker doesn't like the way a young worker talks.
3. A young worker thinks an older worker is inflexible.

TASK 2: Write a Conversation

Adults of all ages work together or attend ESL classes together. Sometimes conflicts happen because of different interests. As a class, brainstorm conflicts that may happen and write them on the board. Write a short conversation about one of these conflicts. Share your conversation with your group.

	Vanessa:	Who cares about Columbus? I need to write a resume to get a job!
	Jean:	It's important to understand history!
	Vanessa:	History won't help me get a job!
	Jean:	But history will help you understand life!

Choose one conversation to share. As a class, answer these questions: What is the problem? Who do you agree with? Explain your answer.

Task 2

Ongoing Assessment

Guide learners in brainstorming conflicts that might occur among members of an ESL class. Then have each write a brief conversation about one of these conflicts.

- As learners write their conversations, take notes on the following criteria:
  a. General quality of description of the conflict
     0 = incomprehensible
     1 = partially formed/partially understood
     2 = clear and appropriate but not perfect
  b. General quality of natural speaking
     0 = incomprehensible pronunciation
     1 = abrupt, halting speech
     2 = clear, understandable speech
- Discuss and model appropriate communication before continuing the lesson.

One Step Up

Discuss resolutions for each conflict and extend the conversations to show these resolutions.

Use Unit Master 14 (Thinking Skill: Negotiate) now or at any time during the rest of the unit.

Lesson 3: Sports to Play and Watch

Follow the suggestions on p. 5 for talking about the lesson title.

If learners do not have experience with playing sports, ask them about sports they watch on television or that are popular in their home countries.

Attention Box

This vocabulary should be understood, but learners should not be expected to produce the words at this point.

Reading Tip

Follow these steps to complete the reading exercise:

- Ask learners to name some benefits of sports.
- List their ideas on the board or an overhead transparency.
- When learners finish the reading, ask them which of those listed benefits were and were not mentioned in the letter.
- Put a check beside each activity that was mentioned.

Talk or Write

This exercise helps learners locate the main idea in what they read.

Answers

1. Sports are beneficial. *OR* Students should join a sports team.
2. Sports can cause or promote positive attributes, including
   - self-discipline
   - respect for others
   - fun
   - friendship
   - good exercise
   - confidence
   - sportsmanship
   - lower risk of drug or alcohol use
   - planning your time

After learners create their main idea/supporting idea charts, create one together on the board or an overhead transparency so that they can check their work.

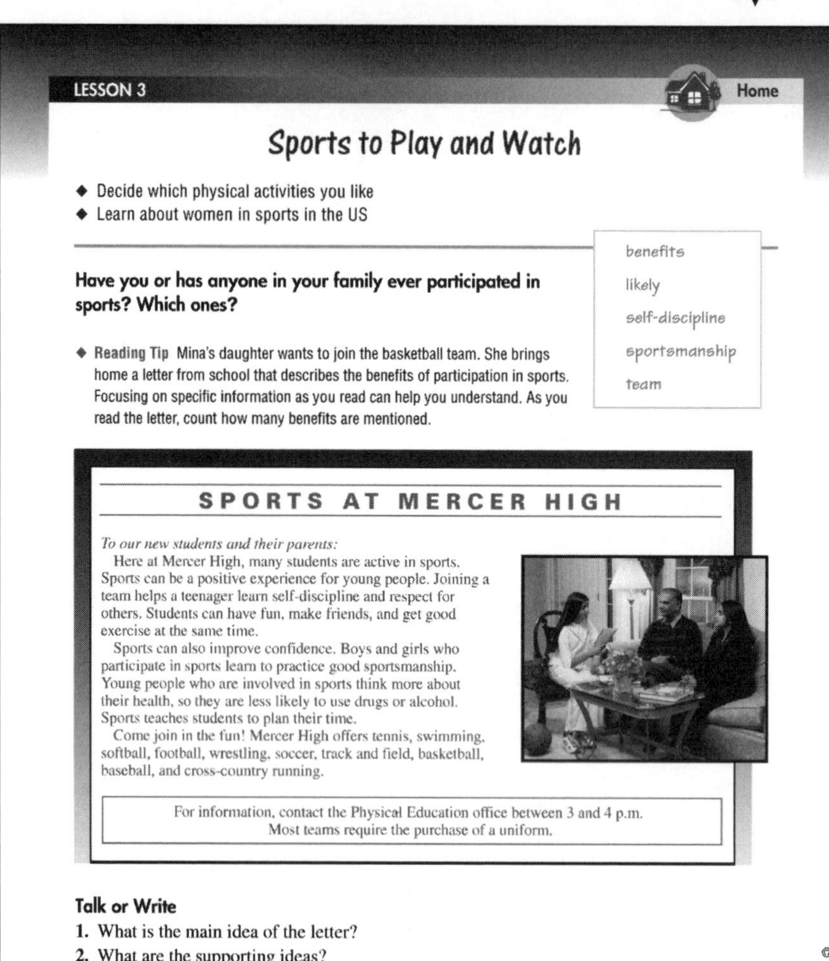

LESSON 3 Home

Sports to Play and Watch

- Decide which physical activities you like
- Learn about women in sports in the US

benefits
likely
self-discipline
sportsmanship
team

Have you or has anyone in your family ever participated in sports? Which ones?

- **Reading Tip** Mina's daughter wants to join the basketball team. She brings home a letter from school that describes the benefits of participation in sports. Focusing on specific information as you read can help you understand. As you read the letter, count how many benefits are mentioned.

SPORTS AT MERCER HIGH

To our new students and their parents:

Here at Mercer High, many students are active in sports. Sports can be a positive experience for young people. Joining a team helps a teenager learn self-discipline and respect for others. Students can have fun, make friends, and get good exercise at the same time.

Sports can also improve confidence. Boys and girls who participate in sports learn to practice good sportsmanship. Young people who are involved in sports think more about their health, so they are less likely to use drugs or alcohol. Sports teaches students to plan their time.

Come join in the fun! Mercer High offers tennis, swimming, softball, football, wrestling, soccer, track and field, basketball, baseball, and cross-country running.

For information, contact the Physical Education office between 3 and 4 p.m.
Most teams require the purchase of a uniform.

Talk or Write

1. What is the main idea of the letter?
2. What are the supporting ideas?

Make a chart in your notebook. Write the main idea at the top of the page. Write the supporting ideas under the main idea.

In the US *Women in US Sports*

Not many years ago, very few women in the US participated in competitive sports. Now, however, many girls and women compete. It's common for girls to join softball, basketball, and soccer teams, as well as individual sports like gymnastics. In 1972, the federal government passed a law that says schools may not discriminate against girls in sports. Since that time, more and more girls have participated in school sports. Women's professional sports have also gained popularity. Although men's professional sports continue to be more popular, many people enjoy watching women's soccer, basketball, and volleyball. The growing popularity of women's sports can be seen in other countries, too. Every year the Olympics add more events for women, and all new Olympic sports must allow women to compete.

Vocabulary

Repeat these words after your teacher. Talk about their meanings. Write the words in your notebook. With a partner, write a sentence using each word.

- challenge/challenging
- compete/competitive
- fitness
- individual
- risky
- team

discriminate

Idiom Watch!
meet someone halfway

☛ **Compare Cultures** Women and girls play all of these sports in the US. Do they play them in your home country? Check "yes" or "no" for each sport on the charts below. Share your information with the class, and write what you've learned in a class chart.

Sports	basketball	soccer	softball	tennis
Yes				
No				

Sports	swimming	golf	volleyball	track and field
Yes				
No				

Activity A Annie's grandfather doesn't want her to join the basketball team. He thinks that Annie needs to spend time with her family. How can he and Annie meet halfway? In your group, discuss possible solutions. Share your ideas with the class. Role-play a conversation between them.

Vocabulary

Follow the suggestions on p. 6 for introducing and reinforcing vocabulary words.

One Step Up 1
The word *challenge* is used as a noun in this unit. Explain that it also can be used as a verb (e.g., He *challenged* me to a game of chess.). Have learners give some other examples using *challenge* as a noun or a verb. Write their sentences on the board or an overhead transparency.

One Step Up 2
After the class has discussed the sentences, write the heads *Noun, Verb,* and *Adjective* on the board or an overhead transparency. Then ask learners to categorize the vocabulary words below:

- Nouns: *fitness, individual, team*
- Verbs: *compete, team*
- Adjectives: *challenging, individual, risky, team*

In the US

Before reading the passage in the student book, discuss these questions with learners to get them thinking about the topic:

1. Do you ever watch girls' or women's sports?
2. What sports do you think women are good at/not good at?
3. Why do you think men's sports are more popular than women's sports?
4. Which sports do women, but not men, compete in?
5. Are there any sports where women's competition is more popular than men's? Why or why not?

Compare Cultures

After creating the class chart, discuss why certain sports traditionally have been played (or have not been played) by women. Consider ways in which boys and girls are raised and schooled; sports available to children and teens through school years; funding available for team and individual sports; training standards for men's and women's teams; and economic factors in fielding a professional sports team.

Activity A

After reading the passage together, have students suggest various "meet halfway" solutions such as those below. Write the solutions on the board or an overhead transparency.

- Annie could spend extra time with her grandfather when she's not practicing.
- Her grandfather could go to her games.
- Annie could postpone basketball until the following year.

Ask volunteers to role-play a conversation for each solution.

Use Unit Master 15 (Vocabulary: Listening) and 16 (Grammar: Jigsaw) now or at any time during the rest of the unit.

Assign Workbook pp. 8–9.

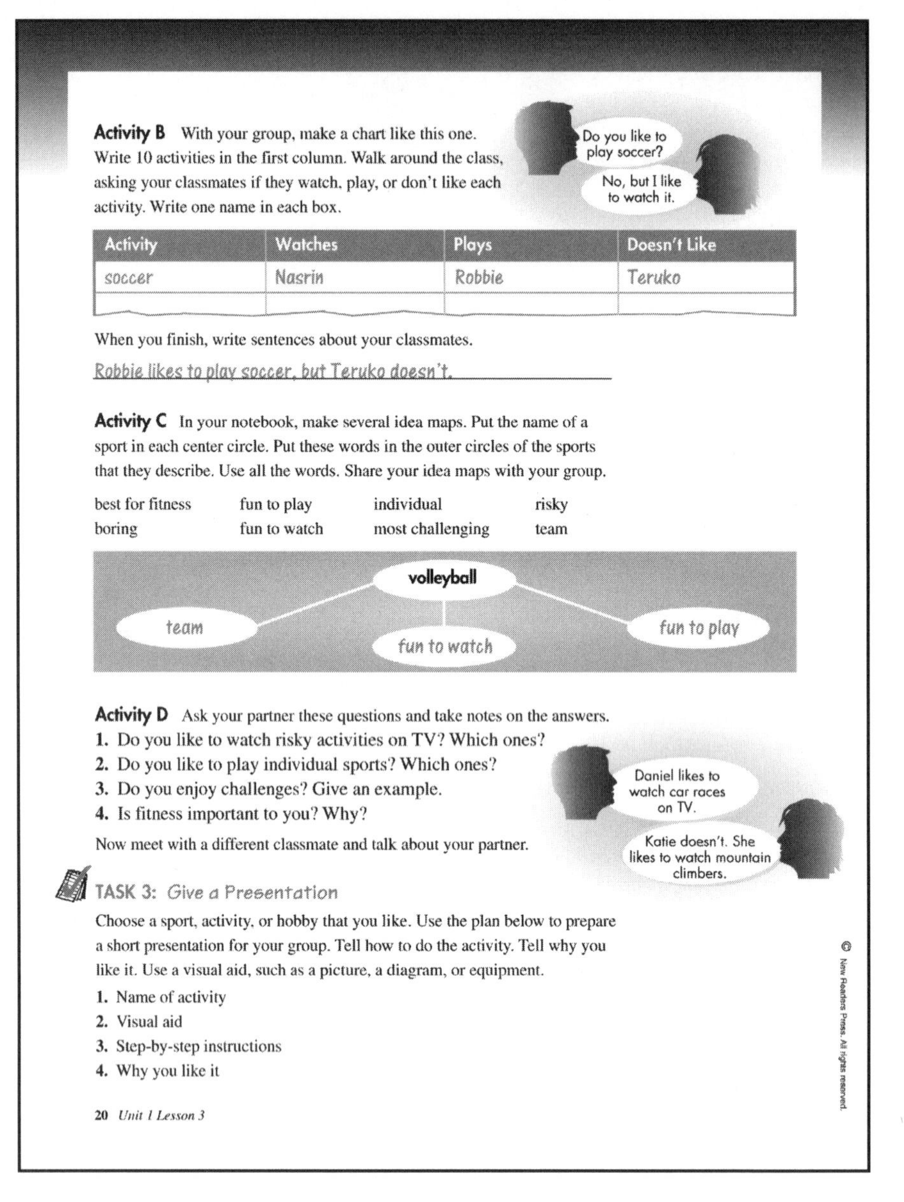

Activity B With your group, make a chart like this one. Write 10 activities in the first column. Walk around the class, asking your classmates if they watch, play, or don't like each activity. Write one name in each box.

Activity	Watches	Plays	Doesn't Like
soccer	Nasrin	Robbie	Teruko

When you finish, write sentences about your classmates.

Robbie likes to play soccer, but Teruko doesn't.

Activity C In your notebook, make several idea maps. Put the name of a sport in each center circle. Put these words in the outer circles of the sports that they describe. Use all the words. Share your idea maps with your group.

best for fitness	fun to play	individual	risky
boring	fun to watch	most challenging	team

Activity D Ask your partner these questions and take notes on the answers.

1. Do you like to watch risky activities on TV? Which ones?
2. Do you like to play individual sports? Which ones?
3. Do you enjoy challenges? Give an example.
4. Is fitness important to you? Why?

Now meet with a different classmate and talk about your partner.

TASK 3: *Give a Presentation*

Choose a sport, activity, or hobby that you like. Use the plan below to prepare a short presentation for your group. Tell how to do the activity. Tell why you like it. Use a visual aid, such as a picture, a diagram, or equipment.

1. Name of activity
2. Visual aid
3. Step-by-step instructions
4. Why you like it

20 *Unit 1 Lesson 3*

Activity B

Use Customizable Master 3 (4-Column Chart). Follow the suggestions on p. 7 for customizing and duplicating the master and distributing the copies.

- Tell learners that the goal of this activity is to fill as many spaces as possible on the chart. If someone likes to both watch and play a sport, learners should write that person's name in both spaces.
- Encourage learners to ask for spellings of classmates' names rather than passing the chart for them to sign. This provides practice in spelling aloud and in listening, and it helps learners memorize one another's names.

Activity C

First, have individual learners quickly create the small idea maps in their notebooks. Then divide learners into small groups.

Have learners share their idea maps with their group. Encourage them to justify their opinions.

Activity D

After the initial pair discussion, have learners change partners and report on their first conversation.

- Some risky activities that learners might like to watch include car racing, mountain climbing, skateboarding, surfing, motocross racing, boxing, downhill skiing, and parachuting.
- Remind learners that challenges do not have to be physical. Encourage them to think of nonphysical challenges as well, e.g., learning English, writing a novel, winning at chess.

Task 3

Have learners sit in small groups. Ask each group to discuss what its members want to present so that each person in the group chooses a different topic. Then do the following:

- Assign a number to each learner.
- After each learner has presented an activity to his or her group, ask learners to regroup according to number (i.e., all ones sit together, all twos sit together, etc.).
- Each learner presents again to the new group.

Use Unit Master 17 (Game: Password) now or at any time during the rest of the unit.

Review Unit Skills

Follow the suggestions on pp. 7–9 for games and activities to review the vocabulary and grammar in this unit.

Unit 1 Project

To do a formal assessment of this project, use Generic Assessment Master 8 (Oral Communication Rubric) to evaluate the presentations.

Learners research classes available in their community. If the community does not offer many services, do the One Step Up as the Unit Project.

Get Ready

If learners are not able to collect information, bring in brochures from local community or senior centers, schools, parks, and cultural organizations.

Use Unit Master 18 (Unit 1 Project: Presentation of Community Classes). Give one copy to each group.

Do the Work

- Write the four age groups from the student book on the board.
- Conduct a hand vote to determine learners' interests.
- Form small groups of learners interested in the same age group.

Present

Give each learner a copy of Generic Assessment Master 12 (Peer Assessment Form).

- Follow the suggestions for peer assessment on p. 4.
- Ask learners to complete and exchange the forms before doing their final presentations.
- Have groups practice their presentations with one another.
- For final presentations, encourage active listening by asking learners follow-up questions.

Writing Extension

Have learners refer to the Writing Checklist on p. 125 of their books for final proofreading.

Technology Extra

If binding is not possible, post the group project pages for all to share.

UNIT 1 Project

Presentation of Community Classes

Find out about classes in your community. Follow these steps:

Get Ready

Research classes that are available in your community.

1. Choose an age group that you are interested in: youth, adults, parents of young children, or the elderly.
2. Ask for written information from schools, churches, or cultural centers that offer classes for the group that you chose.
3. Bring brochures to class.

Do the Work

Work in small groups. Students who are interested in the same age group should work together.

1. Choose activities and classes from the brochures that would be interesting for people in the age group that you chose.
2. Put the information onto one page, including name of organization, place, dates, times, and fees.

Present

Present the information to the class. Each member of the group should present part of the information. After you listen to other groups, ask questions about the activities.

One Step Up

In a small group, create a community organization that fulfills an important need. For example, you could create a center that offers recreational after-school activities for teenagers. You could also form a group that organizes outings to parks for mothers and their young children. Make a brochure that tells the name of the organization, describes the resources that it offers, and lists the schedule of activities.

Writing Extension Write a short letter to a local organization, park service, or community center asking them to offer a class in something you're interested in. Explain what you want them to offer and why you think people would be interested in it.

Technology Extra

Gather your information into a class book to share with others. Each group should type in the information for the age group they chose. Use graphics if possible. Print, laminate, and bind the book or put the pages into a binder with plastic sheet covers. Display the book in the classroom.

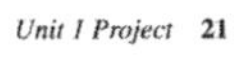

One Step Up

After completing the activity in the student book, follow these steps:

- Discuss how to turn the imaginary organization into a reality.
- Invite a speaker from a community organization to come and describe its services to the class.

Extension

For additional writing practice:

- Find addresses and contact names on the brochures.
- Have learners write letters to these groups asking for information.
- For final drafts of the letters, review block-letter format using p. 16, Unit 2, of their workbook.

Assign Workbook p. 10 (Check Your Progress). Go over the checkup with learners. Be sure they understand how to complete the self-assessment, especially the first part.

- Explain that the numbers represent a rating scale, with *1* being the lowest score and *5* being the highest.
- If learners have difficulty using the scale, explain that a *2* rating means "not very well, but improving" and that a *4* rating means "fairly well."

Use Unit Master 19 (Unit 1 Checkup/Review) whenever you complete this unit.

Unit 2: Smoothing Things Over

Materials for the Unit

- Large sheets of paper or poster board ($8\frac{1}{2} \times 14$ in. or 11×17 in.)
- Sympathy or apology cards (optional)
- Customizable Masters 2, 4, and 5
- Unit Masters 20–27

Smoothing Things Over

Follow the suggestions on p. 5 for talking about the unit title. Then do the following:

- Discuss the meaning of the word *smooth.* One meaning might be "not rough" (e.g., The baby's skin is *smooth.*). Have learners give examples of smooth things.
- Ask learners what they think the idiom *smoothing things over* means. One meaning might be "removing difficulties or obstacles."
- Ask learners when they might use this expression.

Photo

Follow the suggestions on p. 4 for talking about the photo; then read the sentences below the arrow.

Ask learners what they think the word *misunderstanding* means. Explain that it can be defined as "a mistaken idea, a misinterpretation" or as "an argument or disagreement." In this unit, the first definition is more appropriate.

Caption

- Read the photo caption.
- Ask learners to brainstorm communication problems that Jae Lee might have even though he speaks very well.
- Write the problems on the board or an overhead transparency.

Think and Talk

Write learners' answers to the questions on the board.

For question 2, ask learners to explain their answers.

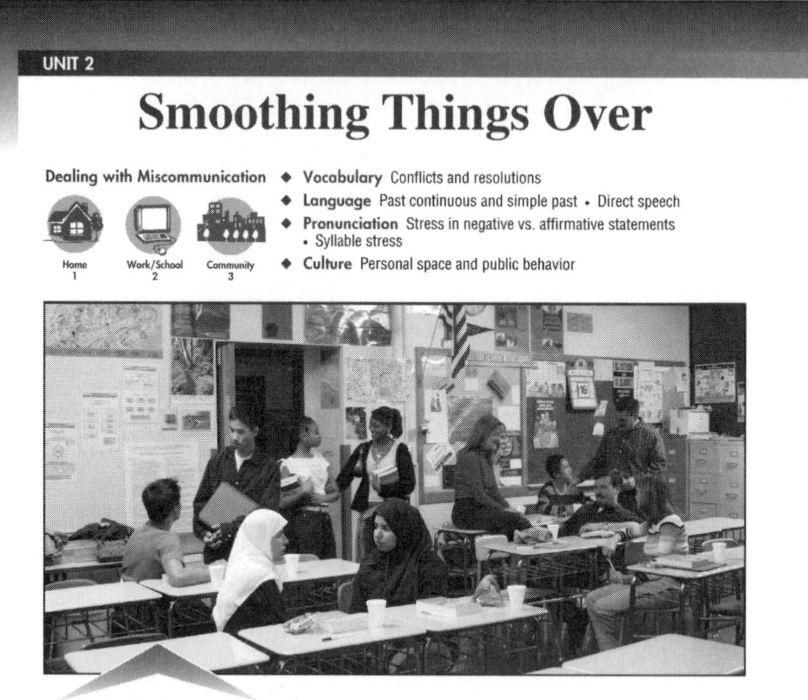

UNIT 2

Smoothing Things Over

Dealing with Miscommunication

Home 1 · Work/School 2 · Community 3

- **Vocabulary** Conflicts and resolutions
- **Language** Past continuous and simple past • Direct speech
- **Pronunciation** Stress in negative vs. affirmative statements • Syllable stress
- **Culture** Personal space and public behavior

Think about a misunderstanding that you had. Tell what happened.

Jae Lee, a 27-year-old from Korea, is talking to his friend, Koji, before English class. Jae Lee has lived in the US for many years. Although he speaks English very well, he sometimes has communication problems for other reasons.

Think and Talk

1. What do you see in the picture?
2. What do you see in this photo that might cause misunderstandings?
3. What happens when people misunderstand each other?
4. How do you feel about the way people are acting in this photo?

What's Your Opinion? In the photo, the instructor has his hand on a student's shoulder. Is this OK? Explain your answer.

22 *Unit 2*

What's Your Opinion?

Have learners consider the issue presented and then explain their opinions.

Vocabulary

Follow the suggestions on p. 6 for introducing and reinforcing the vocabulary words.

One Step Up 1

Follow the suggestions on p. 6 for categorizing the vocabulary words as nouns, verbs, and adjectives.

- Nouns: *expectation, misunderstanding, resolution, body language, gesture*
- Verbs: *expect, misunderstand, offend, resolve*
- Adjectives: *offensive, concerned*

One Step Up 2

Have learners write these headings across the top of a notebook page: *Two-Syllable Words, Three-Syllable Words, Four-Syllable Words, Five-Syllable Words.*

- Model the pronunciation of the words in the Vocabulary box.
- Ask learners to write each word in the correct column.
- Pronounce each word again and ask learners to underline the stressed syllables.

Answers

- Two-Syllable Words: *body, language, gesture, expect, offend, resolve, concerned*
- Three-Syllable Words: *offensive*
- Four-Syllable Words: *expectation, resolution, misunderstand*
- Five-Syllable Words: *misunderstanding*

Gather Your Thoughts

Copy the flow chart from the student book page on the board or an overhead transparency, leaving enough space in each box for one or two sentences. Then do the following:

- Divide learners into small groups.
- Have each group prepare a similar flow chart, enlarged if possible to 8½ × 14 in. or 11 × 17 in.
- Ask group members to choose one example of a misunderstanding and write the story in the boxes on the flow chart.

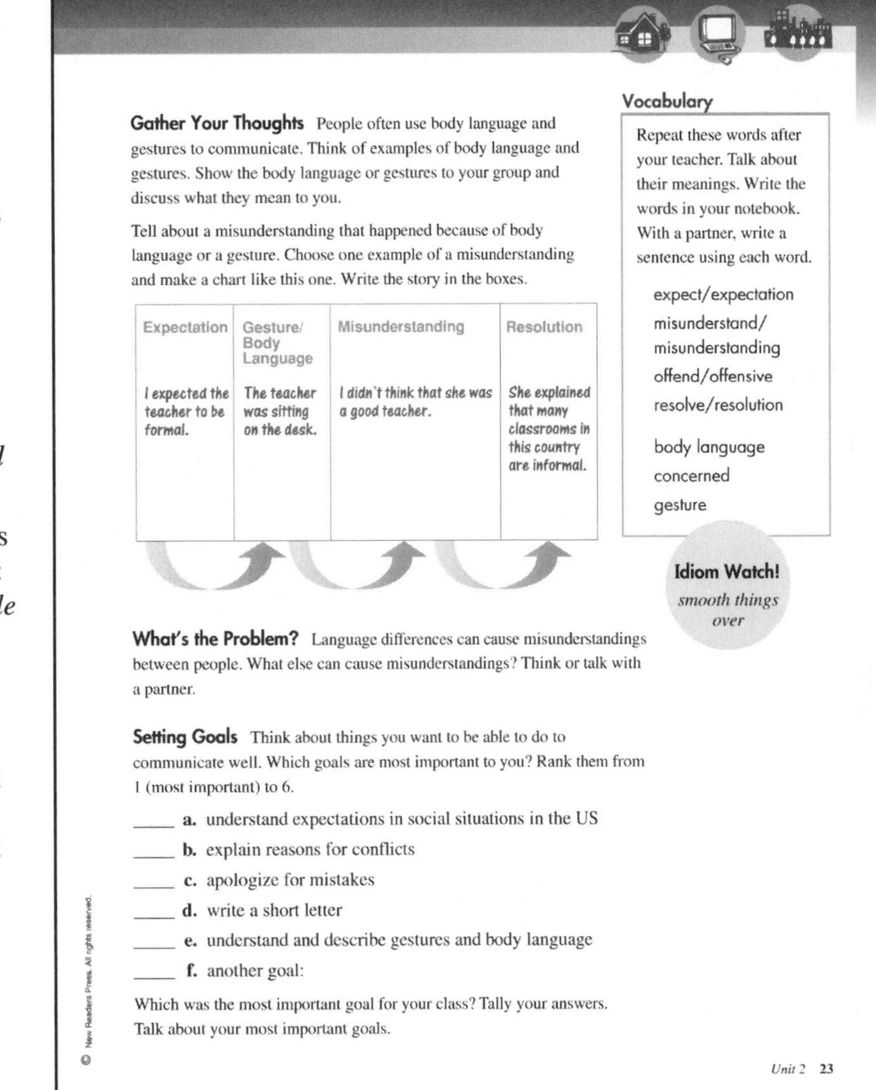

Gather Your Thoughts People often use body language and gestures to communicate. Think of examples of body language and gestures. Show the body language or gestures to your group and discuss what they mean to you.

Tell about a misunderstanding that happened because of body language or a gesture. Choose one example of a misunderstanding and make a chart like this one. Write the story in the boxes.

Expectation	Gesture/ Body Language	Misunderstanding	Resolution
I expected the teacher to be formal.	The teacher was sitting on the desk.	I didn't think that she was a good teacher.	She explained that many classrooms in this country are informal.

Vocabulary

Repeat these words after your teacher. Talk about their meanings. Write the words in your notebook. With a partner, write a sentence using each word.

expect/expectation
misunderstand/misunderstanding
offend/offensive
resolve/resolution
body language
concerned
gesture

Idiom Watch!
smooth things over

What's the Problem? Language differences can cause misunderstandings between people. What else can cause misunderstandings? Think or talk with a partner.

Setting Goals Think about things you want to be able to do to communicate well. Which goals are most important to you? Rank them from 1 (most important) to 6.

____ **a.** understand expectations in social situations in the US
____ **b.** explain reasons for conflicts
____ **c.** apologize for mistakes
____ **d.** write a short letter
____ **e.** understand and describe gestures and body language
____ **f.** another goal:

Which was the most important goal for your class? Tally your answers. Talk about your most important goals.

Unit 2 23

- Ask volunteers from each group to tell their story to the class.
- To generate discussion, have learners ask questions or offer their opinions about each story.

What's the Problem?

Follow the suggestions on p. 5 for thinking about the problem.

Setting Goals

Follow the suggestions on p. 5 for setting goals.

Lesson 1: Body Language

Follow the suggestions on p. 5 for talking about the title.

Act out some of the examples of body language below. Ask learners what feelings the movements convey or what you are trying to communicate with each:

- Shrug your shoulders.
- Slump your shoulders and look down at the floor.
- Pout.
- Wink.
- Raise your eyebrows.
- Motion for someone to come ("Come here.").
- Fold your arms across your chest.

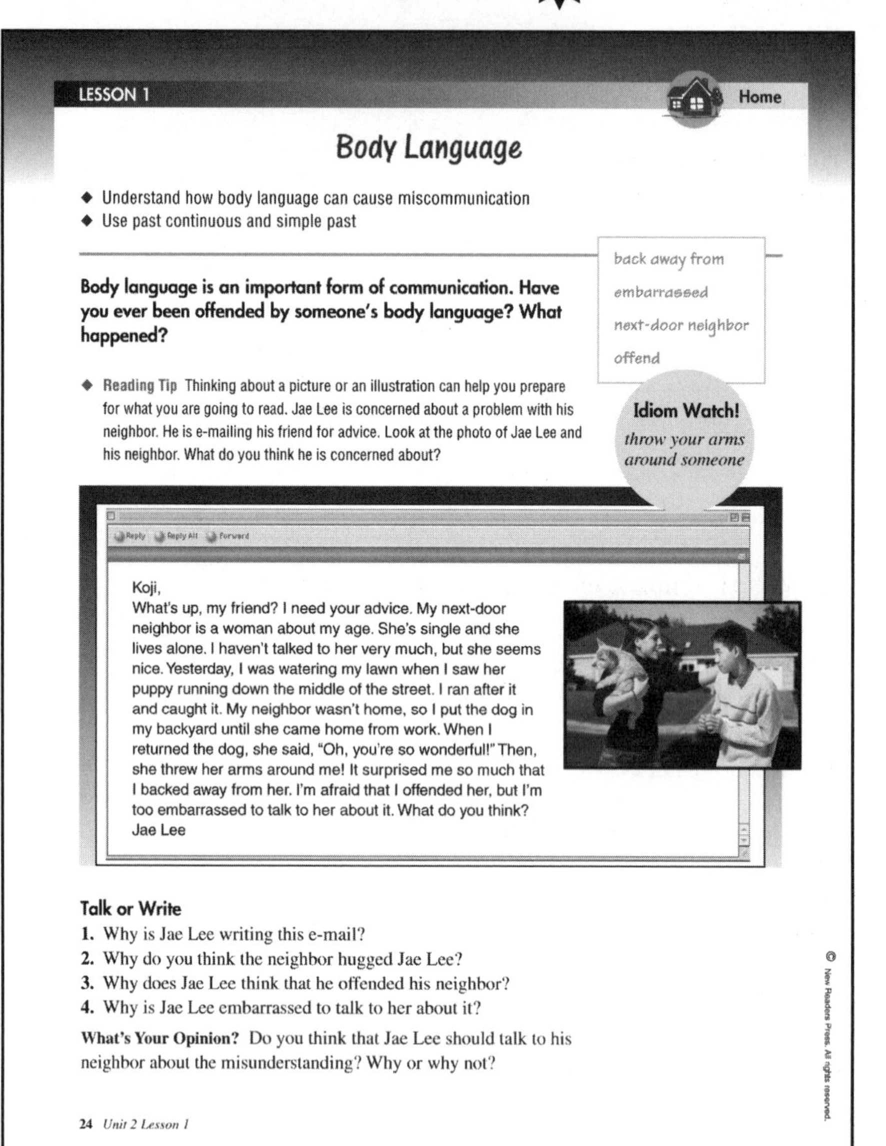

LESSON 1 Home

Body Language

- ◆ Understand how body language can cause miscommunication
- ◆ Use past continuous and simple past

back away from
embarrassed
next-door neighbor
offend

Body language is an important form of communication. Have you ever been offended by someone's body language? What happened?

◆ **Reading Tip** Thinking about a picture or an illustration can help you prepare for what you are going to read. Jae Lee is concerned about a problem with his neighbor. He is e-mailing his friend for advice. Look at the photo of Jae Lee and his neighbor. What do you think he is concerned about?

Idiom Watch!
throw your arms around someone

Reply Reply All Forward

Koji,
What's up, my friend? I need your advice. My next-door neighbor is a woman about my age. She's single and she lives alone. I haven't talked to her very much, but she seems nice. Yesterday, I was watering my lawn when I saw her puppy running down the middle of the street. I ran after it and caught it. My neighbor wasn't home, so I put the dog in my backyard until she came home from work. When I returned the dog, she said, "Oh, you're so wonderful!" Then, she threw her arms around me! It surprised me so much that I backed away from her. I'm afraid that I offended her, but I'm too embarrassed to talk to her about it. What do you think?
Jae Lee

Talk or Write

1. Why is Jae Lee writing this e-mail?
2. Why do you think the neighbor hugged Jae Lee?
3. Why does Jae Lee think that he offended his neighbor?
4. Why is Jae Lee embarrassed to talk to her about it?

What's Your Opinion? Do you think that Jae Lee should talk to his neighbor about the misunderstanding? Why or why not?

24 *Unit 2 Lesson 1*

Questions

Read the questions above the photo, then discuss offensive gestures with learners. Ask them what is offensive in their cultures so they can compare. Use your judgment to avoid situations in which some learners might be offended.

Attention Box

Read the words to learners, pointing or miming to convey meaning. This vocabulary should be understood, but learners should not be expected to produce the words at this point.

Reading Tip

- Have learners cover up the reading while they look at the photo.
- Ask them what they think Jae Lee is concerned about. Write their answers on the board.
- After learners read, review their answers and see which was closest to Jae Lee's problem.

Talk or Write

In this exercise, learners practice reading for a purpose.

Follow the suggestions on pp. 5–6 for in-class reading. Then have learners answer the questions aloud.

Answers

1. Jae Lee is writing the e-mail to get some advice from his friend.
2. She probably hugged him because she was happy that he saved her puppy.
3. He thinks he offended her because he backed away.
4. He's probably embarrassed to talk to her because he feels bad about offending her.

One Step Up

Ask learners to write a return e-mail from Koji giving Jae Lee the advice he is asking for.

What's Your Opinion?

Have learners consider the issue presented in their books and form an opinion. Then ask volunteers to explain their opinions.

Vocabulary

Follow the suggestions on p. 6 for introducing and reinforcing the vocabulary words.

Ask learners to act out the words or model them for the class.

Group Chat

Use Customizable Master 2 (3-Column Chart). Follow the suggestions on p. 7 for customizing and duplicating the master and distributing the copies.

Encourage learners to use classmates' names in the chart, e.g., *Jody was staring at Jerry.*

After groups complete the chat, ask a few learners to read the words and sentences they wrote in their charts. Write the sentences on the board or an overhead transparency. The results might look like this:

1. stare
2. A woman was staring at a man in a classroom.
3. He looked like her old boyfriend.

Grammar Talk

Follow the suggestions on p. 6 for introducing the grammar point.

Suggested Answers

- The first sentence of each pair describes continuous action.
- The second sentence of each pair describes an interrupting action.
- You combine the simple past tense of *be* with the verb plus *-ing*.

Pronunciation Target

Play the audio or read the sentences in the student book.

Extension

Have learners write similar past continuous statements, both affirmative and negative.

- Ask learners from each group to write their sentences on the board and underline the stressed words or syllables, e.g.,
  He was surfing.
  He wasn't surfing.

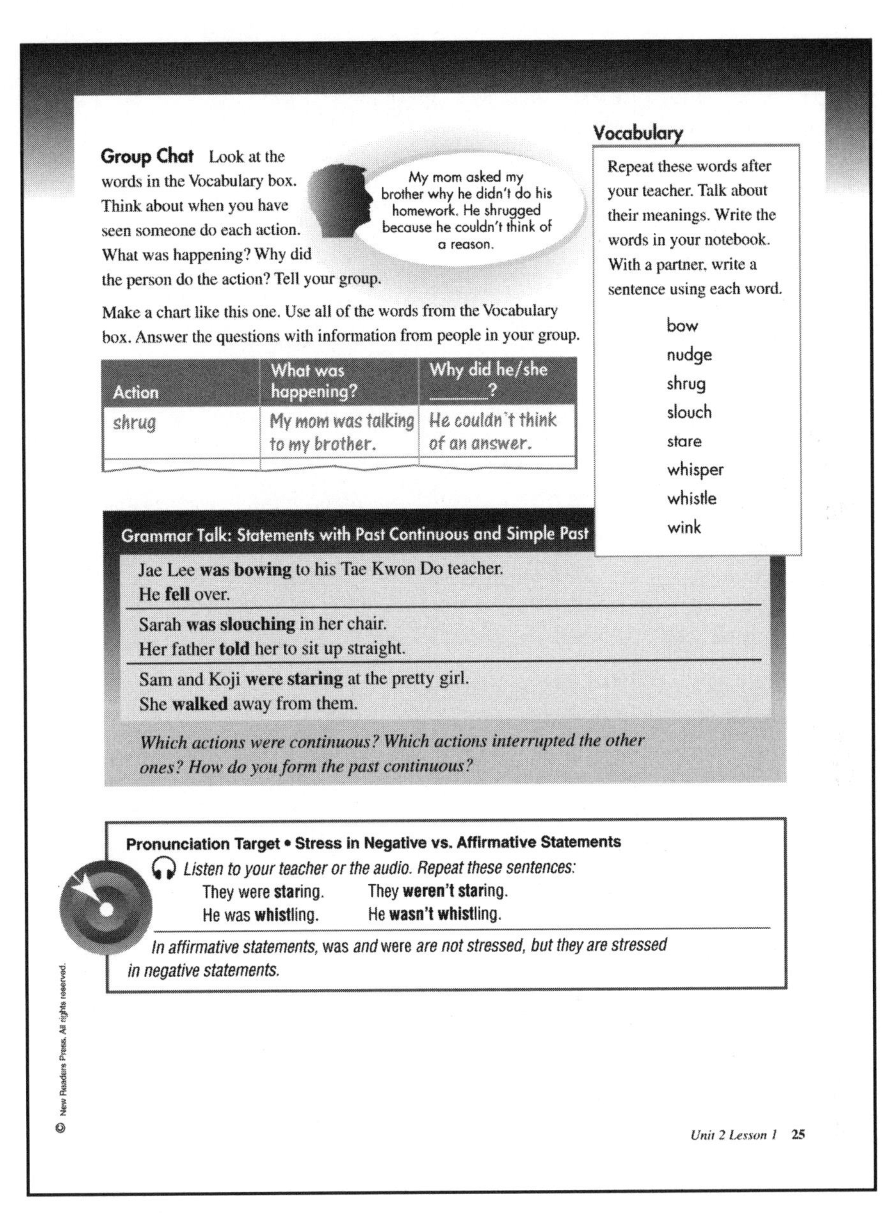

Group Chat Look at the words in the Vocabulary box. Think about when you have seen someone do each action. What was happening? Why did the person do the action? Tell your group.

Make a chart like this one. Use all of the words from the Vocabulary box. Answer the questions with information from people in your group.

Action	What was happening?	Why did he/she ______?
shrug	My mom was talking to my brother.	He couldn't think of an answer.

Vocabulary

Repeat these words after your teacher. Talk about their meanings. Write the words in your notebook. With a partner, write a sentence using each word.

bow
nudge
shrug
slouch
stare
whisper
whistle
wink

Grammar Talk: Statements with Past Continuous and Simple Past

Jae Lee **was bowing** to his Tae Kwon Do teacher.
He **fell** over.

Sarah **was slouching** in her chair.
Her father **told** her to sit up straight.

Sam and Koji **were staring** at the pretty girl.
She **walked** away from them.

Which actions were continuous? Which actions interrupted the other ones? How do you form the past continuous?

Pronunciation Target • Stress in Negative vs. Affirmative Statements

Listen to your teacher or the audio. Repeat these sentences:

They were **star**ing. They **weren't star**ing.
He was **whist**ling. He **wasn't whist**ling.

In affirmative statements, was *and* were *are not stressed, but they are stressed in negative statements.*

Unit 2 Lesson 1 25

- Model the pronunciation and stress patterns for learners, and ask them to repeat.

Assign Workbook pp. 11–12.

Use Unit Master 20 (Grammar: Using Verbs) now or at any time during the rest of the unit.

Activity A

Play the audio or read the listening script below.

Ask learners which are negative and which are affirmative statements.

Listening Script/Answers

Listen:

1. She was shrugging her shoulders. *(affirmative)*
2. The students weren't slouching in their chairs. *(negative)*
3. She was nudging her partner to get his attention. *(affirmative)*
4. He wasn't winking at you. *(negative)*
5. The children were staring out the window. *(affirmative)*

Activity B

Have learners use the vocabulary list and their charts from the Group Chat to write sentences.

Activity C

- Divide learners into small groups.
- Follow the directions for the activity in the student book.
- Set a two-minute time limit for each situation.
- Give small prizes to the group with the most answers.

Activity D

Read the sentences and discuss what each person thought or felt.

Task 1

Draw the outline of a piece of paper on the board or an overhead transparency. Then do the following:

- Draw lines to designate left and right margins. Tell learners not to write in the margins.
- Review paragraph formation, pointing out indentation.
- Remind learners to write from the left to the right margin instead of writing one sentence per line.
- Brainstorm opening lines for the letter, e.g., *I've been thinking about something that happened to me. It was really funny (horrible, uncomfortable, etc.), so I want to tell you about it.*

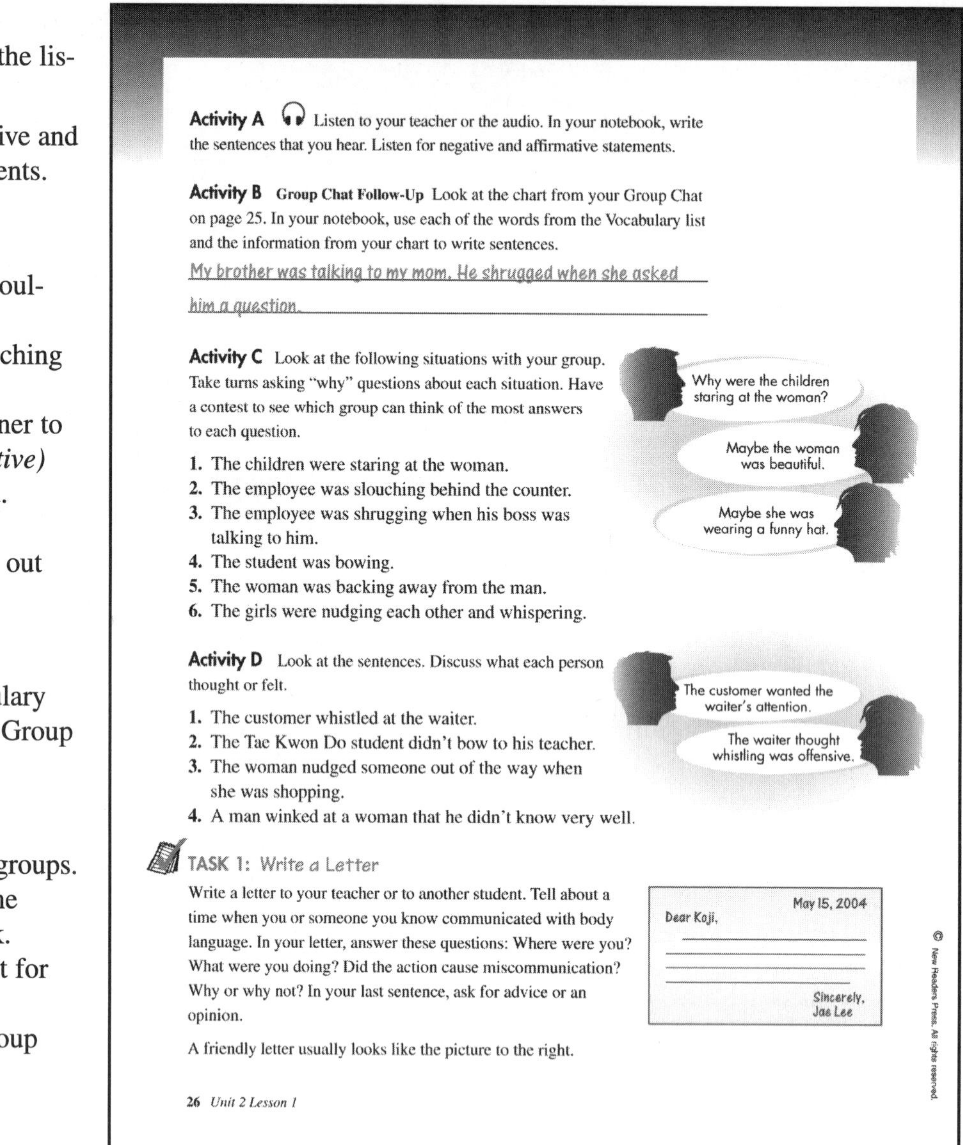

Activity A Listen to your teacher or the audio. In your notebook, write the sentences that you hear. Listen for negative and affirmative statements.

Activity B **Group Chat Follow-Up** Look at the chart from your Group Chat on page 25. In your notebook, use each of the words from the Vocabulary list and the information from your chart to write sentences.

My brother was talking to my mom. He shrugged when she asked him a question.

Activity C Look at the following situations with your group. Take turns asking "why" questions about each situation. Have a contest to see which group can think of the most answers to each question.

1. The children were staring at the woman.
2. The employee was slouching behind the counter.
3. The employee was shrugging when his boss was talking to him.
4. The student was bowing.
5. The woman was backing away from the man.
6. The girls were nudging each other and whispering.

Activity D Look at the sentences. Discuss what each person thought or felt.

1. The customer whistled at the waiter.
2. The Tae Kwon Do student didn't bow to his teacher.
3. The woman nudged someone out of the way when she was shopping.
4. A man winked at a woman that he didn't know very well.

TASK 1: Write a Letter

Write a letter to your teacher or to another student. Tell about a time when you or someone you know communicated with body language. In your letter, answer these questions: Where were you? What were you doing? Did the action cause miscommunication? Why or why not? In your last sentence, ask for advice or an opinion.

A friendly letter usually looks like the picture to the right.

26 *Unit 2 Lesson 1*

Ongoing Assessment

As you read the letters, take notes on the following criteria:

a. Friendly-letter format
   - 0 = no paragraphing, inappropriate or missing salutation and closing
   - 1 = one or two of the above elements done correctly
   - 2 = all of the above elements done correctly

b. Content
   - 0 = content difficult to understand or not related to miscommunication caused by body language
   - 1 = content sometimes difficult to understand because of grammar or word-choice errors; content not difficult to understand, but one or more assignment questions not answered
   - 2 = writing easy to understand and all assignment questions answered

When you return the letters, review problem areas with learners.

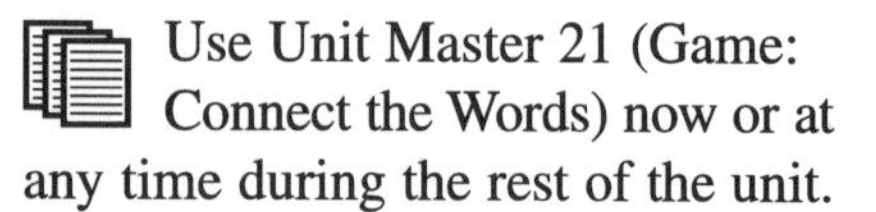

Use Unit Master 21 (Game: Connect the Words) now or at any time during the rest of the unit.

Lesson 2: A Simple Apology

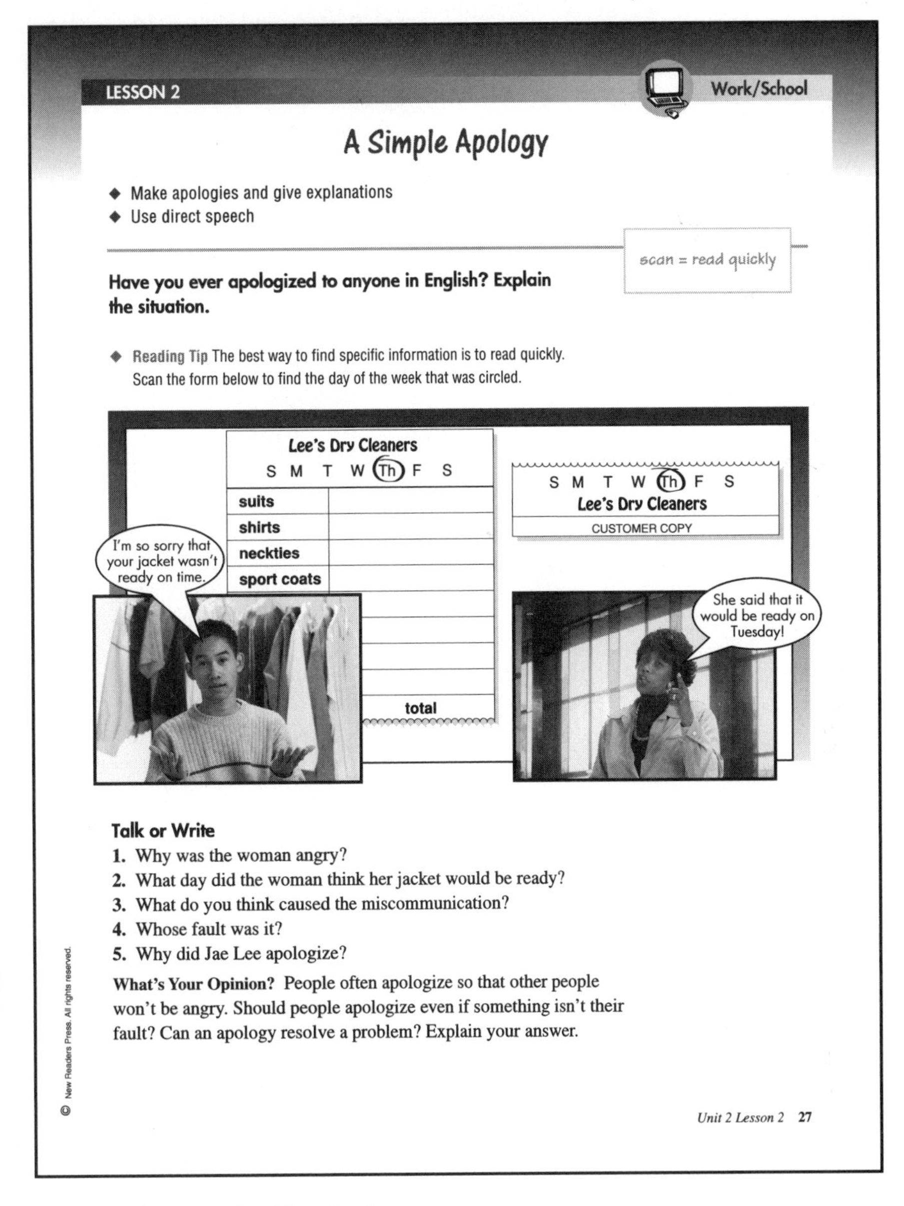

LESSON 2 Work/School

A Simple Apology

- Make apologies and give explanations
- Use direct speech

scan = read quickly

Have you ever apologized to anyone in English? Explain the situation.

- **Reading Tip** The best way to find specific information is to read quickly. Scan the form below to find the day of the week that was circled.

Lee's Dry Cleaners
S M T W (Th) F S

suits	
shirts	
neckties	
sport coats	
total	

S M T W (Th) F S
Lee's Dry Cleaners
CUSTOMER COPY

Talk or Write

1. Why was the woman angry?
2. What day did the woman think her jacket would be ready?
3. What do you think caused the miscommunication?
4. Whose fault was it?
5. Why did Jae Lee apologize?

What's Your Opinion? People often apologize so that other people won't be angry. Should people apologize even if something isn't their fault? Can an apology resolve a problem? Explain your answer.

Unit 2 Lesson 2 27

Follow the suggestions on p. 5 for talking about the title. Then do the following:

- Ask learners to give examples of what a simple apology might be (e.g., *I'm sorry, pardon me*).
- Explain that *simple* may mean "not complex" or "of few words." On the other hand, it can also mean "not difficult." Since many people have trouble saying, "I'm sorry," an apology is seldom simple in this sense.

Question

Ask learners to think of situations that are easy to apologize for and other situations that are not. Discuss reasons why people might have difficulty apologizing (e.g., when they think they're right).

Reading Tip

Answer

If learners have difficulty, tell them that *Th (for Thursday)* was circled.

One Step Up

After learners complete the scanning exercise, ask them to scan again for the following information:

- name of dry cleaners *(Lee's Dry Cleaners)*
- number of clothing words *(4 terms; one—sport coats—has 2 words in it)*

Talk or Write

This exercise helps learners read for details. Follow the suggestions on pp. 5–6 for in-class reading.

Answers

1. Because her jacket wasn't ready.
2. Tuesday
3. Possibly a pronunciation problem or a perception problem, due to similarities in the sounds of Tuesday and Thursday.
4. It's not clear who is at fault. The employee could have pointed to the circled day of the week at the time of the order, or the customer could have looked at the order form to double-check. These actions might have prevented the misunderstanding.
5. He didn't want to lose a customer. (Many business owners, managers, and employees know it's important to apologize to customers for misunderstandings in order not to lose their business.)

What's Your Opinion?

Have learners offer their opinions and explain them.

Vocabulary

Follow the suggestions on p. 6 for introducing and reinforcing the vocabulary words.

<u>One Step Up</u>

Follow the suggestions on p. 6 for categorizing the vocabulary words as nouns and verbs.

- Nouns: *fault, mix-up, apology*
- Verbs: *excuse, forgive, pardon, apologize, fault*

Group Chat

Use Customizable Master 4 (Idea Map). Follow the suggestions on p. 7 for customizing and duplicating the master and distributing the copies.

- Follow the suggestions on p. 7 for debriefing Class Chats.
- When groups finish mapping their ideas, write one problem from each group on the board.
- Talk with the class about each problem. Have learners suggest what people might say because of the problem.

Grammar Talk

Follow the suggestions on p. 6 for introducing the grammar point.

<u>Suggested Answers</u>

- The comma is after the word *said,* just before the direct quote.
- The quotation marks are at the beginning and end of the direct quote.

Pronunciation Target

Play the audio or read the sentences in the student book.

Explain the importance of voice volume and body language in making an apology.

- Repeat an apology using several different levels of volume and different body language.
- Using the expressions below, model the difference in intonation between sincere apologies and sarcastic apologies:

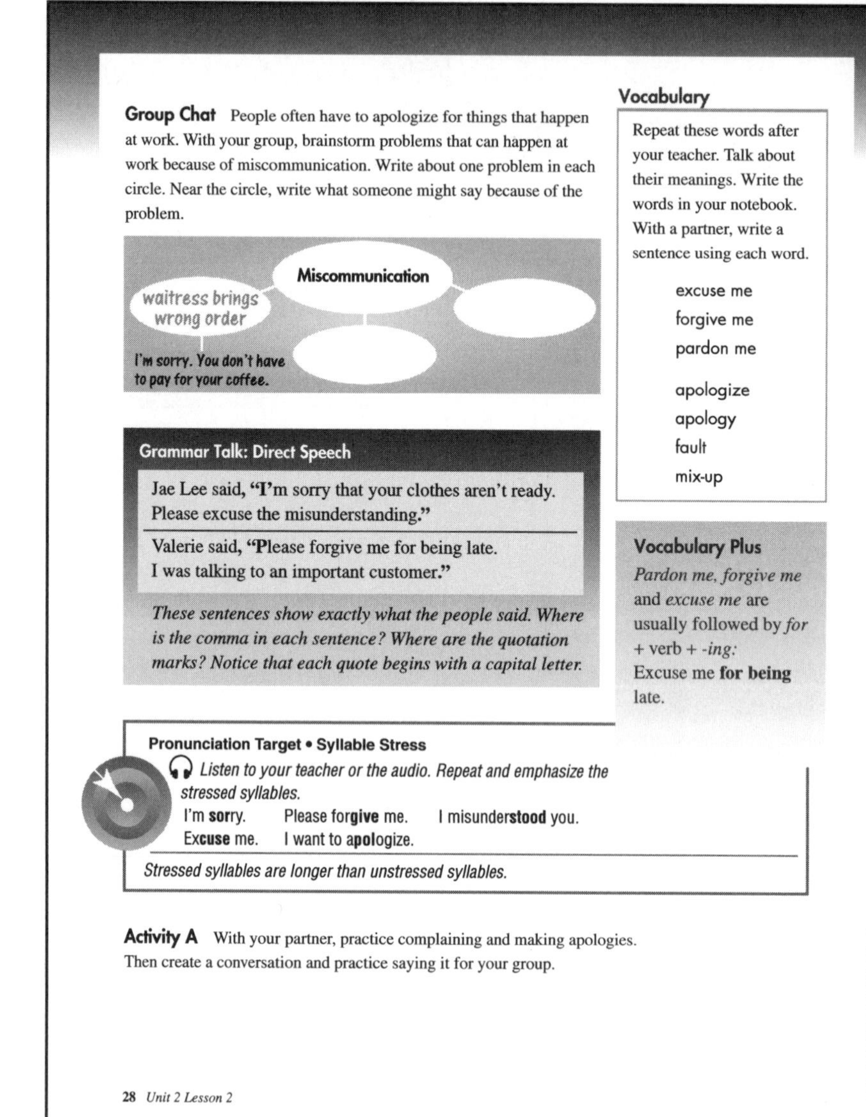

Group Chat People often have to apologize for things that happen at work. With your group, brainstorm problems that can happen at work because of miscommunication. Write about one problem in each circle. Near the circle, write what someone might say because of the problem.

Miscommunication

waitress brings wrong order

I'm sorry. You don't have to pay for your coffee.

Vocabulary

Repeat these words after your teacher. Talk about their meanings. Write the words in your notebook. With a partner, write a sentence using each word.

excuse me
forgive me
pardon me
apologize
apology
fault
mix-up

Grammar Talk: Direct Speech

Jae Lee said, **"I'm** sorry that your clothes aren't ready. Please excuse the misunderstanding.**"**

Valerie said, **"Please** forgive me for being late. I was talking to an important customer.**"**

These sentences show exactly what the people said. Where is the comma in each sentence? Where are the quotation marks? Notice that each quote begins with a capital letter.

Vocabulary Plus

Pardon me, forgive me and *excuse me* are usually followed by *for* + verb + *-ing:*
Excuse me **for being** late.

Pronunciation Target • Syllable Stress

Listen to your teacher or the audio. Repeat and emphasize the stressed syllables.

I'm **sorry**. Please for**give** me. I misunder**stood** you.
Excuse me. I want to a**pol**ogize.

Stressed syllables are longer than unstressed syllables.

Activity A With your partner, practice complaining and making apologies. Then create a conversation and practice saying it for your group.

28 *Unit 2 Lesson 2*

I'm sorry.
Pardon me.
Excuse me.
I apologize.
Forgive me.

Activity A

First, have partners practice making complaints and formulating appropriate apologies. Then have them create full conversations and model them for their groups.

Assign Workbook pp. 13–14.

Use Unit Master 22 (Grammar: Write a Conversation) now or at any time during the rest of the unit.

Activity B

Using sentences from the Group Chat idea map, have learners write them in their notebooks as direct speech.

Activity C

Have partners work together to unscramble the sentences. Remind them to insert commas and quotation marks in the appropriate places.

Answers

2. She said, "Pardon me for keeping you on hold so long."
3. He said, "I'm sorry, but visiting hours are over now."
4. He said, "Please forgive us for the mix-up with your package."

Activity D

Have partners evaluate the situations pictured and then practice making apologies.

Task 2

After the pair practice, have a contest in which learners suggest ridiculous excuses for each of the situations presented. Examples of such excuses include these:

- I think the cook ate your order and gave me this one instead.
- I tripped over my shoelace and fell, then had to find a bandage because I skinned my knee.
- I left my glasses at home and couldn't find the room.
- Your pizza fell out of the truck.

To choose a winner for the contest, write the most ridiculous possibilities on the board and take a hand vote to select the most ridiculous excuse. Explain to learners that, when describing excuses, *lame* is a good synonym for *ridiculous.*

Ongoing Assessment

As learners perform their conversations, circulate and take notes on the following criteria:

Activity B **Group Chat Follow-Up** Look at the sentences that you wrote in your Group Chat idea map. Write them in direct speech in your notebook.

The manager said, "I'm sorry. You don't have to pay for your coffee."

Activity C In your notebook, unscramble the words in each sentence. Work with a partner. Remember to use a comma and quotation marks.

1. forgot / sorry / the / she / to / soda / I'm / said / bring / that / I
   She said, "I'm sorry that I forgot to bring the soda."
2. you / so / me / said / long / pardon / on / she / for / hold / keeping
3. hours / sorry / now / visiting / I'm / but / he / over / said / are
4. for / said / package / your / with / forgive / he / please / us / mix-up / the

Activity D Look at the pictures. With your partner, practice making apologies using the vocabulary words. Think of as many apologies as you can.

TASK 2: Write a Conversation

Look at the following list of problems that could happen at work. In pairs, write a conversation with an appropriate apology and a short explanation. Practice the apologies in pairs.

- A waitress brings the wrong order to a customer.

Customer: Excuse me, this isn't what I ordered. I wanted wheat bread.

Waitress: I'm sorry for the misunderstanding. I thought you said white.

- An employee comes to a meeting at the wrong time.
- A college student goes to the wrong class.
- A pizza place delivers the wrong pizza.

a. General quality of apology
   0 = incorrect apology, or incomprehensible because of pronunciation
   1 = abrupt, halting apology
   2 = smooth, clear, correct apology

b. General quality of excuses
   0 = incomprehensible excuse
   1 = abrupt, halting excuse
   2 = clear, understandable excuse

One Step Up

Bring in sympathy or apology cards and look at the different ways they say, "I'm sorry." Learners can use these cards as models to make their own cards or to write a sympathy note or apology to someone.

Lesson 3: In Public

Follow the suggestions on p. 5 for talking about the title.

Question

Read the question aloud and then follow these steps:

- Ask learners to first think about the question and then make notes about things people do in public that bother them.
- Have a class discussion about the question. Encourage learners to express the ideas in their notes.
- Ask for learners' reactions to behaviors they have observed in classes they have taken.
- Discuss what is appropriate behavior in various public places (e.g., classrooms, shopping malls, restaurants).

Attention Box

These expressions should be understood, but learners should not be expected to produce the phrases at this point.

Listening Tip

Play the audio or read the listening script on p. 119.

Talk or Write

This exercise helps learners to better understand everyday conversation.

Answers

1. She was goofing around with her friend (talking and laughing).
2. He talked to them about appropriate behavior in his class.
3. Jae Lee told Sarah to talk to her instructor.
4. In a martial arts class, the atmosphere is very serious. In an aerobics class, you can talk and have fun while you exercise.
5. Jae Lee wanted Sarah to know that she wasn't the only one who made mistakes.

LESSON 3 — Community

In Public

- Describe public behaviors
- Learn about American public behavior

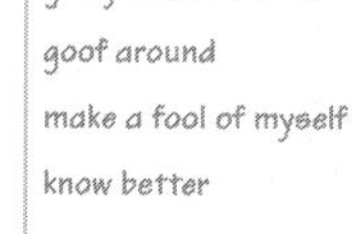

What things do people do in public that bother you?

- **Listening Tip** Thinking about what you already know about a topic can help you understand what you hear. What do you know about martial arts classes? Listen to your teacher or the audio. Listen to the whole conversation once. Then read the questions and listen again. You can read the words on page 118.

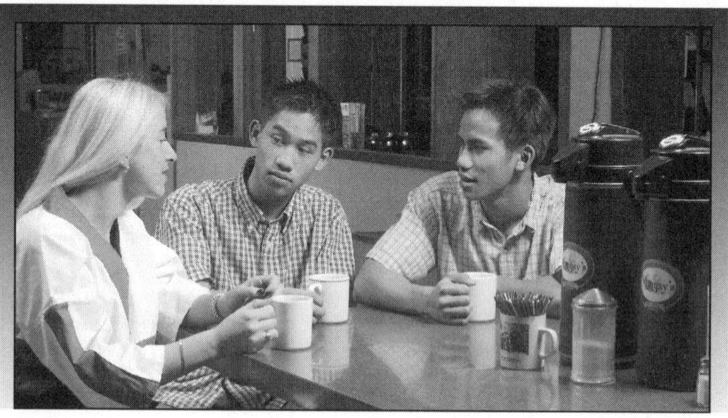

Sarah is telling Jae Lee and Koji about something that she did in Tae Kwon Do class that bothered her instructor.

Talk or Write

1. What was Sarah doing in her Tae Kwon Do class?
2. What did the teacher do?
3. What advice did Jae Lee give her?
4. How is a martial arts class different from an aerobics class?
5. Why did Jae Lee tell Sarah about his experience with his neighbor?

Vocabulary

Follow the suggestions on p. 6 for introducing and reinforcing the vocabulary words.

Ask learners to act out the words or model them for the class.

Pronunciation Tip

Model the pronunciation for the words *impatient, impolite,* and *interrupt,* making sure to stress the difference between *m* and *n* in the prefixes.

One Step Up

Follow the suggestions on p. 6 for categorizing the vocabulary words as verbs or adjectives.

- Verbs: *interrupt, snap*
- Adjectives: *aggressive, impatient, impolite, polite, rude*

In the US

Before reading, relate the topic to learners' experience with these questions:

- How do people act in a supermarket (or other food market) in your home country? How do people act in the US? Is it different or the same?
- Ask learners to demonstrate appropriate distance *(personal space)* between people in their home countries.

Compare Cultures

Use Customizable Master 5 (Venn Diagram). Follow the suggestions on p. 7 for customizing and duplicating the master and distributing the copies.

- After they write their ideas in the diagram, have learners share them with their groups.
- Have a class discussion about similarities and differences between cultures.

Activity A

Have learners sit in small groups to do the activity. Ask each group to share its written sentences with the other groups.

In the US *Personal Space and Public Behavior*

"Personal space" is the distance between two people that seems comfortable. In the US, this distance is about two feet. If you stand or sit too close to someone, the person will feel uncomfortable. If you stand much farther away than two feet, the person will probably move closer to you.

"Public behavior" is the way people act in places like supermarkets and restaurants. When people in the US are shopping, they stand in line to get help, or they take a number. They think it is rude to cut in line. Also, if they want to reach past another customer, they do not touch the other person. People usually say, "Excuse me," and wait for the other person to move. In restaurants, it is impolite to call the waiter by snapping your fingers, whistling, or saying "Psst." People raise one hand and wait for the waiter to see them, or they say "Excuse me" to get the waiter's attention.

Vocabulary

Repeat these words after your teacher. Talk about their meanings. Write the words in your notebook. With a partner, write a sentence using each word.

aggressive
impatient
impolite
interrupt
polite
rude
snap your fingers

Idiom Watch!
cut in line

Compare Cultures Think about how people behave in public places in your home country. Make a diagram like this one. Write the name of your home country in one circle. Write US in the other circle. Choose a public place for the title.

Market

Spain	(both)	US
customers stand in a group and ask who is last	cashier thanks customer	customers stand in line

Activity A Sit in a circle. Tell the student next to you an idea you have about public behavior. That person tells the next student what you said, and adds another idea. The third student tells the fourth student exactly what students 1 and 2 said.

When you have gone around the circle once, write down what each student said in direct speech. Check to see if everyone in your group wrote exactly the same sentences, including punctuation.

I think it's rude to interrupt.

Tony said, "It's rude to interrupt." I think that cheating is dishonest.

Tony said, "It's rude to interrupt." Linh said, "Cheating is dishonest." I think that pushing is aggressive.

Unit 2 Lesson 3 31

Extension

Write the adjectives below on the board or an overhead transparency. Next to each, write the example of that behavior. Ask learners to give you more examples.

- Rude: cutting in line
- Polite: saying "good morning"
- Aggressive: standing very close to a stranger
- Impatient: crossing your arms

Use Unit Master 23 (Vocabulary: Create a Story) and 24 (Thinking Skill: Misunderstandings) now or at any time during the rest of the unit.

Activity B

Have learners do the exercise in pairs.

One Step Up

Have learners sit in small groups.

- Give each group a small card with one of the following adjectives written on it: *aggressive, impatient, polite, impolite, rude, friendly, embarrassed, sorry.*
- Ask each group to act out the word, without using the word. The other learners must guess what the word is.

Task 3

Before beginning the task, discuss the importance of body language:

- Body language affects how people perceive you, so it can influence your chances for success at school or work.
- Behaviors such as slouching, fidgeting, or not looking a teacher or supervisor in the eye are viewed negatively in this culture.
- Since the topic of behavior in school is included in this task, share with learners how such behaviors (and other negative ones you can think of) make you, as a teacher, feel.

One Step Up

Ask each group to create a skit from the story they shared. Have them follow these steps:

- Decide who the characters will be.
- Choose a narrator to set the stage.
- Plan the dialogue.
- Choose props.
- Practice.
- Perform.

Review Unit Skills

Follow the suggestions on pp. 7–9 for games and activities to review the vocabulary and grammar in this unit.

 Assign Workbook pp. 15–16.

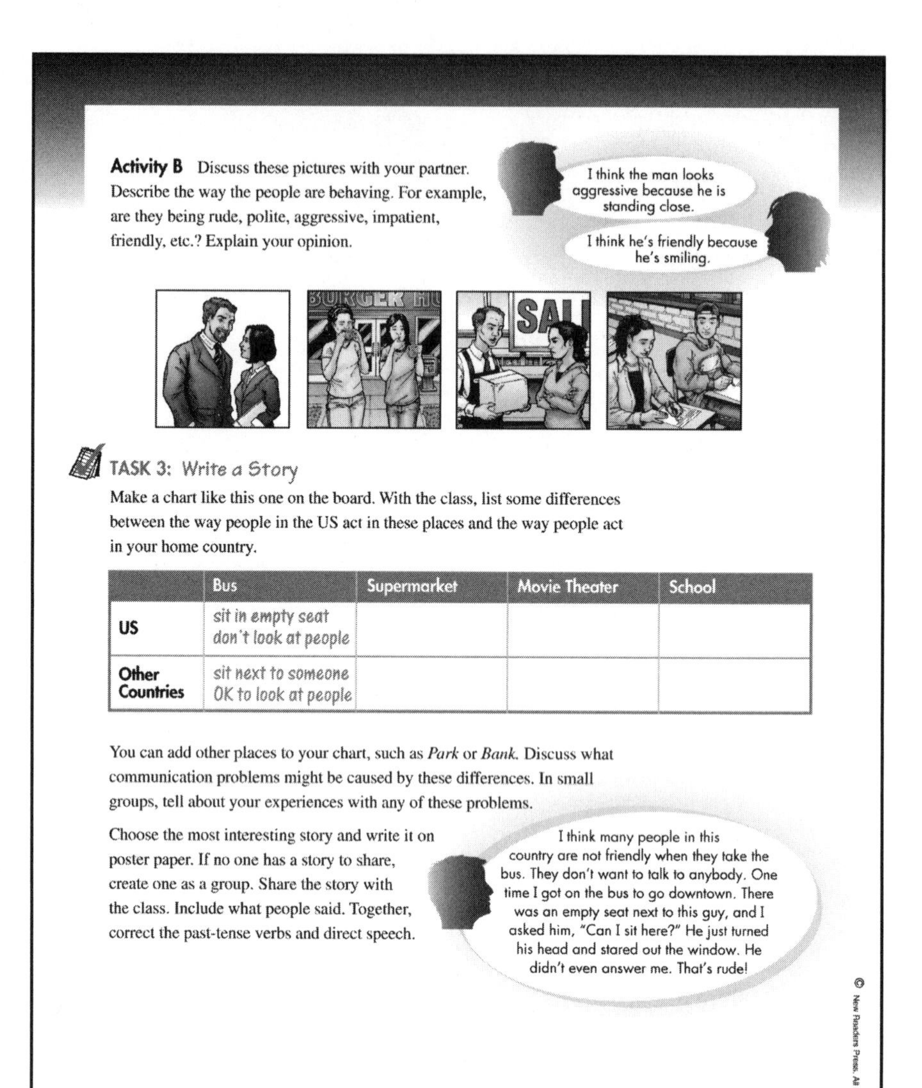

Activity B Discuss these pictures with your partner. Describe the way the people are behaving. For example, are they being rude, polite, aggressive, impatient, friendly, etc.? Explain your opinion.

TASK 3: Write a Story

Make a chart like this one on the board. With the class, list some differences between the way people in the US act in these places and the way people act in your home country.

	Bus	Supermarket	Movie Theater	School
US	sit in empty seat don't look at people			
Other Countries	sit next to someone OK to look at people			

You can add other places to your chart, such as *Park* or *Bank*. Discuss what communication problems might be caused by these differences. In small groups, tell about your experiences with any of these problems.

Choose the most interesting story and write it on poster paper. If no one has a story to share, create one as a group. Share the story with the class. Include what people said. Together, correct the past-tense verbs and direct speech.

Unit 2 Project

Assessment

As each group performs its skit, complete a copy of Unit Master 26 (Project Assessment Form). If possible, make a copy of the form for each group member's portfolio.

Learners work in small groups to write a skit that demonstrates a misunderstanding.

Get Ready

Follow the steps in the student book to prepare the skits.

If learners cannot write in their books, have them copy the form from "Do the Work" and plan their skit.

Do the Work

- Ask group members to agree on a misunderstanding they would like to present. To avoid repetition, monitor and alter the choices before learners begin planning their skits.
- Emphasize that the skit presents the problem but *does not* solve it.
- Encourage learners to exaggerate behaviors in their skits.
- Point out the directions in the student book for developing the skit.

UNIT 2 Project

Write a Skit

Write a skit about a misunderstanding. Follow these steps:

skit

Get Ready

1. In your group, write a skit that demonstrates a misunderstanding between two people. Don't try to solve the problem.
2. You can bring things to class to make your skit more interesting. For example, bring a baseball and talk about a broken window, bring a pizza box and talk about delivering to the wrong house, bring a broken clock and talk about being late.
3. Plan your body language. Include some of the actions from the Vocabulary box on page 25. Memorize your lines.

Do the Work

Use a work sheet like the one to the right to plan and write your skit. Each person should say at least four sentences. Choose two group members to perform the skit.

Title:________
Place:________
Names of characters:_____ and _____
Problem:________

Conversation:

A:_____ B:_____
A:_____ B:_____
A:_____ B:_____
A:_____ B:_____

Present

Present your skit. After each skit is presented, decide how to solve the problem. Work in pairs. Write your solutions on large strips of paper. Tape them on the board. As a class, discuss each solution.

Writing Extension Choose one of the communication problems from the skits and write a paragraph explaining the problem. Tell which solution you think is best and explain why. Remember to indent and stay within the margins.

Technology Extra

Use the following key words to do an Internet search: "cultural diversity," "cultural conflicts," "body language." Choose an article to print and share it with your group.

Unit 2 Project 33

Present

When groups are ready to present their skits, distribute one copy of Unit Master 25 (Unit 2 Project: Alternate Solutions) to each pair of learners.

After learners present their skits, follow the directions in the student book and develop resolutions for each misunderstanding.

- Encourage learners to avoid easy solutions.
- Cut large strips from large sheets of paper or poster board. Provide enough strips to each group for them to write one solution for each skit presented, including their own.
- Ask the groups to agree on the best solution for each problem and to write it on the strip.

Writing Extension

Have learners write a paragraph about one of the misunderstandings from the skits.

Technology Extra

Have learners choose one of the key words suggested in the student book and do an Internet search. Ask them to share the results of their search with their groups.

Assign Workbook p. 17 (Check Your Progress).

Use Unit Master 27 (Unit 2 Checkup/Review) whenever you complete this unit.

Unit 3: Better Safe Than Sorry

Materials for the Unit

- Safety brochures from local police and fire departments (optional)
- Poster paper
- Smoke detector, fire extinguisher, electrical device with plug
- Customizable Masters 1, 4, and 5
- Generic Assessment Masters 8–12
- Unit Masters 28–34

Better Safe Than Sorry

Follow the suggestions on p. 5 for talking about the title.

- Discuss the meanings of the words *safe* and *sorry.* Make sure learners understand that *sorry* can mean "feeling bad" or can be an apology.
- Ask learners what they think the idiom *better safe than sorry* means, e.g., "It's better to be careful, otherwise you can get hurt," or "It's better to take your time than it is to hurry, because you might make a mistake."
- Ask learners when they might use this expression.

Photo

Follow the suggestions on p. 4 for talking about the photo. Then read the question under the arrow.

Think and Talk

Read the questions aloud.

- As learners generate different answers, write them on the board.
- For question 2, encourage learners to be specific when identifying what Miguel might be worried about.

What's Your Opinion?

Discuss the questions in the student book with learners. Be sure they explain their opinions.

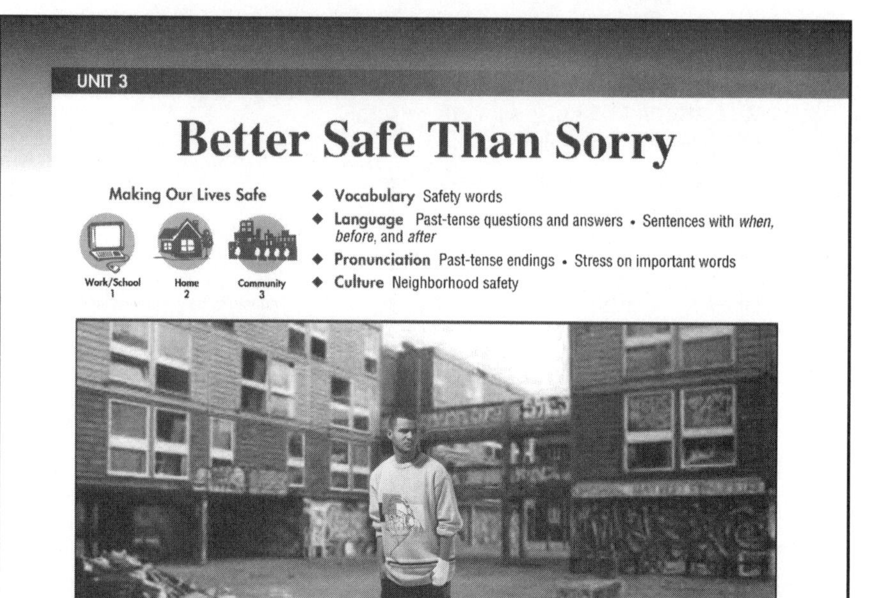

UNIT 3

Better Safe Than Sorry

Making Our Lives Safe

Work/School 1 | Home 2 | Community 3

- **Vocabulary** Safety words
- **Language** Past-tense questions and answers • Sentences with *when, before,* and *after*
- **Pronunciation** Past-tense endings • Stress on important words
- **Culture** Neighborhood safety

Where have you seen a neighborhood like this?

Miguel Jimenez, a 19-year-old from Nicaragua, lives in Rochester, New York, with his parents and younger brother and sisters. Miguel has been worried about safety at his job, at home, and in his neighborhood.

Think and Talk

1. What do you see in the photograph?
2. What do you think Miguel is worried about?
3. What caused the safety problems in his neighborhood?
4. What concerns do you have about your safety?

concerns

What's Your Opinion? Many people notice things that make their homes, workplaces, or neighborhoods unsafe, but they don't do or say anything. Can you explain why? Are those good or bad reasons for not doing anything?

34 *Unit 3*

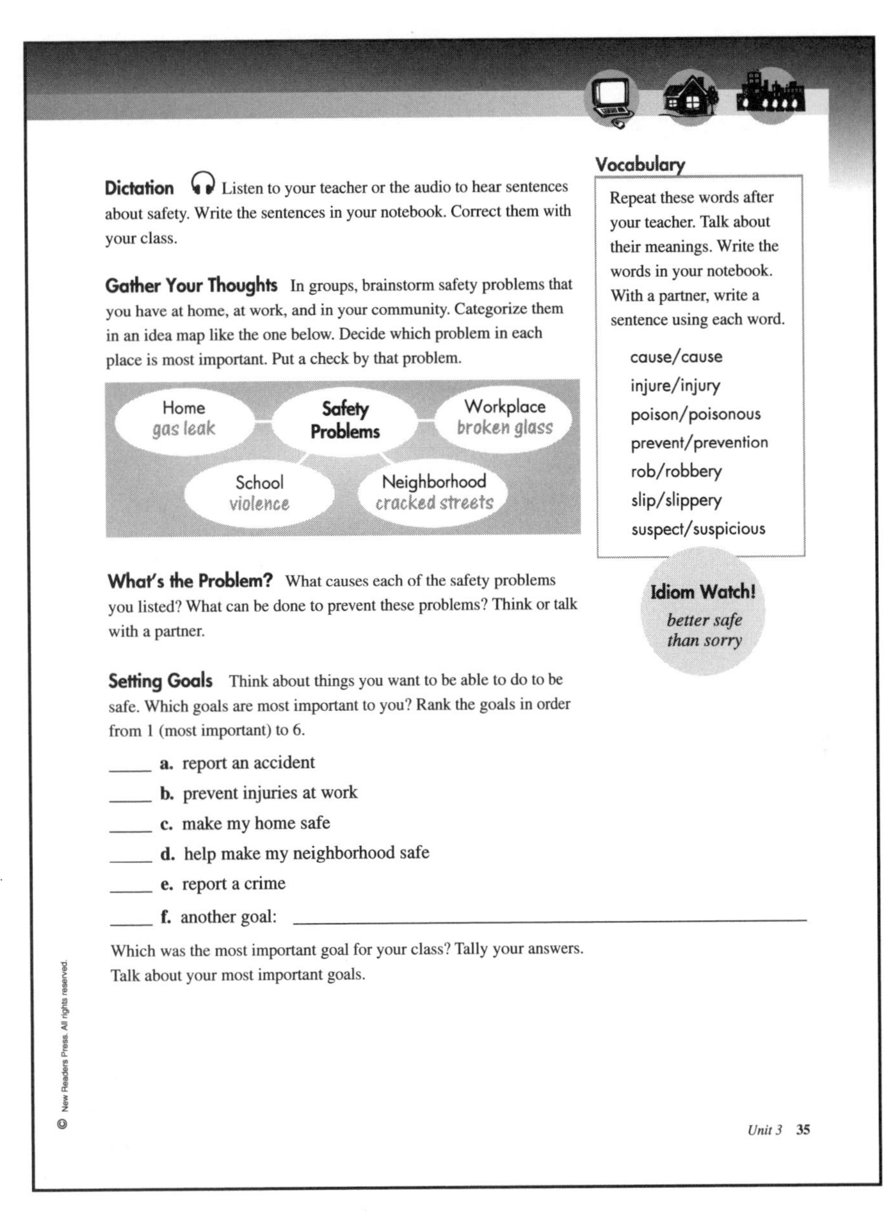

Dictation Listen to your teacher or the audio to hear sentences about safety. Write the sentences in your notebook. Correct them with your class.

Gather Your Thoughts In groups, brainstorm safety problems that you have at home, at work, and in your community. Categorize them in an idea map like the one below. Decide which problem in each place is most important. Put a check by that problem.

What's the Problem? What causes each of the safety problems you listed? What can be done to prevent these problems? Think or talk with a partner.

Setting Goals Think about things you want to be able to do to be safe. Which goals are most important to you? Rank the goals in order from 1 (most important) to 6.

____ **a.** report an accident
____ **b.** prevent injuries at work
____ **c.** make my home safe
____ **d.** help make my neighborhood safe
____ **e.** report a crime
____ **f.** another goal: ______________________

Which was the most important goal for your class? Tally your answers. Talk about your most important goals.

Vocabulary

Repeat these words after your teacher. Talk about their meanings. Write the words in your notebook. With a partner, write a sentence using each word.

cause/cause
injure/injury
poison/poisonous
prevent/prevention
rob/robbery
slip/slippery
suspect/suspicious

Idiom Watch!
better safe than sorry

Vocabulary

Follow the suggestions on p. 6 for introducing and reinforcing the vocabulary words.

Pronunciation Tip

Point out the different pronunciations of *s* in *safety/slippery* and *poison/cause.*

Ask learners to think of other words that have the /s/ or the /z/ sound.

One Step Up

Follow the suggestions on p. 6 for categorizing the vocabulary words as nouns, verbs, and adjectives.

- Nouns: *cause, injury, poison, prevention, robbery, slip, suspect*
- Verbs: *cause, injure, prevent, rob, slip, suspect*
- Adjectives: *poisonous, slippery, suspicious*

Dictation

Play the audio or read the listening script below.

When learners finish writing the dictation sentences, ask volunteers to write them on the board. Correct the sentences together.

Write the sentences that you hear.

1. I want my children to be safe.
2. I want my children to learn about water safety.
3. I slipped on the floor.
4. The floor is slippery.
5. They were robbing the bank.
6. I saw a robbery.
7. Be careful not to injure yourself.
8. I'm sorry that you have an injury.
9. Keep poisons away from children.
10. Some cleaning substances are poisonous.
11. I was trying to prevent an accident.
12. The police help with crime prevention.
13. What was the cause of the fire?
14. A space heater caused the fire.
15. The police arrested the suspect.
16. He had a suspicious manner.

Gather Your Thoughts

Use Customizable Master 4 (Idea Map). Follow the suggestions on p. 7 for customizing and duplicating the master and distributing the copies. Make one copy for each group.

Brainstorm safety issues as a class, and then have small groups categorize them. Lead the class to very specific problems that can be categorized (e.g., cracked sidewalks, streetlights, weapons at school, bullies, unsafe machines at work, no smoke alarms, unfenced pools).

What's the Problem?

Follow the suggestions on p. 5 for identifying and analyzing problems.

Setting Goals

Follow the suggestions on p. 5 for setting goals.

Lesson 1: Safety on the Job

Follow the suggestions on p. 5 for talking about the title.

- Discuss the various meanings of *job* (work, profession, task) and the phrase *Good job!*
- Make sure learners understand that *on the job* means "at work," or "in the workplace."

Questions

Read the introductory questions aloud. Encourage good listening skills by asking follow-up questions about learners' answers, e.g.:

- Where was José's co-worker injured?
- Why was he injured?

Alternatively, have learners make a simple chart in their notebooks using these three heads:

- Who?
- Where?
- What happened?

Have learners fill in the chart as they listen to other learners' answers.

Attention Box

Read the words to learners, pointing or miming to convey meaning. This vocabulary should be understood, but learners should not be expected to produce the words at this point.

<u>One Step Up</u>

Note that *grill, fracture, wound,* and *treat* are both nouns and verbs. The verb *treat* has different meanings:

- The doctor *treats* 15 patients a day.
- I *treat* my children equally.
- I *treat* my daughter to ice cream on Fridays.

Reading Tip

First, have learners read the questions below the accident form. Then ask them to scan the form and find the requested information.

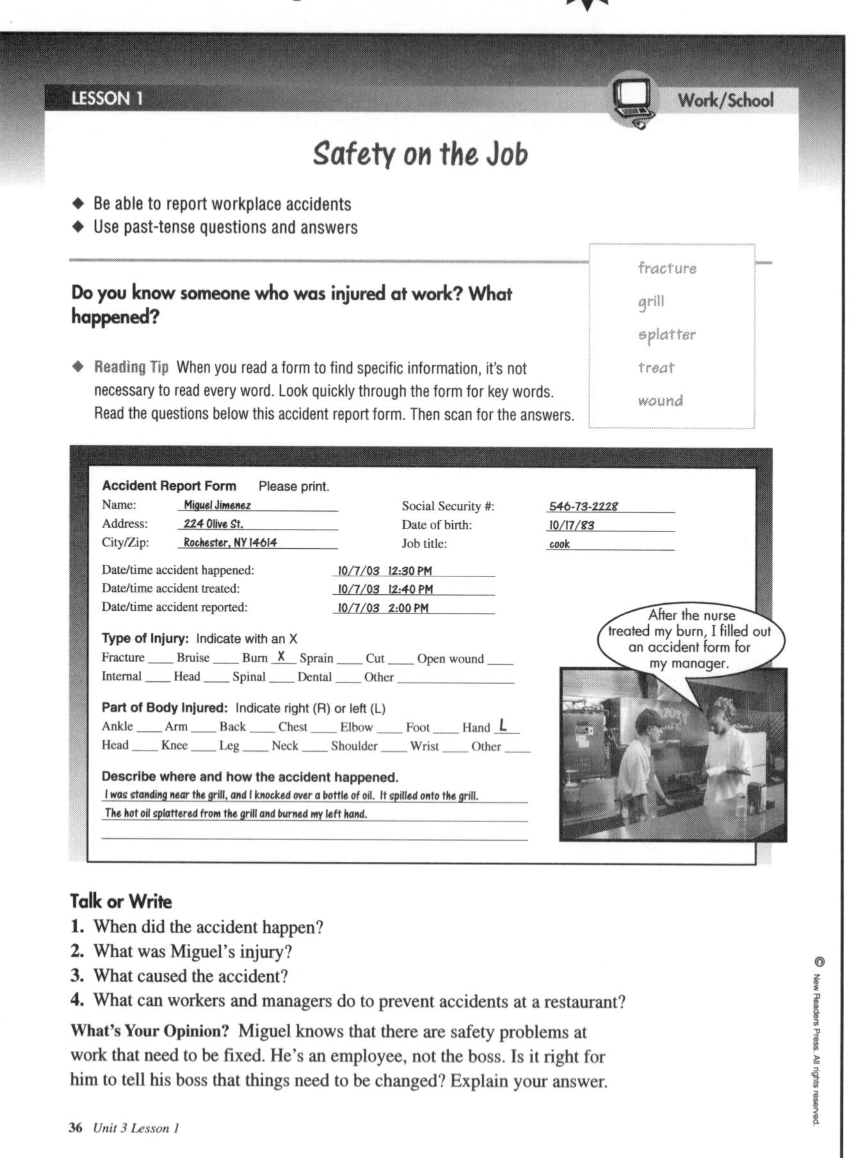

LESSON 1 Work/School

Safety on the Job

- Be able to report workplace accidents
- Use past-tense questions and answers

fracture
grill
splatter
treat
wound

Do you know someone who was injured at work? What happened?

- **Reading Tip** When you read a form to find specific information, it's not necessary to read every word. Look quickly through the form for key words. Read the questions below this accident report form. Then scan for the answers.

Accident Report Form Please print.

Name: Miguel Jimenez
Address: 224 Olive St.
City/Zip: Rochester, NY 14614
Social Security #: 546-73-2228
Date of birth: 10/17/83
Job title: cook

Date/time accident happened: 10/7/03 12:30 PM
Date/time accident treated: 10/7/03 12:40 PM
Date/time accident reported: 10/7/03 2:00 PM

Type of Injury: Indicate with an X
Fracture ___ Bruise ___ Burn _X_ Sprain ___ Cut ___ Open wound ___
Internal ___ Head ___ Spinal ___ Dental ___ Other ___

Part of Body Injured: Indicate right (R) or left (L)
Ankle ___ Arm ___ Back ___ Chest ___ Elbow ___ Foot ___ Hand _L_
Head ___ Knee ___ Leg ___ Neck ___ Shoulder ___ Wrist ___ Other ___

Describe where and how the accident happened.
I was standing near the grill, and I knocked over a bottle of oil. It spilled onto the grill.
The hot oil splattered from the grill and burned my left hand.

Talk or Write

1. When did the accident happen?
2. What was Miguel's injury?
3. What caused the accident?
4. What can workers and managers do to prevent accidents at a restaurant?

What's Your Opinion? Miguel knows that there are safety problems at work that need to be fixed. He's an employee, not the boss. Is it right for him to tell his boss that things need to be changed? Explain your answer.

36 *Unit 3 Lesson 1*

<u>Extension</u>

Have learners scan Miguel's accident form for more information by asking questions like these:

- What's Miguel's last name?
- Did he bruise his hand?

Talk or Write

This exercise help learners read to locate specific information.

<u>Answers</u>

1. 10/7/03 at 12:30 P.M.
2. He burned his left hand.
3. Miguel spilled oil on the hot grill.
4. Answers will vary. Possible answers include *clean up spills* and *put things away.*

What's Your Opinion?

Discuss politeness strategies for making suggestions to the boss. Have learners categorize the suggestions into three types:

- polite
- impolite
- overly polite

Vocabulary

Follow the suggestions on p. 6 for introducing the vocabulary words.

Explain that *trip* can be used without the preposition *over:*

Did you trip?

Note that *trip* takes on a different meaning as a noun:

I took a trip to San Diego.

Partner Chat

Use Customizable Master 4 (Idea Map). Follow the suggestions on p. 7 for customizing and duplicating the master and distributing the copies. Make a copy for each pair of learners.

- Ask learners to think first about different types of work sites.
- Have them identify potential safety problems at those sites and put the problems on an idea map.

Safety problems might include:

- *Restaurant:* dirty hands
- *Factory:* no safety glasses
- *Office*: coffee next to the computer

Grammar Talk

Answers

The main verbs are *knock over, smash,* and *be.* The verb *did* is not used in past-tense questions with the verb *be.*

Pronunciation Target

Play the audio or read the listening script below. Then review these pronunciation rules:

- Words that end in a voiced sound are followed by a /d/ sound. (See p. 7 for an explanation of voiced and voiceless sounds.)
- Words that end in voiceless sounds are followed by a /t/ sound.
- Words that end in *t* and *d* are followed by the additional syllable *-ed.*

Listening Script

Each of these words ends in a different sound: *smashed, bruised, reported.*

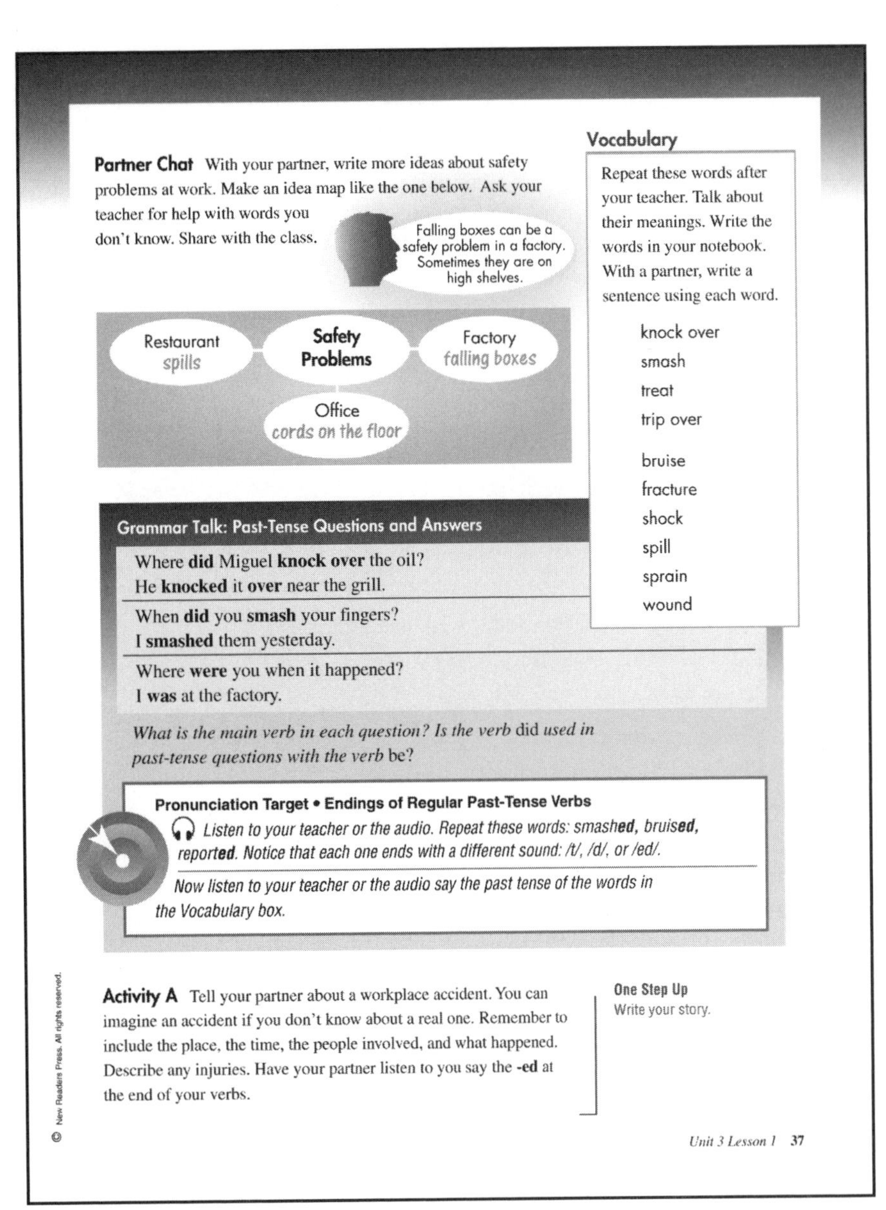

Partner Chat With your partner, write more ideas about safety problems at work. Make an idea map like the one below. Ask your teacher for help with words you don't know. Share with the class.

Vocabulary

Repeat these words after your teacher. Talk about their meanings. Write the words in your notebook. With a partner, write a sentence using each word.

knock over
smash
treat
trip over

bruise
fracture
shock
spill
sprain
wound

Grammar Talk: Past-Tense Questions and Answers

Where **did** Miguel **knock over** the oil? He **knocked** it **over** near the grill.
When **did** you **smash** your fingers? I **smashed** them yesterday.
Where **were** you when it happened? I **was** at the factory.

What is the main verb in each question? Is the verb did *used in past-tense questions with the verb* be?

Pronunciation Target • Endings of Regular Past-Tense Verbs

*Listen to your teacher or the audio. Repeat these words: smash**ed**, bruis**ed**, report**ed**. Notice that each one ends with a different sound: /t/, /d/, or /ed/.*

Now listen to your teacher or the audio say the past tense of the words in the Vocabulary box.

Activity A Tell your partner about a workplace accident. You can imagine an accident if you don't know about a real one. Remember to include the place, the time, the people involved, and what happened. Describe any injuries. Have your partner listen to you say the **-ed** at the end of your verbs.

One Step Up
Write your story.

Listen to these past-tense words. What sound does each one end in?

knocked over, smashed, treated, tripped over, bruised, fractured, shocked, spilled, sprained, wounded

Extension

To emphasize the importance of this additional syllable, create two columns on the board or an overhead transparency. Label them *One-Syllable Words* and *Two-Syllable Words.*

Read the words below. Ask learners to place them in the proper column:

stopped, wanted, rested, helped, needed, tripped

Activity A

One Step Up

Use Customizable Master 4 (Idea Map) to "jump-start" learners for the One Step Up writing.

- Write the word *Accident* in the center circle. In the four peripheral circles write the words *Place, Time, People Involved,* and *What Happened.*
- Make a copy for each learner.
- Have learners complete the map with the information they provided orally in Activity A.

Assign Workbook pp. 18–19.

Activity B

One Step Down

If the One Step Up role-play is difficult for some learners, ask a learner with more developed speaking skills to role-play a supervisor for a group of three employees. The supervisor asks each employee questions about the same accident.

Activity C

Have learners use their idea maps from the Partner Chat to write sentences in their notebooks.

Task 1

Review all vocabulary on the accident report form before learners begin to fill it out.

Have learners identify each part of the body listed by pointing to their own bodies.

One Step Up

Ask learners to talk about their accident reports with their groups. Have them suggest how others can prevent similar accidents.

Pronunciation Tip

Practice pronouncing the words that identify parts of the body, with particular attention to these two contrasting pairs:

- The beginning sounds in *chest* and *shoulder*
- The final /st/ sound in *chest* and *wrist*

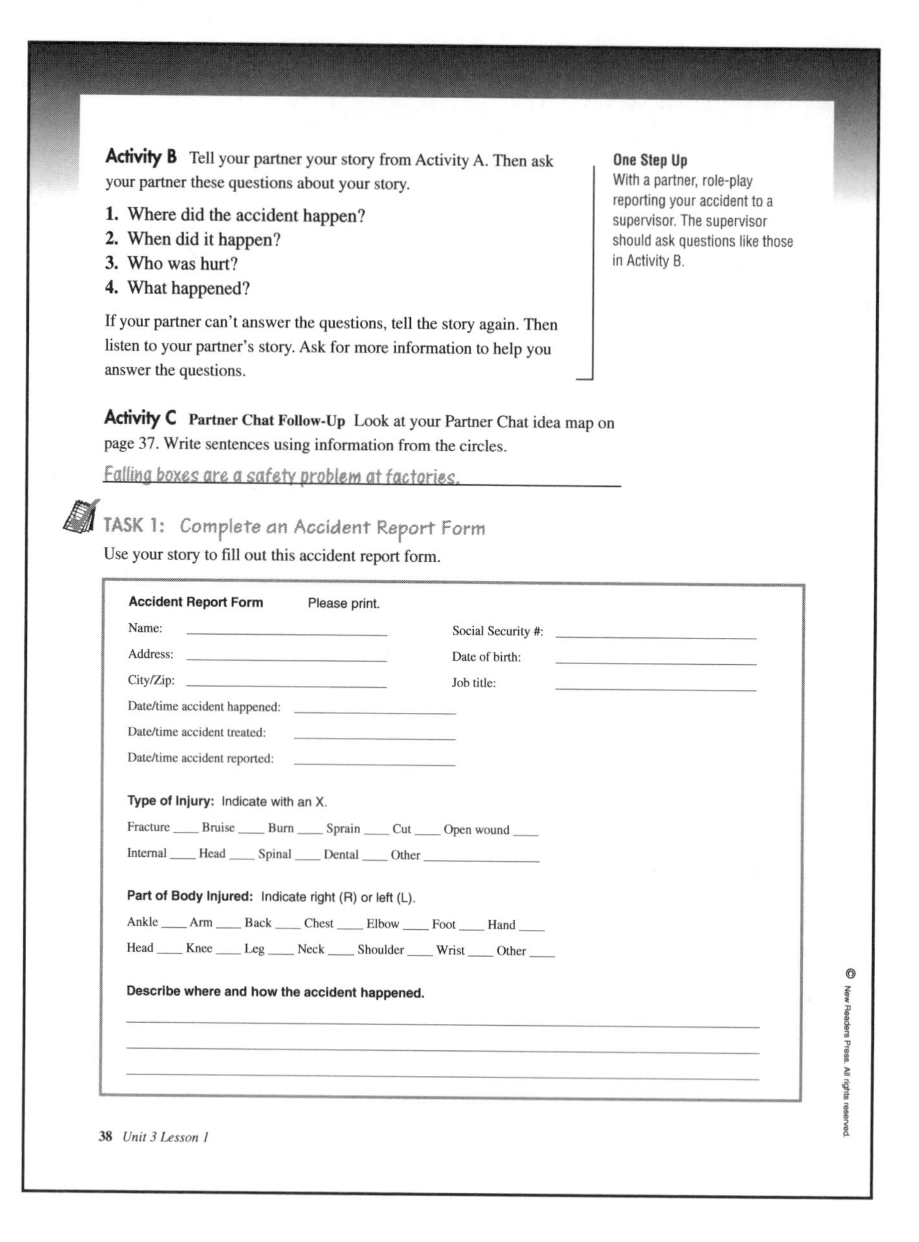

Activity B Tell your partner your story from Activity A. Then ask your partner these questions about your story.

1. Where did the accident happen?
2. When did it happen?
3. Who was hurt?
4. What happened?

If your partner can't answer the questions, tell the story again. Then listen to your partner's story. Ask for more information to help you answer the questions.

One Step Up
With a partner, role-play reporting your accident to a supervisor. The supervisor should ask questions like those in Activity B.

Activity C **Partner Chat Follow-Up** Look at your Partner Chat idea map on page 37. Write sentences using information from the circles.

Falling boxes are a safety problem at factories.

TASK 1: Complete an Accident Report Form

Use your story to fill out this accident report form.

Accident Report Form Please print.

Name: ____ Social Security #: ____
Address: ____ Date of birth: ____
City/Zip: ____ Job title: ____
Date/time accident happened: ____
Date/time accident treated: ____
Date/time accident reported: ____

Type of Injury: Indicate with an X.
Fracture ___ Bruise ___ Burn ___ Sprain ___ Cut ___ Open wound ___
Internal ___ Head ___ Spinal ___ Dental ___ Other ____

Part of Body Injured: Indicate right (R) or left (L).
Ankle ___ Arm ___ Back ___ Chest ___ Elbow ___ Foot ___ Hand ___
Head ___ Knee ___ Leg ___ Neck ___ Shoulder ___ Wrist ___ Other ___

Describe where and how the accident happened.

38 *Unit 3 Lesson 1*

Lesson 2: Safety at Home

Follow the suggestions on p. 5 for talking about the title.

Question

Ask learners what they think a lesson called "Safety at Home" might include. Then read the introductory question.

Attention Box

This vocabulary should be understood, but learners should not be expected to produce the words at this point.

Reading Tip

Read the tip aloud. Ask for volunteers to answer the lead-in question.

Before reading the brochure, have a volunteer read the title aloud. Ask learners to predict some specific tips they think might be in this brochure.

Talk or Write

This exercise helps learners quickly find details.

- Have learners look quickly for the answers. If you know they like competition, have a silent race to find the answers. Say, "Question 1," and have learners raise their hands when they've found the answer. When most hands are up, say, "Question 2."
- Ask learners whether they follow any of the safety tips mentioned in the reading. Find out how many sleep with their doors closed, unplug their appliances, or have talked about an escape plan.
- Discuss whether learners agree with the tip about sleeping with bedroom doors closed for parents with young children in separate rooms.
- Give other suggestions for preventing fires at home.

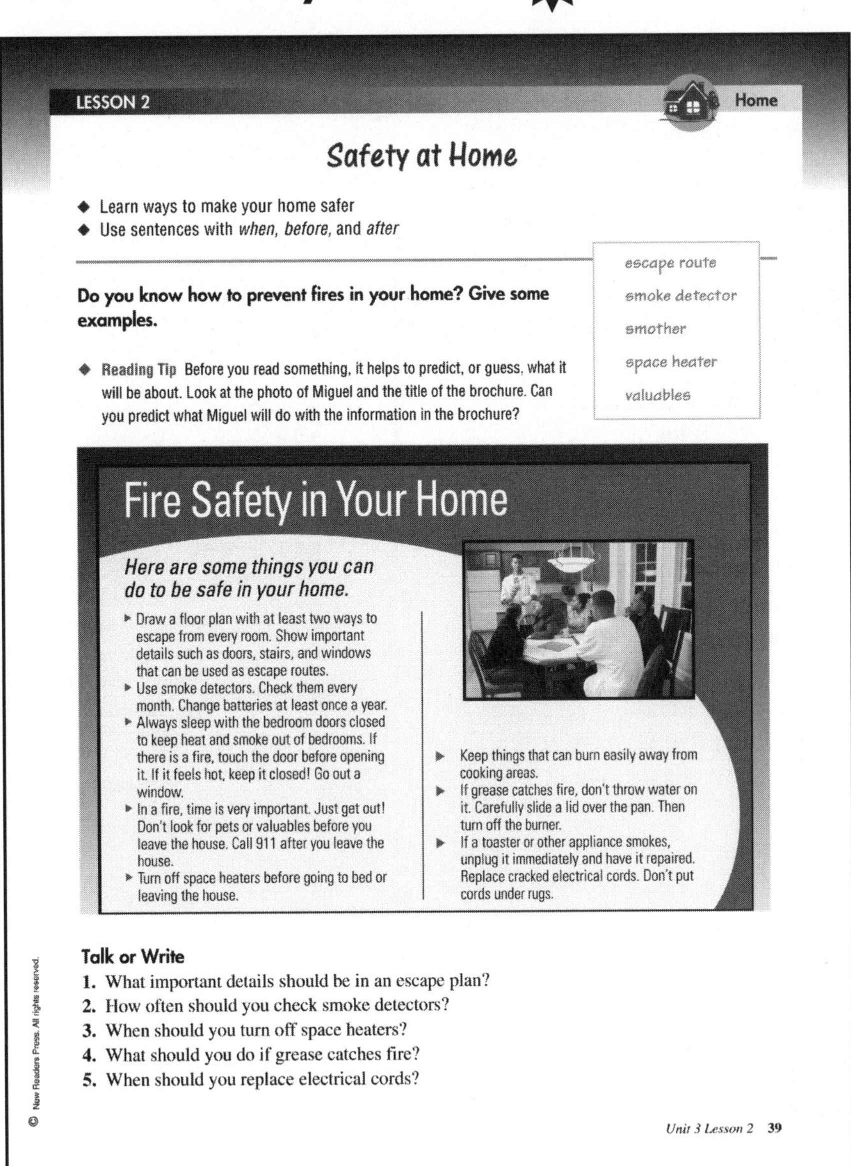

LESSON 2 — Home

Safety at Home

- Learn ways to make your home safer
- Use sentences with *when, before,* and *after*

escape route
smoke detector
smother
space heater
valuables

Do you know how to prevent fires in your home? Give some examples.

- **Reading Tip** Before you read something, it helps to predict, or guess, what it will be about. Look at the photo of Miguel and the title of the brochure. Can you predict what Miguel will do with the information in the brochure?

Talk or Write

1. What important details should be in an escape plan?
2. How often should you check smoke detectors?
3. When should you turn off space heaters?
4. What should you do if grease catches fire?
5. When should you replace electrical cords?

Answers

1. doors, stairs, and windows
2. once a month
3. before you go to bed or leave the house
4. slide a lid over the pan and turn off the burner
5. when they are cracked

Vocabulary

Bring in a fire extinguisher and smoke detector to illustrate these words. Demonstrate *plug in* and *unplug* with any electrical device.

Group Chat

Use Customizable Master 1 (2-Column Chart). Follow the suggestions on p. 7 for customizing and duplicating the master. Give a copy to each learner.

Grammar Talk

If learners are unsure of the meaning of *after* or *before,* the order shift may confuse them.

- If possible, use the experiences reported in the Group Chat to model the grammar.
- Point out that in an adverbial clause, words following *after* happen first:

  Linh was scared after she heard the loud noise.
- Words that follow *before* happen second:

  Marco was scared before he took his daughter to the hospital.
- Reverse the order of the clauses to show that the meaning does not change.

Answers

Clauses with *when, before,* or *after* can be at the beginning or the end of a sentence.

Use a comma after the clause when the sentence begins with *when, before,* or *after.*

Pronunciation Target

Play the audio or read the sentences in the student book.

- Read sentences from the Group Chat, exaggerating pitch differences. Pause after each and ask learners which words are stressed.
- Read the sentences again, this time exaggerating length differences in important words.

Group Chat After Miguel's accident, he became concerned about safety. Most people can remember a time when they didn't feel safe. Talk to several classmates about a time when they were concerned about safety at home. Take notes about their answers on your chart.

When were you concerned about safety at home?

When my front window broke.

What's your name?	When were you concerned about safety at home?
Fatuum Added	front window broke

Vocabulary

Repeat these words after your teacher. Talk about their meanings. Write the words in your notebook. With a partner, write a sentence using each word.

escape route
fire extinguisher
smoke detector

lock up
plug in
put away
replace
unplug

Grammar Talk: Sentences with *when, before,* and *after*

when	I was scared **when** the smoke detector went off. **When** the smoke detector went off, I was scared.
before	Turn the heater off **before** you go to bed. **Before** you go to bed, turn the heater off.
after	They called the firefighters **after** they left the house. **After** they left the house, they called the firefighters.

Idiom Watch! *go off*

A clause with when, before, *or* after *is not a complete thought. It is only part of a sentence. What can you say about the position of these clauses in a sentence? When do you need to use a comma with these clauses?*

Pronunciation Target • Stress on Important Words

I was **scared** when the **smoke** detector went **off.**
Do **not** place **cords** under **rugs.**

In English, important words are stressed. This means that they are ***longer*** *than unstressed words.*

Activity A Listen to your teacher or the audio. Write the sentences that you hear in your notebook. Write *T (true)* or *F (false)* after each sentence.

40 *Unit 3 Lesson 2*

Activity A

Play the audio or read the listening script below. Then have learners correct the false sentences.

Listening Script / Answers

1. You should put away a ladder after you use it. *(T)*
2. You should unplug the iron before you use it. *(F)*
3. You should lock up medicines after you take them. *(T)*
4. You should close the bedroom door before you go to sleep. *(T)*
5. You should turn heaters off after you go to bed. *(F)*

Use Unit Master 28 (Grammar: Find Your Partner) now or at any time during the rest of the unit.

Assign Workbook pp. 20–21.

Activity B

Answers

2. e   4. f   6. c
3. a   5. b

One Step Up

Have partners write their own items and safety rules.

Circulate to help learners word their examples correctly.

Extension

Ask learners to sit in small groups.

- Using the words and phrases in Activity B as examples, have each learner write the name of an item on a large strip of paper. Then, on another strip, have a different group member write the corresponding safety rule.
- Tape the strips to the board or wall out of order.
- Ask learners to match items and strips.

Request that learners not participate when their own sentence is in question because they already know the match.

Activity C

Have learners use the information in their Group Chat charts to write sentences in their notebooks.

Remember?

Ask learners when a person might use *should.*

Remind learners that the verb that comes after *should* is always in the base (or simple) form.

Activity D

Possible Answers

1. You should dry your hands before you plug in a hair dryer.
2. You should get under a table when you feel an earthquake.
3. You should protect your windows before a big storm.
4. You should stay low after a fire starts.
5. You should clean brushes well after you use paint.

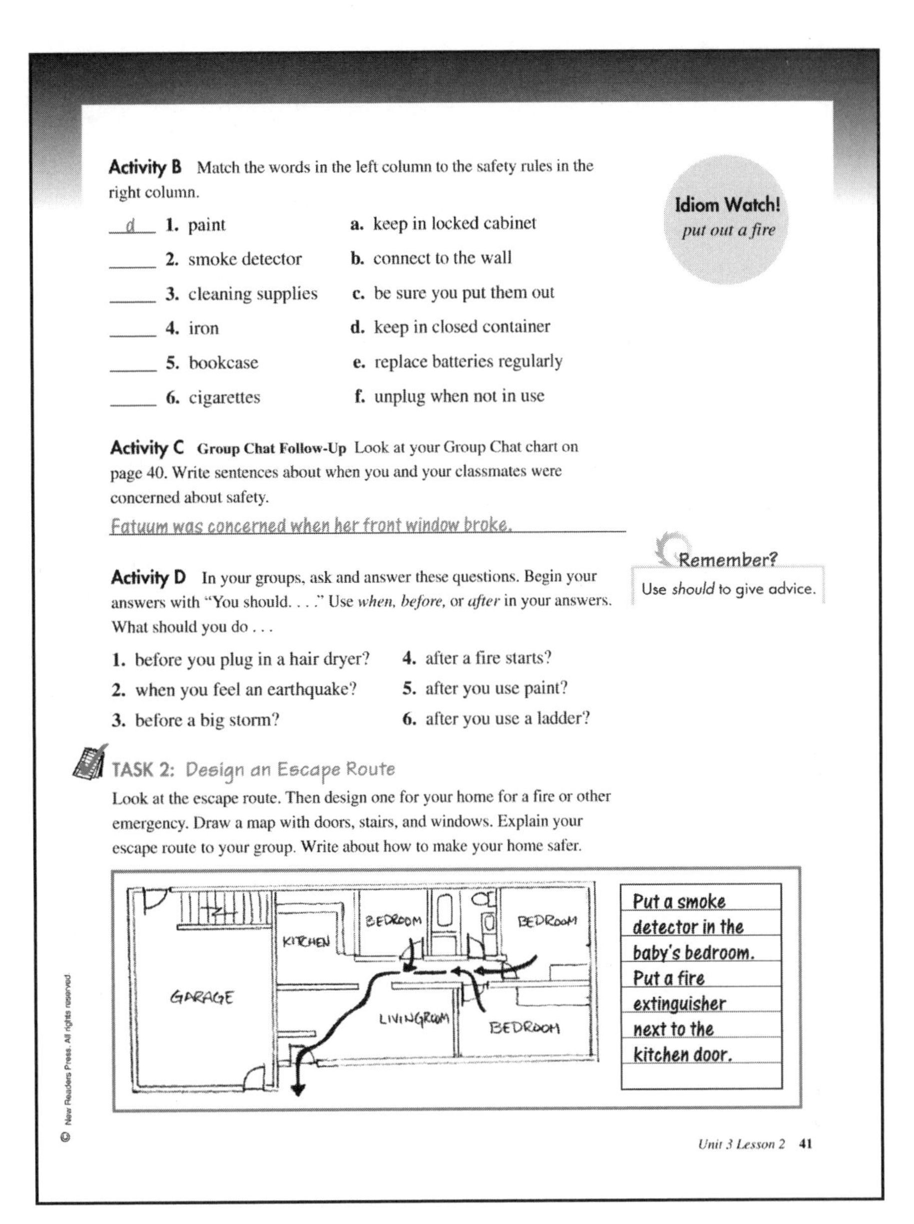

Activity B Match the words in the left column to the safety rules in the right column.

d	1. paint	a.	keep in locked cabinet
____	2. smoke detector	b.	connect to the wall
____	3. cleaning supplies	c.	be sure you put them out
____	4. iron	d.	keep in closed container
____	5. bookcase	e.	replace batteries regularly
____	6. cigarettes	f.	unplug when not in use

Idiom Watch! *put out a fire*

Activity C **Group Chat Follow-Up** Look at your Group Chat chart on page 40. Write sentences about when you and your classmates were concerned about safety.

Fatuum was concerned when her front window broke.

Activity D In your groups, ask and answer these questions. Begin your answers with "You should. . . ." Use *when, before,* or *after* in your answers. What should you do . . .

1. before you plug in a hair dryer?
2. when you feel an earthquake?
3. before a big storm?
4. after a fire starts?
5. after you use paint?
6. after you use a ladder?

Remember? Use *should* to give advice.

TASK 2: Design an Escape Route

Look at the escape route. Then design one for your home for a fire or other emergency. Draw a map with doors, stairs, and windows. Explain your escape route to your group. Write about how to make your home safer.

6. You should put away a ladder after you use it.

One Step Up

Ask learners to answer the questions again, this time beginning their sentences with *when, before,* or *after.*

Task 2

Following the model, have learners map emergency escape routes for their own homes. After learners discuss their maps with their groups, ask them to write safety procedures for their homes.

Use Unit Master 29 (Vocabulary: Scrambled Sentences) and 30 (Game: Safety Awareness Concentration) now or at any time during the rest of the unit.

Lesson 3: At the Bus Stop

Follow the suggestions on p. 5 for talking about the title.

Questions

Read the introductory questions. If any learners have witnessed or been a victim of a crime, ask if they will explain who was involved, where it took place, and what happened.

Attention Box

Read the words to learners, pointing or miming to convey meaning. This vocabulary should be understood, but learners should not be expected to produce the words at this point.

Listening Tip

Before beginning this exercise, do the following:

- Ask, "What questions do you think the police officer is asking Miguel?"
- Discuss how learners would feel if they were stopped for questioning by the police. Ask, "Would you want to provide information or would you be uncomfortable about getting involved?"

Then play the audio or read the listening script on p. 120.

Talk or Write

This exercise helps learners listen for details. Have learners discuss the questions with a partner or write down their answers individually. Then discuss their answers as a group.

Possible Answers

1. Two guys asked an older couple what time it was and then grabbed the woman's purse.
2. The older couple were the victims.
3. They looked like teenagers.
4. They were afraid, or they didn't want to get involved.

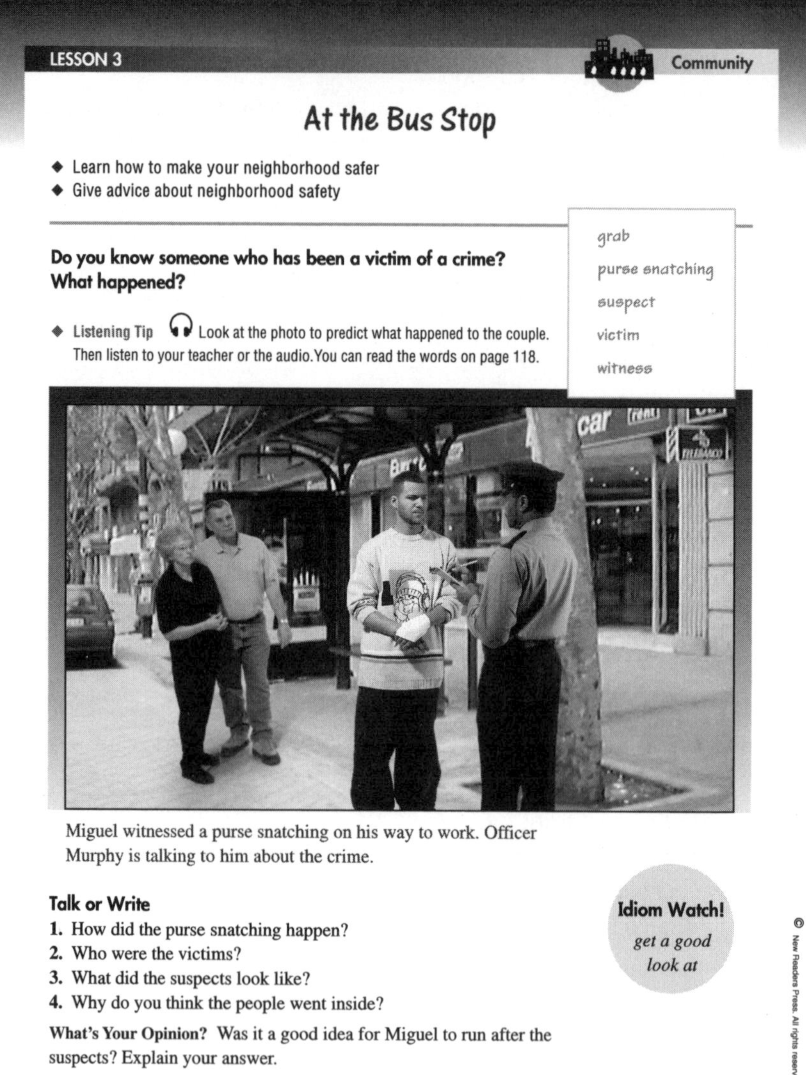

LESSON 3 — Community

At the Bus Stop

- Learn how to make your neighborhood safer
- Give advice about neighborhood safety

Do you know someone who has been a victim of a crime? What happened?

grab
purse snatching
suspect
victim
witness

- Listening Tip — Look at the photo to predict what happened to the couple. Then listen to your teacher or the audio. You can read the words on page 118.

Miguel witnessed a purse snatching on his way to work. Officer Murphy is talking to him about the crime.

Talk or Write

1. How did the purse snatching happen?
2. Who were the victims?
3. What did the suspects look like?
4. Why do you think the people went inside?

Idiom Watch! *get a good look at*

What's Your Opinion? Was it a good idea for Miguel to run after the suspects? Explain your answer.

42 *Unit 3 Lesson 3*

What's Your Opinion?

Have learners give and explain their opinions on the issue.

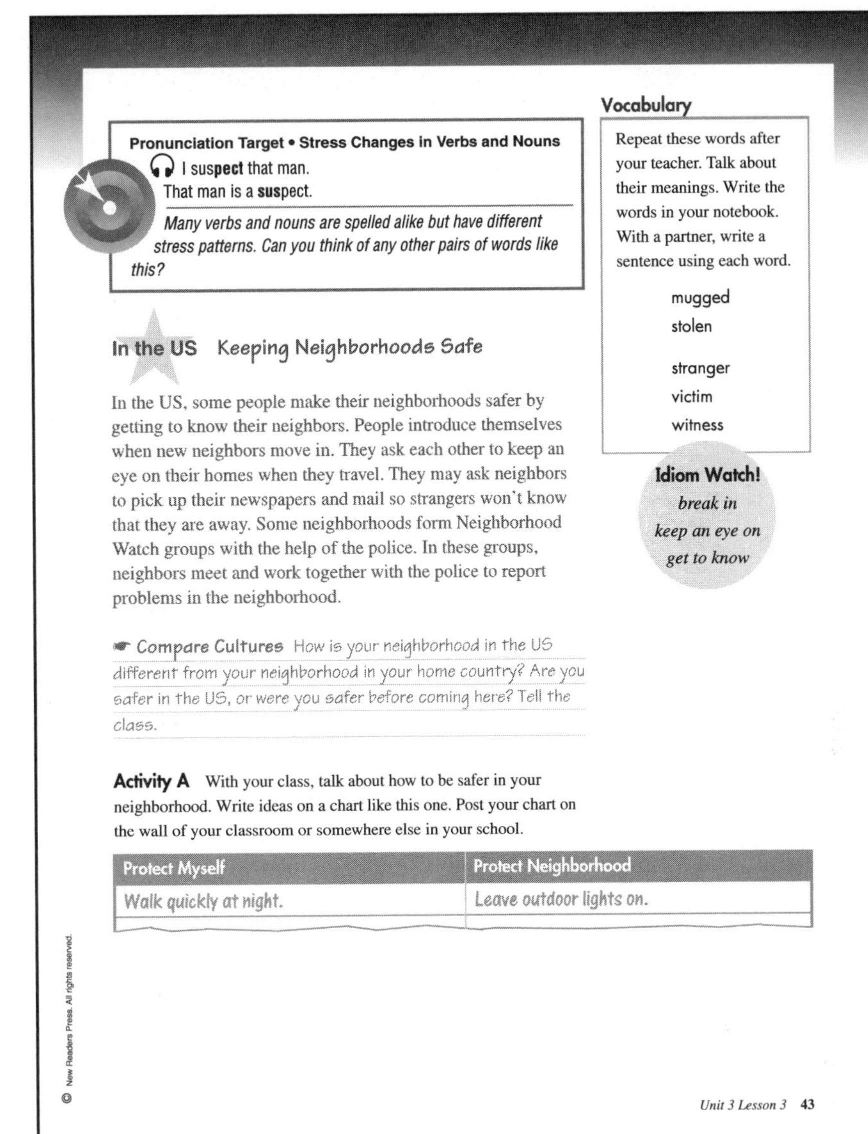
Pronunciation Target • Stress Changes in Verbs and Nouns

I sus**pect** that man.
That man is a **sus**pect.

Many verbs and nouns are spelled alike but have different stress patterns. Can you think of any other pairs of words like this?

In the US Keeping Neighborhoods Safe

In the US, some people make their neighborhoods safer by getting to know their neighbors. People introduce themselves when new neighbors move in. They ask each other to keep an eye on their homes when they travel. They may ask neighbors to pick up their newspapers and mail so strangers won't know that they are away. Some neighborhoods form Neighborhood Watch groups with the help of the police. In these groups, neighbors meet and work together with the police to report problems in the neighborhood.

Compare Cultures How is your neighborhood in the US different from your neighborhood in your home country? Are you safer in the US, or were you safer before coming here? Tell the class.

Activity A With your class, talk about how to be safer in your neighborhood. Write ideas on a chart like this one. Post your chart on the wall of your classroom or somewhere else in your school.

Protect Myself	Protect Neighborhood
Walk quickly at night.	Leave outdoor lights on.

Vocabulary

Repeat these words after your teacher. Talk about their meanings. Write the words in your notebook. With a partner, write a sentence using each word.

mugged
stolen
stranger
victim
witness

Idiom Watch!
break in
keep an eye on
get to know

Pronunciation Target

Play the audio or read the sentences in the student book.

- Explain that many verbs and nouns are spelled alike but have different stress patterns.
- Ask learners what other noun/verb words they know.

Vocabulary

Follow the suggestions on p. 6 for introducing and reinforcing the vocabulary words.

Point out that *witness* can be a verb or a noun.

In the US

Before reading, get learners thinking about the topic by asking these questions:

1. Do you talk to your neighbors?
2. What is your relationship with your neighbors?
3. Do you feel safe in your neighborhood? Why or why not?

Tell them about your relationship with your neighbors.

After reading, ask if anyone has seen Neighborhood Watch signs around town. Discuss what the signs look like and what their purpose is.

Extension

You may wish to invite a police officer to speak to the class about neighborhood safety. Have learners prepare questions in advance.

Compare Cultures

Use Customizable Master 5 (Venn Diagram) to help learners complete this activity.

Model the use of the graphic organizer by comparing your current neighborhood to one you lived in previously.

Activity A

Use Customizable Master 1 (2-Column Chart). Follow the suggestions on p. 7 for customizing and duplicating the master and distributing the copies. Make a copy for each learner and have learners work in small groups.

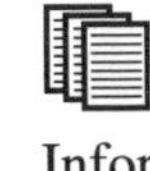
Use Unit Master 31 (Grammar: Past-Tense Question Information Gap) now or at any time during the rest of the unit.

Assign Workbook pp. 22–23.

Review Unit Skills

Follow the suggestions on pp. 7–9 for games and activities to review the vocabulary and grammar in this unit.

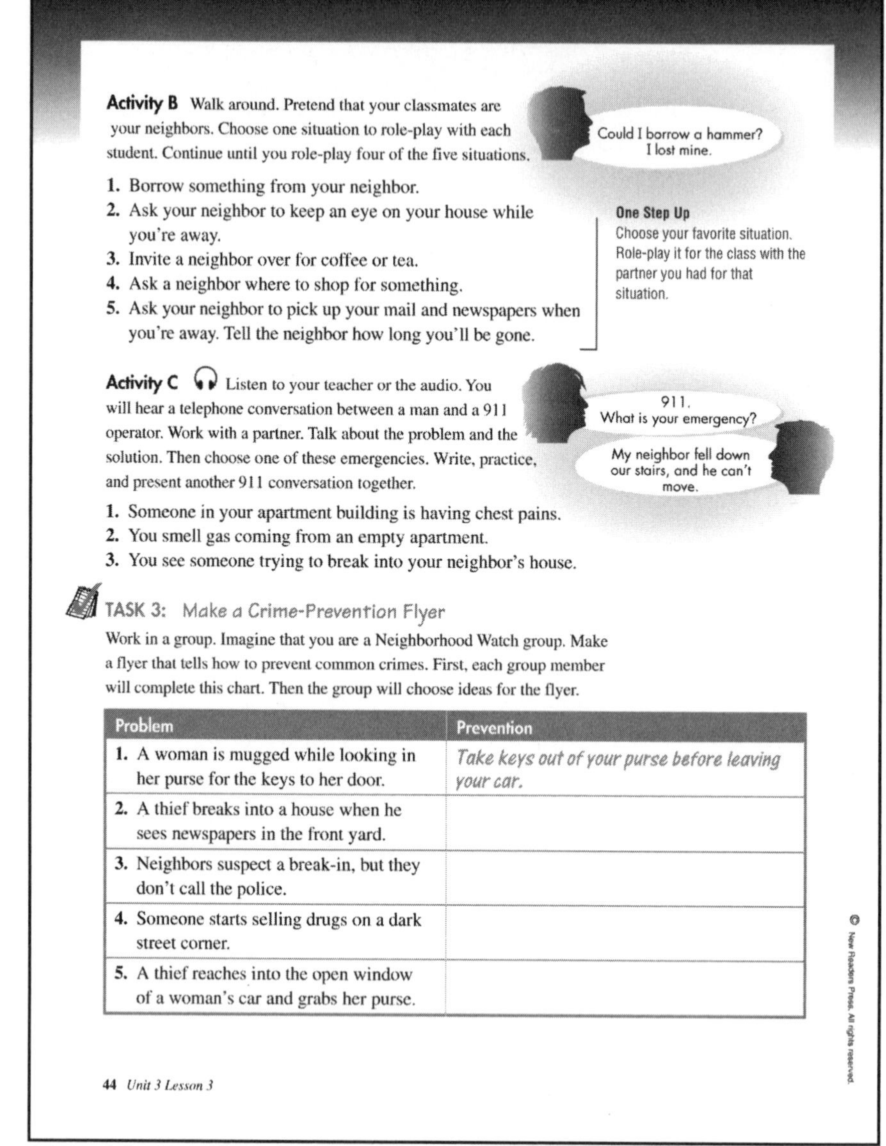

Activity B Walk around. Pretend that your classmates are your neighbors. Choose one situation to role-play with each student. Continue until you role-play four of the five situations.

1. Borrow something from your neighbor.
2. Ask your neighbor to keep an eye on your house while you're away.
3. Invite a neighbor over for coffee or tea.
4. Ask a neighbor where to shop for something.
5. Ask your neighbor to pick up your mail and newspapers when you're away. Tell the neighbor how long you'll be gone.

One Step Up
Choose your favorite situation. Role-play it for the class with the partner you had for that situation.

Activity C Listen to your teacher or the audio. You will hear a telephone conversation between a man and a 911 operator. Work with a partner. Talk about the problem and the solution. Then choose one of these emergencies. Write, practice, and present another 911 conversation together.

1. Someone in your apartment building is having chest pains.
2. You smell gas coming from an empty apartment.
3. You see someone trying to break into your neighbor's house.

TASK 3: *Make a Crime-Prevention Flyer*

Work in a group. Imagine that you are a Neighborhood Watch group. Make a flyer that tells how to prevent common crimes. First, each group member will complete this chart. Then the group will choose ideas for the flyer.

Problem	Prevention
1. A woman is mugged while looking in her purse for the keys to her door.	*Take keys out of your purse before leaving your car.*
2. A thief breaks into a house when he sees newspapers in the front yard.	
3. Neighbors suspect a break-in, but they don't call the police.	
4. Someone starts selling drugs on a dark street corner.	
5. A thief reaches into the open window of a woman's car and grabs her purse.	

Activity B

Ongoing Assessment

- While learners are completing this activity, circulate to monitor the conversations.
- Take notes on how well learners perform on the following criteria:
  - a. General quality of introductions
    - 0 = no introductions
    - 1 = abrupt, halting introductions
    - 2 = smooth, clear introductions
  - b. General quality of questions
    - 0 = lack of questions or incomprehensible
    - 1 = partially formed/partially understood
    - 2 = clear and appropriate but not perfect
  - c. Features of language functions (borrow, ask, tell, invite)
    - 0 = many problems or not understandable
    - 1 = some problems with clarity
    - 2 = clear and appropriate but not perfect

One Step Down

Help learners compose mini-dialogues they can use to role-play situations 1–5. Write the dialogues on the board or an overhead transparency. Follow this example:

A: Excuse me. Do you think I could borrow a hammer?

B: No problem! I'm not using it now.

Activity C

Play the audio or read the listening script below.

Listening Script

Listen to the 911 emergency call.

Operator: 911. What is your emergency?

Man: My neighbor fell down our stairs, and he can't move.

Operator: Is he breathing?

Man: Yes, he's crying in pain.

Operator: Is he bleeding?

Man: No, I don't see any blood.

Operator: OK, don't move him. Stay with him. Tell me your address and give me the major cross streets near your home.

Man: 445 West Palm Avenue near Glendale Boulevard and Bell Avenue.

Operator: Stay calm. The ambulance will be right there.

Ask learners to perform their conversations for the class. Alternatively, have pairs rotate from group to group:

- Divide each group into "Pair One" and "Pair Two."
- After both pairs have performed their conversations, ask all "Pair Ones" to move to the next group.
- The new pairs then perform for each other.
- Continue rotating pairs until all have returned to their original groups.

Task 3

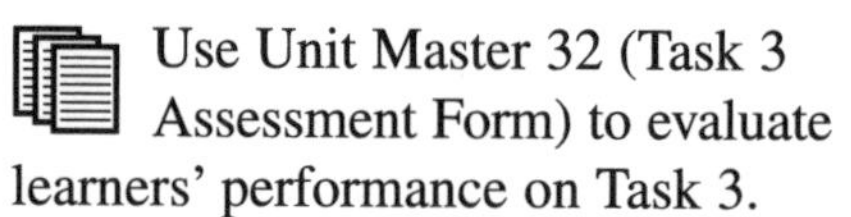

Use Unit Master 32 (Task 3 Assessment Form) to evaluate learners' performance on Task 3.

Unit 3 Project

Assessment

To evaluate learner performance on this project, use Generic Assessment Masters 8 (Oral Communication Rubric) and 9 (Written Communication Rubric). Follow the instructions on p. 4 for using these masters.

Learners make a safety poster for a place in their neighborhood or town.

Get Ready

Use Unit Master 33 (Unit 3 Project: Make a Safety Poster). Distribute a copy to each group along with a large sheet of poster paper.

Do the Work

- Have groups start by brainstorming ideas. Assign a recorder in each group to write the ideas on the group master.
- Ask groups to choose one person to draw the escape route, another to design the poster, and a third to write the final text.

Present

Give each learner a copy of Generic Assessment Master 12 (Peer Assessment Form).

- Have each group practice its presentation in front of another group.
- Learners complete and exchange the assessment forms before giving their final presentations.

One Step Up

Bring in safety brochures or ask learners to go out into the community to collect safety information about the place they chose for their poster.

Writing Extension

Use the illustration of the poster in the student book to compose a model paragraph titled, "Playground Safety." Write the paragraph on the board or an overhead transparency.

UNIT 3 Project

Make a Safety Poster

Make a safety poster for a place in your neighborhood or town. Follow these steps:

Get Ready

1. With your group, choose a workplace, school, park, or public building.
2. Study this safety poster that one class made.

Playground Safety

- *Use park equipment properly*
- *Stay out of the playground after dark*
- *Watch children at all times*

Do the Work

1. Plan your poster. Use the Unit Project handout that your teacher will give you.
2. Give the poster a title.
3. Include illustrations, if possible. You can draw them, cut them from magazines or brochures, or find them on the Internet. You can include a drawing of an escape route.

Present

Present your poster to the class.

Writing Extension Write a letter to the Mayor or the City Council about the place that you chose for your poster. Follow these steps:

1. In your first paragraph, tell about the place. Explain why it is important to you.
2. In your second paragraph, tell why the place is dangerous and explain your safety plan.
3. If you can, attach photos or illustrations of the problem and a small version of your poster. (See Technology Extra below.)

One Step Up
Ask for permission to put up your poster in the community.

Technology Extra
Make a small version of your poster on the computer. Add graphics or clip art. Put a border around the rules. Print copies for everyone in your class.

Ask questions like these to elicit content for the paragraph:

- Why is the playground important to you?
- What are some safety rules for the playground?

Point out important elements of paragraphs, including

- main ideas and details
- connected sentences as opposed to list form
- indentation
- left and right margins.

Ask learners to check their finished paragraphs for correct formation. For final proofreading, learners can use the Writing Checklist on p. 125 of their books.

Assign Workbook p. 24 (Check Your Progress).

Use Unit Master 34 (Unit Checkup/Review) whenever you complete this unit.

Self-Assessment

Give each learner a copy of the Speaking and Listening Self-Checks and the Writing and Reading Self-Checks (Generic Assessment Masters 10–11). Go over the assessment together. The completed form will become part of each learner's portfolio.

Unit 4: Planning Ahead

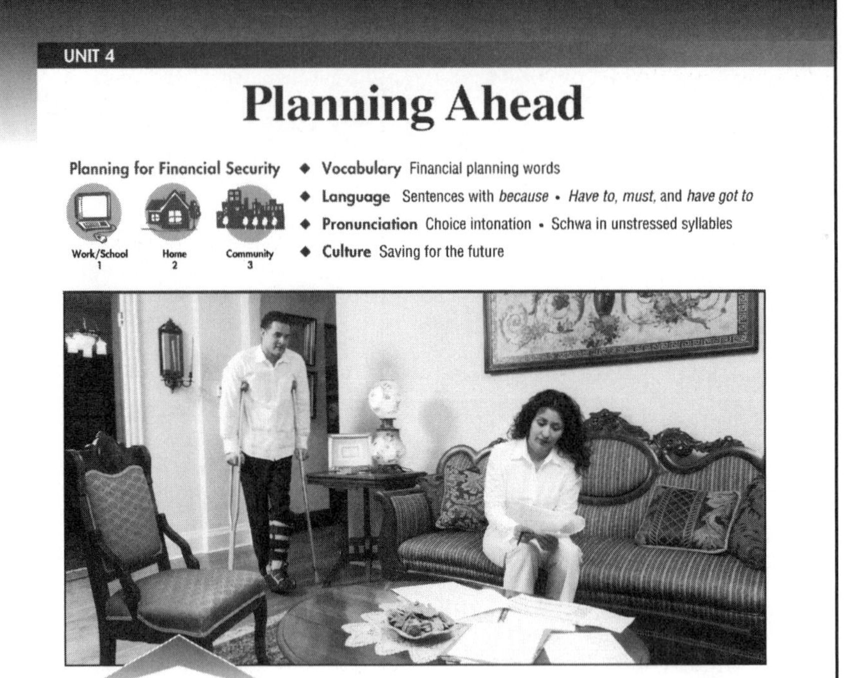
UNIT 4

Planning Ahead

Planning for Financial Security

Work/School 1 · Home 2 · Community 3

- **Vocabulary** Financial planning words
- **Language** Sentences with *because* • *Have to, must,* and *have got to*
- **Pronunciation** Choice intonation • Schwa in unstressed syllables
- **Culture** Saving for the future

What things can people do to have more financial security?

Olivia is 35 years old. She and her husband, Victor, live in a small rented house. She recently inherited some furniture from her grandmother. She is concerned about protecting her valuables, paying medical bills, and saving for the future.

Think and Talk

1. What do you see in the photo?
2. What can Olivia do to have more financial security?
3. What kinds of papers do you think she is looking at?
4. What concerns do you have about financial security?

valuables
coverage

What's Your Opinion? Sometimes when people apply for insurance, they don't tell the insurance company about a medical problem that they have. They are afraid that they won't get coverage. Do you think it's OK for a person to hide a medical problem from an insurance company in order to get coverage? Explain your answer.

46 *Unit 4*

Materials for the Unit

- Brochures and magazine ads with the symbols +, *, and **.
- Customizable Masters 2, 4, and 6
- Generic Assessment Masters 8–9
- Unit Masters 35–39

Planning Ahead

Follow the suggestions on p. 5 for talking about the title.

Point out that *ahead* can refer to time or space.

Ask these questions:

- Do you usually plan ahead when you have something important to do? Why or why not?
- When is it necessary to plan ahead?
- Do you ever prefer to do things without planning ahead?

Photo

Follow the suggestions on p. 4 for talking about the photo. Then read the question below the arrow.

Attention Box

This vocabulary should be understood, but learners should not be expected to produce the words at this point.

Caption

Follow the suggestions on p. 5 for talking about captions.

Think and Talk

As learners generate answers, write them on the board or an overhead transparency.

For question 3, discuss the ideas offered and then vote on which answer learners think is most likely.

What's Your Opinion?

Read the paragraph in the student book aloud. Then ask learners what they think about these cases:

- Someone with a very serious illness who can't afford medication
- Someone who has just lost a job and medical coverage
- Someone whose child is diagnosed with a life-threatening disease

Also discuss the insurance companies' perspective—that being forced to cover everyone would raise rates too high or put them out of business.

Vocabulary

Follow the suggestions on p. 6 for introducing and reinforcing vocabulary words.

Vocabulary Plus

Answers

- Two-syllable words: *agent, payments, afford, cover*
- Three-syllable words: *coverage, policy, premium, financial* (Explain that although the word *coverage* has three syllables, it is often pronounced as two.)
- Four-syllable words: *deductible, security, affordable, eligible*

Gather Your Thoughts

Write the expressions on the board or an overhead transparency. As learners discuss their ideas, write them next to the appropriate expressions.

What's the Problem?

Follow the suggestions on p. 5 for identifying and analyzing problems.

Setting Goals

Follow the suggestions on p. 5 for setting goals.

Gather Your Thoughts Many people don't buy insurance. Use the expressions in the chart to talk about reasons why they don't. Write your ideas next to the expressions.

Vocabulary	Why don't people buy insurance?
financial security	People don't think insurance will give them financial security.
affordable coverage	
deductible amount	
monthly payments	
insurance agent	
eligible for coverage	

Idiom Watch! *plan ahead*

What's the Problem? What prevents people from having financial security? Think or talk with a partner.

Setting Goals Insurance policies and savings accounts are important parts of financial planning. Which goals are most important to you? Rank them from 1 (most important) to 6.

_____ **a.** understand health insurance policies
_____ **b.** understand renters and home insurance policies
_____ **c.** learn names of medical specialists
_____ **d.** ask for information about savings accounts
_____ **e.** compare different kinds of savings accounts
_____ **f.** another goal: ______________________________

Which was the most important goal for your class? Tally your answers. Talk about your most important goals. Explain your choices.

Vocabulary

Repeat these words after your teacher. Talk about their meanings. Write the words in your notebook. With a partner, write a sentence using each word.

agent
coverage
deductible
payments
policy
premium
security

afford
cover

affordable
eligible
financial

Vocabulary Plus

In your notebook, write these words across the top of a page: *Two-Syllable, Three-Syllable, Four-Syllable.* Listen to your teacher say the words in the Vocabulary box. Write each word in the correct column. Listen again, and underline the stressed syllables.

Lesson 1: Decisions, Decisions!

Follow the suggestions on p. 5 for talking about the title.

Explain that people sometimes say, "Decisions, decisions!" when they are having difficulty making a choice. Often the choice is between two equally desirable—or equally undesirable—things.

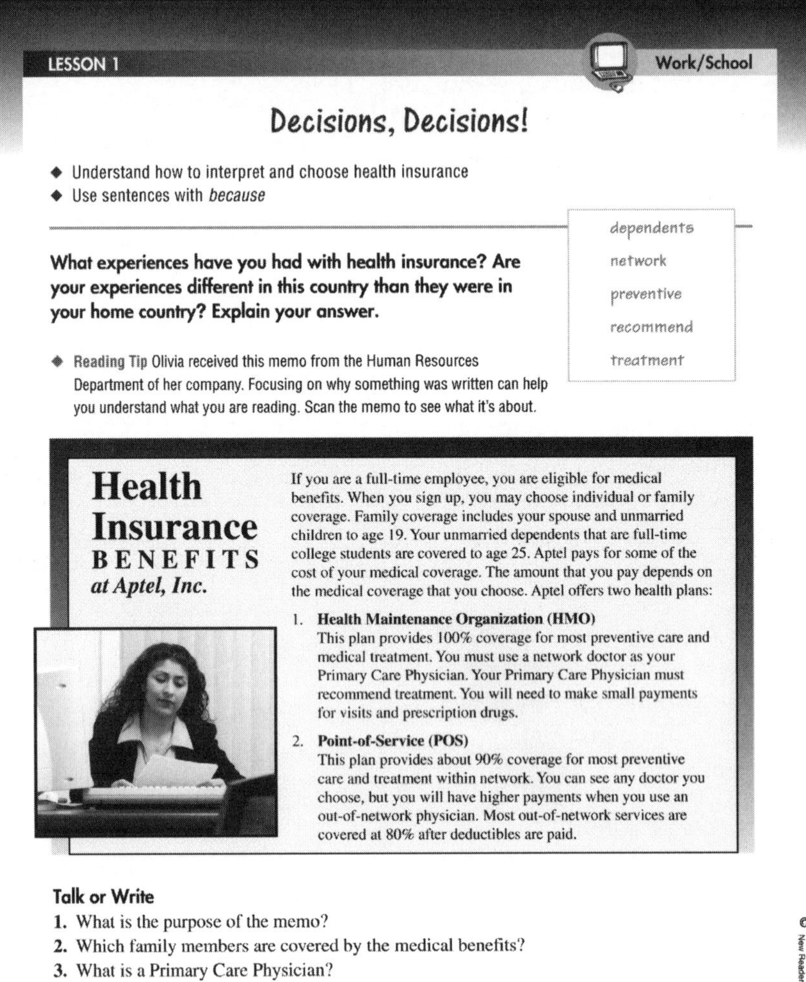

LESSON 1 Work/School

Decisions, Decisions!

- Understand how to interpret and choose health insurance
- Use sentences with *because*

dependents
network
preventive
recommend
treatment

What experiences have you had with health insurance? Are your experiences different in this country than they were in your home country? Explain your answer.

- **Reading Tip** Olivia received this memo from the Human Resources Department of her company. Focusing on why something was written can help you understand what you are reading. Scan the memo to see what it's about.

Health Insurance BENEFITS *at Aptel, Inc.*

If you are a full-time employee, you are eligible for medical benefits. When you sign up, you may choose individual or family coverage. Family coverage includes your spouse and unmarried children to age 19. Your unmarried dependents that are full-time college students are covered to age 25. Aptel pays for some of the cost of your medical coverage. The amount that you pay depends on the medical coverage that you choose. Aptel offers two health plans:

1. **Health Maintenance Organization (HMO)**
   This plan provides 100% coverage for most preventive care and medical treatment. You must use a network doctor as your Primary Care Physician. Your Primary Care Physician must recommend treatment. You will need to make small payments for visits and prescription drugs.
2. **Point-of-Service (POS)**
   This plan provides about 90% coverage for most preventive care and treatment within network. You can see any doctor you choose, but you will have higher payments when you use an out-of-network physician. Most out-of-network services are covered at 80% after deductibles are paid.

Talk or Write

1. What is the purpose of the memo?
2. Which family members are covered by the medical benefits?
3. What is a Primary Care Physician?
4. How are the two health plans similar? How are they different?

48 *Unit 4 Lesson 1*

© New Readers Press. All rights reserved.

Questions

Read the introductory questions aloud. As learners share their experiences, write on the board or an overhead transparency the different kinds of health-care options they report (e.g., care for everyone provided by the government, care for the poor provided by the government, care provided by employers, care provided by charitable organizations, private insurance coverage).

Attention Box

This vocabulary should be understood, but learners should not be expected to produce the words at this point.

- Discuss the word *network.* Demonstrate its meaning by drawing a number of intersecting lines on the board or an overhead transparency. Place circles at some of the intersecting points to show the connections within a network.
- Elicit examples of networks (e.g., a TV or radio network, the Internet, a network of related businesses, a network of friends).

Reading Tip

Read the tip aloud.

- Tell learners that they will have 30 seconds to look over, or *scan,* the entire reading and get a very general idea of what it is about.
- Tell them to move their eyes rapidly over the memo, looking for familiar key words.
- When 30 seconds are up, ask learners to cover the text and share ideas on what it is about.

Talk or Write

This exercise helps learners improve reading for details.

Ask learners to read the questions first and then re-read the memo carefully as they look for the answers.

<u>Answers</u>

1. to describe options available to employees for benefits
2. spouse; unmarried children up to age 19, or up to age 25 if they are in college
3. a network doctor who recommends treatment
4. Both cover preventive care and medical treatments. HMO pays 100 percent, but you can't choose your doctor. POS covers 80 or 90 percent after deductibles, but you can choose your own doctor.

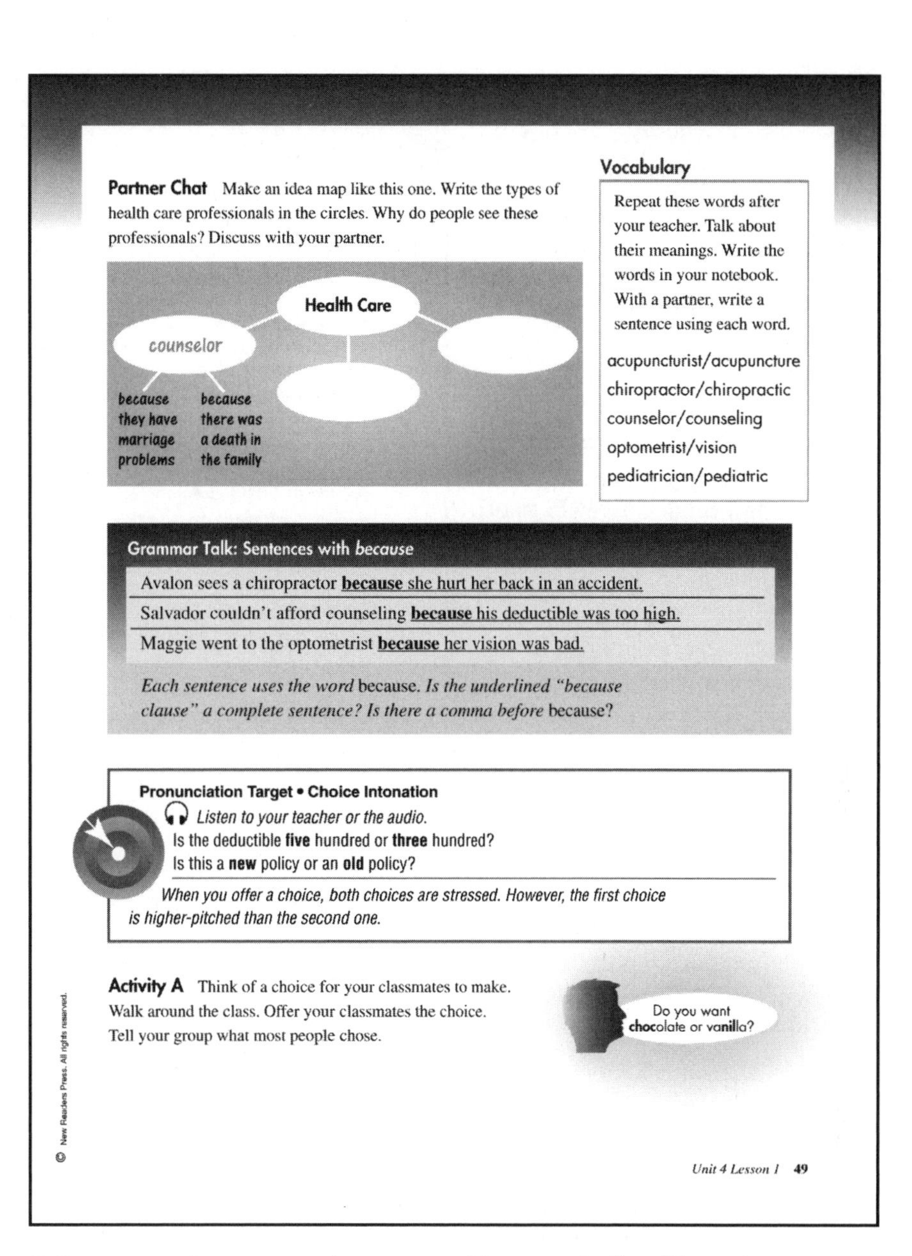

Partner Chat Make an idea map like this one. Write the types of health care professionals in the circles. Why do people see these professionals? Discuss with your partner.

Vocabulary

Repeat these words after your teacher. Talk about their meanings. Write the words in your notebook. With a partner, write a sentence using each word.

acupuncturist/acupuncture
chiropractor/chiropractic
counselor/counseling
optometrist/vision
pediatrician/pediatric

Grammar Talk: Sentences with *because*

Avalon sees a chiropractor **because** she hurt her back in an accident.
Salvador couldn't afford counseling **because** his deductible was too high.
Maggie went to the optometrist **because** her vision was bad.

Each sentence uses the word because. *Is the underlined "because clause" a complete sentence? Is there a comma before* because?

Pronunciation Target • Choice Intonation

Listen to your teacher or the audio.
Is the deductible **five** hundred or **three** hundred?
Is this a **new** policy or an **old** policy?

When you offer a choice, both choices are stressed. However, the first choice is higher-pitched than the second one.

Activity A Think of a choice for your classmates to make. Walk around the class. Offer your classmates the choice. Tell your group what most people chose.

Unit 4 Lesson 1 49

Vocabulary

Follow the suggestions on p. 6 for introducing and reinforcing vocabulary words.

Note that all the words are nouns except *pediatric.*

- Explain that the noun form of *pediatric (pediatrics)* is used to describe the field of study.
- Brainstorm more words that designate types of doctors.

Partner Chat

Use Customizable Master 4 (Idea Map). Follow the suggestions on p. 7 for customizing and duplicating the master and distributing the copies. Make a copy for each pair of learners.

Grammar Talk

Follow the suggestions on p. 6 for introducing the grammar point.

Suggested Answers

- No, a "because clause" is not a complete sentence.
- No, there is no comma before *because.*

One Step Up

Read the Grammar Talk sentences aloud. Then write them on the board or an overhead transparency with the clauses reversed:

Because she hurt her back in an accident, Avalon sees a chiropractor.

Because his deductible was too high, Salvador couldn't afford counseling.

Because her vision was bad, Maggie went to the optometrist.

- Point out that *because* follows the same grammatical rules as *when, before,* and *after,* which were presented in Unit 3.
- Write the sentences and clauses below on the board to illustrate how confusing reading can be if punctuation is not correct:

Julie went to the optometrist. Because she couldn't see well. The doctor gave her an eye test.

Mr. Kim went to the acupuncturist. Because his neck was hurting. He felt better after the treatment.

- Ask learners to connect the *because* clause in each group to one of the two sentences. (In the first example, the clause can be connected to either sentence. In the second example, it must be connected to the first sentence.)

Pronunciation Target

Play the audio or read the sentences in the student book.

Activity A

Circulate among the learners and participate in the activity. This will give you an opportunity to correct each person's pronunciation.

Assign Workbook pp. 25–26.

Use Unit Master 35 (Grammar: The Chain Game) now or at any time during the rest of the unit.

Activity B

Have learners write *because* sentences in their notebooks using the ideas from the Partner Chat.

Activity C

If learners have difficulty making a choice, help them determine the main issues:

- On the one hand, because medical care is so expensive, even paying 10 or 20 percent of a medical bill (under the POS plan) can be very expensive.
- On the other hand, having a limited choice of doctors (HMO) could deprive a patient of a trusted doctor or of necessary specialist care.

Activity D

After learners rank their choices, do the following:

- Ask learners if any type of important coverage is missing from the list.
- Point out that serious emergencies are not on the list because they typically are covered by any health plan.
- Take a hand vote to determine which kinds of coverage learners most often ranked as number 1.
- Ask volunteers to explain why the coverage they picked is so important.

Task 1

Before learners discuss their choices, review forming comparative adjectives. Use these examples:

Maternity care is cheaper at Health Guard than at Sana Delta.

Maternity care is more expensive at Sana Delta than at Health Guard.

Ask pairs of learners to explain their choices to another pair. Then ask volunteers to explain their choices to the class.

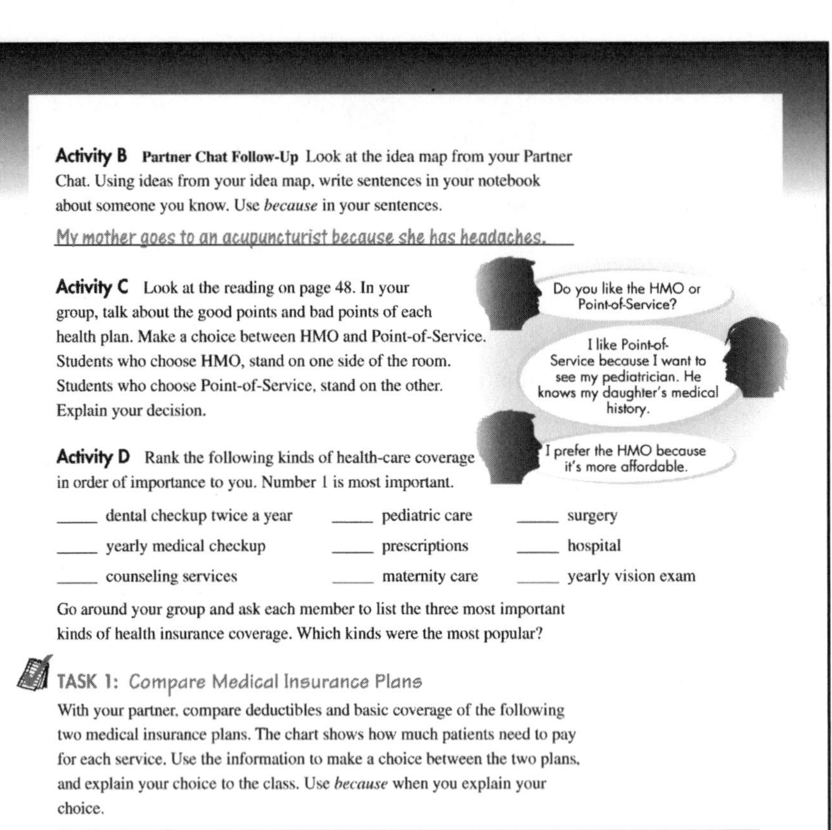

Activity B **Partner Chat Follow-Up** Look at the idea map from your Partner Chat. Using ideas from your idea map, write sentences in your notebook about someone you know. Use *because* in your sentences.

My mother goes to an acupuncturist because she has headaches.

Activity C Look at the reading on page 48. In your group, talk about the good points and bad points of each health plan. Make a choice between HMO and Point-of-Service. Students who choose HMO, stand on one side of the room. Students who choose Point-of-Service, stand on the other. Explain your decision.

Activity D Rank the following kinds of health-care coverage in order of importance to you. Number 1 is most important.

____ dental checkup twice a year ____ pediatric care ____ surgery

____ yearly medical checkup ____ prescriptions ____ hospital

____ counseling services ____ maternity care ____ yearly vision exam

Go around your group and ask each member to list the three most important kinds of health insurance coverage. Which kinds were the most popular?

TASK 1: Compare Medical Insurance Plans

With your partner, compare deductibles and basic coverage of the following two medical insurance plans. The chart shows how much patients need to pay for each service. Use the information to make a choice between the two plans, and explain your choice to the class. Use *because* when you explain your choice.

	Health Guard Insurance Co.	Sana Delta Insurance Co.
Yearly deductible	$500	$1,200
Lifetime maximum	none	$1,000,000
Office visits	$15.00	$5.00
Yearly check-up	$30.00	$20.00
Emergency care	20%	$50.00
Hospital services	10%	none
X-rays	30%	20%
Maternity care	$15.00 each visit	20%
Prescription drugs	20%	none

50 *Unit 4 Lesson 1*

<u>Assessment</u>

To use this task as an opportunity for formal evaluation, have learners present their choices to the class.

 Use Generic Assessment Master 8 (Oral Communication Rubric) to evaluate the presentations. Follow the suggestions on p. 4.

Lesson 2: Protecting Your Home

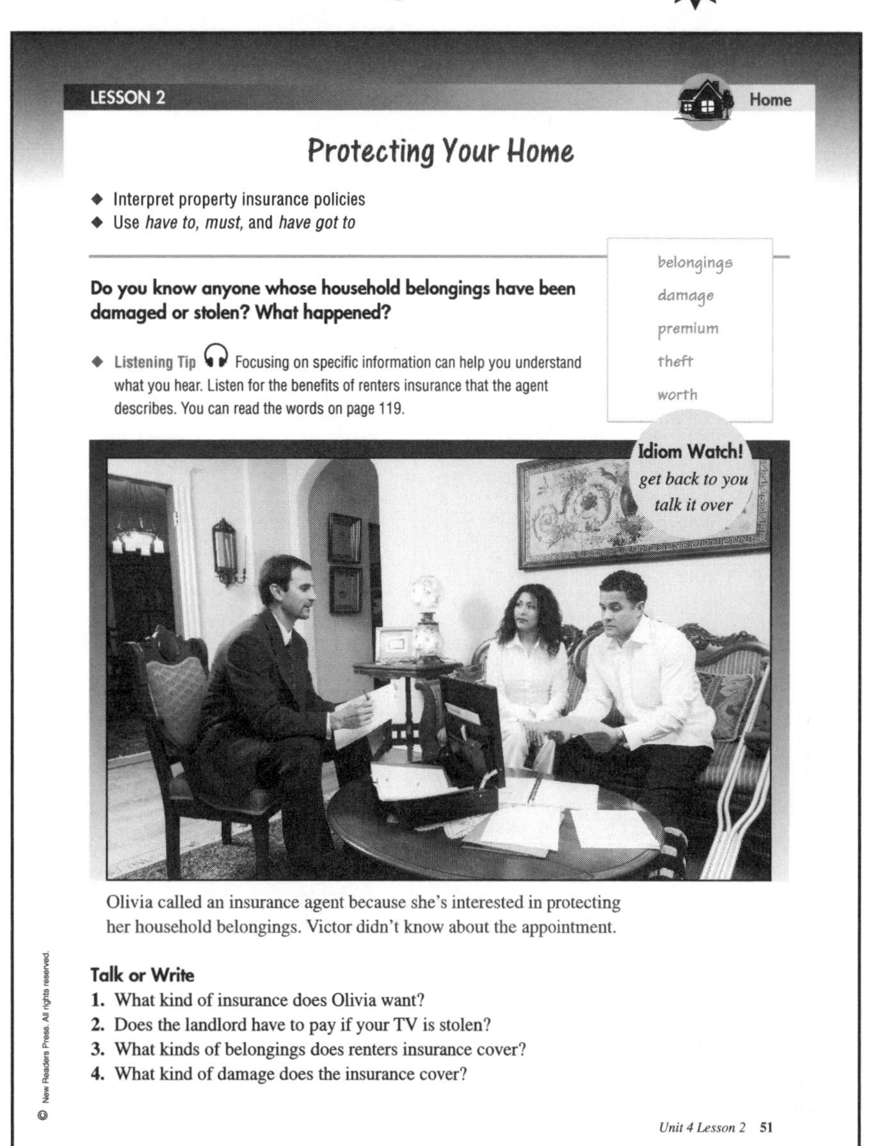

LESSON 2 Home

Protecting Your Home

- Interpret property insurance policies
- Use *have to, must,* and *have got to*

belongings
damage
premium
theft
worth

Do you know anyone whose household belongings have been damaged or stolen? What happened?

- Listening Tip Focusing on specific information can help you understand what you hear. Listen for the benefits of renters insurance that the agent describes. You can read the words on page 119.

Idiom Watch!
get back to you
talk it over

Olivia called an insurance agent because she's interested in protecting her household belongings. Victor didn't know about the appointment.

Talk or Write

1. What kind of insurance does Olivia want?
2. Does the landlord have to pay if your TV is stolen?
3. What kinds of belongings does renters insurance cover?
4. What kind of damage does the insurance cover?

Unit 4 Lesson 2 51

Follow the suggestions on p. 5 for talking about the title.

Ask learners what they think a lesson called "Protecting Your Home" might be about.

Question

Read the introductory questions aloud. Encourage good listening skills for the introductory questions by asking follow-up questions about the learners' answers, e.g.:

- What was stolen from Juan's uncle?
- What happened?

Attention Box

Read the words to learners, pointing or miming to convey meaning. This vocabulary should be understood, but learners should not be expected to produce the words at this point.

Listening Tip

Read the caption below the photo. Then introduce the listening exercise by asking these questions:

- Would you invite an insurance agent (or any salesperson) to your house or would you prefer an appointment in that person's office? Explain your answer.
- What is your *image* of an insurance agent? What kind of person do you picture or imagine?
- What do you think the agent will say to Olivia and Victor?

Play the audio or read the listening script on p. 120–121.

Have learners listen to the conversation twice. Then ask them what are the benefits of renters insurance, according to the agent. Write their answers on the board or an overhead transparency.

Talk or Write

This exercise helps learners improve listening for details.

As you discuss the questions, refer to the benefits listed on the board during the listening exercise.

<u>Answers</u>

1. renters insurance
2. no
3. stereo, furniture, television, jewelry, computer, bicycles, and other belongings
4. damage from fire or smoke, lightning, explosions, and windstorms; water damage from plumbing problems

<u>What's Your Opinion?</u>

Remind learners that, according to the caption, Victor did not know about the appointment with the insurance agent.

- Ask learners if they approve of Olivia making the appointment without first consulting Victor.
- If not, ask if they would also disapprove if the roles were reversed, i.e., if a husband made an appointment without first consulting his wife.

Vocabulary

Follow the suggestions on p. 6 for introducing and reinforcing vocabulary words.

One Step Up

Follow the suggestions on p. 6 for categorizing vocabulary words as nouns, verbs, and adjectives.

- Nouns: *antiques, belongings, valuables, damage, flood, hail, theft, vandalism*
- Verbs: *damage, destroy, flood, hail, vandalize*

Group Chat

Use Customizable Master 6 (Pie Chart). Follow the suggestions on p. 7 for customizing and duplicating the master and distributing the copies. Pass out colored pencils or crayons.

Ask learners which things have happened to them or to people they know. This discussion may help them decide which things are more likely to happen in the future.

Grammar Talk

Follow the suggestions on p. 6 for introducing the grammar point.

Suggested Answers

- *must not; don't have to*
- *Have got to* is never used in the negative.

Although the meaning of these three expressions is the same, *must* is the most formal and *have got to* the least formal. Emphasize that *must* is usually used in formal circumstances and not for everyday activities (e.g., *"I have to* go shopping," not *"I must* go shopping").

Pronunciation Target

Play the audio or read the sentences in the Grammar Talk box.

Activity A

Learners often have difficulty with the difference in meaning between

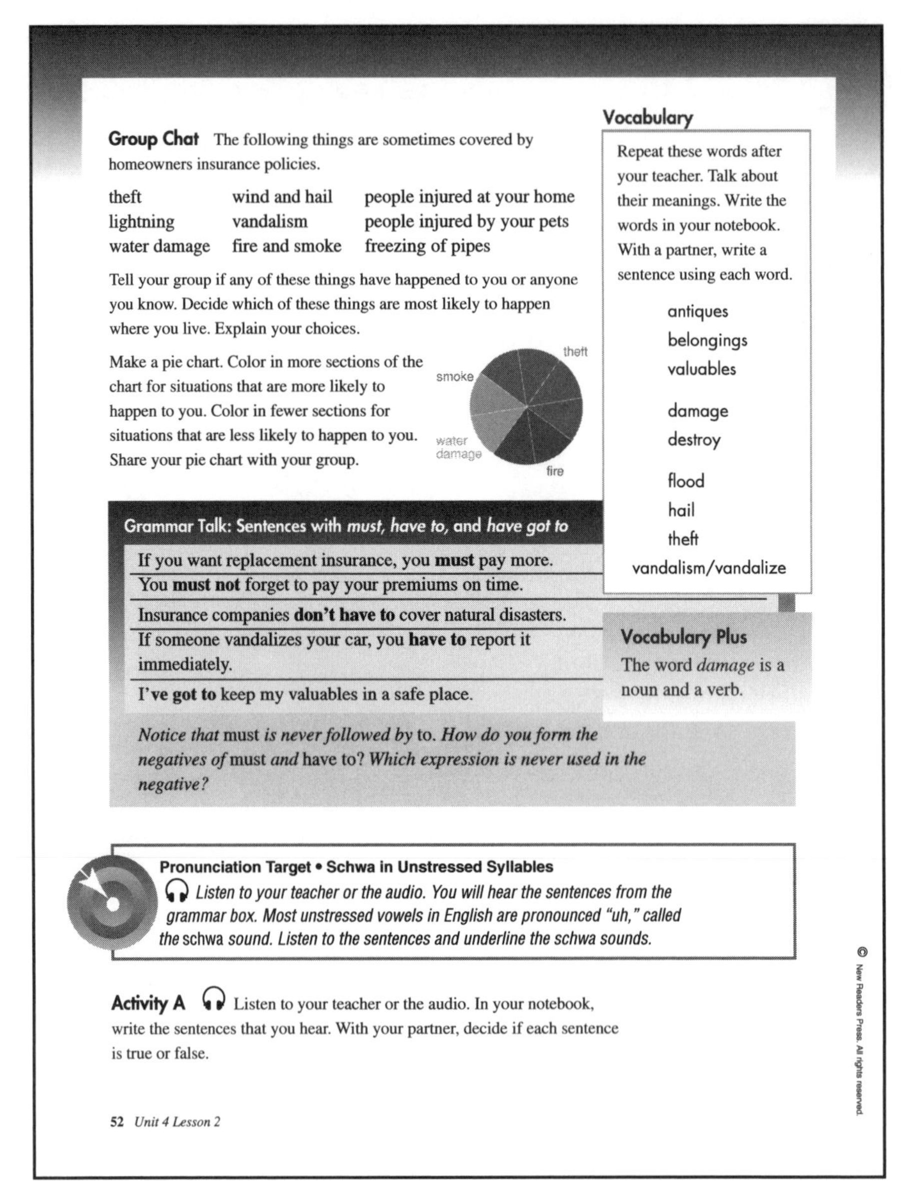

Group Chat The following things are sometimes covered by homeowners insurance policies.

theft	wind and hail	people injured at your home
lightning	vandalism	people injured by your pets
water damage	fire and smoke	freezing of pipes

Tell your group if any of these things have happened to you or anyone you know. Decide which of these things are most likely to happen where you live. Explain your choices.

Make a pie chart. Color in more sections of the chart for situations that are more likely to happen to you. Color in fewer sections for situations that are less likely to happen to you. Share your pie chart with your group.

Vocabulary

Repeat these words after your teacher. Talk about their meanings. Write the words in your notebook. With a partner, write a sentence using each word.

antiques
belongings
valuables

damage
destroy

flood
hail
theft
vandalism/vandalize

Grammar Talk: Sentences with *must, have to,* and *have got to*

If you want replacement insurance, you **must** pay more.
You **must not** forget to pay your premiums on time.

Insurance companies **don't have to** cover natural disasters.
If someone vandalizes your car, you **have to** report it immediately.

I've got to keep my valuables in a safe place.

Notice that must *is never followed by* to. *How do you form the negatives of* must *and* have to? *Which expression is never used in the negative?*

Vocabulary Plus

The word *damage* is a noun and a verb.

Pronunciation Target • Schwa in Unstressed Syllables

Listen to your teacher or the audio. You will hear the sentences from the grammar box. Most unstressed vowels in English are pronounced "uh," called the schwa *sound. Listen to the sentences and underline the schwa sounds.*

Activity A Listen to your teacher or the audio. In your notebook, write the sentences that you hear. With your partner, decide if each sentence is true or false.

52 *Unit 4 Lesson 2*

must not and *don't have to.* Before doing the dictation, provide these example sentences:

You don't have to wear a uniform to work.

You must not park in front of the store.

You don't have to chew gum in class.

You must not bring flowers when you come to dinner.

Ask learners which sentences are more logical *(the first two).*

- *Don't have to* means something is not necessary.
- *Must not* means something is prohibited.

Play the audio or read the listening script below.

Listening Script / Answers

1. Renters have to get renters insurance. *(F)*
2. You don't have to insure your valuables. *(T)*
3. Insurance companies must not cover flood damage. *(F)*
4. You must not buy insurance if you have a lot of antiques. *(F)*

Assign Workbook pp. 27–28.

Use Unit Master 36 (Grammar: Complete the Sentences) now or at any time during the rest of the unit.

Activity B

Ask learners to select two choices from their Group Chat pie charts. Then have them write sentences in their notebooks explaining those choices.

Activity C

Before beginning the listening exercise, tell learners that each blank contains several words. Ask them to fill in the missing words as they listen. Then play the audio or read the listening script below.

Listening Script / Answers

Olivia: How much does renters insurance cost?

Agent: You've got to think about how much your belongings are worth. For example, if you want $30,000 worth of coverage, you have to spend about $200 a year. For replacement insurance, you must pay a little more.

Olivia: What's replacement insurance?

Agent: The company will pay you enough money to buy new belongings. Without replacement insurance, the company only has to pay what your belongings are worth now. For example, your five-year-old TV may only be worth $50, but if you have to buy a new one, you'll spend a lot more.

Task 2

Answers

1. yes (theft)
2. yes (wind/hail)
3. no (doesn't cover damage from pets)
4. yes (vandalism)
5. yes (people injured at your home)
6. no (only covers damage to the home)

Use Unit Master 37 (Vocabulary: Disaster Poll) now or at any time during the rest of this unit.

Activity B **Group Chat Follow-Up** Look at your pie chart. Explain two of the choices you made for your pie chart. Write in your notebook.

I chose "theft" because it's a problem in my neighborhood.

Activity C Listen to your teacher or the audio. You will hear more of Olivia's conversation with the insurance agent. Write the missing words in the blanks.

Olivia: How much does renters insurance cost?

Agent: You ________ about how much your belongings are worth. For example, if you want $30,000 worth of coverage, you ________ about $200 a year. For replacement insurance, you ________ a little more.

Olivia: What's replacement insurance?

Agent: The company will pay you enough money to buy new belongings. Without replacement insurance, the company only ________ what your belongings are worth now. For example, your five-year-old TV may only be worth $50, but if you ________ a new one, you'll spend a lot more.

TASK 2: Analyze an Insurance Policy

With your partner, look at the homeowners insurance policy to see if the following situations are covered. Write *yes* or *no* next to each sentence. When you've finished, compare your answers with the rest of your group.

plumbing

The Security Plus Homeowners Policy

Provides complete coverage for your home in case of fire, lightning, wind and hail, smoke, vandalism, theft, water damage from plumbing, freezing of plumbing, people injured at your home, and people injured by your pets.

____ 1. Someone breaks into the house and takes the TV and stereo.

____ 2. A bad storm damages the roof.

no 3. Your cat destroys the new curtains.

____ 4. Someone breaks into the garage and sprays paint on the walls.

____ 5. Your Aunt Nancy falls down the stairs and breaks her ankle.

____ 6. The fruit tree in your backyard freezes and dies.

For each situation that is not covered, explain why in your notebook.

3. The policy doesn't cover damage from pets.

Lesson 3: Saving for a Rainy Day

Follow the suggestions on p. 5 for talking about the title.

Ask learners what "a rainy day" might represent *(bad times, trouble, illness).*

Questions

Read the introductory questions aloud.

The question "How do you save money for the future?" can be considered in different ways. It may refer to ways for actually saving money (e.g., sending it to one's home country, putting it in a savings account) or it could refer to saving money in daily activities (e.g., looking for bargains in the newspaper, using coupons when shopping, conserving energy at home).

Attention Box

This vocabulary should be understood, but learners should not be expected to produce the words at this point.

Reading Tip

Read the tip aloud. To illustrate the point, bring in brochures or magazine advertisements using the symbols. (Ads containing health warnings, such as those for prescription drugs and alcohol, often include asterisks.)

Talk or Write

This exercise gives learners practice with reading a table.

<u>Answers</u>

1. 2.47%
2. $2,500
3. higher
4. 48-month CD

Use Unit Master 38 (Life Skill: Gather Information) now or at any time during the rest of the unit.

LESSON 3 — Community

Saving for a Rainy Day

- Learn about different kinds of savings plans
- Learn about saving and spending in the US

withdrawal
maturity
penalty
term

Is it important to you to save money? How do you save money for the future?

◆ **Reading Tip** When you see symbols like + and * in something you are reading, look for an explanation of what they mean. Before you read this flyer, look for the following symbols: +, *, and **. What do they mean?

Premier National Bank

Account	Minimum Deposit	Term	Interest Rate	Minimum Balance
Regular Savings	$5.00		2.47%	$5.00
CD*	$1,000	3 month +	3.73%	$1,000
		12 month +	4.40%	
		36 month +	4.64%	
		48 month +	4.88%	
Money Market Account**	$2,500		2.97%	$2,500
			3.16%	$10,000
			3.54%	$25,000
			3.82%	$50,000 and above

We offer regular savings accounts; CDs, or certificates of deposit; and money market accounts.

* There is a penalty for withdrawals before the maturity date.
**A total of six withdrawals per month

Talk or Write

1. What is the interest rate for a regular savings account?
2. What is the minimum deposit for a money market account?
3. Does a 3-month CD with $1,000 have a lower or higher interest rate than a money market account of $2,500?
4. Which savings plan has the highest interest rate?

54 *Unit 4 Lesson 3*

Vocabulary

Follow the suggestions on p. 6 for introducing and reinforcing the vocabulary words.

Attention Box

This vocabulary should be understood, but learners should not be expected to produce the words at this point.

In the US

Before reading, discuss these questions to get learners thinking about the topic:

- How do retired people live in this country?
- How is this different from your home country?
- What is *credit?*
- What kinds of things do many people buy on credit?
- Are credit cards difficult to get?
- What is good about using credit?
- What is bad about using credit?
- What kind of person should *not* have a credit card?

Compare Cultures

Use Customizable Master 2 (3-Column Chart).

After learners have completed their charts, have a class discussion. Ask learners if people prepare better for retirement in their home countries or in the US.

Activity A

Use Customizable Master 4 (Idea Map). Follow the suggestions on p. 7 for customizing and duplicating the master and distributing the copies. Give one copy to each pair of learners.

Read the directions with learners. Circulate to verify comprehension.

After learners complete the activity, have a class discussion using these questions:

- What are some common savings goals for people you know?

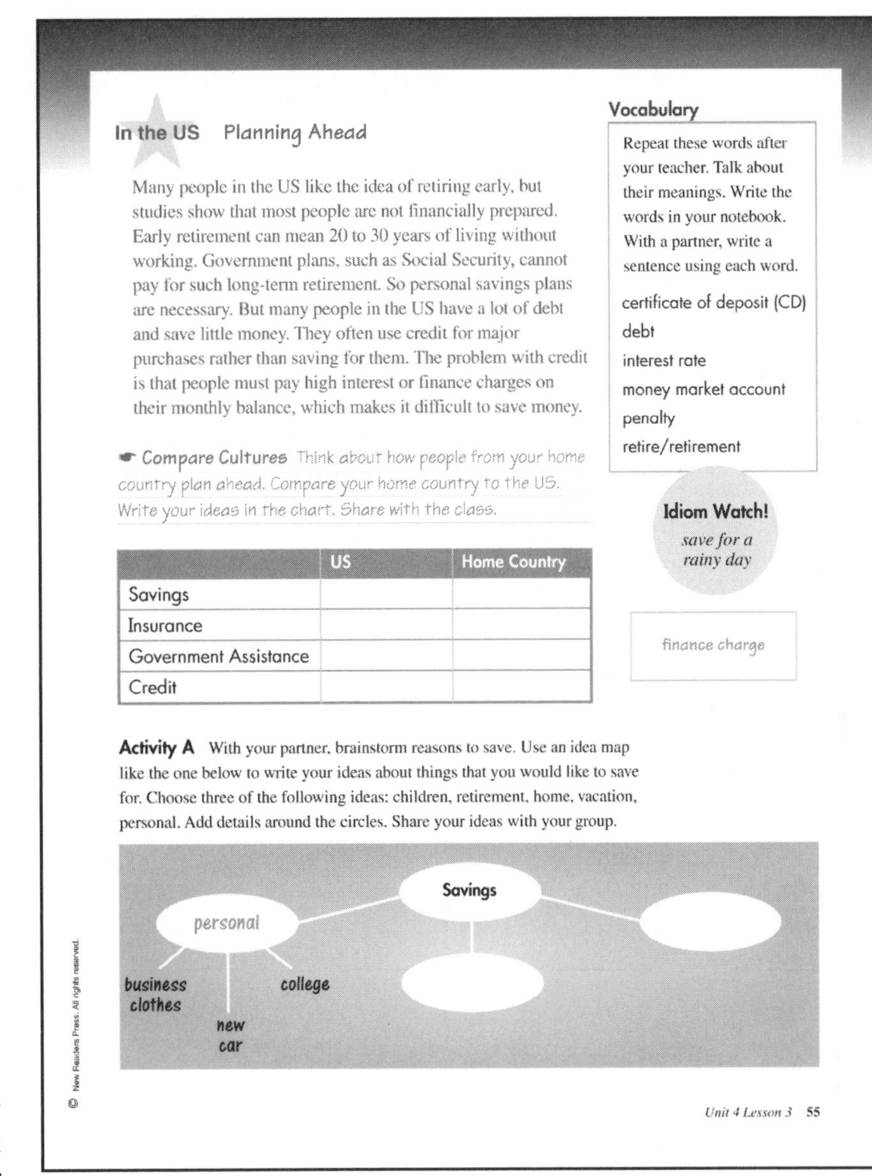

In the US Planning Ahead

Many people in the US like the idea of retiring early, but studies show that most people are not financially prepared. Early retirement can mean 20 to 30 years of living without working. Government plans, such as Social Security, cannot pay for such long-term retirement. So personal savings plans are necessary. But many people in the US have a lot of debt and save little money. They often use credit for major purchases rather than saving for them. The problem with credit is that people must pay high interest or finance charges on their monthly balance, which makes it difficult to save money.

Vocabulary

Repeat these words after your teacher. Talk about their meanings. Write the words in your notebook. With a partner, write a sentence using each word.

certificate of deposit (CD)
debt
interest rate
money market account
penalty
retire/retirement

Compare Cultures Think about how people from your home country plan ahead. Compare your home country to the US. Write your ideas in the chart. Share with the class.

	US	Home Country
Savings		
Insurance		
Government Assistance		
Credit		

Idiom Watch!
save for a rainy day

finance charge

Activity A With your partner, brainstorm reasons to save. Use an idea map like the one below to write your ideas about things that you would like to save for. Choose three of the following ideas: children, retirement, home, vacation, personal. Add details around the circles. Share your ideas with your group.

- Does anyone have an unusual savings goal they would like to share with the class?

Assign Workbook pp. 29–30.

Activity B

Ask learners to sit in pairs for the banking role-play. Then do the following:

- Using the chart from the beginning of the lesson, write the kinds of accounts (regular savings, CD, money market) on the board so that the "customer" does not have to refer to the book.
- To do this activity as a telephone role-play, write these examples of telephone language on the board or an overhead transparency:

  Good morning, Midwest Bank. May I help you?

  Yes, I'm calling to ask about your savings accounts.

  What would you like to know?

  Thanks for calling.
- For the telephone activity, ask partners to sit back-to-back so that they have to listen carefully to each other. Circulate; monitor pair work.
- After learners have sufficient time to practice, ask volunteers to perform role-plays for the class.

Attention Box

Provide sample sentences with the noun and verb forms of the expressions (e.g., I *wasted money* in the slot machine. That concert was a *waste of money.*).

Encourage learners to tell about a time when they wasted money on something.

Activity C

After learners complete the activity, tape five pieces of butcher paper to the board or wall. Number the sheets 1 through 5, then do the following:

- Assign one group to each piece of paper.
- Have each group answer the question that corresponds to the number on the sheet.

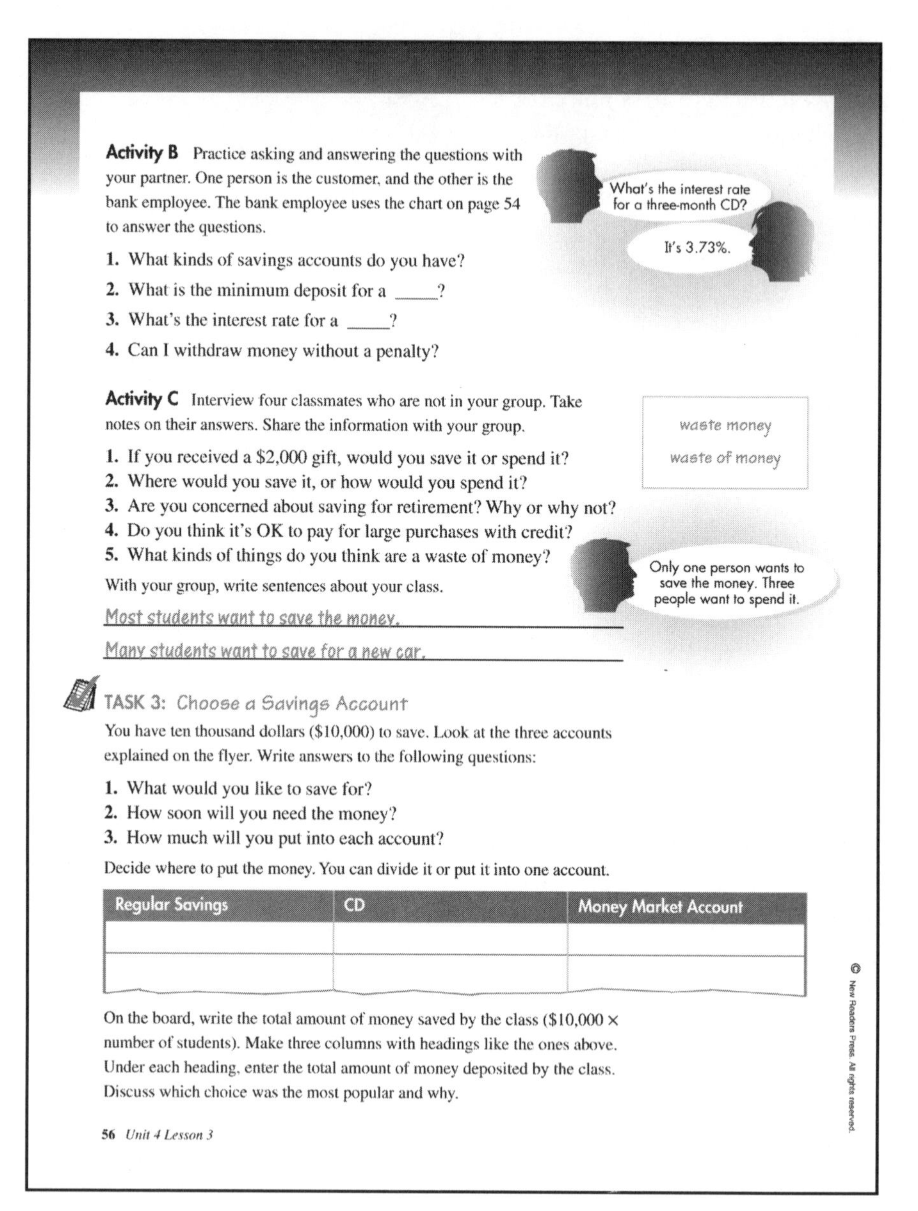

Activity B Practice asking and answering the questions with your partner. One person is the customer, and the other is the bank employee. The bank employee uses the chart on page 54 to answer the questions.

1. What kinds of savings accounts do you have?
2. What is the minimum deposit for a ____?
3. What's the interest rate for a ____?
4. Can I withdraw money without a penalty?

Activity C Interview four classmates who are not in your group. Take notes on their answers. Share the information with your group.

1. If you received a $2,000 gift, would you save it or spend it?
2. Where would you save it, or how would you spend it?
3. Are you concerned about saving for retirement? Why or why not?
4. Do you think it's OK to pay for large purchases with credit?
5. What kinds of things do you think are a waste of money?

With your group, write sentences about your class.

Most students want to save the money.

Many students want to save for a new car.

TASK 3: Choose a Savings Account

You have ten thousand dollars ($10,000) to save. Look at the three accounts explained on the flyer. Write answers to the following questions:

1. What would you like to save for?
2. How soon will you need the money?
3. How much will you put into each account?

Decide where to put the money. You can divide it or put it into one account.

Regular Savings	CD	Money Market Account

On the board, write the total amount of money saved by the class ($10,000 × number of students). Make three columns with headings like the ones above. Under each heading, enter the total amount of money deposited by the class. Discuss which choice was the most popular and why.

56 *Unit 4 Lesson 3*

- As groups finish their answers, they move on to a different sheet with a different number. Continue until each group has written an answer for every question.
- Discuss the answers and correct the sentences together.

Task 3

Make sure that learners write their ideas in their notebooks before the class tally. If they change their minds at the last minute, it will invalidate the final count.

Review Unit Skills

See pp. 7–9 for suggestions on games and activities to review the vocabulary and grammar in this unit.

Unit 4 Project

Learners survey friends or classmates to find out their savings and insurance needs.

Get Ready

Ask learners to make a four-column chart like the one in the student book. The chart may be drawn in their notebooks or on a separate sheet of paper.

- Have learners copy the four headings in the student book across the top of their charts.
- If the class is large and learners are interviewing classmates only, you may want them to interview only 3 to 5 people to avoid overlap among the group members.

Do the Work

Remind learners that they should not discuss amounts of insurance or savings while doing this activity. Explain that details about personal finance are considered very private information in the US.

Present

After groups tally their results, tally results for the class on the board or an overhead transparency.

Writing Extension

Use Generic Assessment Master 9 (Written Communication Rubric) to evaluate the paragraph. Follow the instructions on p. 4.

Extension

English has many proverbs about money. Write the following proverbs on the board:

- *The best things in life are free.*
- *Time is money.*
- *Money talks.*
- *You can't take it with you.*
- *Money doesn't grow on trees.*

Ask groups to restate each proverb using different words.

Ask learners these questions:

- Do you have proverbs similar to any of these in your language?

UNIT 4 Project

Do a Survey

Do a survey of your friends or classmates to find out their savings and insurance needs. Follow these steps:

Get Ready
Work with your group. Make a list of eight to ten people that you want to survey about their savings and insurance needs. Include family, friends, or classmates. Make sure each group member is talking to different people. Make a chart like the one to the right.

Number of People Interviewed ______			
Insurance/Savings Account	**Have**	**Don't Have**	**Want**
Homeowners			
Renters			
Auto			
Earthquake			
Flood		✓	✓
Medical			
Dental			
Vision			
Life			
Regular Savings Account			
CD			
Money Market Account			

Do the Work
Talk with eight to ten people. Find out what types of insurance and savings accounts they have, don't have, and want. Put check marks in the correct columns in the chart.

Present
Tally the number of check marks in each column. Share your results with your group. Tell which kinds of savings plans most people have, don't have, and want.

Writing Extension Write a paragraph about the kinds of insurance many people have and the kinds few people have. Explain the results.

Technology Extra
Search the Web for information on affordable insurance. Use the key words "renters insurance," "homeowners insurance," "health insurance," "medical insurance," "dental insurance," and "vision insurance."

Unit 4 Project 57

- Do you agree with every one of these proverbs? Explain.
- Can you give an example of when you might say one of these proverbs?

One Step Up

Have learners write a short paragraph explaining why they agree or disagree with one of these proverbs.

Technology Extra

Assist any learners who have difficulty finding or using a search engine.

Assign Workbook p. 31 (Check Your Progress).

Use Unit Master 39 (Unit 4 Checkup/Review) whenever you complete this unit.

Unit 5: Making Ends Meet

Materials for the Unit

- Magazines and catalogs with pictures showing items that might be sold at a garage sale
- Aquarium, blender, crib, hamper, nightstand, recliner, stroller—or pictures of these items (optional)
- Construction paper
- Index cards
- Customizable Masters 1–2
- Unit Masters 40–46

Making Ends Meet

Follow the suggestions on p. 5 for talking about the title.

Write a definition of the idiom *making ends meet* on the board or an overhead transparency. One definition might be "to have enough money to pay bills, but with little or nothing left over."

Questions

Read the questions below the arrow.

- Have learners brainstorm answers in pairs or groups.
- Ask learners to share their answers. Write them on the board or an overhead transparency.

Photo

Follow the suggestions on p. 4 for talking about the photo.

Caption

Follow the suggestions on p. 5 for talking about captions.

Think and Talk

- Write learners' responses for questions 1, 2, and 4 on the board or an overhead transparency.
- For question 4, have learners share the location of the places they shop for bargains.

What's Your Opinion?

Encourage learners to talk about their own shopping habits at different stages of their lives or shopping habits at various life stages in general. Discuss key economic factors such as the following:

- Personal budgets
- Family size
- Specific life situations (e.g., college students putting themselves through school)
- Proper use of credit versus use of credit without cash to back it up

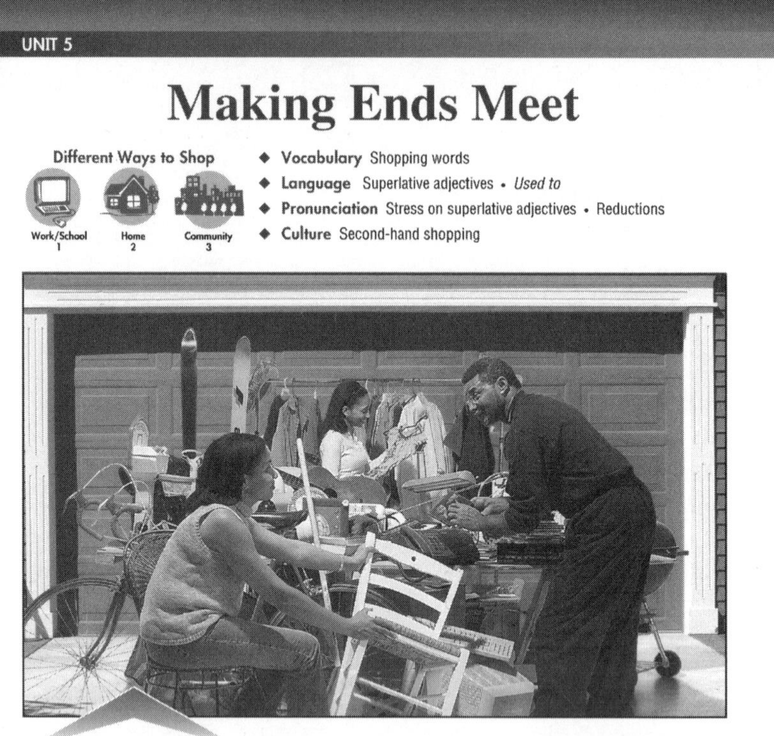

UNIT 5

Making Ends Meet

Different Ways to Shop

Work/School 1 · Home 2 · Community 3

- **Vocabulary** Shopping words
- **Language** Superlative adjectives • *Used to*
- **Pronunciation** Stress on superlative adjectives • Reductions
- **Culture** Second-hand shopping

Which things are important to you when you buy something? Quality? Price? Warranty?

Gail and Trevor Granville and their daughter, Tremaine, need to buy some new items, but they don't have a lot of money. They are looking for good quality at bargain prices.

Think and Talk

1. Describe what you see in the picture.
2. What do you think each of the Granvilles wants to buy?
3. Do you think a garage sale is a good place for them to shop?
4. Where do you shop for bargains?

What's Your Opinion? Is it OK to buy things that you want instead of things that you need? When is it OK? When is it not OK?

58 *Unit 5*

Vocabulary

Follow the suggestions on p. 6 for introducing and reinforcing vocabulary words.

One Step Up

Follow the suggestions on p. 6 for categorizing vocabulary words as nouns, verbs, and adjectives.

- Nouns: *condition, quality, warranty, exchange, guarantee, refund*
- Verbs: *exchange, guarantee, refund*
- Adjectives: *defective, second-hand*

Gather Your Thoughts

Use Customizable Master 1 (2-Column Chart). Follow the suggestions on p. 7 for customizing and duplicating the master and distributing the copies.

- For the third question, learners should write examples of different kinds of stores and which products those stores might guarantee.
- For the sixth question, ask learners to give specific examples.

When partners finish, ask them to share first with their group and then with the class.

What's the Problem?

Follow the suggestions on p. 5 for identifying and analyzing problems.

Possible Answers

- Busy schedules/lack of time to compare
- Children needing parent's constant attention in store
- Transportation limitations
- Lack of knowledge about how to comparison shop
- Lack of interest or desire

Setting Goals

Follow the suggestions on p. 5 for setting goals.

Gather Your Thoughts Discuss these questions with your partner. Take notes in the chart.

I always want a warranty when I buy a machine.

Questions	Answers
When do you think it's important to have a warranty?	*expensive items; machines*
Did you ever buy something defective? What happened?	
What kinds of things do stores guarantee?	
Did you ever exchange an item? What item?	
Did you ever ask for a refund? What happened?	
Do you care more about quality or price?	
What would you buy that wasn't in perfect condition?	

What's the Problem? Comparison shopping is important for saving money. What makes it difficult for people to do comparison shopping? Think or talk with a partner. Tell your group your ideas.

Setting Goals Shopping is an important part of everyone's life. Which of the following goals are most important to you? Rank them from 1 (most important) to 6.

_____ **a.** describe items that I want to return
_____ **b.** understand catalog descriptions
_____ **c.** interpret newspaper ads
_____ **d.** ask for information about products
_____ **e.** describe items that I want to sell
_____ **f.** another goal: ______________________________

Which was the most important goal for your class? Tally your answers. Talk about your most important goals.

Vocabulary

Repeat these words after your teacher. Talk about their meanings. Write the words in your notebook. With a partner, write a sentence using each word.

condition
defective
quality
second-hand
warranty

exchange
guarantee
refund

Idiom Watch!
make ends meet

Vocabulary Plus
The words *exchange, guarantee,* and *refund* can be nouns or verbs.
refund = noun or verb
re**fund** = verb

Lesson 1: Getting the Most for Your Money

Follow the suggestions on p. 5 for talking about the lesson title.

Discuss the meaning of the idiom *getting the most for your money.* One definition might be "getting the best quality possible at the best price when making a purchase."

To illustrate this concept, write the following examples on the board:

- The same quality item at different stores, with different prices
- Different quality items at different stores, with the same price

Questions

Discuss the meaning of the verb *break down.* One definition might be "to stop working or to malfunction."

There are other meanings that do not apply here but that you may wish to discuss:

- To take something apart (e.g., to *break down* into smaller parts)
- To be overcome by emotion (e.g., to *break down* and cry)

You may also want to introduce the noun *breakdown.*

Read the introductory questions aloud. Encourage good listening skills by asking follow-up questions about the learners' answers, e.g.:

- Whose washing machine broke down?
- Was he or she able to return it?

One Step Up

More advanced learners may enjoy learning the term *lemon*. One definition of *lemon* might be "a badly made machine that constantly breaks down and needs repair."

- Explain that some states have *lemon laws* that protect buyers from defective automobiles.
- Ask learners why calling a badly made machine "a lemon" might be an appropriate way to describe it.

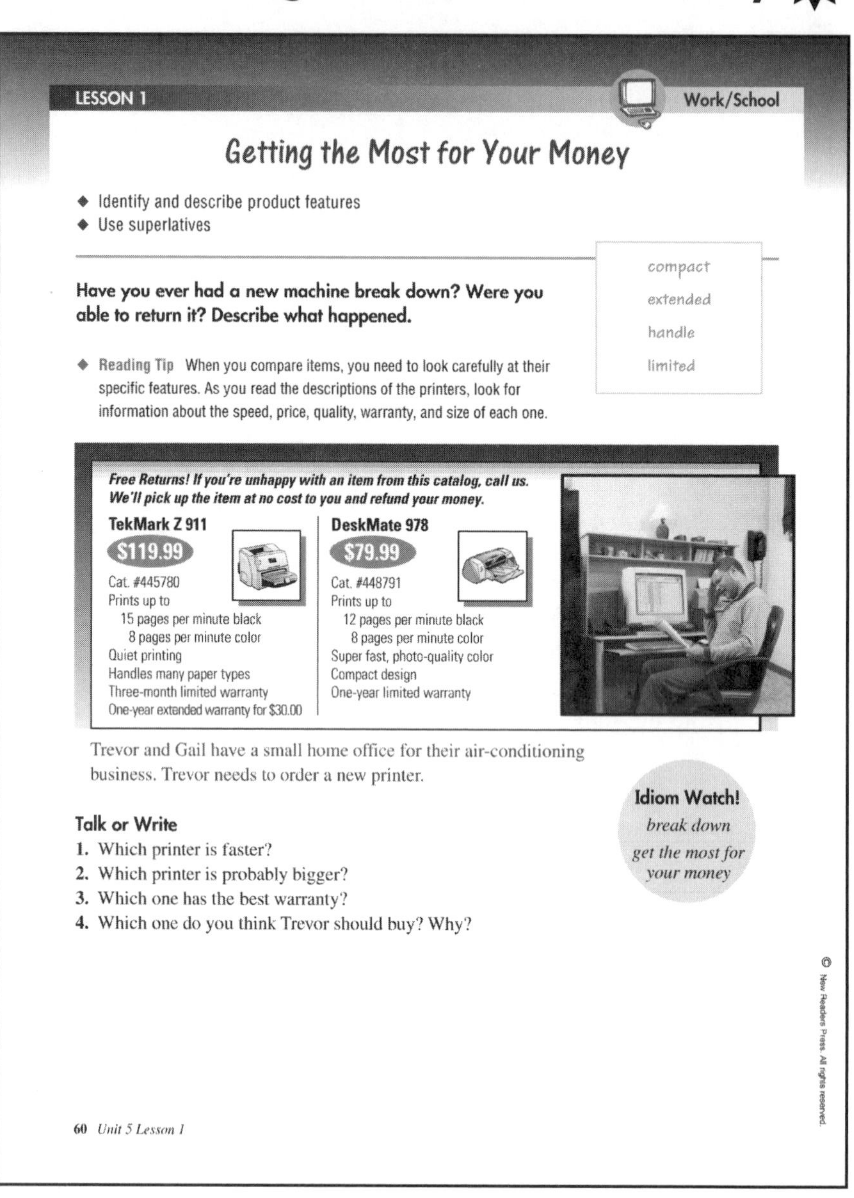

LESSON 1 — Work/School

Getting the Most for Your Money

- Identify and describe product features
- Use superlatives

compact
extended
handle
limited

Have you ever had a new machine break down? Were you able to return it? Describe what happened.

- **Reading Tip** When you compare items, you need to look carefully at their specific features. As you read the descriptions of the printers, look for information about the speed, price, quality, warranty, and size of each one.

Free Returns! If you're unhappy with an item from this catalog, call us. We'll pick up the item at no cost to you and refund your money.

TekMark Z 911	**DeskMate 978**
$119.99	$79.99
Cat. #445780	Cat. #448791
Prints up to	Prints up to
15 pages per minute black	12 pages per minute black
8 pages per minute color	8 pages per minute color
Quiet printing	Super fast, photo-quality color
Handles many paper types	Compact design
Three-month limited warranty	One-year limited warranty
One-year extended warranty for $30.00	

Trevor and Gail have a small home office for their air-conditioning business. Trevor needs to order a new printer.

Idiom Watch!
break down
get the most for your money

Talk or Write

1. Which printer is faster?
2. Which printer is probably bigger?
3. Which one has the best warranty?
4. Which one do you think Trevor should buy? Why?

60 *Unit 5 Lesson 1*

Attention Box

Read the words to learners, pointing or miming to convey meaning. This vocabulary should be understood, but learners should not be expected to produce the words at this point.

Reading Tip

Read the tip aloud, then have learners complete the reading.

Extension

You may wish to use Customizable Master 1 (2-Column Chart) to enhance this comparison activity.

Ask learners to read the details of the catalog and take notes in the chart to compare the printers. Reinforce the idea of *getting the most for your money.*

Talk or Write

This exercise helps learners become skilled at comparing information.

Answers

1. TekMark, for black and white printing
2. TekMark (DeskMate is compact)
3. DeskMate
4. DeskMate for warranty, price, and size; TekMark for speed (TekMark also advertises quiet printing.)

Vocabulary

Follow the suggestions on p. 6 for introducing and reinforcing vocabulary words.

Group Chat

- Ask each group to make two 5-column charts, following the models in their book.
- Have each group choose a recorder to write the information in the charts.
- Ask the recorder to write each group member's name in the margin next to his or her answers in the charts.
- Group members can take turns using the vocabulary words to ask the questions. For example, Student 1 can ask each group member about the most *compact* item; Student 2 can ask about the most *durable,* etc.
- Encourage group members to ask each other specific questions about the items.

One Step Down

Give learners a list of nouns to talk about (e.g., *tablecloth, television, phone, dishwasher*) before beginning the Group Chat.

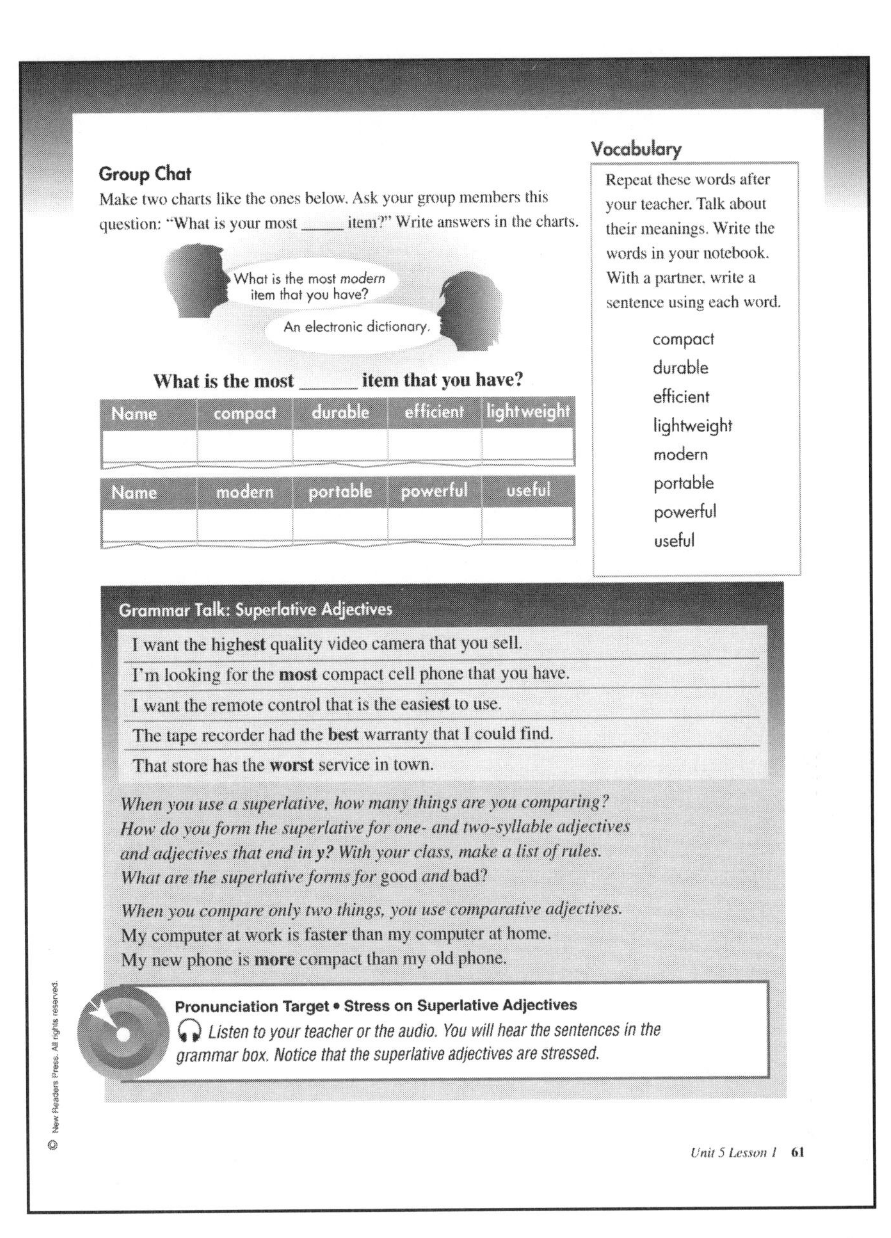

Group Chat

Make two charts like the ones below. Ask your group members this question: "What is your most _____ item?" Write answers in the charts.

What is the most _____ item that you have?

Name	compact	durable	efficient	lightweight

Name	modern	portable	powerful	useful

Vocabulary

Repeat these words after your teacher. Talk about their meanings. Write the words in your notebook. With a partner, write a sentence using each word.

compact
durable
efficient
lightweight
modern
portable
powerful
useful

Grammar Talk: Superlative Adjectives

I want the high**est** quality video camera that you sell.
I'm looking for the **most** compact cell phone that you have.
I want the remote control that is the easi**est** to use.
The tape recorder had the **best** warranty that I could find.
That store has the **worst** service in town.

When you use a superlative, how many things are you comparing?
How do you form the superlative for one- and two-syllable adjectives and adjectives that end in **y**? *With your class, make a list of rules.*
What are the superlative forms for good *and* bad?

When you compare only two things, you use comparative adjectives.
My computer at work is fast**er** than my computer at home.
My new phone is **more** compact than my old phone.

Pronunciation Target • Stress on Superlative Adjectives

Listen to your teacher or the audio. You will hear the sentences in the grammar box. Notice that the superlative adjectives are stressed.

Grammar Talk

Follow the suggestions on p. 6 for introducing the grammar point.

Suggested Answers

To make sure that learners understand these points, write them on the board or an overhead transparency:

- Superlatives compare three or more things.
- The superlative form for one-syllable adjectives is adjective + *-est* (e.g., *highest, tallest*).
- The superlative form for two- and three-syllable adjectives is *most* + adjective.
- The superlative form for words that end in *y* is adjective + *-est.* Note that with two-syllable adjectives that end in *y,* such as *happy* or *easy,* the spelling rule for changing the *y* to *i* before adding the ending *-est* applies.
- The superlative forms for *good* and *bad* are *best* and *worst.*

Pronunciation Target

Play the audio or read the listening script below.

Have learners listen for the stressed syllables or words in each sentence.

Listening Script

1. I want the highest quality video camera that you sell. *(highest)*
2. I'm looking for the most compact cell phone that you have. *(most compact)*
3. I want the remote control that is the easiest to use. *(easiest)*
4. The tape recorder had the best warranty that I could find. *(best)*
5. That store has the worst service in town. *(worst)*

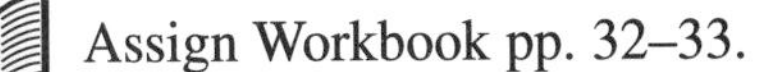

Assign Workbook pp. 32–33.

Use Unit Master 40 (Thinking Skill: Jigsaw) now or at any time during the rest of the unit.

Activity A

Before learners begin the activity, write these examples on the board or an overhead transparency:

- The most compact item that Stephen has is a cell phone.
- The most efficient item that Lana has is a laptop computer.

Activity B

Encourage learners to share their ideas and to openly disagree with each other. Remind them that there are no right answers, only opinions. Model ways to disagree politely:

- *Do you think so?*
- *Really?*
- *Maybe you're right, but I think . . .*
- *I agree, but I also think . . .*

One Step Up

Ask learners to write pairs or sets of sentences that report their ideas from the discussion. Their sentences might look like these:

Lisa thinks that cell phones are the most useful item on the chart because people can use them anywhere. But I think that they aren't the most efficient because they don't always work.

Activity C

One Step Down

If learners have difficulty writing a conversation, write this portion of a phone conversation on the board:

Fernando: Kramer Office Supply. How may I help you?

Trevor: Hello. I'd like to order a printer from your catalog.

Fernando: I can help you with that. May I have your name?

Trevor: Yes, my name is Trevor Granville. That's G-R-A-N-V-I-L-L-E.

Fernando: Thank you. And which printer would you like to order?

Have learners finish writing the conversation in pairs or groups. Then ask them to share what they have written with the class.

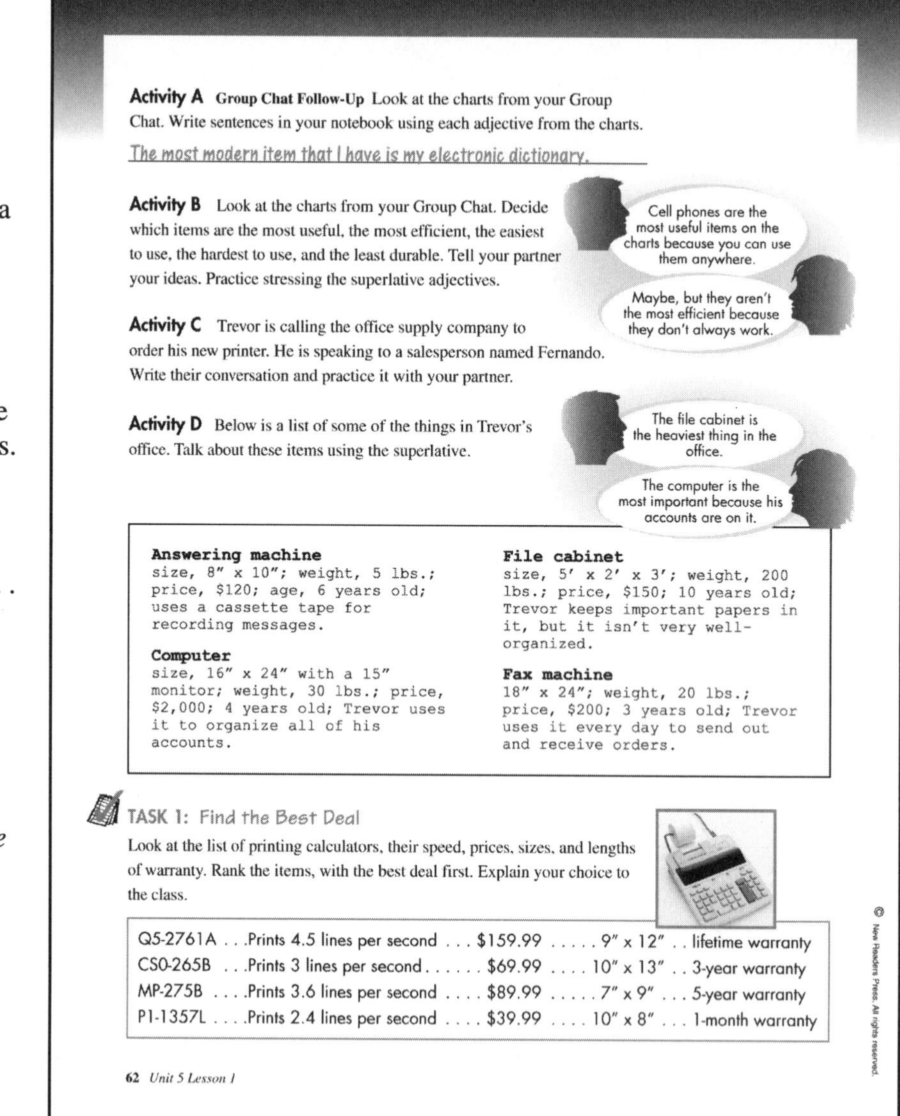

Activity A **Group Chat Follow-Up** Look at the charts from your Group Chat. Write sentences in your notebook using each adjective from the charts.

The most modern item that I have is my electronic dictionary.

Activity B Look at the charts from your Group Chat. Decide which items are the most useful, the most efficient, the easiest to use, the hardest to use, and the least durable. Tell your partner your ideas. Practice stressing the superlative adjectives.

Activity C Trevor is calling the office supply company to order his new printer. He is speaking to a salesperson named Fernando. Write their conversation and practice it with your partner.

Activity D Below is a list of some of the things in Trevor's office. Talk about these items using the superlative.

Answering machine
size, 8" x 10"; weight, 5 lbs.; price, $120; age, 6 years old; uses a cassette tape for recording messages.

Computer
size, 16" x 24" with a 15" monitor; weight, 30 lbs.; price, $2,000; 4 years old; Trevor uses it to organize all of his accounts.

File cabinet
size, 5' x 2' x 3'; weight, 200 lbs.; price, $150; 10 years old; Trevor keeps important papers in it, but it isn't very well-organized.

Fax machine
18" x 24"; weight, 20 lbs.; price, $200; 3 years old; Trevor uses it every day to send out and receive orders.

TASK 1: Find the Best Deal

Look at the list of printing calculators, their speed, prices, sizes, and lengths of warranty. Rank the items, with the best deal first. Explain your choice to the class.

Q5-2761A	Prints 4.5 lines per second	$159.99	9" x 12"	lifetime warranty
CS0-265B	Prints 3 lines per second	$69.99	10" x 13"	3-year warranty
MP-275B	Prints 3.6 lines per second	$89.99	7" x 9"	5-year warranty
P1-1357L	Prints 2.4 lines per second	$39.99	10" x 8"	1-month warranty

62 Unit 5 Lesson 1

Activity D

Possible Answers

- The answering machine is the smallest, cheapest, and lightest machine in Trevor's office.
- The fax machine is the newest thing in his office.
- The file cabinet is the oldest, biggest, and heaviest thing in the office.

Task 1

Possible Answers

- Q5-2761A prints the fastest, is of average size, and has the best warranty. But it's the most expensive. Someone with more money might rank this model highest.
- MP-275B prints second fastest, is $70 cheaper than the Q5 model, is more compact, and has a good warranty. This would be the number 1 choice for someone looking for the best price, good quality, and decent warranty. Size is more important than speed for this choice.

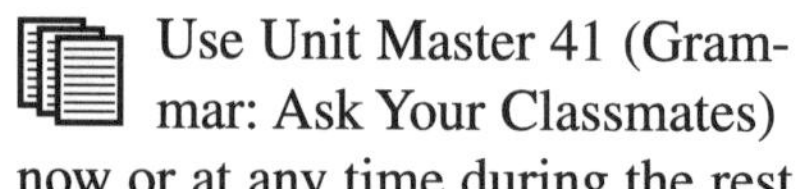

Use Unit Master 41 (Grammar: Ask Your Classmates) now or at any time during the rest of the unit.

Lesson 2: Second-Hand Rose

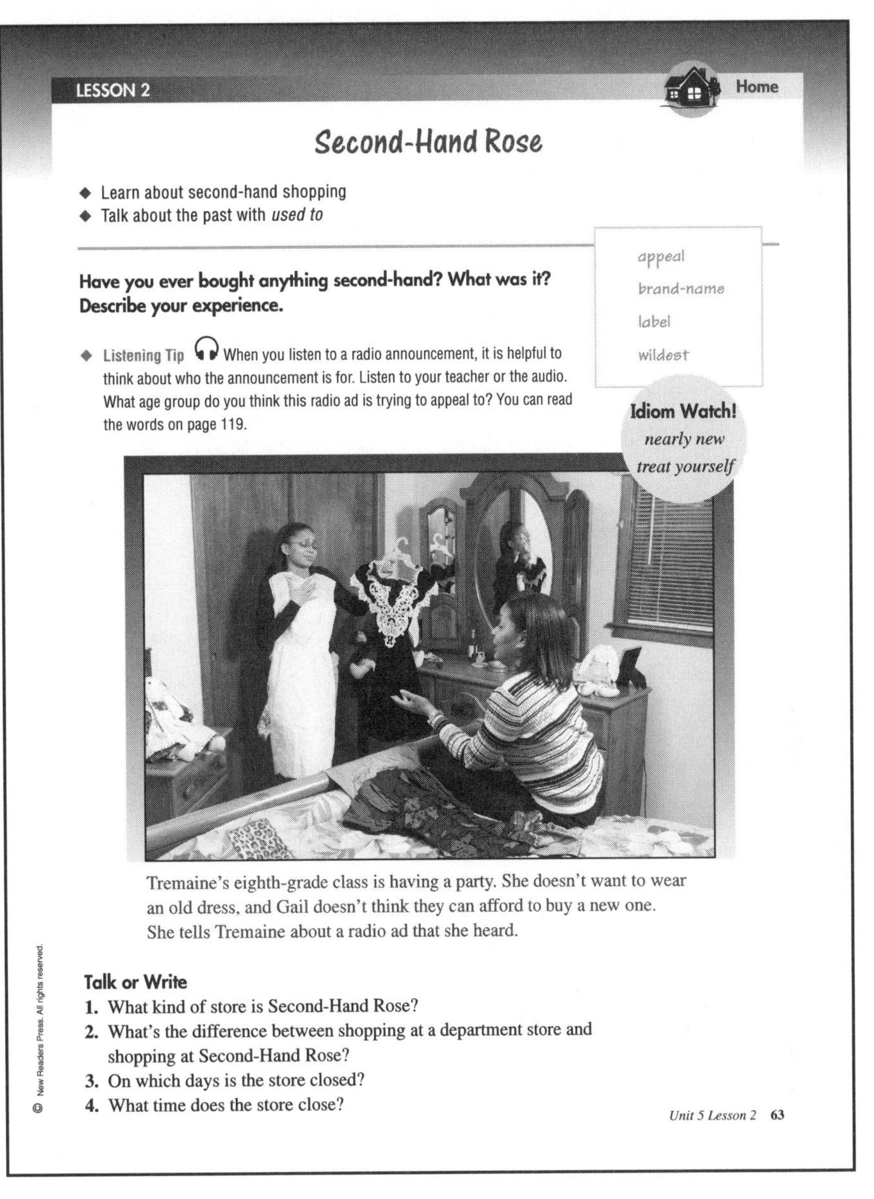
LESSON 2 Home

Second-Hand Rose

- Learn about second-hand shopping
- Talk about the past with *used to*

appeal
brand-name
label
wildest

Have you ever bought anything second-hand? What was it? Describe your experience.

- Listening Tip When you listen to a radio announcement, it is helpful to think about who the announcement is for. Listen to your teacher or the audio. What age group do you think this radio ad is trying to appeal to? You can read the words on page 119.

Idiom Watch!
nearly new
treat yourself

Tremaine's eighth-grade class is having a party. She doesn't want to wear an old dress, and Gail doesn't think they can afford to buy a new one. She tells Tremaine about a radio ad that she heard.

Talk or Write

1. What kind of store is Second-Hand Rose?
2. What's the difference between shopping at a department store and shopping at Second-Hand Rose?
3. On which days is the store closed?
4. What time does the store close?

Unit 5 Lesson 2 **63**

Follow the suggestions on p. 5 for talking about the title.

Explain that *second-hand* means "owned or used by someone else before." Ask learners if they have heard the song "Second-Hand Rose." Explain that *Rose* is a woman's first name. Tell them they will learn the song later in the unit.

Questions

Read the introductory questions aloud, and encourage learners to share their experiences.

Extension

A logical follow-up to *second-hand* is *hand-me-down.* A definition of this term is "a used article, mainly clothing, given to another person."

Ask learners what their experiences are with hand-me-downs in their families.

Attention Box

Read the words to learners, pointing or miming to convey meaning. This vocabulary should be understood, but learners should not be expected to produce the words at this point.

Idiom Watch!

The expression *nearly new* can be defined as "used, but in very good condition." One meaning of the idiom *treat yourself* might be "to do something special for yourself."

Ask several learners what they think would be a treat for themselves. Write their examples on the board.

Listening Tip

Read the listening tip aloud.

Answer

teenagers or young adults

Play the audio or read the listening script on p. 121.

After learners listen to the passage, ask their opinions on whether it is possible for something to be "better than new." Ask learners if they would consider shopping at a store like Second-Hand Rose.

Talk or Write

This exercise helps learners listen for details.

Possible Answers

1. A second-hand store that sells used clothing and accessories
2. Department stores are bigger and they sell new products. Returned items might be sold at sale prices, but everything else is new.
3. Monday and Tuesday
4. 9:00 P.M.

Use Unit Master 42 (Song: Unscramble the Lines) now or at any time during the rest of the unit.

Vocabulary

Follow the suggestions on p. 6 for introducing and reinforcing vocabulary words.

One Step Up

Follow the suggestions on p. 6 for categorizing the vocabulary words as nouns, verbs, and adjectives.

- Nouns: *defect, flaw, rip, scratch*
- Verbs: *rip, scratch*
- Adjectives: *faded, ripped, scratched, stained*

Attention Box

Introduce the word *equipment* for use in the Partner Chat. Read the word to learners, pointing or miming to convey meaning. This word should be understood, but learners should not be expected to produce it at this point.

One definition for *equipment* might be "useful items needed for a purpose, such as work or sports."

Partner Chat

Use Customizable Master 2 (3-Column Chart). Follow the suggestions on p. 7 for customizing and duplicating the master and distributing the copies.

When learners have finished filling in their charts, ask for volunteers to provide a few examples for you to write on the board or an overhead transparency. Their sentences might look like this:

Nicole usually shops for clothes at department stores. She used to shop at dress shops in Argentina.

Grammar Talk

Follow the suggestions on p. 6 for introducing the grammar point.

Possible Answers

- *Used to* refers to a habitual past action—something you often did in the past, but no longer do.
- The simple, or base, form of the verb follows *used to.*

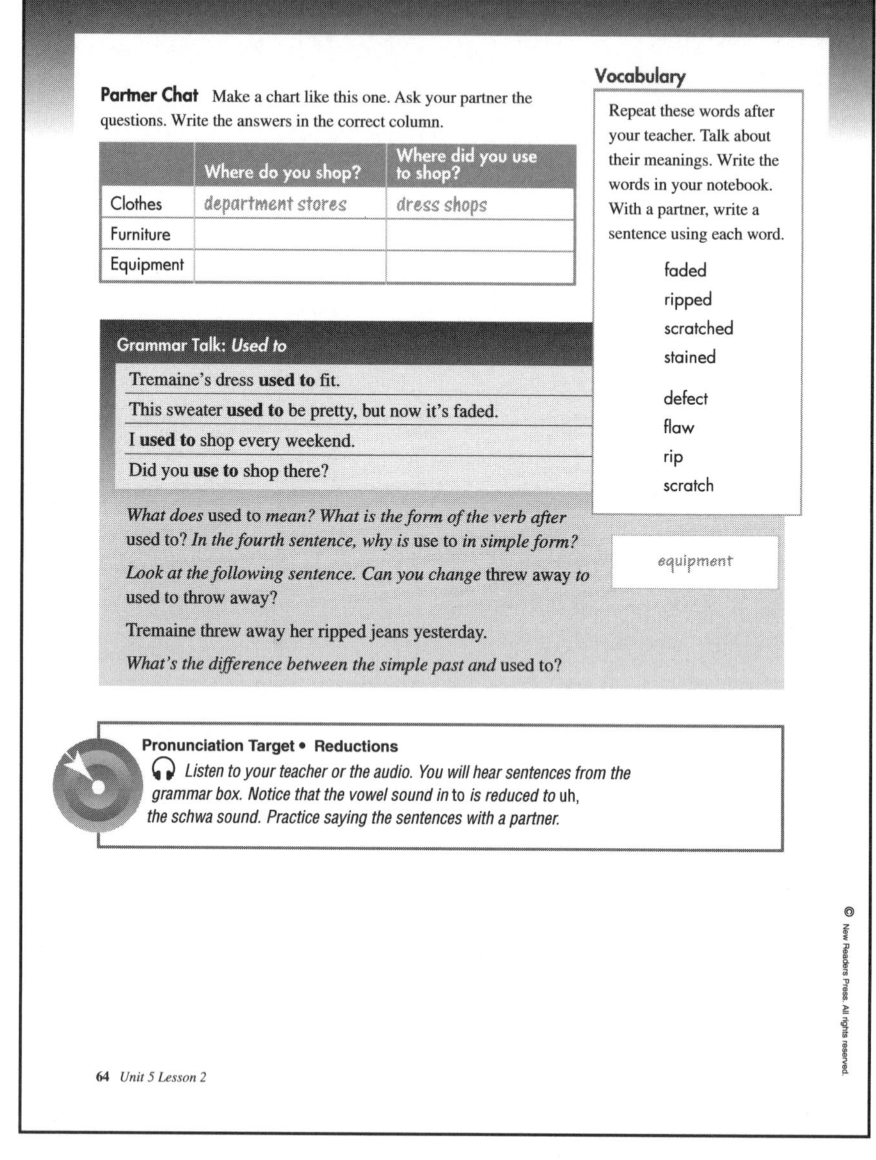

Partner Chat Make a chart like this one. Ask your partner the questions. Write the answers in the correct column.

	Where do you shop?	Where did you use to shop?
Clothes	department stores	dress shops
Furniture		
Equipment		

Vocabulary

Repeat these words after your teacher. Talk about their meanings. Write the words in your notebook. With a partner, write a sentence using each word.

faded
ripped
scratched
stained

defect
flaw
rip
scratch

equipment

Grammar Talk: *Used to*

Tremaine's dress **used to** fit.
This sweater **used to** be pretty, but now it's faded.
I **used to** shop every weekend.
Did you **use to** shop there?

What does used to *mean? What is the form of the verb after* used to? *In the fourth sentence, why is* use to *in simple form?*

Look at the following sentence. Can you change threw away *to* used to throw away?

Tremaine threw away her ripped jeans yesterday.

What's the difference between the simple past and used to?

Pronunciation Target • Reductions

Listen to your teacher or the audio. You will hear sentences from the grammar box. Notice that the vowel sound in to *is reduced to* uh, *the schwa sound. Practice saying the sentences with a partner.*

64 *Unit 5 Lesson 2*

- In sentence 4, *use to* is in simple form because it is a past-tense question with *did.*
- "Tremaine threw away her ripped jeans yesterday" cannot be changed to "used to throw away" because the sentence describes a single past action, which requires the simple past tense.
- The simple past tense refers to a single past action or an action that took place at one specific time or several specific times in the past. *Used to* refers to past action that was habitual (recurrent) and is no longer happening.

Introduce the negative form *didn't use to.* Provide these examples on the board or an overhead transparency:

- I didn't use to work here.
- I didn't use to stay up so late.

Pronunciation Target

Play the audio or read the sentences in Grammar Talk aloud.

Assign Workbook pp. 34–35.

Use Unit Master 43 (Grammar: Listen and Write) now or at any time during the rest of the unit.

Activity A

Learners should write at least six sentences—one about themselves and one about their partners for each category: clothing, furniture, and equipment.

Activity B

Ask volunteers to write some of their sentences on the board.

Grammar Talk

Ask learners to provide more sentences comparing the use of *one* and *ones.* Have them follow these examples:

- *This sweatshirt is too small. That one fits well.*
- *I like these sunglasses. The other ones are too narrow for my face.*

Model a natural speaking pace for sentences with *that one* and *the other ones.* Exaggerate the stress on *that* and *other* so learners can hear the natural stress pattern. Then ask learners to practice their sentences with a partner.

Activity C

Play the audio or read the listening script below. Have learners use the conversation as a model for the rest of the activity.

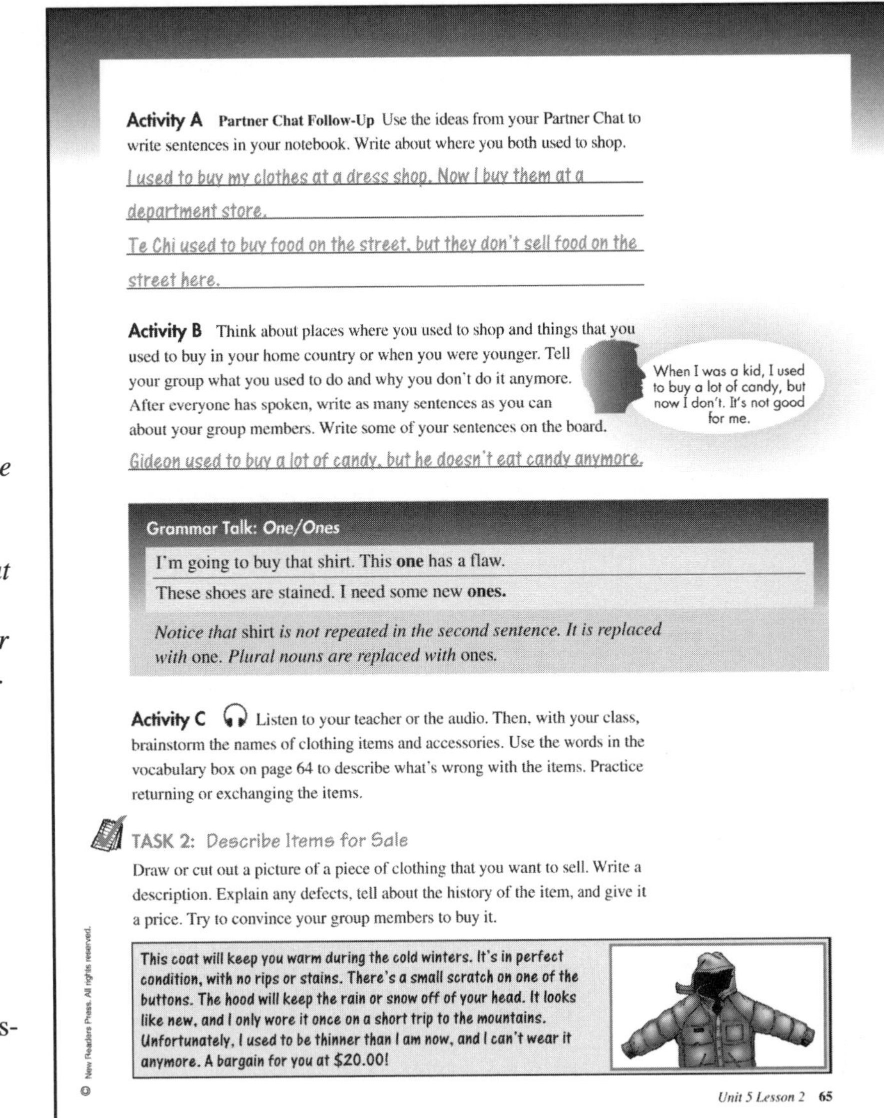

Activity A **Partner Chat Follow-Up** Use the ideas from your Partner Chat to write sentences in your notebook. Write about where you both used to shop.

I used to buy my clothes at a dress shop. Now I buy them at a department store.

Te Chi used to buy food on the street, but they don't sell food on the street here.

Activity B Think about places where you used to shop and things that you used to buy in your home country or when you were younger. Tell your group what you used to do and why you don't do it anymore. After everyone has spoken, write as many sentences as you can about your group members. Write some of your sentences on the board.

Gideon used to buy a lot of candy, but he doesn't eat candy anymore.

Grammar Talk: One/Ones

I'm going to buy that shirt. This **one** has a flaw.
These shoes are stained. I need some new **ones.**

Notice that shirt *is not repeated in the second sentence. It is replaced with* one. *Plural nouns are replaced with* ones.

Activity C Listen to your teacher or the audio. Then, with your class, brainstorm the names of clothing items and accessories. Use the words in the vocabulary box on page 64 to describe what's wrong with the items. Practice returning or exchanging the items.

TASK 2: Describe Items for Sale

Draw or cut out a picture of a piece of clothing that you want to sell. Write a description. Explain any defects, tell about the history of the item, and give it a price. Try to convince your group members to buy it.

This coat will keep you warm during the cold winters. It's in perfect condition, with no rips or stains. There's a small scratch on one of the buttons. The hood will keep the rain or snow off of your head. It looks like new, and I only wore it once on a short trip to the mountains. Unfortunately, I used to be thinner than I am now, and I can't wear it anymore. A bargain for you at $20.00!

© New Readers Press. All rights reserved.

Unit 5 Lesson 2 65

Listening Script

Salesperson: May I help you?
Gail: Yes. I'd like to return these sunglasses.
Salesperson: What's the problem?
Gail: They're scratched!
Salesperson: Oh, I see. Would you like a refund or an exchange?
Gail: I'd like to exchange them.
Salesperson: No problem. I'll get you some new ones.

When learners change *sunglasses* to *CD,* for example, the new dialogue might look like this:

Salesperson: May I help you?
Gail: Yes. I'd like to return this CD.
Salesperson: What's the problem?
Gail: It's scratched!
Salesperson: Oh, I see. Would you like a refund or an exchange?
Gail: I'd like to exchange it.
Salesperson: No problem. I'll get you a new one.

Task 2

Ongoing Assessment

- After learners have written their descriptions, check their writing and listen to their conversations.
- Take notes on how well learners perform on the following criteria:
  a. Quality of descriptions
     0 = incorrect grammar and word choice that make comprehension very difficult
     1 = incorrect grammar and word choice that occasionally make comprehension difficult
     2 = descriptions of clothing items understandable but not perfect
  b. Features of language functions (tell, convince)
     0 = many problems/not understandable
     1 = some problems with clarity or pronunciation
     2 = clear and appropriate but not perfect

Lesson 3: Bargain Hunting

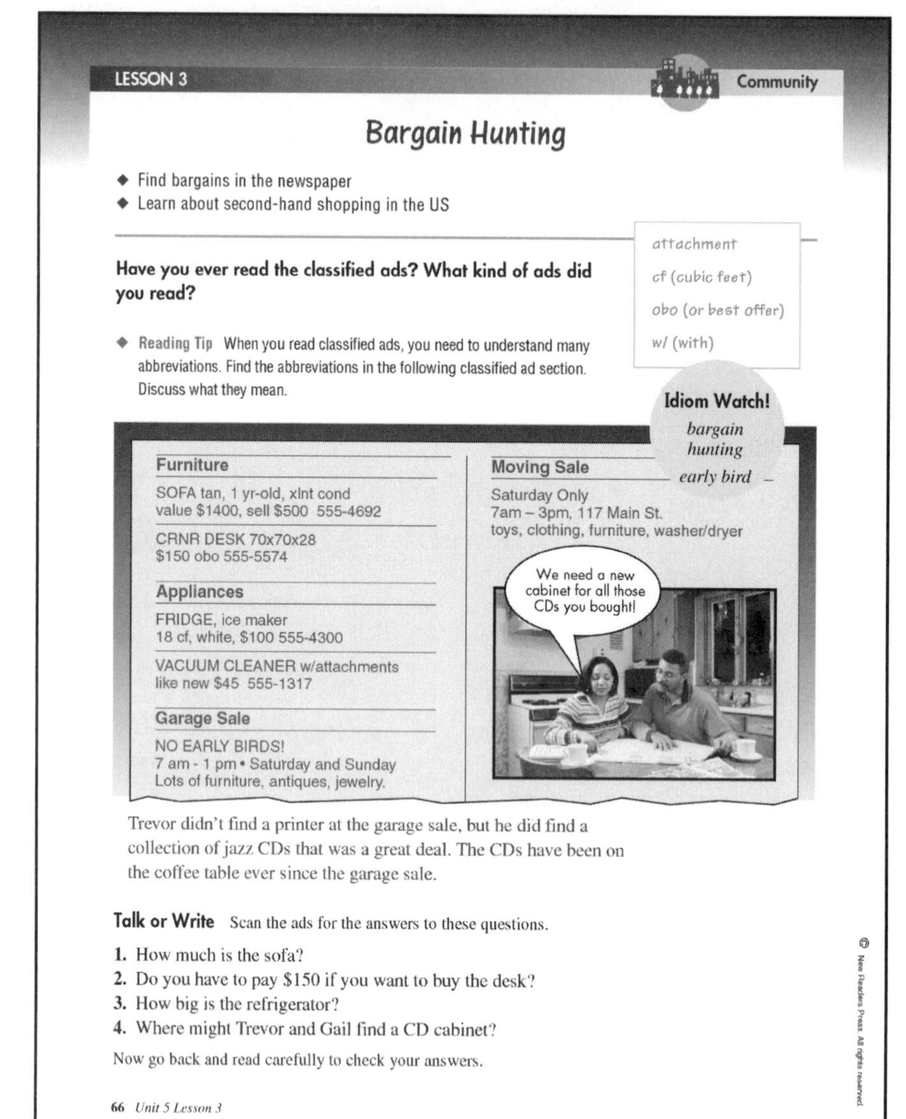

LESSON 3 Community

Bargain Hunting

- Find bargains in the newspaper
- Learn about second-hand shopping in the US

attachment
cf (cubic feet)
obo (or best offer)
w/ (with)

Have you ever read the classified ads? What kind of ads did you read?

◆ **Reading Tip** When you read classified ads, you need to understand many abbreviations. Find the abbreviations in the following classified ad section. Discuss what they mean.

Idiom Watch!
bargain hunting
early bird

Furniture
SOFA tan, 1 yr-old, xlnt cond value $1400, sell $500 555-4692
CRNR DESK 70x70x28 $150 obo 555-5574

Appliances
FRIDGE, ice maker 18 cf, white, $100 555-4300
VACUUM CLEANER w/attachments like new $45 555-1317

Garage Sale
NO EARLY BIRDS!
7 am - 1 pm • Saturday and Sunday
Lots of furniture, antiques, jewelry.

Moving Sale
Saturday Only
7am – 3pm, 117 Main St.
toys, clothing, furniture, washer/dryer

Trevor didn't find a printer at the garage sale, but he did find a collection of jazz CDs that was a great deal. The CDs have been on the coffee table ever since the garage sale.

Talk or Write Scan the ads for the answers to these questions.

1. How much is the sofa?
2. Do you have to pay $150 if you want to buy the desk?
3. How big is the refrigerator?
4. Where might Trevor and Gail find a CD cabinet?

Now go back and read carefully to check your answers.

66 *Unit 5 Lesson 3*

Follow the suggestions on p. 5 for talking about the title.

Give learners this definition of *bargain hunting:* "searching/looking/shopping for good, low prices." In bargaining, a buyer asks for a lower price.

Introduce these ideas to begin a discussion about bargains:
- Looking for a bargain involves comparison shopping.
- In some cultures, it is common for buyers and sellers to bargain.

Questions

Read the questions aloud.
- Have learners give detailed examples of any classified ads they have read.
- Also ask if learners have ever purchased an item through the classifieds. If so, ask them to describe their experience.

Attention Box

This vocabulary should be understood when reading the ads, but learners should not be expected to produce the words at this point.

Early bird refers to someone who gets up early or arrives early. *Early birds* are not always welcomed at garage sales because they try to get the best items before the sale has officially opened.

Caption

Follow the suggestions on p. 5 for talking about captions.
- Discuss the meaning of *deal* (an agreement, trade, or transaction).
- Point out that some people will buy an item because it is a "great deal" but then rarely use it once they take it home.
- Discuss the difference between a *big deal* and a *great deal.*

Reading Tip

Answers

yr = year
xlnt cond = excellent condition
CRNR = corner
obo = or best offer
fridge = refrigerator
cf = cubic feet
w/ = with

Extension

Ask learners to compare the abbreviations from the ads in the reading with those found in the classified ads of a local newspaper.

One Step Up

Ask learners to bring in ads that have other abbreviations. Discuss the abbreviations with the learners.

Discuss the term *moving sale.* When people move long distances, they can't always take everything with them. They sell their excess furnishings at a *moving sale.*

Talk or Write

This exercise helps learners scan for information.

Answers

1. $500
2. No. The offer that's closest to $150 will be accepted.
3. 18 cubic feet
4. At the garage sale or moving sale

Vocabulary

Follow the suggestions on p. 6 for introducing and reinforcing vocabulary words. If possible, bring in the items themselves (e.g., a blender) or pictures of them to show learners.

Pronunciation Tip

The final *-er* sound in the words *blender, hamper, recliner,* and *stroller* may be difficult for some learners to pronounce.

- Demonstrate how the lips tighten at the corners of the mouth when this sound is produced. The tip of the tongue is pulled back and tightened, and the base of the tongue is curved upward.
- Emphasize that the final *-er* is a complete syllable and needs to be drawn out. Many learners cut the sound short, making the word difficult to understand.

In the US

To enhance this activity, make a list of names and locations of local thrift stores, second-hand stores, consignment shops, and pawnshops in your area. Be sure to include flea markets and swap meets.

Compare Cultures

Use Customizable Master 1 (2-Column Chart). Divide the second column into two columns labeled *Yes* and *No*. Follow the suggestions on p. 7 for customizing and duplicating the master and distributing the copies.

Ask learners to write the name of their home countries as the heading for the second and third columns.

Activity A

Encourage learners to share some of their ideas. Write various reasons for buying or not buying items second-hand on the board or an overhead transparency.

In the US Second-Hand Shopping

In the US there are many kinds of places to buy and sell second-hand items. Thrift stores sell clothing and items that people give away. Second-hand clothing stores sell used clothing and accessories that have been chosen carefully. Sometimes these stores sell other items on *consignment*. This means that people bring in items they want to sell. If the items are sold, the store receives a percentage of the price. A pawn shop is another place to buy used items. People sell valuable items, such as jewelry and musical instruments, to pawn-shop owners. The pawn shop sells the items back to the owner or to other customers for a higher price.

One popular place to buy and sell used items is a garage sale or sidewalk sale. Some people buy used items because they need to save money. Other people just like to shop at garage sales and find bargains. Many people in the US move frequently. When they move, they often sell items that they no longer want. Sometimes neighborhoods have group garage sales. Everyone on the block sells items on the same day. It's OK to bargain for a cheaper price at a garage sale.

Vocabulary

Repeat these words after your teacher. Talk about their meanings. Write the words in your notebook. With a partner, write a sentence using each word.

aquarium
blender
crib
hamper
nightstand
recliner
stroller

give away

Compare Cultures

Does your home country have these kinds of stores and sales? Fill in the chart by putting a check under yes or no.

US	Your Home Country	
	yes	no
thrift stores		
second-hand stores		
consignment shops		
pawn shops		
garage sales		

Activity A Make a list of things you have bought or would buy second-hand and things you wouldn't. Compare your lists in a small group and explain reasons for your choices.

Assign Workbook pp. 36–37.

Use Unit Master 44 (Vocabulary: Tell a Story) now or at any time during the rest of the unit.

Activity B

Write learners' suggestions under the appropriate heading on the board or an overhead transparency. If some items don't fit the categories, ask learners to suggest a new category name.

Activity C

Follow the suggestions on p. 6 for partner conversations.

- Before learners begin, model the conversation, paying particular attention to question intonation.
- After partners practice the new conversation, ask one or two sets of volunteers to model their conversation for the class.
- Point out that the expression "Would you take $ ____?" (line 5) is very common in bargaining.
- Explain that the expression "Well, I guess that's OK" shows slight disappointment, but acceptance nevertheless.

Task 3

Possible Answers

When buying a used item, questions to ask might include these:

- How old is it?
- How big is it?
- What color is it?
- What condition is it in?
- Does it work?
- Could you give me a detailed description?
- What is the asking price?

Review Unit Skills

Follow the suggestions on pp. 7–9 for games and activities to review the vocabulary and grammar in this unit.

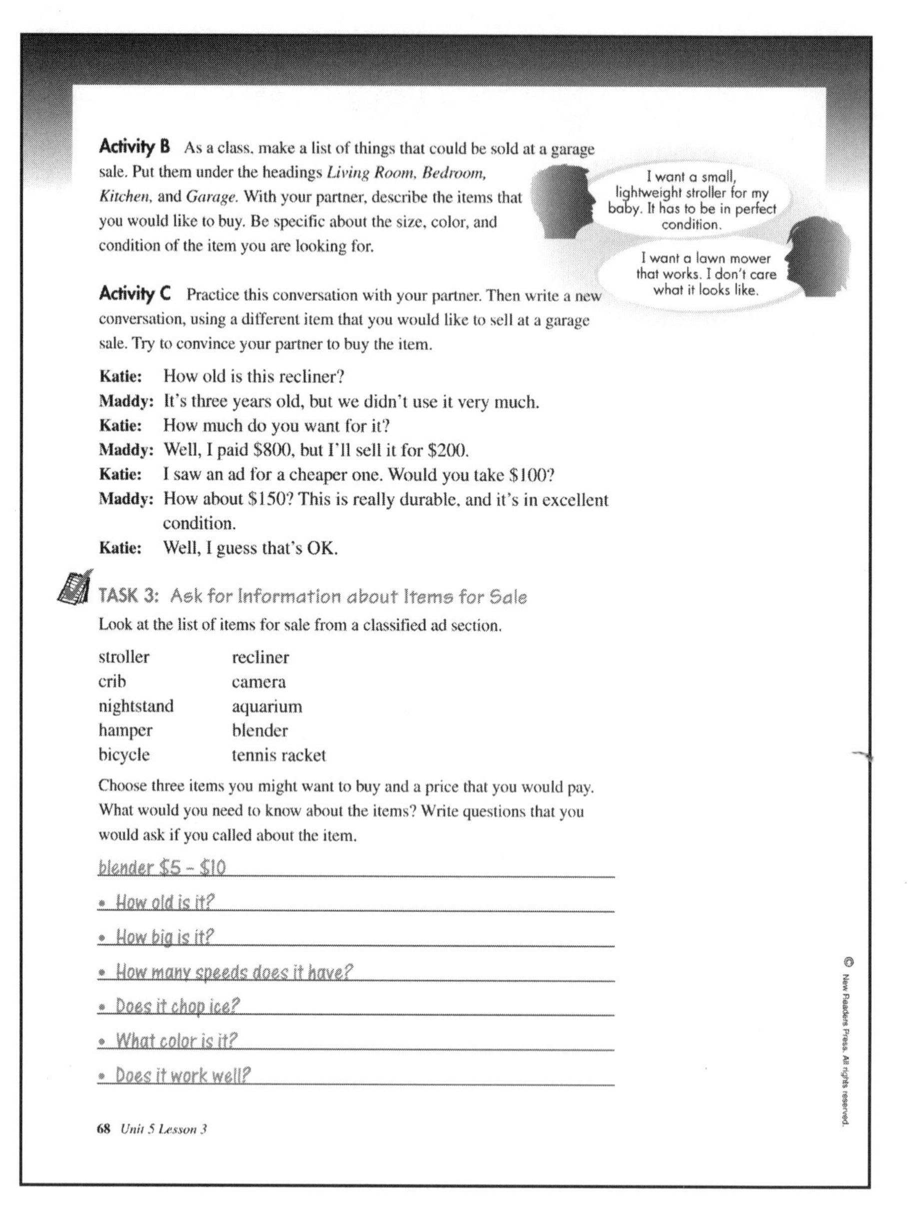

Activity B As a class, make a list of things that could be sold at a garage sale. Put them under the headings *Living Room, Bedroom, Kitchen,* and *Garage.* With your partner, describe the items that you would like to buy. Be specific about the size, color, and condition of the item you are looking for.

Activity C Practice this conversation with your partner. Then write a new conversation, using a different item that you would like to sell at a garage sale. Try to convince your partner to buy the item.

Katie: How old is this recliner?
Maddy: It's three years old, but we didn't use it very much.
Katie: How much do you want for it?
Maddy: Well, I paid $800, but I'll sell it for $200.
Katie: I saw an ad for a cheaper one. Would you take $100?
Maddy: How about $150? This is really durable, and it's in excellent condition.
Katie: Well, I guess that's OK.

TASK 3: Ask for Information about Items for Sale

Look at the list of items for sale from a classified ad section.

stroller	recliner
crib	camera
nightstand	aquarium
hamper	blender
bicycle	tennis racket

Choose three items you might want to buy and a price that you would pay. What would you need to know about the items? Write questions that you would ask if you called about the item.

blender $5 – $10
- How old is it?
- How big is it?
- How many speeds does it have?
- Does it chop ice?
- What color is it?
- Does it work well?

Unit 5 Project

Learners hold a classroom "garage sale."

Get Ready

Provide learners with magazines, catalogs, scissors, and index cards.

Assessment

As learners engage in the garage sale activity, complete a copy of Unit Master 45 (Project Assessment Form) for as many learners as you can. If possible, copy the completed form for each learner's portfolio.

Do the Work

Extensions

1. Have learners bring items from home that they really want to sell. If learners agree, tell them they can use the money earned from the sale to plan a class outing or party.

   Then proceed as follows:
   - Turn desks and tables into selling booths.
   - Have learners take turns buying and selling their items. Encourage them to bargain if that is the norm in your area.
   - Assign a detail-oriented, trustworthy student to be in charge of collecting and counting all the money earned at the sale.
2. Invite other classes to conduct garage sales in their classrooms and pool the money with them for a school outing.

Present

Have volunteers begin the series of class presentations.

Writing Extension

After learners have written their paragraphs, refer them to the Writing Checklist on p. 125 of their books. Ask volunteers to share their stories with the class.

Technology Extra

Assist any learners who have difficulty searching the web site.

UNIT 5 Project

Classroom "Garage Sale"

Have a classroom garage sale. Follow these steps:

Get Ready

Draw or cut out pictures of five items that you would like to sell. If possible, choose items that you actually have at home and would like to sell. Write information about the item on an index card like the one at the right. In your description, use adjectives and give other information about the item.

Name:
How Old:
Price:
Description:

Do the Work

Divide the class into "buyers" and "sellers." The sellers spread their pictures out on their desks or tables. The buyers walk around deciding what they want to buy. The sellers try to convince the buyers to choose their items. When an agreement is reached, the buyer takes the picture. After 15 minutes, the sellers put away the unsold items. Buyers become sellers, and the new sellers display their items. Repeat the process for 15 more minutes.

Present

Tell the class which items you sold, which items you couldn't sell, and why.

Writing Extension Write a paragraph about what you chose to buy. Explain why you bought the items.

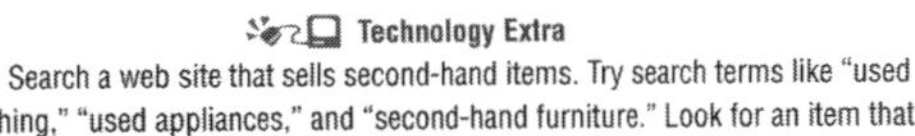

Technology Extra

Search a web site that sells second-hand items. Try search terms like "used clothing," "used appliances," and "second-hand furniture." Look for an item that you are interested in buying. Report back to the class on what you find. Discuss the advantages and disadvantages of purchasing on the Internet.

Assign Workbook p. 38 (Check Your Progress).

Use Unit Master 46 (Unit 5 Checkup/Review) whenever you complete this unit.

Unit 6: Facing Problems Head On

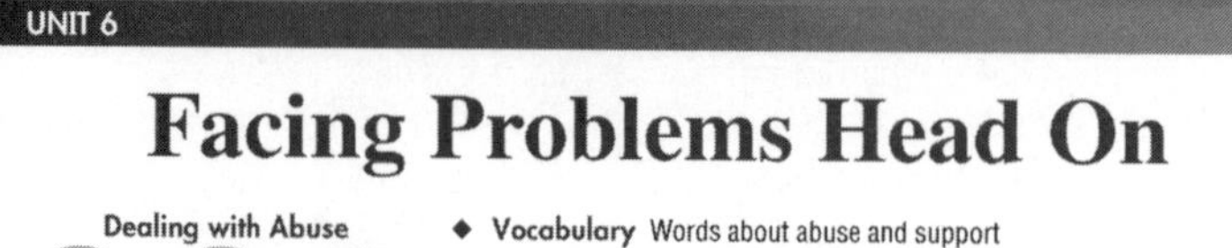

UNIT 6

Facing Problems Head On

Dealing with Abuse

Work/School 1 · Home 2 · Community 3

- **Vocabulary** Words about abuse and support
- **Language** Gerunds as subjects and objects • Present perfect
- **Pronunciation** Reduction of *-ing* • Disappearing initial *h*
- **Culture** Disciplining children

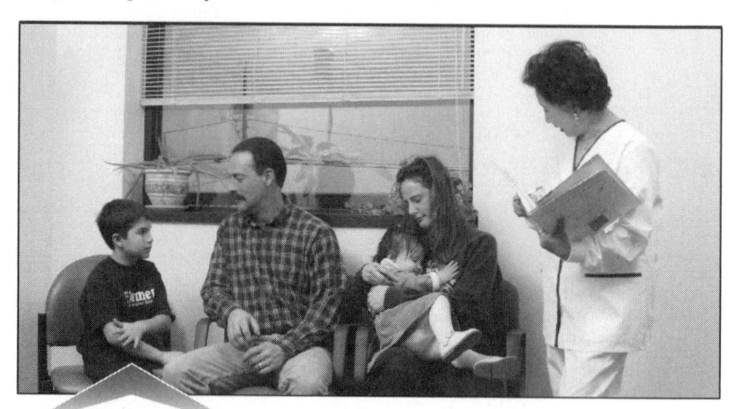

What are some reasons people go to a medical clinic?

Leticia Medina is a nurse in a medical clinic. She often sees the results of violence, neglect, and abuse. Lately, however, these problems have affected people that she knows. She wants to learn more about drug abuse and child abuse and how to help people who struggle with these problems.

Think and Talk

1. What do you see in the picture?
2. What kinds of problems do you think the patients have?
3. Do you think that these problems are common? Explain.
4. Why do you think people have these problems?

What's Your Opinion? Which of the following causes more problems in society: tobacco, alcohol, or illegal drugs? Explain your answer.

70 *Unit 6*

Materials for the Unit

- Construction paper
- Brochures, booklets, or pages from the Internet about child abuse or drug and alcohol abuse (optional)
- Customizable Masters 1, 2, and 5
- Generic Assessment Masters 8–12
- Unit Masters 47–52

Facing Problems Head On

Follow the suggestions on p. 5 for talking about the title. Then do the following:

- Discuss the meaning of the verb *face* and the expression *head on.*
- Ask learners what they think the title might mean. One meaning might be "to confront directly."
- Discuss why a person should *face problems head on.* Ask, "What can happen if you run away from a problem instead of facing it?"

Photo

Follow the suggestions on p. 4 for talking about the photo, then read the question below the arrow.

Caption

Follow the suggestions on p. 5 for talking about captions.

Think and Talk

As learners give different answers, write them on the board or an overhead transparency.

Ask learners if they think these problems are as common in their home countries as they are in the US.

What's Your Opinion?

As part of this discussion, ask the following questions:

- Which substance is the most dangerous?
- Which is the most addictive?
- Which is used the most?
- Which costs the most for society? (Consider social as well as economic costs.)

Vocabulary

Follow the suggestions on p. 6 for introducing and reinforcing vocabulary words.

One Step Up

Follow the suggestions on p. 6 for categorizing the vocabulary words as nouns, verbs, and adjectives.

- Nouns: *abuse, alcoholic, addict, alcoholism, support, symptom*
- Verbs: *abuse, addict, recover, support*
- Adjectives: *abusive, addicted, alcoholic, anonymous*

Vocabulary Plus

Point out the difference in pronunciation between the noun and verb forms of the word *abuse.*

Gather Your Thoughts

Use Customizable Master 2 (3-Column Chart). Follow the suggestions on p. 7 for customizing and duplicating the master and distributing the copies.

- Follow the directions for the activity in the student book.
- If pairs of learners have difficulty generating ideas on their own, brainstorm activities together and then have the partners categorize.

What's the Problem?

Follow the suggestions on p. 5 for identifying and analyzing problems.

Setting Goals

Follow the suggestions on p. 5 for setting goals.

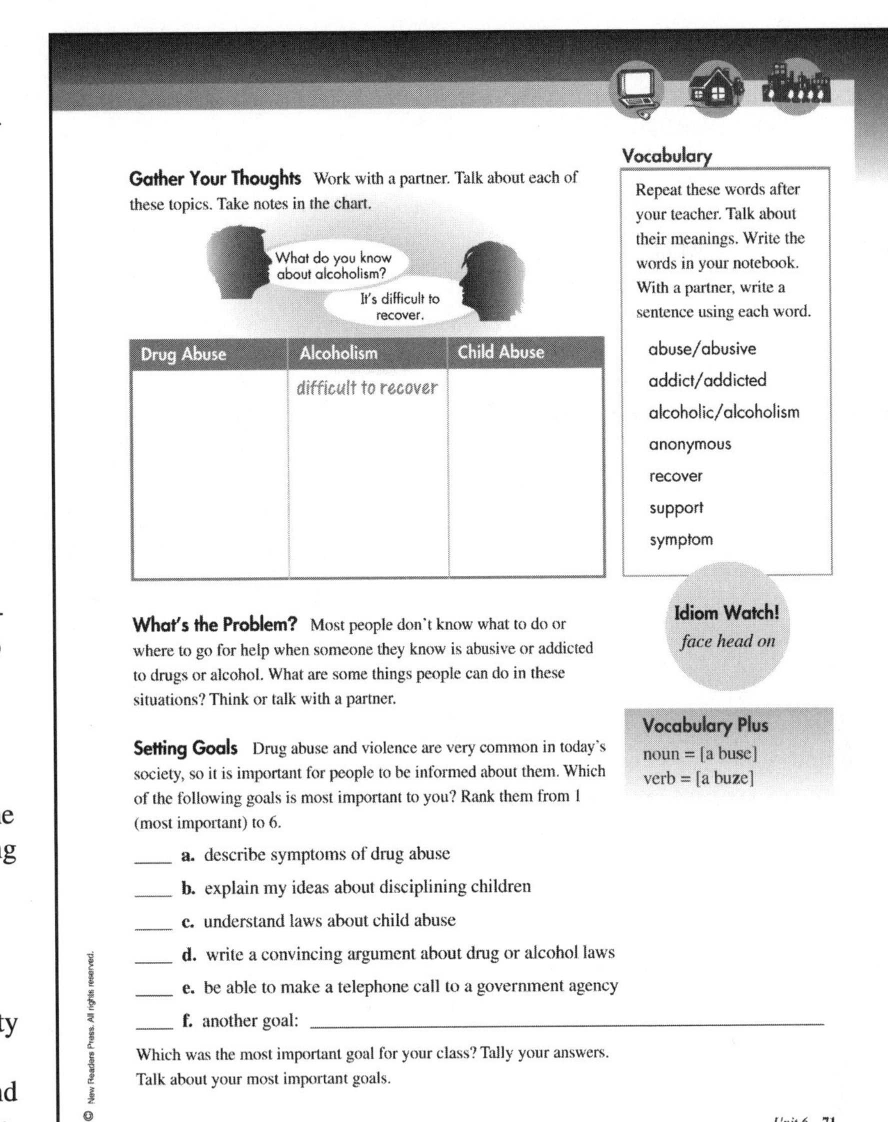

Gather Your Thoughts Work with a partner. Talk about each of these topics. Take notes in the chart.

What do you know about alcoholism?

It's difficult to recover.

Drug Abuse	Alcoholism	Child Abuse
	difficult to recover	

Vocabulary

Repeat these words after your teacher. Talk about their meanings. Write the words in your notebook. With a partner, write a sentence using each word.

abuse/abusive
addict/addicted
alcoholic/alcoholism
anonymous
recover
support
symptom

Idiom Watch!
face head on

What's the Problem? Most people don't know what to do or where to go for help when someone they know is abusive or addicted to drugs or alcohol. What are some things people can do in these situations? Think or talk with a partner.

Vocabulary Plus
noun = [a buse]
verb = [a buze]

Setting Goals Drug abuse and violence are very common in today's society, so it is important for people to be informed about them. Which of the following goals is most important to you? Rank them from 1 (most important) to 6.

____ **a.** describe symptoms of drug abuse
____ **b.** explain my ideas about disciplining children
____ **c.** understand laws about child abuse
____ **d.** write a convincing argument about drug or alcohol laws
____ **e.** be able to make a telephone call to a government agency
____ **f.** another goal: ______________________

Which was the most important goal for your class? Tally your answers. Talk about your most important goals.

Unit 6 71

Lesson 1: Laying Down the Law

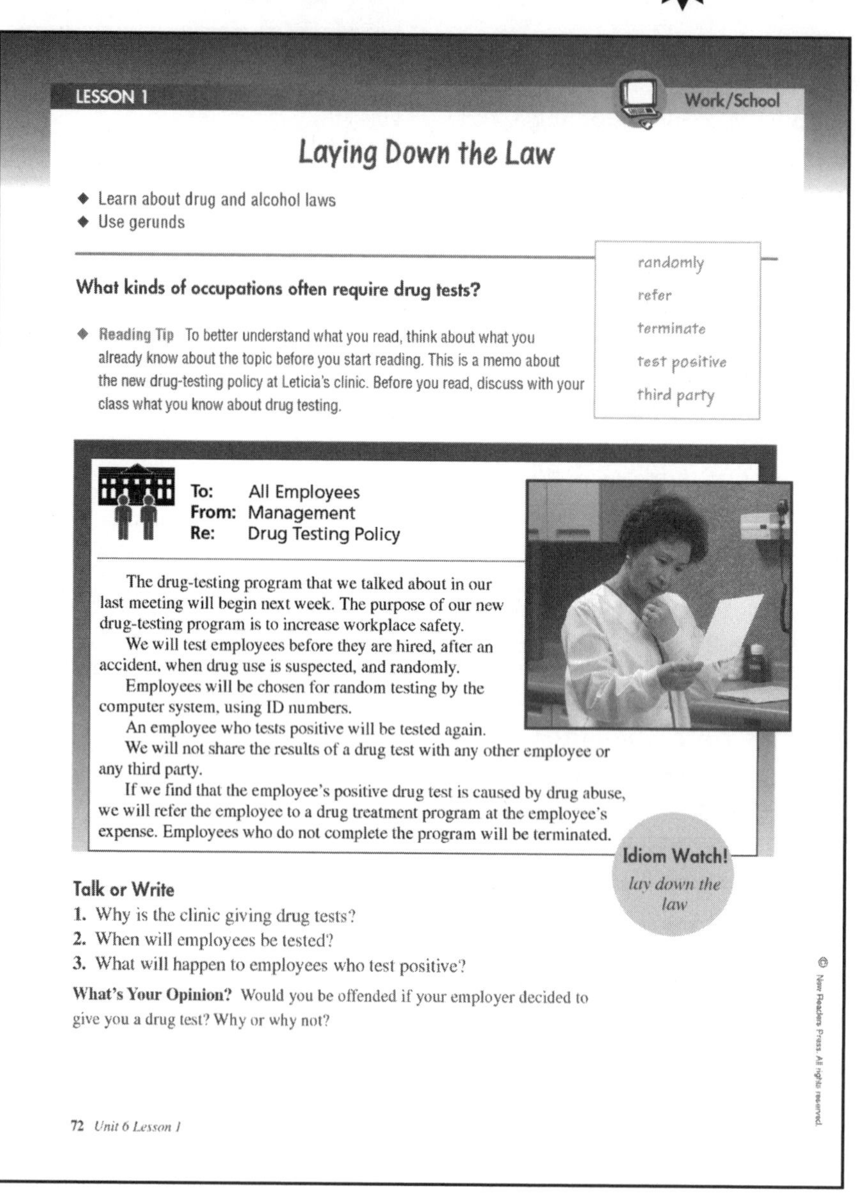

LESSON 1 Work/School

Laying Down the Law

- Learn about drug and alcohol laws
- Use gerunds

randomly
refer
terminate
test positive
third party

What kinds of occupations often require drug tests?

- **Reading Tip** To better understand what you read, think about what you already know about the topic before you start reading. This is a memo about the new drug-testing policy at Leticia's clinic. Before you read, discuss with your class what you know about drug testing.

To: All Employees
From: Management
Re: Drug Testing Policy

The drug-testing program that we talked about in our last meeting will begin next week. The purpose of our new drug-testing program is to increase workplace safety.

We will test employees before they are hired, after an accident, when drug use is suspected, and randomly.

Employees will be chosen for random testing by the computer system, using ID numbers.

An employee who tests positive will be tested again.

We will not share the results of a drug test with any other employee or any third party.

If we find that the employee's positive drug test is caused by drug abuse, we will refer the employee to a drug treatment program at the employee's expense. Employees who do not complete the program will be terminated.

Idiom Watch! *lay down the law*

Talk or Write

1. Why is the clinic giving drug tests?
2. When will employees be tested?
3. What will happen to employees who test positive?

What's Your Opinion? Would you be offended if your employer decided to give you a drug test? Why or why not?

72 *Unit 6 Lesson 1*

Follow the suggestions on p. 5 for talking about the title.

Explain that parents and teachers sometimes say, "I'm going to lay down the law," meaning "I'm going to strictly enforce the rules."

Question

Read the questions.

Possible Answers

Truck, bus, or ambulance driver; athlete; hospital worker; factory worker; people who work with machines

Attention Box

This vocabulary should be understood, but learners should not be expected to produce the words at this point.

Note that *terminate* is a very formal word meaning "fire" or "end." It is not often used in everyday speech.

Reading Tip

Read the tip aloud. Before initiating discussion, point out these elements of an office memo:

- No signature at the bottom
- *To:, From:,* and *Re:* at the top left
- *Re:* stands for *regarding* and marks the line that tells you what the memo will be about.

Talk or Write

In this exercise, learners practice scanning for specific information.

Answers

1. To increase workplace safety.
2. Before they are hired, after an accident, when drug use is suspected, and randomly.
3. They'll be tested again. After that, they'll be referred to a drug treatment program. If they don't finish their treatment, they'll be fired.

Extensions

1. Ask groups of learners to imagine that they have management positions at a company and are going to begin a new policy at the workplace. They need to write a memo to the employees telling them what is going to happen. As a group, have them write the memo on the board, butcher paper, or an overhead transparency, using correct memo format.
2. As an alternative, have the new policy be something ridiculous, (e.g., a crazy new dress code). Then ask the learners to vote on which memo is the funniest.

What's Your Opinion?

Tell learners to think about the issue. Then have them give and explain their opinions.

Vocabulary

Follow the suggestions on p. 6 for introducing and reinforcing vocabulary words.

Note that these words are clustered by part of speech—as verbs, nouns, and adjectives. Point out to learners that while *fine* and *sentence* are in the noun cluster, they can also be verbs. In addition, *fine* can be used as an adjective and *arrest* can be a noun.

Class Chat

Use Customizable Master 1 (2-Column Chart). Follow the suggestions on p. 7 for customizing and duplicating the master and distributing the copies.

When the chart is full, ask learners whether they agree with all of the rules/laws they have written down.

Grammar Talk

Follow the suggestions on p. 6 for introducing the grammar point.

- *Smoking* is a subject in the sentence. Point out that "to smoke" is *not* correct in this sentence. Learners often want to use infinitives as subjects, but such usage is very uncommon in modern English.
- Learners often confuse gerunds with progressive verbs. Emphasize that gerunds are nouns, which is one reason why it is important not to forget the verb *be* when writing progressive sentences.

Answers

- Subjects: *smoking* in the first sentence.
- Objects: *going* and *smoking* in the last two sentences.

Pronunciation Target

Play the audio or read the sentences from the grammar box. Be sure to reduce the *-ing* sound.

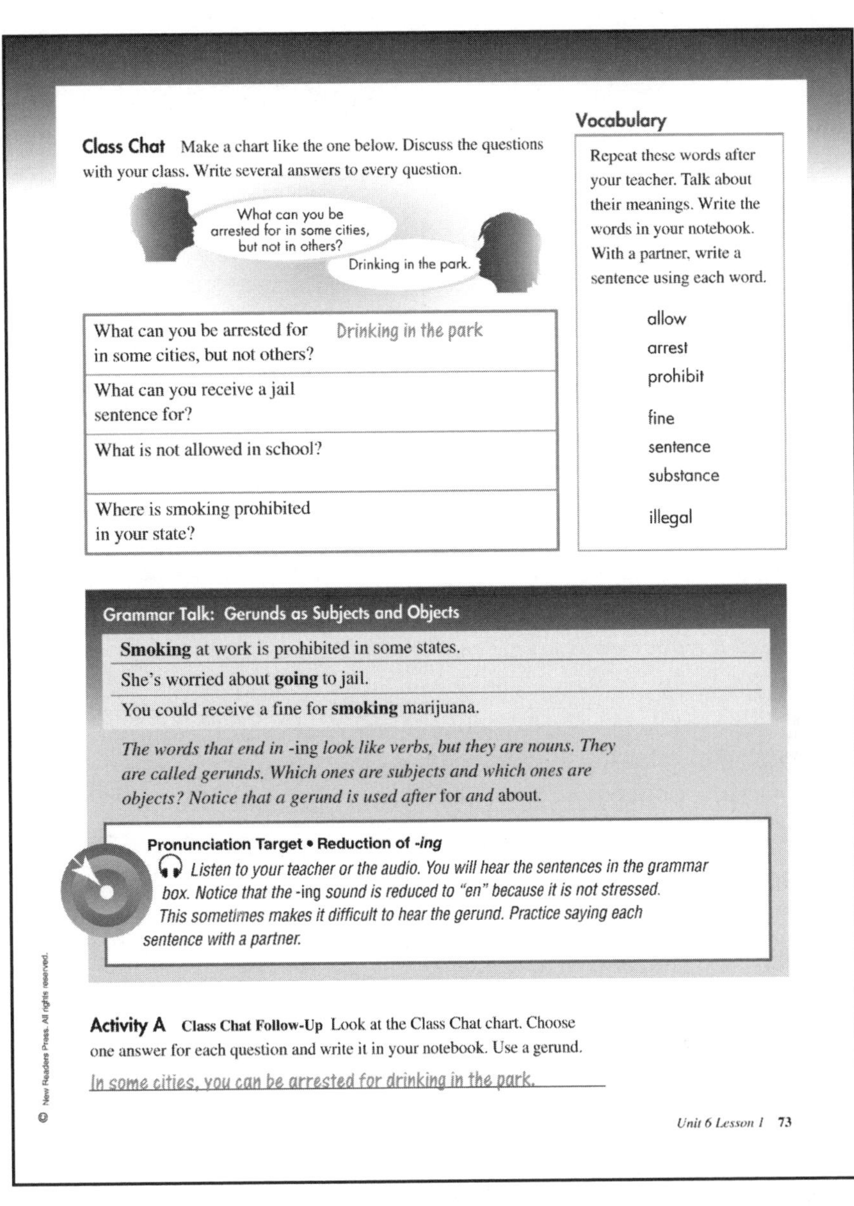

Class Chat Make a chart like the one below. Discuss the questions with your class. Write several answers to every question.

What can you be arrested for in some cities, but not others?	Drinking in the park
What can you receive a jail sentence for?	
What is not allowed in school?	
Where is smoking prohibited in your state?	

Vocabulary

Repeat these words after your teacher. Talk about their meanings. Write the words in your notebook. With a partner, write a sentence using each word.

allow
arrest
prohibit

fine
sentence
substance

illegal

Grammar Talk: Gerunds as Subjects and Objects

Smoking at work is prohibited in some states.
She's worried about **going** to jail.
You could receive a fine for **smoking** marijuana.

The words that end in -ing *look like verbs, but they are nouns. They are called gerunds. Which ones are subjects and which ones are objects? Notice that a gerund is used after* for *and* about.

Pronunciation Target • Reduction of *-ing*

Listen to your teacher or the audio. You will hear the sentences in the grammar box. Notice that the -ing sound is reduced to "en" because it is not stressed. This sometimes makes it difficult to hear the gerund. Practice saying each sentence with a partner.

Activity A **Class Chat Follow-Up** Look at the Class Chat chart. Choose one answer for each question and write it in your notebook. Use a gerund.

In some cities, you can be arrested for drinking in the park.

Unit 6 Lesson 1 73

Extension

Read the sentences below aloud. Ask learners to write only the gerund.

1. We talked about *working* there.
2. *Eating* healthy food is important.
3. I'm tired of *seeing* that TV show.
4. I know all about *fixing* cars.
5. *Reading* is very good practice.

Activity A

Ask learners to write sentences containing gerunds in their notebooks. Have them use the information in the charts from the Class Chat.

Assign Workbook pp. 39–40.

Use Unit Master 47 (Grammar: Round Table) now or at any time during the rest of the unit.

Activity B

Ask learners to write prohibitive rules for their classroom using a gerund in each.

Activity C

Play the audio or read the listening script below. Have learners write the sentences they hear in their notebooks.

Listening Script

1. They arrested him for drinking in his car.
2. Selling alcohol to teenagers is prohibited.
3. Bringing drugs across the border is illegal.
4. Drinking alcohol was not allowed in the 1930s.
5. He got a $300 fine for carrying an illegal substance.

Activity D

Have learners sit in small groups. Ask them to discuss the questions and take notes. Then have them use their notes to complete the activity.

One Step Up

After the class discussion, ask each learner to choose the question that interested him or her most and write a one-paragraph answer.

- Tell learners to begin their paragraphs by stating an opinion (e.g., "I think 21 is a reasonable drinking age limit.").
- Explain that they should follow the opinion statement with supporting examples from their own experience or from news reports they have seen or read.

Extension

Invite a police officer or a social worker from a drug treatment center to talk to your class about drug laws and treatment options in your area.

Task 1

Following the steps in the student book, have learners practice their arguments after they write them.

Activity B With your group, write sentences about your classroom. Use *prohibited, allowed,* or *not allowed.* Use a gerund subject.

Using dictionaries is not allowed during tests.

Activity C Listen to your teacher or the audio. You will hear sentences about drugs and alcohol. Write them in your notebook. Listen for the gerund. Check the sentences with your class. Then read them with your partner.

Activity D Discuss these questions with your group. Take notes.

1. What problems do drugs and alcohol cause in your home country? How do they compare to problems in the US?
2. How does the government handle drug use in your home country?
3. What do you think the US government should do about drugs and alcohol?
4. Does your home country have a drinking age limit? What is it? Do you think it's appropriate?
5. What do you think about the drinking age limits in the US?
6. What are other laws about alcohol use in this country?

Put the headings below on the board. Use your notes to write some ideas under each heading. Have a class discussion.

Drug and Alcohol Problems **Government Solutions** **Your Solutions**

TASK 1: Write a Convincing Argument

With your partner, choose to agree or disagree with one of these statements:

- All employers should be able to randomly drug test their employees.
- Marijuana should be legal.
- Smoking should not be allowed in public.
- The drinking age should be 18.
- If people use drugs, they should go to jail.
- Alcohol should not be allowed at sporting events.
- Drug addicts should go to treatment centers, not to jail.

Write an argument explaining your opinion. Include an example to make your opinion convincing. Specific examples are more convincing. Compare the two arguments to the right.

Teenagers drink anyway, so why not make it legal? [weak]

In my home country, teenagers are allowed to drink alcohol. Drinking wasn't exciting to us because it wasn't prohibited. I didn't know many people who abused alcohol. [more convincing]

Share your argument with another pair. Try to convince them that you are right. Talk to two more pairs. When everyone finishes, decide which pair was the most convincing and tell why.

74 *Unit 6 Lesson 1*

Extension

- After learners complete the activity, discuss which arguments were the most convincing and why.
- Ask volunteers to read their arguments for the class.
- Make suggestions for more specific and compelling examples.

Assessment

To use this task as a formal evaluation, ask learners to turn in a written version of their argument. Use Generic Assessment Master 9 (Written Communication Rubric) to evaluate the writing. Follow the suggestions on p. 4.

Lesson 2: Protecting Children

Follow the suggestions on p. 5 for talking about the title.

Discuss ways that people protect their children.

Question

Read the question aloud. Note that someone could be shocked by parental treatment that was either too harsh or too lenient. Ask the question, "Do you think more parents are too strict with their children or not strict enough?"

Attention Box

Read the words to learners, pointing or miming to convey meaning. This vocabulary should be understood, but learners should not be expected to produce the words at this point.

Reading Tip

Before reading, have learners cover the text. Ask the four questions that are highlighted in the passage and have learners predict answers. Then read the tip aloud and complete the exercise.

Talk or Write

This exercise helps learners become skilled at applying what they read.

<u>Answers</u>

1. Abuse is injuring a child. Neglect is not taking proper care of a child or leaving a child in a situation where he or she could be harmed.
2. Examples of neglect might be
   - Leaving a child in a car or outside at night
   - Not feeding a child enough
   - Not taking a child to the doctor when he or she is very ill or injured
3. A teacher could lose his or her license, be fined $2,000, or go to jail.

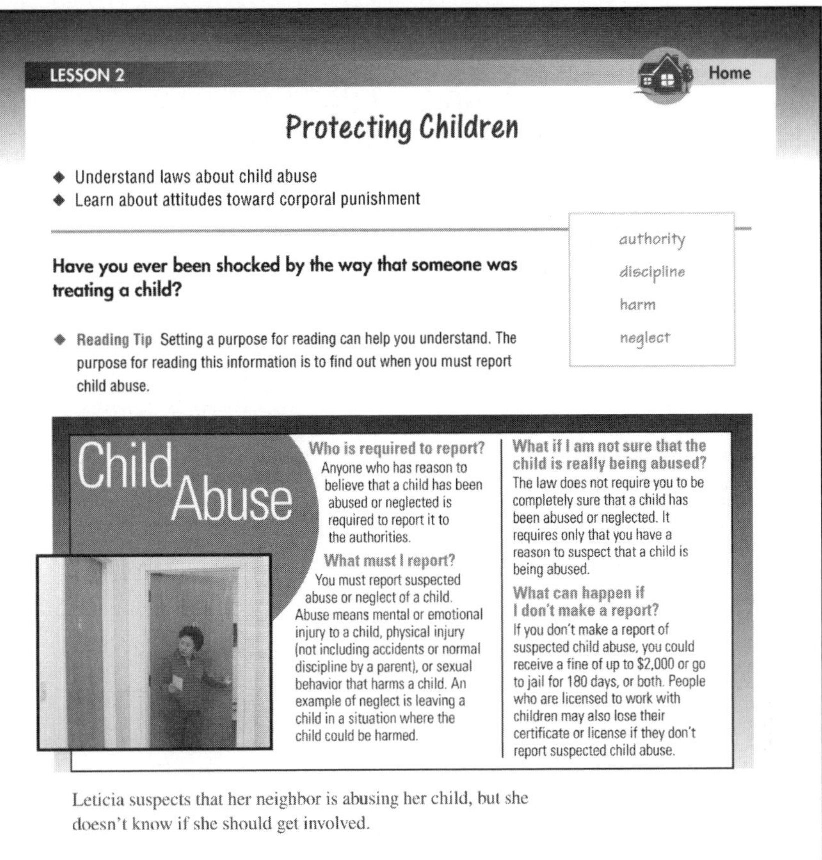

LESSON 2 Home

Protecting Children

- Understand laws about child abuse
- Learn about attitudes toward corporal punishment

authority
discipline
harm
neglect

Have you ever been shocked by the way that someone was treating a child?

- **Reading Tip** Setting a purpose for reading can help you understand. The purpose for reading this information is to find out when you must report child abuse.

Child Abuse

Who is required to report?
Anyone who has reason to believe that a child has been abused or neglected is required to report it to the authorities.

What must I report?
You must report suspected abuse or neglect of a child. Abuse means mental or emotional injury to a child, physical injury (not including accidents or normal discipline by a parent), or sexual behavior that harms a child. An example of neglect is leaving a child in a situation where the child could be harmed.

What if I am not sure that the child is really being abused?
The law does not require you to be completely sure that a child has been abused or neglected. It requires only that you have a reason to suspect that a child is being abused.

What can happen if I don't make a report?
If you don't make a report of suspected child abuse, you could receive a fine of up to $2,000 or go to jail for 180 days, or both. People who are licensed to work with children may also lose their certificate or license if they don't report suspected child abuse.

Leticia suspects that her neighbor is abusing her child, but she doesn't know if she should get involved.

Talk or Write

1. What is the difference between abuse and neglect?
2. What are some behaviors you think would be neglect rather than abuse?
3. If a teacher suspects child abuse but doesn't report it, what can happen?

Unit 6 Lesson 2 75

Vocabulary

Follow the suggestions on p. 6 for introducing and reinforcing vocabulary words.

The word *ground* is often used in its adjective form, as in "You are grounded!" The expression comes from aviation. When an airplane isn't permitted to fly, it is *grounded.*

In the US

To introduce the reading, ask these questions:

- Is corporal punishment common in your home country?
- Are children spanked or hit in school there?
- In what ways can adults discipline children without hitting them?

Compare Cultures

Use Customizable Master 5 (Venn Diagram).

Ask learners to offer some examples of attitudes toward disciplining children.

When you have three examples, decide if they belong in the left circle, the right circle, or the middle circle.

Activity A

- While brainstorming, encourage learners to be specific (e.g., "staying out late" as opposed to "disobeying parents").
- When learners finish brainstorming, ask whether the behavior is more likely by a teenager or a young child. For behaviors that could involve younger children or teenagers, ask what difference in discipline, if any, would be appropriate and why.
- Pairs should discuss the behaviors listed on the board and determine the appropriate discipline, depending on the age group.

In the US Disciplining Children

Corporal punishment, such as hitting or spanking, is one form of disciplining children. People in the US have strong feelings about it. Some people believe that corporal punishment may harm children. Others believe that corporal punishment is sometimes necessary. Some parents use spanking for discipline, but few use it as the most important form. Most parents prefer talking to children, or using *time out,* where children are made to sit quietly. Parents often punish older children by *grounding* them—not allowing them to leave home except to go to school.

About half of the states in the US have laws that forbid corporal punishment in schools. Where it is permitted, it is often not done. However, some people believe that it is a good way to control students' behavior. Corporal punishment in schools is called *paddling* because students are hit with a flat wooden paddle. Schools that use paddling must have a policy defining how it may be used. The policy explains what the paddle is made of and how many times the student may be hit.

Vocabulary

Repeat these words after your teacher. Talk about their meanings. Write the words in your notebook. With a partner, write a sentence using each word.

beat
forbid
ground
harm
permit
slap
spank

corporal punishment
discipline
neglect

Idiom Watch!
get involved

Compare Cultures Are attitudes toward disciplining children different in your home country than they are in the US? How? Write your ideas in circles like the ones below. Discuss with your group.

Home Country
Spanking kids in school is OK.

US
Spanking kids in most schools is not OK.

Vocabulary Plus
The words *discipline* and *neglect* are nouns and verbs.

Activity A As a class, make a list of behaviors that children and teenagers are often punished for. Make another list of ways that children are disciplined. Talk to your partner about your ideas on using corporal punishment to discipline children in school and at home.

I think it's OK to spank children if they do something dangerous.

It's important not to hit a child when you're angry.

76 *Unit 6 Lesson 2*

Possible Answers

- *Behaviors:* talking back, not cleaning up, not doing homework, hitting, being noisy, drinking alcohol, dating without permission, lying, acting wild, destroying property
- *Ways to Discipline:* redirecting or distracting the child (for very young children), time out, withholding privileges, grounding the child, scolding, discussing why the behavior is wrong

Assign Workbook pp. 41–42.

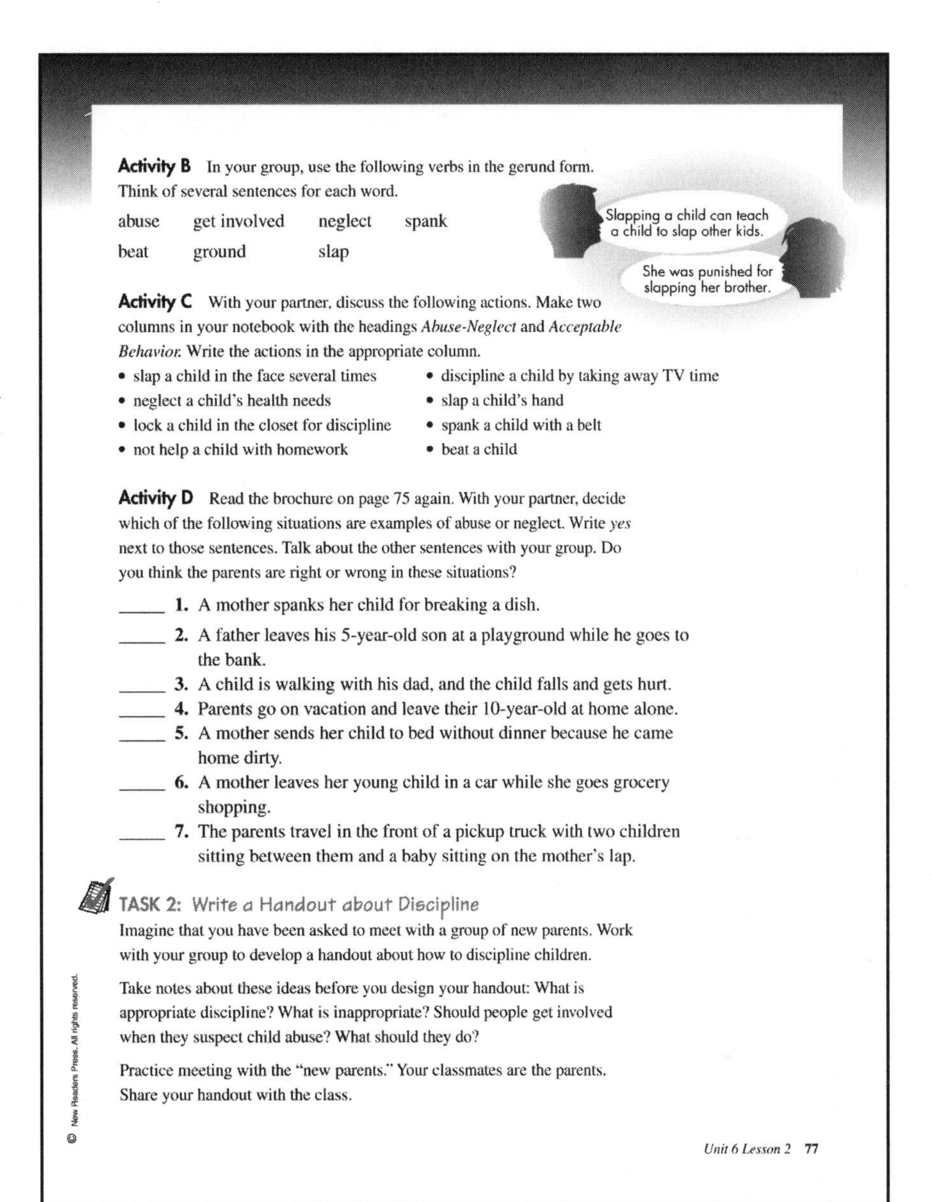

Activity B In your group, use the following verbs in the gerund form. Think of several sentences for each word.

abuse get involved neglect spank

beat ground slap

Activity C With your partner, discuss the following actions. Make two columns in your notebook with the headings *Abuse-Neglect* and *Acceptable Behavior*. Write the actions in the appropriate column.

- slap a child in the face several times
- neglect a child's health needs
- lock a child in the closet for discipline
- not help a child with homework
- discipline a child by taking away TV time
- slap a child's hand
- spank a child with a belt
- beat a child

Activity D Read the brochure on page 75 again. With your partner, decide which of the following situations are examples of abuse or neglect. Write *yes* next to those sentences. Talk about the other sentences with your group. Do you think the parents are right or wrong in these situations?

_____ **1.** A mother spanks her child for breaking a dish.

_____ **2.** A father leaves his 5-year-old son at a playground while he goes to the bank.

_____ **3.** A child is walking with his dad, and the child falls and gets hurt.

_____ **4.** Parents go on vacation and leave their 10-year-old at home alone.

_____ **5.** A mother sends her child to bed without dinner because he came home dirty.

_____ **6.** A mother leaves her young child in a car while she goes grocery shopping.

_____ **7.** The parents travel in the front of a pickup truck with two children sitting between them and a baby sitting on the mother's lap.

TASK 2: Write a Handout about Discipline

Imagine that you have been asked to meet with a group of new parents. Work with your group to develop a handout about how to discipline children.

Take notes about these ideas before you design your handout: What is appropriate discipline? What is inappropriate? Should people get involved when they suspect child abuse? What should they do?

Practice meeting with the "new parents." Your classmates are the parents. Share your handout with the class.

Unit 6 Lesson 2 77

Activity B

Have learners sit in small groups and work together to develop the sentences.

Activity C

Tell learners that the word *acceptable* means "OK."

After learners complete the categorization, have a discussion together. There may be some disagreement about categorizing these means of discipline. Encourage learners to explain why they think the behavior is acceptable or unacceptable.

Activity D

Answers

1. No (Spanking may be considered normal discipline if it doesn't injure the child.)
2. Yes (neglect)
3. No (accident)
4. Yes (neglect)
5. No (One missed meal won't injure the child.)
6. Yes (neglect)
7. Yes (neglect)

After learners have finished the pair discussion, review each situation and its answers together. Then discuss the *no* answers, which, although not illegal, may be considered unacceptable by some.

Task 2

Give a copy of Generic Assessment Master 12 (Peer Assessment Form for Projects and Tasks) to each learner.

Ask groups of learners to prepare handouts explaining how to discipline children. Have them share the handouts with the class.

- Ask each group to rehearse its presentation with another group.
- Have learners fill out and exchange assessment forms before doing their final presentations.
- Before learners address the class, choose a piece of text (e.g., the sentences in Activity D) and practice reading aloud together in very loud voices. This activity can release tension and warm up vocal cords.
- Encourage each member of the group to say at least one sentence about the handout during the presentation.

Assessment

Use Generic Assessment Master 8 (Oral Communication Rubric) to evaluate the presentation. Follow the suggestions on p. 4.

Use Unit Master 48 (Vocabulary: Remember When) now or at any time during the rest of the unit.

Lesson 3: A Helping Hand

Follow instructions on p. 5 for talking about the title.

Question

Read the question aloud, and encourage learners to make suggestions.

Possible Answers
doctor, clinic, drug treatment center, church, family, friends

Attention Box

Read the words to learners, pointing or miming to convey meaning. This vocabulary should be understood, but learners should not be expected to produce the words at this point.

Listening Tip

Read the listening tip aloud. Then play the audio or read the listening script on p. 122 twice. The first time, ask learners to just listen. The second time, have them take notes on what they hear.

Talk or Write

This exercise helps learners recall main ideas.

- After learners have listened twice and taken notes during the listening exercise, ask them to call out some of the key words in the questions they heard. Write the words on the board or an overhead transparency.
- Play the tape or read the listening script again and allow groups to share ideas.
- Elicit a question from each group and write it on the board or transparency. It is not important that learners reproduce word-for-word the questions in the listening passage, but, if they wish, they can compare their versions with the listening script on p. 119 of the student book.

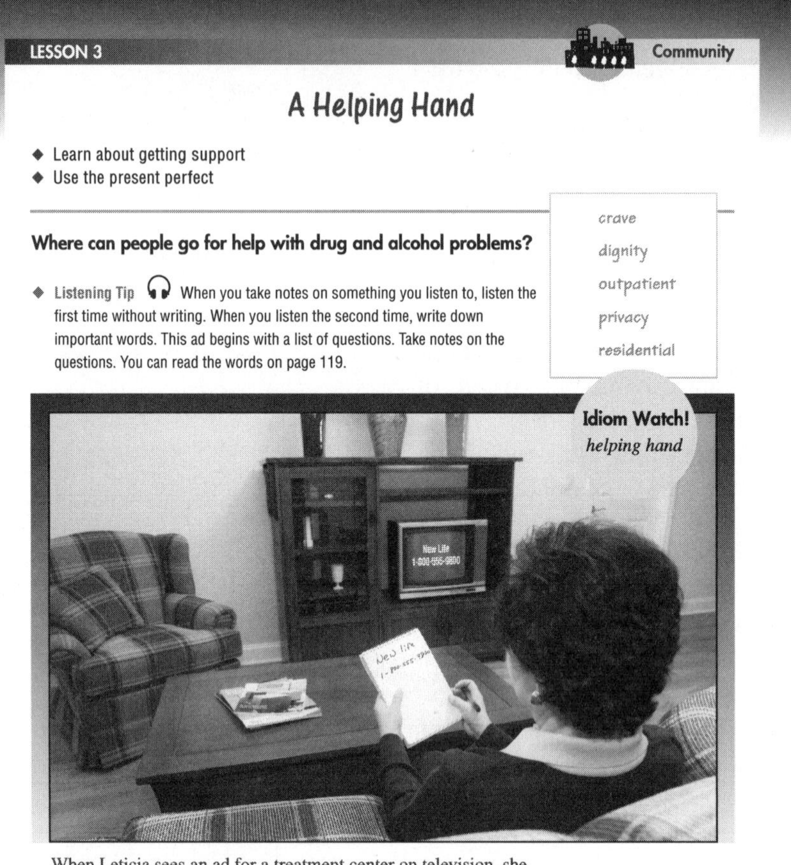

LESSON 3 Community

A Helping Hand

- Learn about getting support
- Use the present perfect

crave
dignity
outpatient
privacy
residential

Where can people go for help with drug and alcohol problems?

- Listening Tip When you take notes on something you listen to, listen the first time without writing. When you listen the second time, write down important words. This ad begins with a list of questions. Take notes on the questions. You can read the words on page 119.

Idiom Watch!
helping hand

When Leticia sees an ad for a treatment center on television, she realizes that the treatment center might be able to give her advice about helping her neighbor.

Talk or Write

Try to remember the main ideas of the questions. Using your notes, write questions like the ones in the ad. Don't worry about the exact words. There are seven questions in the ad. Write as many as you can remember.

78 *Unit 6 Lesson 3*

Vocabulary

Follow the suggestions on p. 6 for introducing and reinforcing vocabulary words.

Each adjective describes a feeling most people experience at some time. Discuss situations in which it is normal to experience these feelings (e.g., aggressive while playing a competitive sport; depressed after someone dies; enthusiastic when beginning a new job; irrational when very tired).

Group Chat

Use Customizable Master 1 (2-Column Chart). Follow the suggestions on p. 7 for customizing and duplicating the master and distributing the copies.

- Leave enough space between rows for learners to write short sentences in the second column.
- Emphasize that this second column should include *symptoms* of the emotion (e.g., how they knew the person was depressed), but not *causes.*

Grammar Talk

Follow the suggestions on p. 6 for introducing the grammar point.

Answers

- The helping verb is *have* or *has.*
- The main verb is a *past participle.*
- The word *ever* means "at any time."
- The sentences in column two cannot be changed to present perfect because they contain time expressions that specify a time in the past. They have no connection to the present.

Point out that the sentences in column one can be changed to the simple past, but doing so eliminates their connection to the present. For example, the sentence *He has been arrested three times* implies that the action is likely to happen again. *He was arrested three times* does not carry that implication.

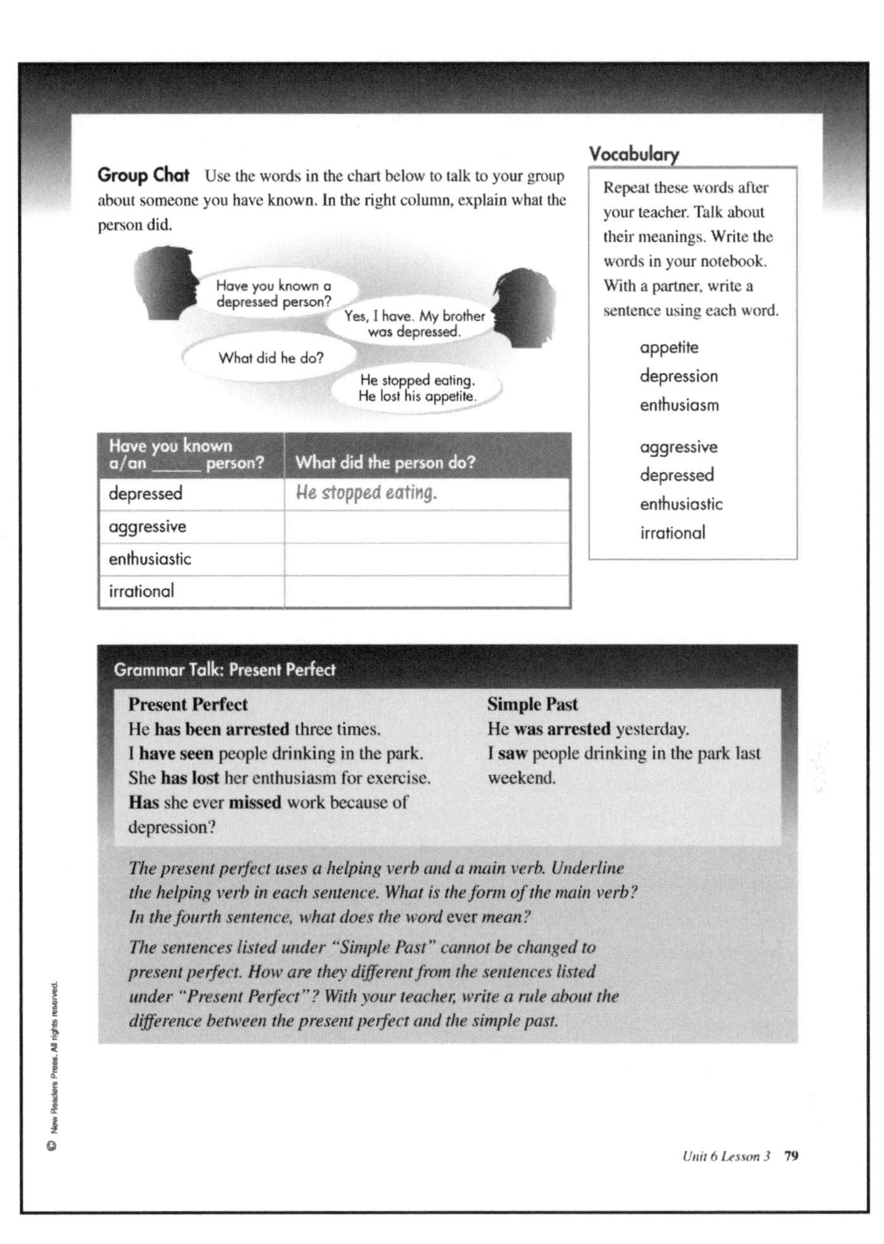

Group Chat Use the words in the chart below to talk to your group about someone you have known. In the right column, explain what the person did.

Have you known a/an _____ person?	What did the person do?
depressed	He stopped eating.
aggressive	
enthusiastic	
irrational	

Vocabulary

Repeat these words after your teacher. Talk about their meanings. Write the words in your notebook. With a partner, write a sentence using each word.

appetite
depression
enthusiasm

aggressive
depressed
enthusiastic
irrational

Grammar Talk: Present Perfect

Present Perfect	Simple Past
He **has been arrested** three times.	He **was arrested** yesterday.
I **have seen** people drinking in the park.	I **saw** people drinking in the park last weekend.
She **has lost** her enthusiasm for exercise.	
Has she ever **missed** work because of depression?	

The present perfect uses a helping verb and a main verb. Underline the helping verb in each sentence. What is the form of the main verb? In the fourth sentence, what does the word ever *mean?*

The sentences listed under "Simple Past" cannot be changed to present perfect. How are they different from the sentences listed under "Present Perfect"? With your teacher, write a rule about the difference between the present perfect and the simple past.

Possible Rule

The *present perfect* describes actions that happened in the past but have a connection to the present. It cannot be used with actions that occurred at a specific time in the past. The *simple past* does not show any connection to the present.

 Assign Workbook pp. 43–44.

Use Unit Master 49 (Grammar: Listening) now or at any time during the rest of the unit.

Activity A
Using the charts from the Group Chat, have learners write sentences in their notebooks.

Pronunciation Target
Play the audio or read the sentences in the student book.

Activity B
One Step Down
To help learners form sentences, write a number of time expressions on the board, e.g., *last year, yesterday, two weeks ago, in 1999, thousands of years ago, last summer, last night, five minutes ago.*

Activity C
Answers
- My friend has gotten drunk three times this month.
- My teenager has come home late every night this week.
- My son's room has smelled like tobacco a few times.
- My daughter hasn't eaten anything all day.
- My niece has been arrested twice for selling drugs.

Task 3
To help learners get started, write some expressions on the board for beginning and ending telephone conversations:
- ______ *Hotline, how can I help you?*
- *I have a problem with my _______ (friend, sister, father-in-law, etc.).*
- *Please feel free to call again any time.*
- *Thank you for your help.*

Ask volunteers to read their conversation for the class.

Ongoing Assessment
While learners complete this activity, circulate to listen to as many conversations as possible. Take

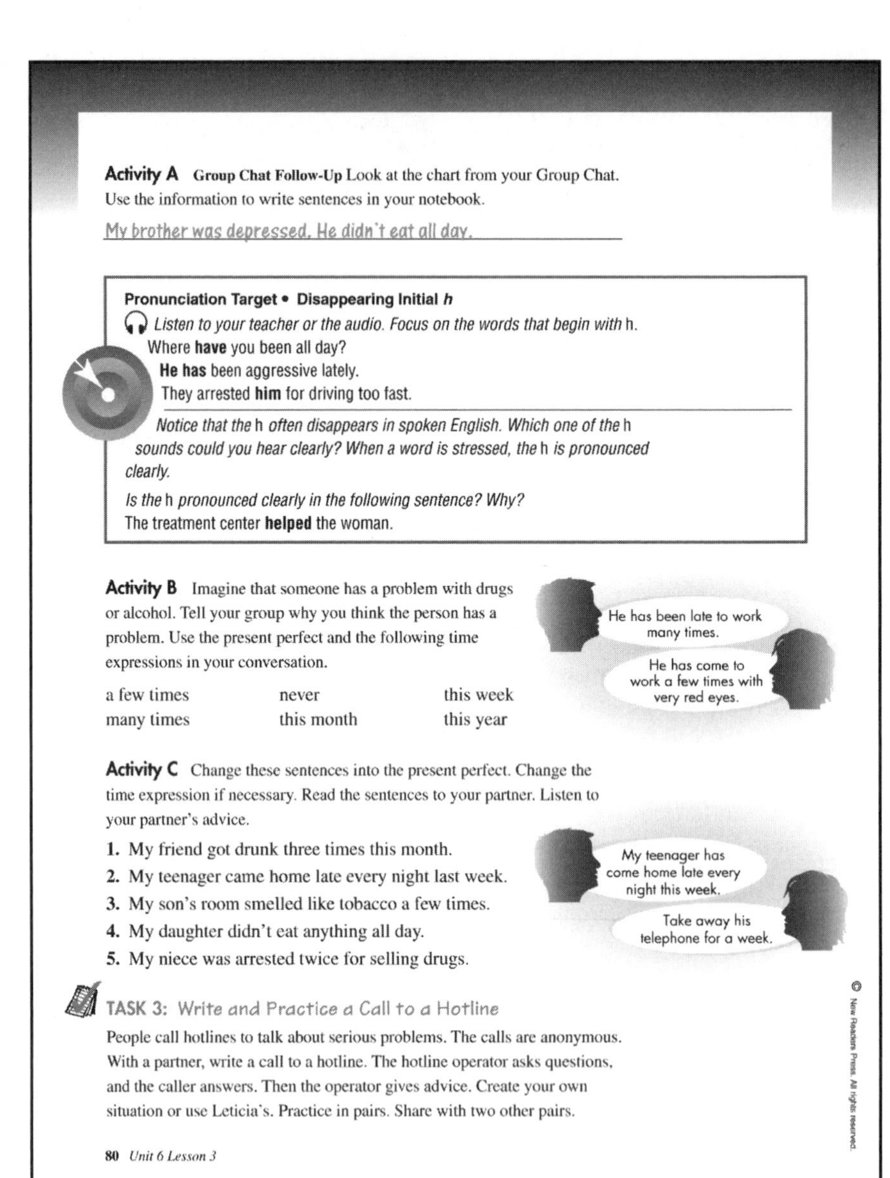

Activity A **Group Chat Follow-Up** Look at the chart from your Group Chat. Use the information to write sentences in your notebook.

My brother was depressed. He didn't eat all day.

Pronunciation Target • Disappearing Initial *h*
Listen to your teacher or the audio. Focus on the words that begin with h.
Where **have** you been all day?
He has been aggressive lately.
They arrested **him** for driving too fast.

Notice that the h *often disappears in spoken English. Which one of the* h *sounds could you hear clearly? When a word is stressed, the* h *is pronounced clearly.*
Is the h *pronounced clearly in the following sentence? Why?*
The treatment center **helped** the woman.

Activity B Imagine that someone has a problem with drugs or alcohol. Tell your group why you think the person has a problem. Use the present perfect and the following time expressions in your conversation.

a few times	never	this week
many times	this month	this year

Activity C Change these sentences into the present perfect. Change the time expression if necessary. Read the sentences to your partner. Listen to your partner's advice.

1. My friend got drunk three times this month.
2. My teenager came home late every night last week.
3. My son's room smelled like tobacco a few times.
4. My daughter didn't eat anything all day.
5. My niece was arrested twice for selling drugs.

TASK 3: Write and Practice a Call to a Hotline
People call hotlines to talk about serious problems. The calls are anonymous. With a partner, write a call to a hotline. The hotline operator asks questions, and the caller answers. Then the operator gives advice. Create your own situation or use Leticia's. Practice in pairs. Share with two other pairs.

80 *Unit 6 Lesson 3*

notes on how well learners perform on the following criteria:

a. Beginnings and endings of phone conversations
   0 = missing or incomprehensible
   1 = incomplete or partially understandable
   2 = clear and understandable but not perfect
b. Quality of questions and descriptions
   0 = incorrect grammar, word choice, and pronunciation that make comprehension very difficult
   1 = incorrect grammar, word choice, and pronunciation that occasionally make comprehension difficult
   2 = problems and questions understandable but not perfect

Use Unit Master 50 (Thinking Skill: Guide and Support Others) and 51 (Game: Match the Definition) now or at any time during the rest of the unit.

Review Unit Skills
See pp. 7–9 for suggestions on games and activities to review the vocabulary and grammar in this unit.

Unit 6 Project

Learners make a booklet about different types of abuse.

Get Ready

Give learners two or three days to collect the information. Ask them to follow the suggestions in the student book for topics and sources.

One Step Down

Gather information from brochures, booklets, and Internet pages and bring it in for learners to use.

Do the Work

Before learners make the final booklet, do the following:

- Ask learners to summarize the booklet information in their notebooks as practice for each booklet page.
- Have them prepare sketches of any drawings they want to use.
- Make your suggestions and corrections before they transfer the information and pictures onto a booklet page.

Give each group seven sheets of construction paper to make the final booklet.

Present

If possible, laminate and bind the books so they can be easily passed around. If binding is not possible, post the booklets in a bulletin board display.

Writing Extension

Point out that examples do not have to be from personal experience. Learners can use an example of someone they have heard about, read about, or seen in a movie.

Assign Workbook p. 45 (Check Your Progress).

Use Unit Master 52 (Unit 6 Checkup/Review) whenever you complete this unit.

Technology Extra

Assist any learners who have difficulty using a search engine.

UNIT 6 Project

Make a Booklet

Make a booklet about drug abuse, alcohol abuse, and child abuse. Follow these steps:

Get Ready

With your group, collect information about the topics below. Divide the research among your group members. You can use information from this unit. You can also look in the phone book or on the Internet, or go to a local library, hospital, or police station. Organize the information that your group has gathered under the correct headings.

- Alcohol Laws
- Drug Laws
- Drug Testing
- Drug Abuse Symptoms
- Drug and Alcohol Treatment Centers
- Child Abuse Laws
- Corporal Punishment

Do the Work

Make a booklet with one page about each of the topics. If possible, include phone numbers and other important information about your community. Draw or cut out pictures to illustrate your work.

Present

Share your booklet with other groups. Display the booklets, if possible, for other classes as well.

Writing Extension Write a paragraph about why you think people use drugs and alcohol. Include at least one example.

Technology Extra

Use the Internet to get more information about hotlines and local support groups. Use the search terms "substance abuse hotlines," "substance abuse treatment centers," "substance abuse support," "Alcoholics Anonymous," "Al-Anon," and "Child Protective Services."

Self-Assessment

Give each learner a copy of the Speaking and Listening Self-Checks and the Writing and Reading Self-Checks (Generic Assessment Masters 10–11) when they complete Unit 6. Go over the items together. The completed forms will become part of each learner's portfolio.

Unit 7: Pitching In

UNIT 7

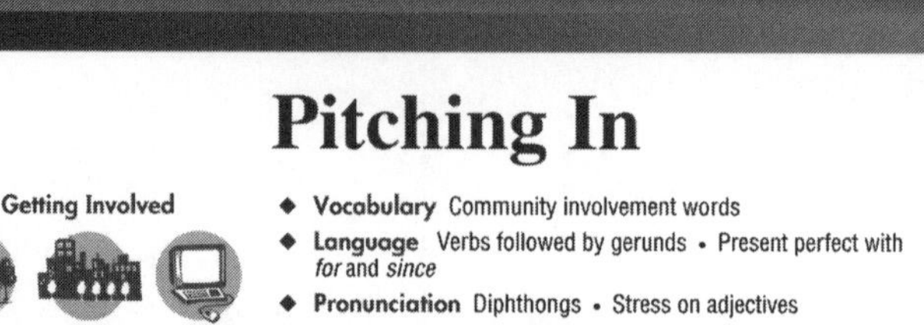

Pitching In

- **Vocabulary** Community involvement words
- **Language** Verbs followed by gerunds • Present perfect with *for* and *since*
- **Pronunciation** Diphthongs • Stress on adjectives
- **Culture** Processes for change

Do you know of a place that has problems like the ones that you see in this picture?

Marlene and her daughter, Jenny, are talking to their neighbors at a park near their homes. They both enjoy being involved in their community. They know that they can help improve things in their neighborhood.

Think and Talk

1. What do you see in the photograph?
2. What do you think Marlene and Jenny are talking about to their neighbors?
3. What can they do to create change in their neighborhood?
4. What can you do to get involved in your community?

What's Your Opinion? If you saw people throwing trash on the ground, would you ask them to pick it up? Explain your answer.

82 *Unit 7*

Materials for the Unit

- Poster paper
- Customizable Masters 1, 2, and 4
- Generic Assessment Master 12
- Unit Masters 53–58

Pitching In

Follow the suggestions on p. 5 for talking about the title.

- Discuss the meaning of the verb *pitch* (to throw or toss).
- Ask learners what they think the idiom *pitch in* might mean. One meaning might be "to join with others or contribute to an activity," e.g., We all *pitched in* to help the homeless people in our community.

Photo

Follow the suggestions on p. 4 for talking about the photo. Then read the question below the arrow.

Brainstorm a list of things people might want to do to improve their neighborhoods. If learners have difficulty, suggest the following:

- Put in stop signs or speed bumps.
- Lower speed limits.
- Clean up litter.
- Plant more trees.
- Create a safe neighborhood.

Think and Talk

Possible Answers

1. Litter, dirty area, graffiti
2. Answers will vary.
3. Get help from neighbors to clean up park, ask city to help
4. Vote; pick up litter, keep neighborhoods clean; talk to neighbors about problems in neighborhood and community; go to city hall for help; organize committees to improve areas in the community; help create Neighborhood Watches; volunteer to help with community events

What's Your Opinion?

Provide these scenarios:

- Someone is littering on or near a learner's property, outside a restaurant, at the mall, in a strange neighborhood.
- The person littering is a friend, a stranger, a small child.

Vocabulary

Follow the suggestions on p. 6 for introducing and reinforcing vocabulary words.

- Before writing sentences, talk about what happens at these events.
- Ask learners to bring in family photos or pictures from magazines depicting these events.

Gather Your Thoughts

Use Customizable Master 2 (3-Column Chart). Follow the suggestions on p. 7 for customizing and duplicating the master and distributing the copies.

- Have group leaders ask group members this question about each event: "How can you help at the _________?"
- Write learners' ideas on the board or an overhead transparency and have the class discuss them.

One Step Down

If groups have difficulty generating ideas, first brainstorm activities with all learners together. Then ask the groups to categorize them.

What's the Problem?

Follow the suggestions on p. 5 for identifying and analyzing problems.

Possible Answers

busy schedules, work, caring for children, lack of knowledge or confidence, family or educational obligations

Setting Goals

Follow the suggestions on p. 5 for setting goals.

- For goal b, discuss the meaning of the phrase *to speak up.* One meaning might be "to express one's interests strongly" (e.g., Don't be afraid to *speak up* at the meeting.). Point out that another common meaning of *speak up* is "talk louder."
- For goal e, personal qualities might include friendly, hardworking, reliable, and organized.

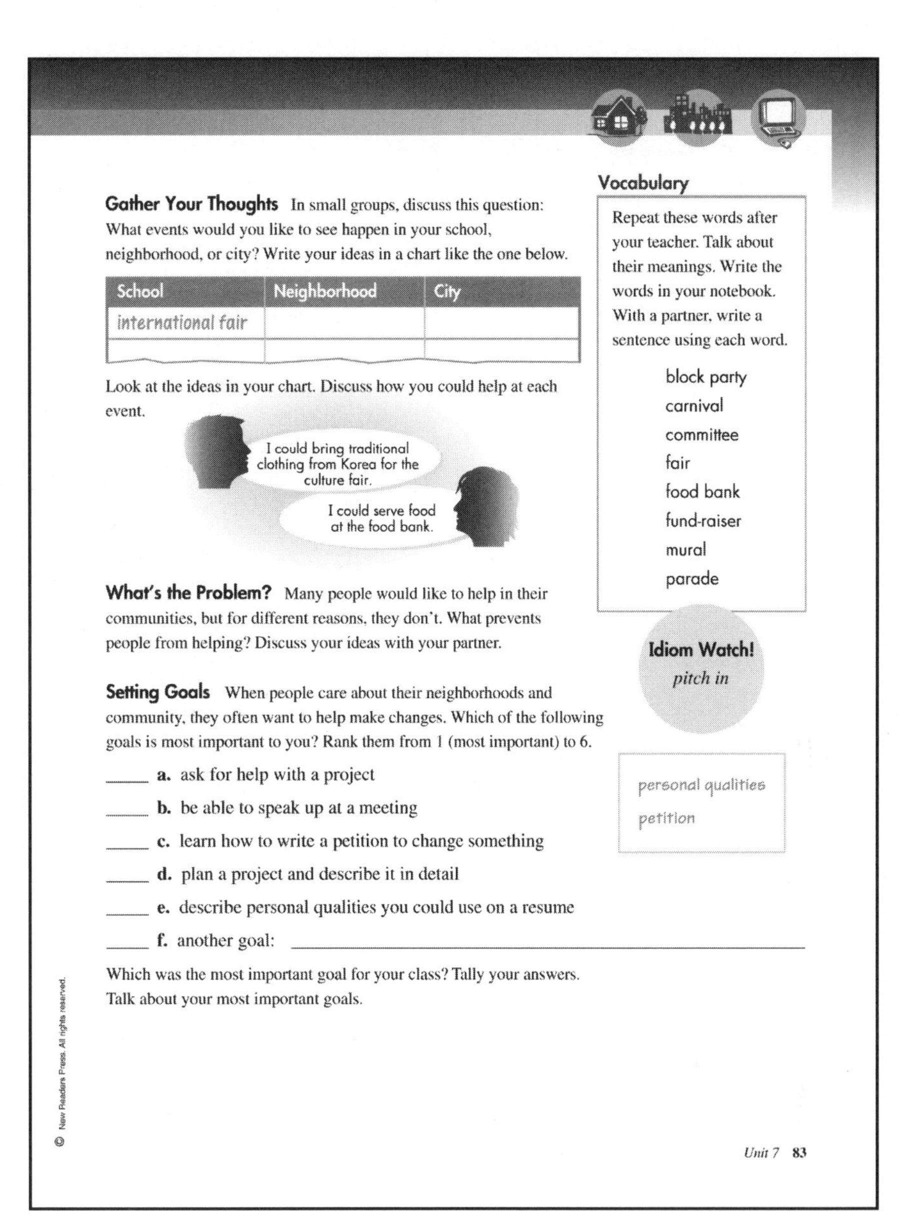

Gather Your Thoughts In small groups, discuss this question: What events would you like to see happen in your school, neighborhood, or city? Write your ideas in a chart like the one below.

School	Neighborhood	City
international fair		

Look at the ideas in your chart. Discuss how you could help at each event.

What's the Problem? Many people would like to help in their communities, but for different reasons, they don't. What prevents people from helping? Discuss your ideas with your partner.

Setting Goals When people care about their neighborhoods and community, they often want to help make changes. Which of the following goals is most important to you? Rank them from 1 (most important) to 6.

_____ **a.** ask for help with a project

_____ **b.** be able to speak up at a meeting

_____ **c.** learn how to write a petition to change something

_____ **d.** plan a project and describe it in detail

_____ **e.** describe personal qualities you could use on a resume

_____ **f.** another goal: ______________________________

Which was the most important goal for your class? Tally your answers. Talk about your most important goals.

Vocabulary

Repeat these words after your teacher. Talk about their meanings. Write the words in your notebook. With a partner, write a sentence using each word.

block party
carnival
committee
fair
food bank
fund-raiser
mural
parade

Idiom Watch!
pitch in

personal qualities
petition

Lesson 1: Get the Ball Rolling

Follow the suggestions on p. 5 for talking about the title.

Discuss the meaning of the verb *roll.*

- Ask learners what they think *get the ball rolling* means. One meaning might be "to start an activity or process."
- Ask learners when they might use this expression.

Attention Box

This vocabulary should be understood, but learners should not be expected to produce the words at this point.

- Ask learners what they think the compound word *eyesore* might mean. Tell them to look at the two small words in it. One meaning might be "an unpleasant sight" (e.g., The neighbors said that the graffiti was an *eyesore.*).
- Discuss the meaning of the phrase *give someone a hand.* One meaning might be "to help or give assistance" (e.g., Please let me *give you a hand.*).

Listening Tip

Read the tip aloud, then play the audio or read the listening script on p. 122.

Talk or Write

In this exercise, learners practice listening for details.

Answers

1. Marlene wants to clean up the park.
2. She has to make a list of different jobs, get the neighbors to help, and call Parks and Recreation.
3. Jenny isn't convinced at first because she thinks the park is too big and that it's the city's responsibility.
4. Jenny is going to help by calling Parks and Recreation and asking her children to help.

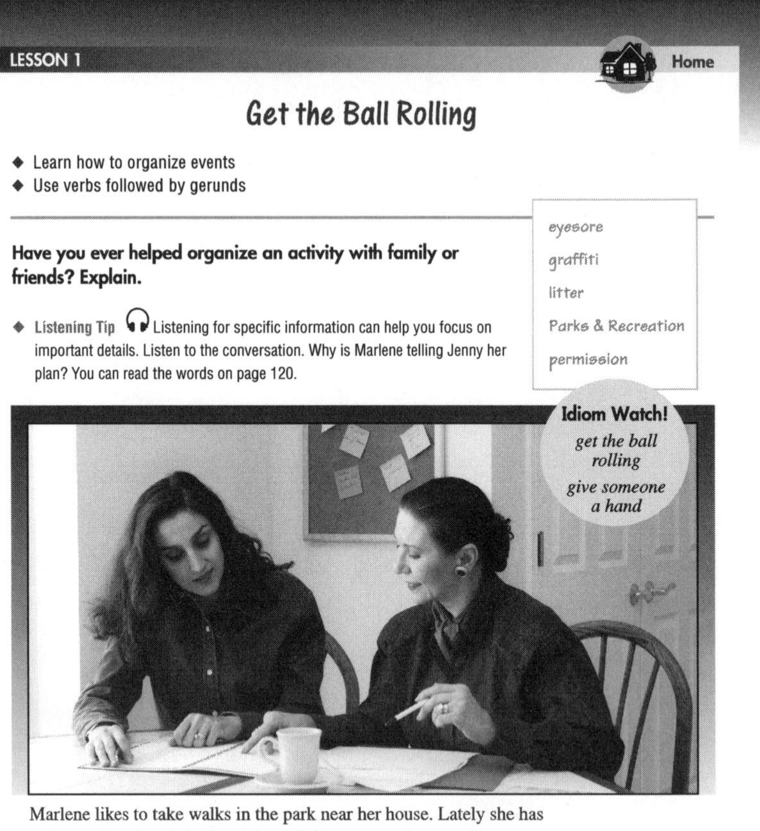

LESSON 1 Home

Get the Ball Rolling

- Learn how to organize events
- Use verbs followed by gerunds

eyesore
graffiti
litter
Parks & Recreation
permission

Have you ever helped organize an activity with family or friends? Explain.

- Listening Tip Listening for specific information can help you focus on important details. Listen to the conversation. Why is Marlene telling Jenny her plan? You can read the words on page 120.

Idiom Watch!
get the ball rolling
give someone a hand

Marlene likes to take walks in the park near her house. Lately she has noticed a lot of trash in the park, and she wants to do something about it. She is talking to Jenny about her plan.

Talk or Write

1. What does Marlene want to do?
2. What does she have to do to get started?
3. Why isn't Jenny convinced at first?
4. How is Jenny going to help?

84 *Unit 7 Lesson 1*

© New Readers Press. All rights reserved.

Vocabulary

Follow the suggestions on p. 6 for introducing and reinforcing vocabulary words.

Vocabulary Plus

Explain that the words *request* and *volunteer* can be nouns or verbs:

- *She is a volunteer at the hospital.*
- *She volunteered to bring cookies.*
- *She made a request for supplies.*
- *He requested help with his yard.*

One Step Up

Have learners write these headings across the top of a notebook page: *One-Syllable, Two-Syllable, Three-Syllable,* and *Four-Syllable.*

Say the vocabulary words again. Ask learners to write the words they hear in the correct column and underline the stressed syllables.

Answers

- One-syllable word: *mind*
- Two-syllable words: *avoid, request, suggest*
- Three-syllable words: *consider, recommend, volunteer*
- Four-syllable word: *appreciate*

Group Chat

Use Customizable Master 1 (2-Column Chart). Follow the suggestions on p. 7 for customizing and duplicating the master and distributing the copies. Give one to each learner.

- Encourage group members to pass their charts around so that each person has a chance to ask questions and write responses.
- When learners have finished their charts, ask for volunteers to read their answers. If learners use gerunds in their charts *(working, cleaning, organizing),* write sentences using the gerunds on the board or an overhead transparency. If learners use only simple verbs *(work, clean, organize),* write sentences with the simple forms.

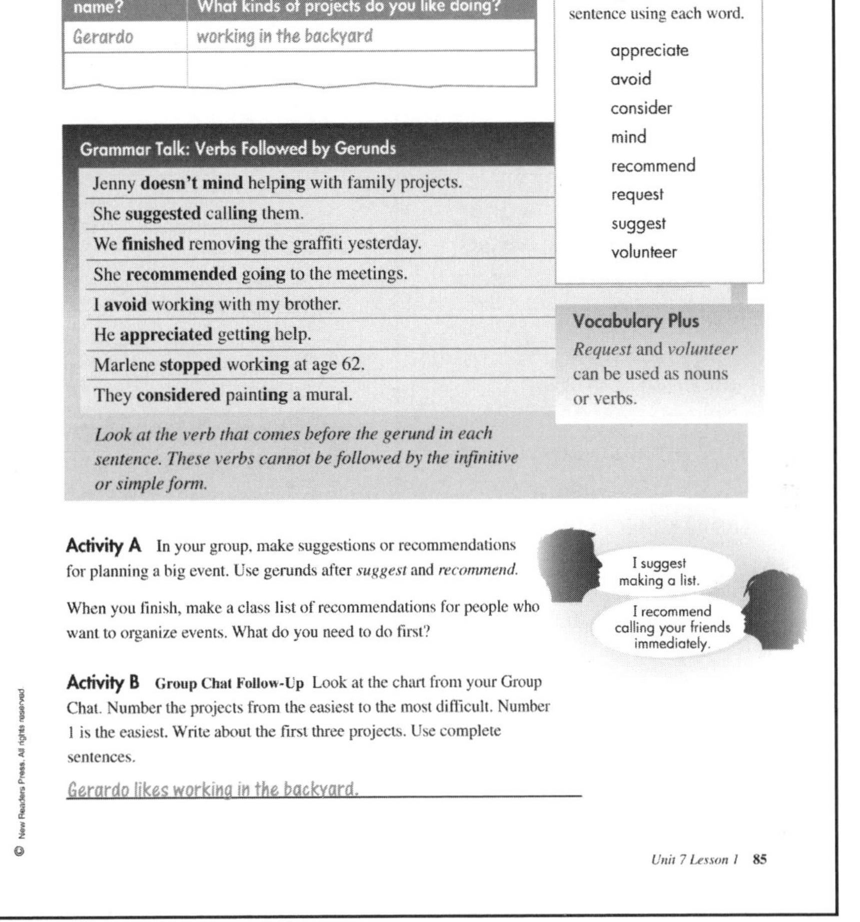

Group Chat Talk about activities, events, or projects that you like doing around your house or in your neighborhood. Write the names of the people in your group in a chart like this one. Write what they like to do. Talk to your group about the events or projects in your chart.

What's your name?	What kinds of projects do you like doing?
Gerardo	working in the backyard

Vocabulary

Repeat these words after your teacher. Talk about their meanings. Write the words in your notebook. With a partner, write a sentence using each word.

appreciate
avoid
consider
mind
recommend
request
suggest
volunteer

Grammar Talk: Verbs Followed by Gerunds

Jenny **doesn't mind** help**ing** with family projects.
She **suggested** call**ing** them.
We **finished** remov**ing** the graffiti yesterday.
She **recommended** go**ing** to the meetings.
I **avoid** work**ing** with my brother.
He **appreciated** gett**ing** help.
Marlene **stopped** work**ing** at age 62.
They **considered** paint**ing** a mural.

Look at the verb that comes before the gerund in each sentence. These verbs cannot be followed by the infinitive or simple form.

Vocabulary Plus

Request and *volunteer* can be used as nouns or verbs.

Activity A In your group, make suggestions or recommendations for planning a big event. Use gerunds after *suggest* and *recommend.*

When you finish, make a class list of recommendations for people who want to organize events. What do you need to do first?

Activity B **Group Chat Follow-Up** Look at the chart from your Group Chat. Number the projects from the easiest to the most difficult. Number 1 is the easiest. Write about the first three projects. Use complete sentences.

Gerardo likes working in the backyard.

Grammar Talk

Follow the suggestions on p. 6 for introducing the grammar point.

For each verb in the box, write sentences on the board or an overhead transparency that will demonstrate correct and incorrect usage of verbs followed by gerunds. Follow these examples:

- *I don't mind driving.*
- *I don't mind to drive.*
- *I don't mind drive.*

Ask learners to tell which sentence is correct *(the first one).*

Activity A

If learners have difficulty thinking of events, suggest the following: birthday or graduation party, wedding reception, retirement party, holiday party.

Possible Answers

Making a list of people to invite; *planning* or *reserving* a location; *planning* food, drinks, music, and decorations; *making* a list of supplies; *asking* people to help; *planning* a schedule for *buying* food and supplies; *preparing* food

Assign Workbook pp. 46–47.

Pronunciation Target

Play the audio or read the words in the student book aloud.

Use Customizable Master 1 (2-Column Chart). Follow the suggestions on p. 7 for customizing and duplicating the master. Distribute one copy to each group. Then do the following:

- Have learners follow the directions in their books.
- Set a three- to five-minute time limit to see which group writes the most words and spells them correctly.
- Write a class word list on the board or an overhead transparency.
- Model the pronunciation of the words.
- Ask learners to practice in pairs.

Activity C

- Ask learners to use their list from Activity A for this activity.
- When learners finish the oral activity, ask volunteers to write their questions on the board or an overhead transparency.

Task 1

Use Customizable Master 1 (2-Column Chart). Follow the suggestions on p. 7 for customizing and duplicating the master and distributing the copies. Give one copy to each learner.

Tell learners to estimate what their expenses might be.

Extension

Ask learners to write about their plans for the project. Share this example with them:

I'm going to have a baby soon, and I want to fix up the bedroom before she's born. I need help planning what it will look like. I want to use the colors white, pink, and yellow. I need help painting and making curtains. I'd like someone to help me pick out furniture, too. I can't spend much money, so I want help finding inexpensive furniture stores. I want to ask three people to help me with this. My husband's co-worker is a very good painter, and my neighbor is really good at decorating. My sister-in-law knows how to sew. My English teacher might know where to get good bargains on furniture.

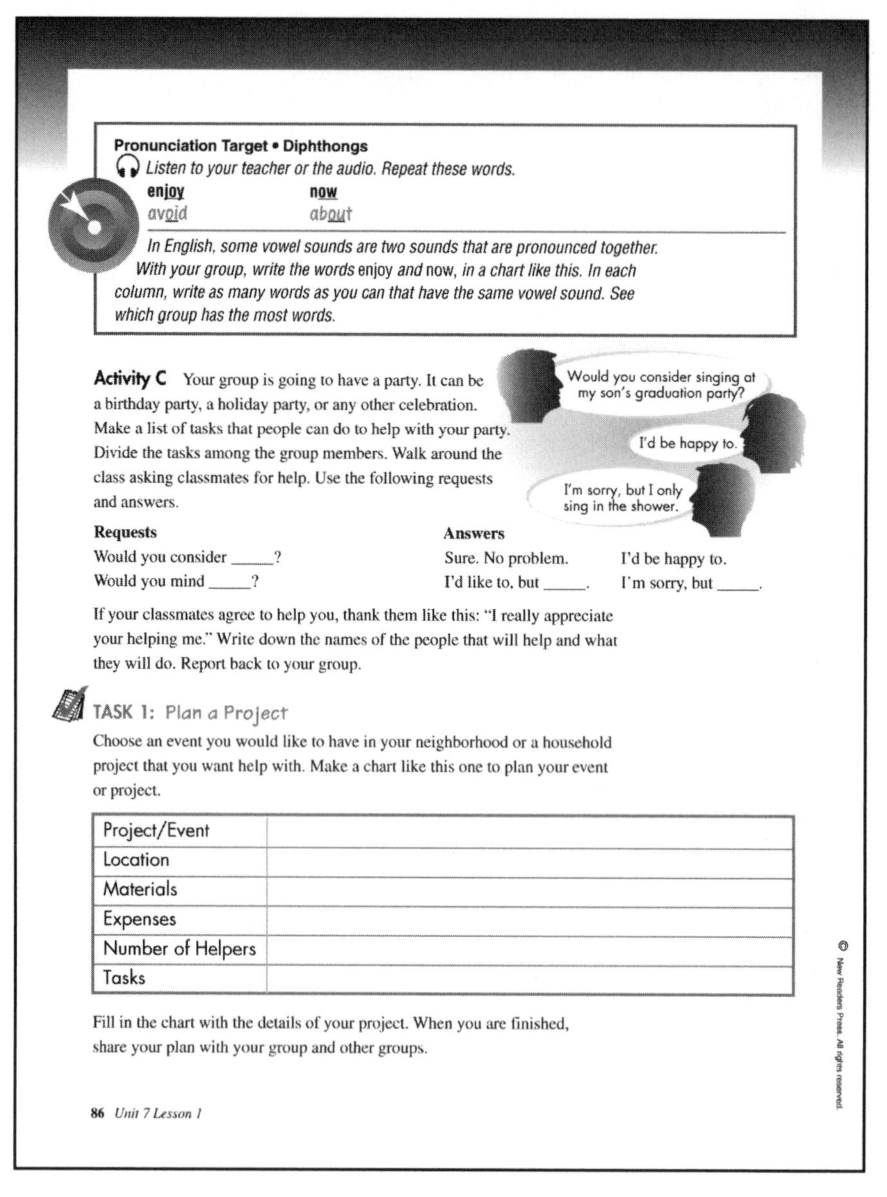

Pronunciation Target • Diphthongs

Listen to your teacher or the audio. Repeat these words.

enjoy	now
avoid	about

In English, some vowel sounds are two sounds that are pronounced together. With your group, write the words enjoy *and* now, *in a chart like this. In each column, write as many words as you can that have the same vowel sound. See which group has the most words.*

Activity C Your group is going to have a party. It can be a birthday party, a holiday party, or any other celebration. Make a list of tasks that people can do to help with your party. Divide the tasks among the group members. Walk around the class asking classmates for help. Use the following requests and answers.

Requests	Answers	
Would you consider _____?	Sure. No problem.	I'd be happy to.
Would you mind _____?	I'd like to, but _____.	I'm sorry, but _____.

If your classmates agree to help you, thank them like this: "I really appreciate your helping me." Write down the names of the people that will help and what they will do. Report back to your group.

TASK 1: Plan a Project

Choose an event you would like to have in your neighborhood or a household project that you want help with. Make a chart like this one to plan your event or project.

Project/Event	
Location	
Materials	
Expenses	
Number of Helpers	
Tasks	

Fill in the chart with the details of your project. When you are finished, share your plan with your group and other groups.

86 *Unit 7 Lesson 1*

One Step Up

- Plan a class party, and ask learners to comparison shop before buying food, supplies, etc.
- After the party, check the project plan for accuracy, and write a detailed follow-up list of actual expenses, including where supplies were purchased. This information might be helpful for future planning.

Use Unit Master 53 (Grammar: Tell about Something) now or at any time during the rest of the unit.

Lesson 2: Sign on the Dotted Line

Follow the suggestions on p. 5 for talking about the title.

- Explain that a *dot* is a small point or mark. Draw a dotted line on the board to help illustrate the idiom.
- Explain that *sign on the dotted line* is a common expression meaning "sign your name to show agreement."

Questions

If learners have signed petitions, ask them if they know whether any changes occurred because of their action.

Attention Box

Read the words to learners, pointing or miming to convey meaning. This vocabulary should be understood, but learners should not be expected to produce the words at this point.

- Tell learners that the word *limit* can be a noun or a verb, but in the reading, it is a verb.
- Share this sentence for using *limit* as a noun: The *limit* for visitor parking is two hours.

Reading Tip

- Read the tip aloud.
- The general idea of the reading is that Marlene wants to change parking regulations. Explain that *regulations* are rules or statements of what can and cannot be done.

Use the information in the petition to practice pronunciation of names and the most common ways to say numbers in addresses and phone numbers. Use these examples:

- The *h* is usually silent in *Cohen.*
- 985: *nine, eight, five* or *nine eighty-five* rather than *nine hundred eighty-five*
- 310: *three, one, oh* or *three ten*
- 555: *five, five, five* rather than *five hundred fifty-five*
- 2987: *two, nine, eight, seven* rather than *two thousand nine hundred eighty-seven*

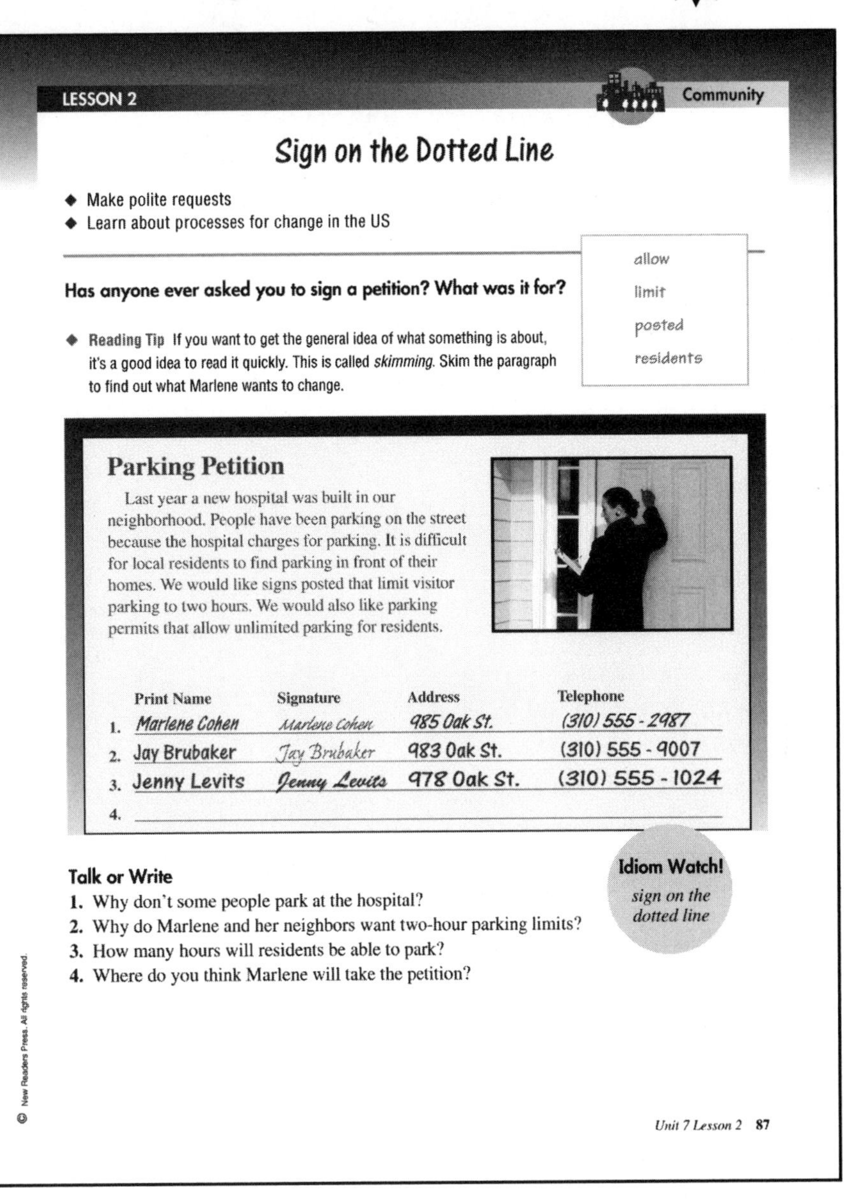

LESSON 2 — Community

Sign on the Dotted Line

- Make polite requests
- Learn about processes for change in the US

allow
limit
posted
residents

Has anyone ever asked you to sign a petition? What was it for?

- **Reading Tip** If you want to get the general idea of what something is about, it's a good idea to read it quickly. This is called *skimming.* Skim the paragraph to find out what Marlene wants to change.

Parking Petition

Last year a new hospital was built in our neighborhood. People have been parking on the street because the hospital charges for parking. It is difficult for local residents to find parking in front of their homes. We would like signs posted that limit visitor parking to two hours. We would also like parking permits that allow unlimited parking for residents.

	Print Name	Signature	Address	Telephone
1.	Marlene Cohen	Marlene Cohen	985 Oak St.	(310) 555-2987
2.	Jay Brubaker	Jay Brubaker	983 Oak St.	(310) 555-9007
3.	Jenny Levits	Jenny Levits	978 Oak St.	(310) 555-1024
4.				

Talk or Write

1. Why don't some people park at the hospital?
2. Why do Marlene and her neighbors want two-hour parking limits?
3. How many hours will residents be able to park?
4. Where do you think Marlene will take the petition?

Idiom Watch! *sign on the dotted line*

Unit 7 Lesson 2 87

Talk or Write

This exercise helps learners locate cause and effect.

Answers

1. Some people don't park at the hospital because the hospital charges for parking.
2. They want two-hour parking limits because people stay longer than two hours, and the residents don't have enough parking spaces.
3. Residents will be able to park for an unlimited time.
4. Marlene will probably take the petition to city hall.

Vocabulary

Follow the suggestions on p. 6 for introducing and reinforcing vocabulary words.

Point out that *influence* is both a noun and a verb:

- He is a good *influence* on his little sister.
- He tried to *influence* me to vote for him.

Point out that *opposed* is used as an adjective in the reading, but that it is also the simple past form of the verb *oppose. Petition* is also a verb, and *representative* can be an adjective.

<u>One Step Up</u>
Follow the suggestions on p. 6 for categorizing vocabulary words as nouns, verbs, and adjectives.

Write the words on the board or an overhead transparency. Have learners come and underline the stressed syllables.

Practice saying the words with correct stress.

- Nouns: *ad<u>min</u>istrator, ap<u>prov</u>al, <u>in</u>fluence, <u>is</u>sues, pe<u>ti</u>tion, repre<u>sen</u>tative*
- Verbs: *ap<u>prove</u>, <u>in</u>fluence*
- Adjectives: *op<u>posed</u>*

Remember?

Discuss the meaning of *federal* (related to the national government), *state* (related to state government) and *local* (related to city, town, or county government).

In the US

As a pre-reading activity, have a class discussion about changes in life. Ask these questions:

- Do you like things to stay the same, or do you like change?
- What are some changes you've experienced that you like?
- If you aren't happy with something, do you speak out, or do you let things stay the same? Why?

In the US Speaking Out

In the US, there are many ways for people to change situations. Sometimes, a phone call to complain or report a dangerous situation is enough. Sometimes people start the change process with a petition. People do this at schools, in their communities, and at the state and federal levels. People can express their opinions or influence decision making in this way.

Someone who is not happy with something at a school can talk about the issue or present a petition to a school administrator, at a PTA (Parent and Teacher Association) meeting, or at a school board meeting. The members of the school board are elected by the people in the community. They give final approval on many decisions made by school administrators.

Sometimes, people want to make changes in their local community. For example, a city can decide to cut down trees because they are breaking the sidewalks. If the residents of that neighborhood don't agree with the city, they can present a petition or speak at a City Hall meeting.

People can also help make changes at the state and federal level. People make phone calls, write letters, and send e-mails to their representatives to express their opinions about issues.

Vocabulary

Repeat these words after your teacher. Talk about their meanings. Write the words in your notebook. With a partner, write a sentence using each word.

administrator
approve/approval
influence
issues
opposed
petition
representative

Idiom Watch!
speak out

Remember?
federal state local

Compare Cultures With your group, talk about how people make changes in their schools and communities. Compare the US to your home country. Take notes in a chart like this one.

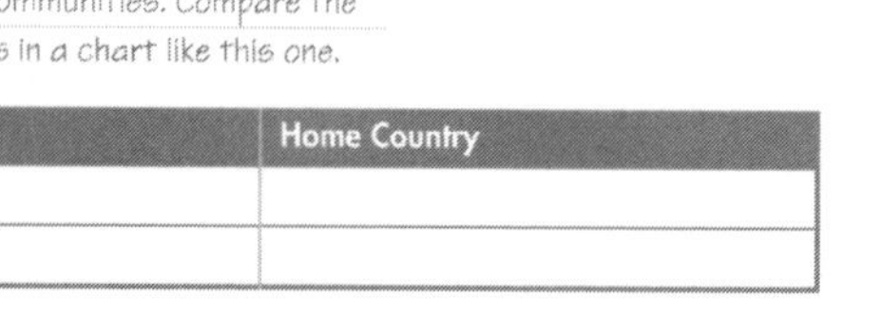

	US	Home Country
School		
Community		

Activity A Think of something you'd like to change or improve in your school or program. Make a list with your group and vote on the most popular idea.

88 *Unit 7 Lesson 2*

Brainstorm a list of positive changes and a list of difficult or negative changes in life.

Compare Cultures

Use Customizable Master 2 (3-Column Chart). Follow the suggestions on p. 7 for customizing and duplicating the master. Distribute a copy to each group.

Ask learners to use the information from the reading "Speaking Out" to fill in the *US* portion of the chart. Then have them fill in information about their home countries.

Activity A

<u>Possible Answers</u>
improved parking, more tables and chairs in student areas, more classes, up-to-date technology in classrooms, improved communication between learners and teachers, changes in rules and regulations

 Assign Workbook pp. 48–49.

Attention Box

This vocabulary should be understood, but learners should not be expected to produce the words at this point.

- Discuss the meaning of the word *nightclub*. One meaning might be "a place where people can go to eat, drink, and dance" (e.g., We usually go to a *nightclub* on Saturday nights.).
- Discuss the meaning of the word *fireworks*. One meaning might be "colorful explosives used for celebrations" (e.g., The Fourth of July *fireworks* were beautiful.).

Activity B

Ask volunteers to present their conversation to the class.

Activity C

One Step Up

Include issues related to the environment, immigration, and taxes. Ask all learners together to choose one of these broad topics and create a problem situation. Then do the following together:

- Decide who you should talk to about the problem.
- Write a conversation on the board.
- Practice the conversation in pairs.

Activity D

One Step Up

To encourage good listening and retention skills, tell learners that they will be expected to answer questions about their classmates' responses.

After learners report back to their groups, ask everyone the same questions, randomly using names of specific learners:

- Has _____ ever signed a petition?
- What would _____ do if he or she were opposed to a decision made by his or her school?
- Does _____ think that he or she could influence change?

Learners who interviewed the persons named in the questions should volunteer the answers.

Task 2

Remind learners to use gerunds after asking questions with *would you mind* and *would you consider*. Review this usage with these examples:

- *Would you mind reading this petition?*
- *Would you consider signing this petition?*

For final proofreading, learners should refer to the Writing Checklist on p. 125 of their books.

Use Unit Master 54 (Thinking Skill: Making a Difference) now or at any time during the rest of the unit.

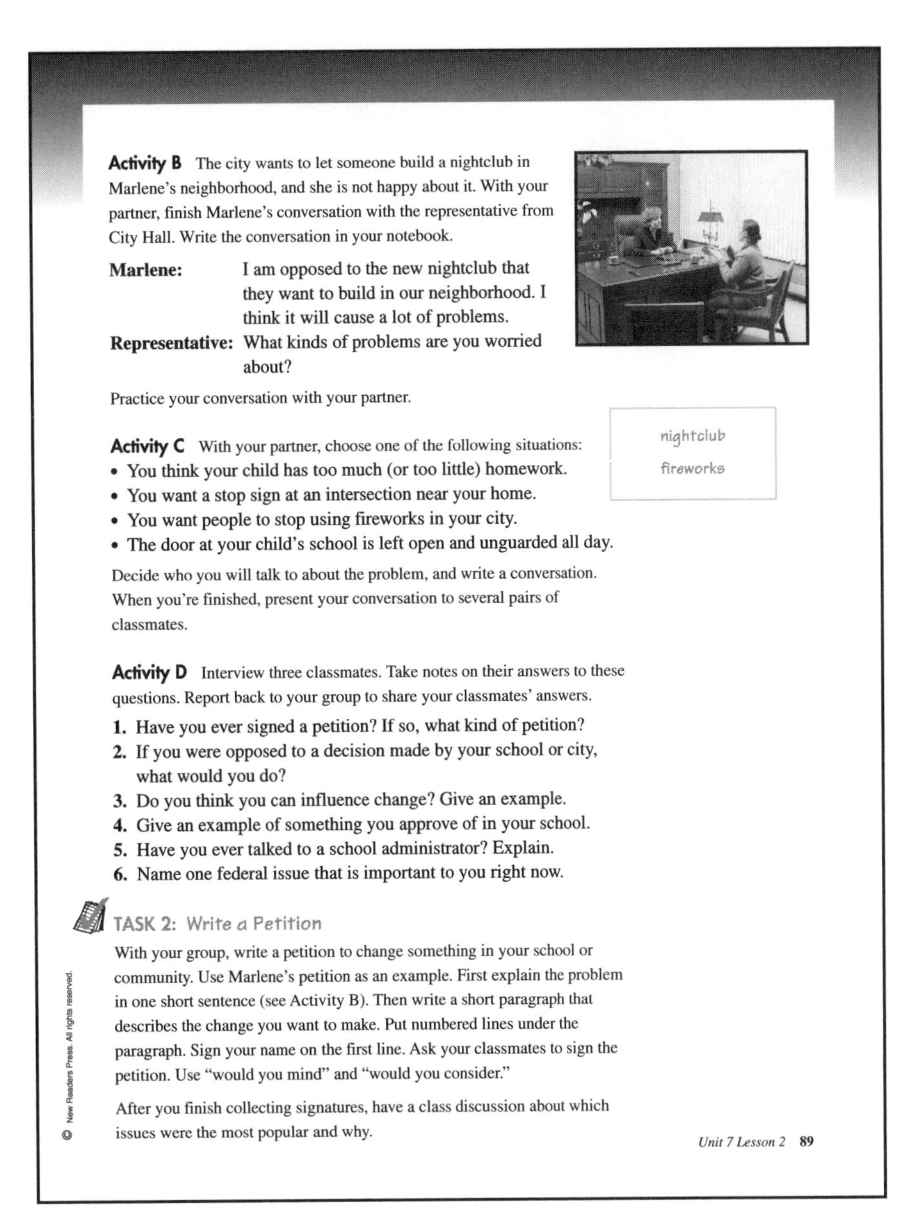

Activity B The city wants to let someone build a nightclub in Marlene's neighborhood, and she is not happy about it. With your partner, finish Marlene's conversation with the representative from City Hall. Write the conversation in your notebook.

Marlene: I am opposed to the new nightclub that they want to build in our neighborhood. I think it will cause a lot of problems.

Representative: What kinds of problems are you worried about?

Practice your conversation with your partner.

nightclub
fireworks

Activity C With your partner, choose one of the following situations:

- You think your child has too much (or too little) homework.
- You want a stop sign at an intersection near your home.
- You want people to stop using fireworks in your city.
- The door at your child's school is left open and unguarded all day.

Decide who you will talk to about the problem, and write a conversation. When you're finished, present your conversation to several pairs of classmates.

Activity D Interview three classmates. Take notes on their answers to these questions. Report back to your group to share your classmates' answers.

1. Have you ever signed a petition? If so, what kind of petition?
2. If you were opposed to a decision made by your school or city, what would you do?
3. Do you think you can influence change? Give an example.
4. Give an example of something you approve of in your school.
5. Have you ever talked to a school administrator? Explain.
6. Name one federal issue that is important to you right now.

TASK 2: Write a Petition

With your group, write a petition to change something in your school or community. Use Marlene's petition as an example. First explain the problem in one short sentence (see Activity B). Then write a short paragraph that describes the change you want to make. Put numbered lines under the paragraph. Sign your name on the first line. Ask your classmates to sign the petition. Use "would you mind" and "would you consider."

After you finish collecting signatures, have a class discussion about which issues were the most popular and why.

Unit 7 Lesson 2 89

Lesson 3: Actions Speak Louder Than Words

Follow the suggestions on p. 5 for talking about the title.

Discuss the meaning of *words* in this idiom. One meaning might be "what people tell you they're going to do or what they promise you."

Share these three equivalents of the idiom *actions speak louder than words* with learners:

- Your actions don't support what you say.
- I don't believe you because you're not doing what you promised.
- Prove it. Stop talking about what you're going to do, and just do it.

Ask learners when they might use this idiom.

Question

Read the question aloud. Then brainstorm a list of qualities with learners. Elicit words they are familiar with, and write the list on the board or an overhead transparency.

Photo

Ask learners if doing volunteer work is common in their countries. Then ask if they have ever done volunteer work or volunteered to work on a community event or project. Have them give specific examples.

Attention Box

This vocabulary should be understood, but learners should not be expected to produce the words at this point.

Reading Tip

Read the tip aloud, then ask learners to complete the reading exercise.

Answers

organize, contact, arrange, collect, assign, coordinate, request, attend, participate, keep track of

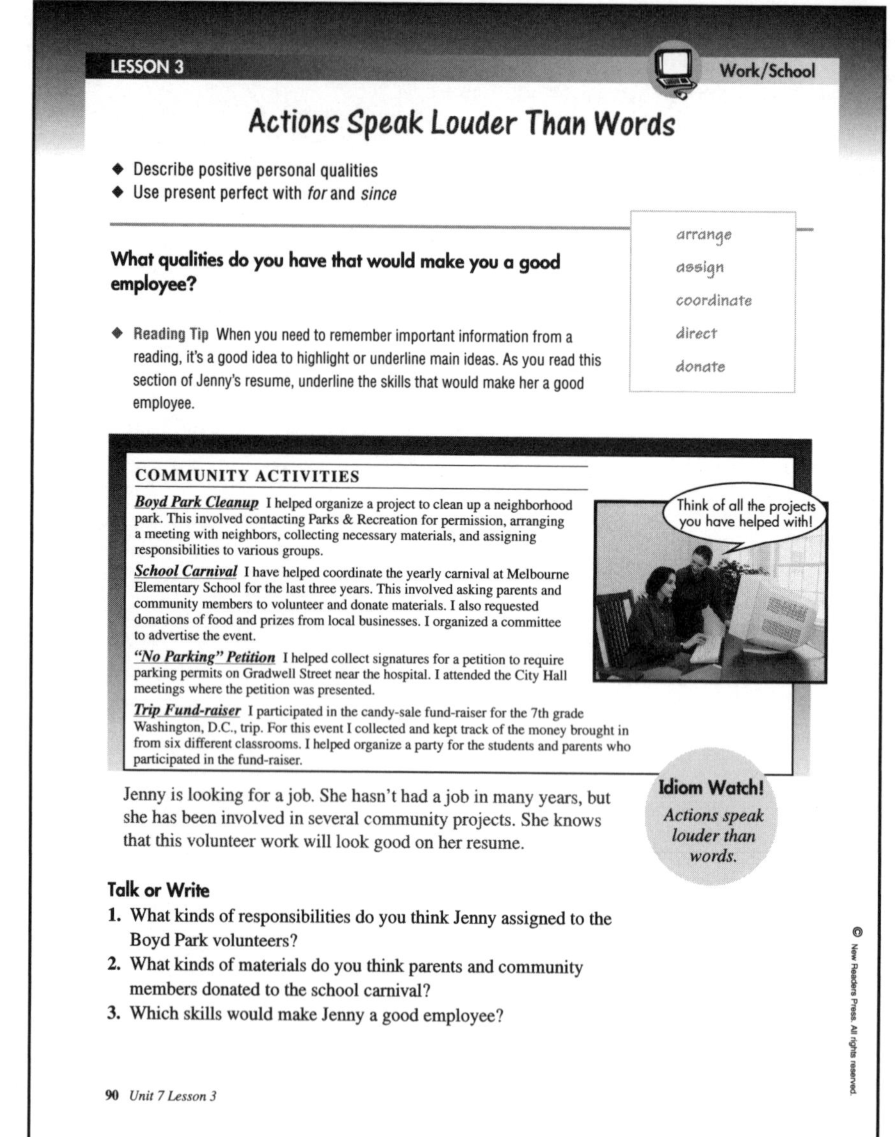

LESSON 3 Work/School

Actions Speak Louder Than Words

- Describe positive personal qualities
- Use present perfect with *for* and *since*

arrange
assign
coordinate
direct
donate

What qualities do you have that would make you a good employee?

- **Reading Tip** When you need to remember important information from a reading, it's a good idea to highlight or underline main ideas. As you read this section of Jenny's resume, underline the skills that would make her a good employee.

COMMUNITY ACTIVITIES

Boyd Park Cleanup I helped organize a project to clean up a neighborhood park. This involved contacting Parks & Recreation for permission, arranging a meeting with neighbors, collecting necessary materials, and assigning responsibilities to various groups.

School Carnival I have helped coordinate the yearly carnival at Melbourne Elementary School for the last three years. This involved asking parents and community members to volunteer and donate materials. I also requested donations of food and prizes from local businesses. I organized a committee to advertise the event.

"No Parking" Petition I helped collect signatures for a petition to require parking permits on Gradwell Street near the hospital. I attended the City Hall meetings where the petition was presented.

Trip Fund-raiser I participated in the candy-sale fund-raiser for the 7th grade Washington, D.C., trip. For this event I collected and kept track of the money brought in from six different classrooms. I helped organize a party for the students and parents who participated in the fund-raiser.

Think of all the projects you have helped with!

Jenny is looking for a job. She hasn't had a job in many years, but she has been involved in several community projects. She knows that this volunteer work will look good on her resume.

Idiom Watch! *Actions speak louder than words.*

Talk or Write

1. What kinds of responsibilities do you think Jenny assigned to the Boyd Park volunteers?
2. What kinds of materials do you think parents and community members donated to the school carnival?
3. Which skills would make Jenny a good employee?

90 *Unit 7 Lesson 3*

Talk or Write

This exercise helps learners practice drawing conclusions from what they read.

Possible Answers

1. Cleaning up litter, painting over graffiti, cleaning tables and benches
2. Food, drinks, paper goods, prizes, decorations, materials for booths and games
3. Organization skills, active participant, good at making arrangements, leadership skills, good coordinator, asks others for help

Vocabulary

Follow the suggestions on p. 6 for introducing and reinforcing vocabulary words.

Discuss the meaning of the expression *team player.* One meaning might be "a person who works well with others and doesn't look for personal glory" (e.g., It's important to be a *team player* in many areas of our lives.).

One Step Up

Follow the suggestions on p. 6 for categorizing the vocabulary words as nouns, verbs, and adjectives.

- Ask groups to write noun forms for the vocabulary words. Set a two-minute time limit to see which group can write the most words. Point out that although *outgoing* does have a noun form—outgoingness—it is not used very often and will probably sound funny to native English speakers.
- Write the nouns on the board or an overhead transparency and give a sample sentence for each.

Answers

arrangement, donation, improvement, confidence, dedication, generosity, persistence, punctuality

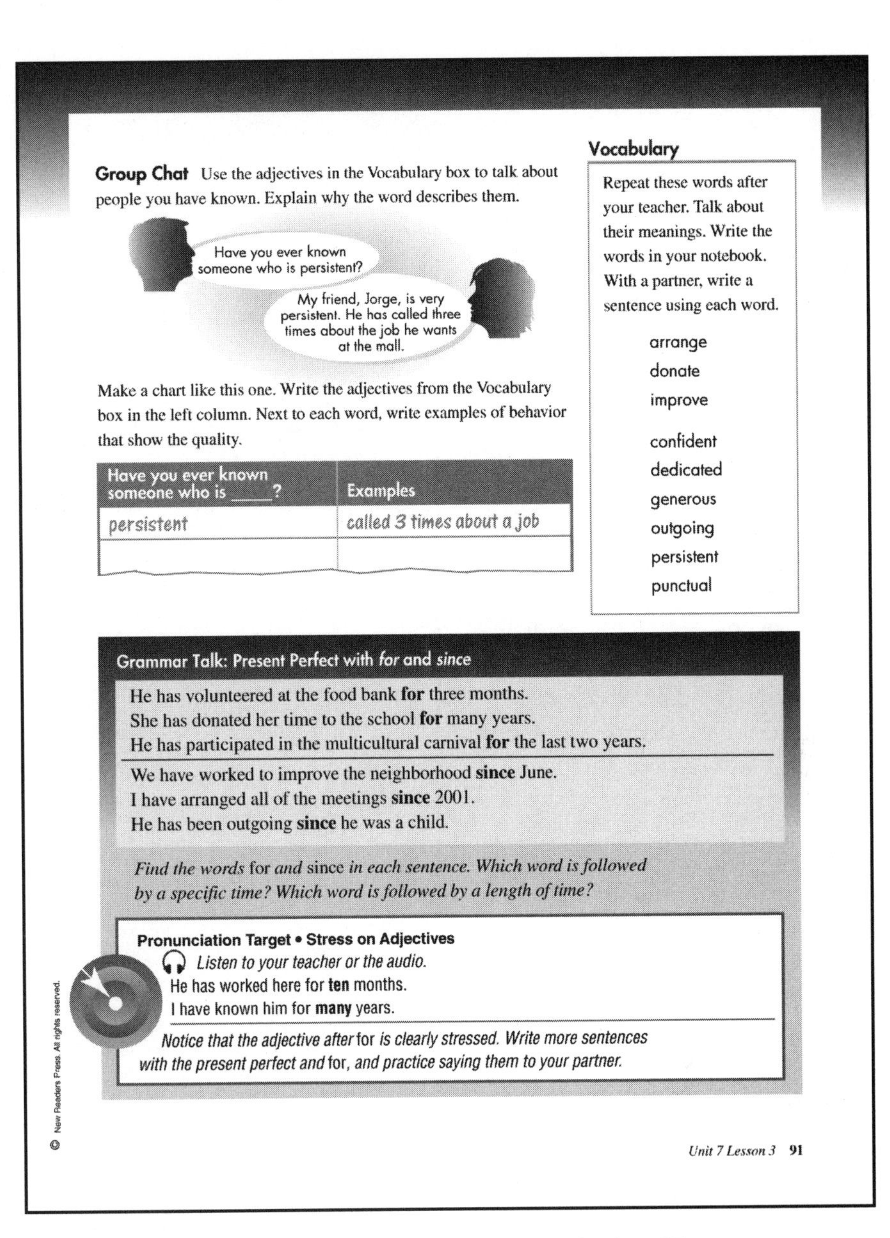

Group Chat Use the adjectives in the Vocabulary box to talk about people you have known. Explain why the word describes them.

Make a chart like this one. Write the adjectives from the Vocabulary box in the left column. Next to each word, write examples of behavior that show the quality.

Have you ever known someone who is ____?	Examples
persistent	called 3 times about a job

Vocabulary

Repeat these words after your teacher. Talk about their meanings. Write the words in your notebook. With a partner, write a sentence using each word.

arrange
donate
improve

confident
dedicated
generous
outgoing
persistent
punctual

Grammar Talk: Present Perfect with *for* and *since*

He has volunteered at the food bank **for** three months.
She has donated her time to the school **for** many years.
He has participated in the multicultural carnival **for** the last two years.

We have worked to improve the neighborhood **since** June.
I have arranged all of the meetings **since** 2001.
He has been outgoing **since** he was a child.

Find the words for *and* since *in each sentence. Which word is followed by a specific time? Which word is followed by a length of time?*

Pronunciation Target • Stress on Adjectives

Listen to your teacher or the audio.
He has worked here for **ten** months.
I have known him for **many** years.

Notice that the adjective after for *is clearly stressed. Write more sentences with the present perfect and* for, *and practice saying them to your partner.*

Group Chat

Use Customizable Master 1 (2-Column Chart). Follow the suggestions on p. 7 for customizing and duplicating the master. Give a copy to each group.

- Help learners identify the adjectives from the Vocabulary box.
- Encourage each learner to ask another group member the question at least once. Each group member should also give at least one answer.
- After the groups have completed their charts, ask learners to report the information from the group (e.g., "Who did your group describe as dedicated? What behavior shows this?).

Grammar Talk

Follow the suggestions on p. 6 for introducing the grammar point.

- Explain that *since* is followed by a specific time. *For* is followed by a length of time.
- Tell learners that the use of present perfect indicates that the action began in the past and continues in the present, or that something was true in the past and is still true in the present.

Answers

- *Since* is followed by a specific time.
- *For* is followed by a length of time.

Pronunciation Target

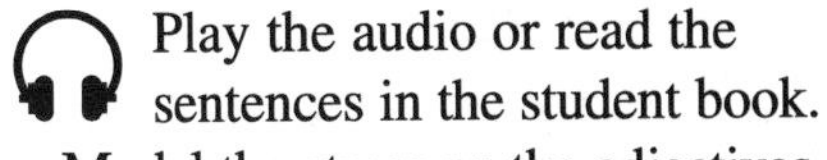

Play the audio or read the sentences in the student book.

- Model the stress on the adjectives.
- Point out that the words in bold type in the pronunciation box are stressed.

Use Unit Master 55 (Vocabulary: Describing People) now or at any time during the rest of the unit.

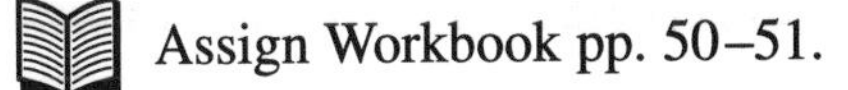

Assign Workbook pp. 50–51.

Activity A

Ask for volunteers to share some of their sentences with the class. Have them write their sentences on the board or an overhead transparency.

Activity B

- Note the cultural importance of being positive in job interviews. Talk about the fact that it is often difficult to say positive things about ourselves. This activity provides learners with an opportunity to think about and express their positive attributes.
- Introduce the word *brag* as a negative concept. Show animated examples of bragging about yourself. Compare these examples with talking positively about yourself without bragging.

Activity C

Extension

Conduct a poll to find out which quality is most admired by learners and which they believe would be most admired in the US. Then open a discussion with these questions:

- Are you usually/always on time?
- Do you feel that you can do many things well?
- Are you comfortable participating in class discussions?
- Is your job important to you?
- Do you always help family members and friends who need your help?
- Do you like to spend time helping other people?
- Do you buy things for other people?

During the discussion, use learners' responses to write sample sentences on the board or an overhead transparency.

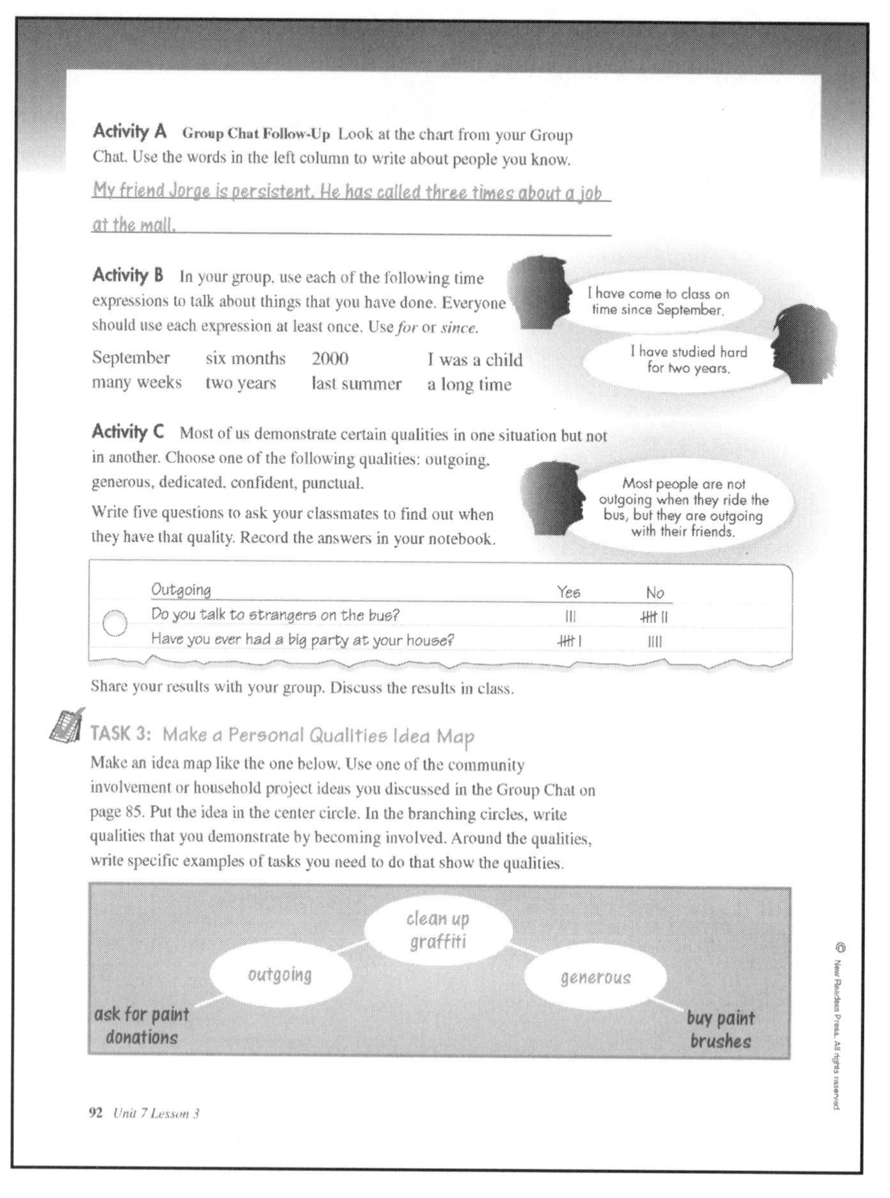

Activity A **Group Chat Follow-Up** Look at the chart from your Group Chat. Use the words in the left column to write about people you know.

My friend Jorge is persistent. He has called three times about a job at the mall.

Activity B In your group, use each of the following time expressions to talk about things that you have done. Everyone should use each expression at least once. Use *for* or *since*.

September	six months	2000	I was a child
many weeks	two years	last summer	a long time

Activity C Most of us demonstrate certain qualities in one situation but not in another. Choose one of the following qualities: outgoing, generous, dedicated, confident, punctual.

Write five questions to ask your classmates to find out when they have that quality. Record the answers in your notebook.

Outgoing	Yes	No
Do you talk to strangers on the bus?	III	~~IIII~~ II
Have you ever had a big party at your house?	~~IIII~~ I	IIII

Share your results with your group. Discuss the results in class.

TASK 3: Make a Personal Qualities Idea Map

Make an idea map like the one below. Use one of the community involvement or household project ideas you discussed in the Group Chat on page 85. Put the idea in the center circle. In the branching circles, write qualities that you demonstrate by becoming involved. Around the qualities, write specific examples of tasks you need to do that show the qualities.

92 *Unit 7 Lesson 3*

Task 3

Use Customizable Master 4 (Idea Map). Follow the suggestions on p. 7 for customizing and duplicating the master and distributing the copies.

Divide learners into small groups. Give one copy of the master to each group.

One Step Up

Write this sample paragraph on the board or an overhead transparency to show learners how to write about their ideas.

People who become involved in community projects demonstrate positive qualities. An outgoing person might ask for paint donations to help clean up graffiti. A generous person might buy the paintbrushes.

Ask learners to write a similar paragraph using ideas from their idea maps.

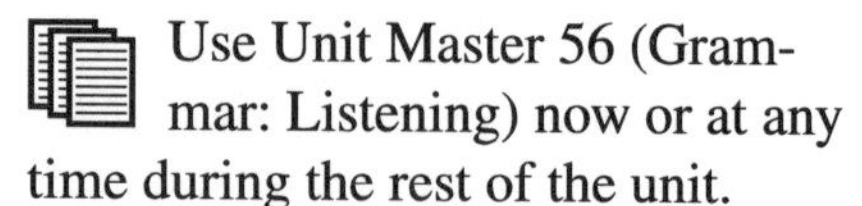

Use Unit Master 56 (Grammar: Listening) now or at any time during the rest of the unit.

Review Unit Skills

See pp. 7–9 for suggestions on games and activities to review the vocabulary and grammar in this unit.

Unit 7 Project

Learners prepare a poster about a community project.

Get Ready

Help learners choose topics for their projects. Make sure that each group chooses a different project.

Do the Work

Give a copy of Generic Assessment Master 12 (Peer Assessment Form) to each group.

- Follow the suggestions for peer assessment on p. 4.
- Identify a recorder in each group to take notes and a reporter to share them with the class.

Present

Assessment

Use Unit Master 57 (Project Assessment Form) to assess the project presentations. As each group presents its project, fill out a copy of the form. If possible, make a copy of the completed form for each group member's portfolio.

- After learners have picked officers for the town hall meeting, assist the president, if necessary, in developing opening and closing remarks. Follow these examples: *Welcome and thank you for attending this very important meeting. This meeting is now in session. We are here tonight to discuss ideas for changes in our community. Members of the community will present their ideas for changes they would like to see happen. First on our agenda is a group of people who would like to clean up Boyd Park . . .*
- Sample closure to the meeting: *This meeting is now adjourned. Thank you for coming.*
- When all groups have finished presenting, ask the recorders to compare their notes.

UNIT 7 Project

Make a Poster for a Community Project

Prepare a poster about a community project. Follow these steps:

Get Ready

In groups, choose an idea for getting involved or changing something in your community. Write a description of the project. The description should answer the following questions:

- How will the project benefit the community?
- How will it benefit the people who get involved?
- What tasks does the project require?
- How many people will need to help?
- What materials will you need?
- How much will the materials cost?

Do the Work

Write the information on a large poster.

Present

Sometimes city officials organize town hall meetings to discuss important changes in the community. Have a town hall meeting with your class. Select a president to lead the meeting and two secretaries to take notes. Each group will present their project plan. Take a vote on which project the class would like to do first. Have a class discussion about any changes or additions that you want to make to the plan.

Idiom Watch! *team player*

Writing Extension Write a letter to a friend. Tell him or her about one of the class projects. Tell why you think it is good.

 **Technology Extra**

Use the computer to make a flyer that announces your project and asks for volunteers. Use computer art to make it more interesting. Exchange flyers with another group. Ask questions about anything you do not understand.

Unit 7 Project 93

Writing Extension

For final proofreading of the letter, refer learners to the Writing Checklist on p. 125 of their books.

Technology Extra

If necessary, show learners how to add computer art to their flyers.

Assign Workbook p. 52 (Check Your Progress).

Use Unit Master 58 (Unit 7 Checkup/Review) whenever you complete this unit.

Unit 8: Into Your Own Hands

Materials for the Unit

- Three-hole punch
- Dividers for binders or colored card stock
- Customizable Masters 1, 2, and 4
- Generic Assessment Master 9
- Unit Masters 59–64

Into Your Own Hands

Follow the suggestions on p. 5 for talking about the title.

Question

Read the question below the arrow. Encourage learners to think beyond the obvious reason of getting a better job. Adults also want to continue learning because their interests or circumstances change, they want to keep mentally active, they want to help their children, they think learning is fun, etc.

Photo

Follow the suggestions on p. 4 for talking about the photo.

Think and Talk

For question 2, ask learners what they think the teacher might say to describe Cameron's "poor behavior."

What's Your Opinion?

Ask learners if they have had any experience with a doctor, teacher, or other authority figure giving them bad advice. If so, what did they do?

UNIT 8

Into Your Own Hands

Becoming a Lifelong Learner

Home 1 · Community 2 · Work/School 3

- **Vocabulary** Words for learning and planning
- **Language** Future with *will* and *be going to* • Polite requests with modals
- **Pronunciation** Reduction of *be* and *will* • Reduction of *would you* and *could you*
- **Culture** Opportunities for lifelong learning

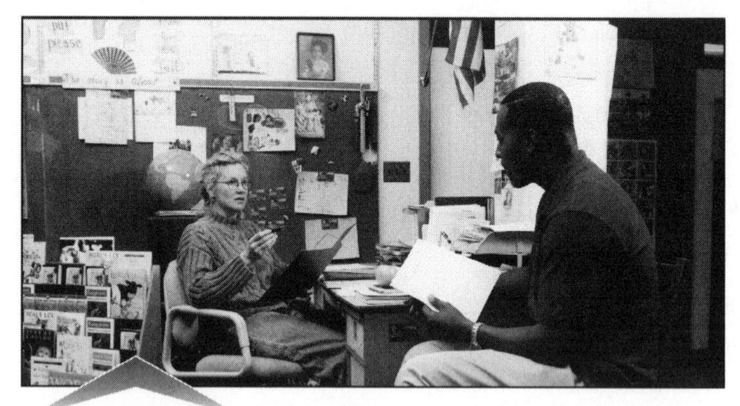

Why do adults want to continue learning after they finish high school or college?

Anthony Robinson is talking to his 8-year-old son's teacher about problems that his son, Cameron, is having at school. Lately, Cameron's behavior has been poor, and he hasn't been completing his homework. Anthony wants to help his son, but he needs to learn more about his son's behavior.

Think and Talk

1. What do you see in the photograph?
2. What do you think that Anthony is saying to the teacher?
3. What can Anthony do to learn more about his son's problem?
4. If you want to learn more about a topic, where can you get information or who can you talk to?

What's Your Opinion? Many people go to doctors and teachers for advice. Do you think doctors and teachers always give good advice? Explain your answer.

94 *Unit 8*

Vocabulary

Follow the suggestions on p. 6 for introducing and reinforcing vocabulary words.

Dictation

Play the audio or read the listening script below.

When learners finish writing the dictation sentences, ask volunteers to write them on the board. Correct the sentences together.

Listening Script/Answers

Listen. Write the sentences that you hear.

1. It is very fulfilling to get a college degree.
2. Learning about interesting topics is meaningful.
3. Using the Internet is a practical skill.
4. Many people change careers more than once.
5. I haven't had an opportunity to learn about computers.
6. Are you going to enroll next semester?

Gather Your Thoughts

Use Customizable Master 4 (Idea Map). Follow the suggestions on p. 7 for customizing and duplicating the master and distributing the copies. Make a copy for each learner.

What's the Problem?

Follow the suggestions on p. 5 for identifying and analyzing problems.

Setting Goals

Follow the suggestions on p. 5 for setting goals.

Dictation Listen to your teacher or the audio. Write the sentences that you hear.

Gather Your Thoughts There are many reasons for being a lifelong learner. Some reasons are practical and others are personal. What is practical for one person might not be practical for another person.

Use the idea map below to brainstorm topics that you could learn more about. Decide why you want to learn more about the topics. Write where you can learn more about them.

What do you want to learn?
word processing
Why? Where?
get a better job
community college
about heart problems
Why? Where?
Why? Where?

Vocabulary

Repeat these words after your teacher. Talk about their meanings. Write the words in your notebook. With a partner, write a sentence using each word.

advantage
career
lifelong learning
opportunity

fulfilling
meaningful
practical
resource

enroll/enrollment
register/registration

Idiom Watch!
take something into your own hands

What's the Problem? Look at your idea map again. What things can get in the way of becoming a lifelong learner? Think or talk with a partner.

Setting Goals Think about things you want to be able to do to continue learning. Which goals are most important to you? Rank them from 1 (most important) to 6.

_____ **a.** talk about future plans
_____ **b.** learn ways to improve study habits
_____ **c.** learn how to use library resources
_____ **d.** learn how to ask politely for information or help
_____ **e.** understand recorded enrollment procedures for college
_____ **f.** another goal: ______________________________

Which was the most important goal for your class? Tally your answers. Talk about your most important goals.

Lesson 1: Study Habits

Follow the suggestions on p. 5 for talking about the title.

Questions

Read the introductory questions aloud. Then ask volunteers to talk about the following topics:

- How much time they spent studying as children
- Where they studied
- What their study environment was like

Introduce the word *procrastinate* or the idiom *put off* + gerund (e.g., *put off* studying).

Attention Box

Read the words to learners, pointing or miming to convey meaning. This vocabulary should be understood, but learners should not be expected to produce the words at this point.

Reading Tip

- Discuss the title of the reading. Ask learners if they think it is likely that a dog would eat someone's homework. Explain that this is a well-known example of a bad excuse for not doing homework.
- Ask learners to think of other excuses that students might give for not doing homework.
- After learners scan the article and write down ideas, review their ideas as a class. Then have them read the article more carefully.

Talk or Write

This exercise helps learners draw conclusions from what they read.

- Have learners describe their own study environments.
- Ask them which suggestions in the article, if any, they would like to follow.

<u>One Step Up</u>

Ask learners to look through their binders for English class and consider these questions:

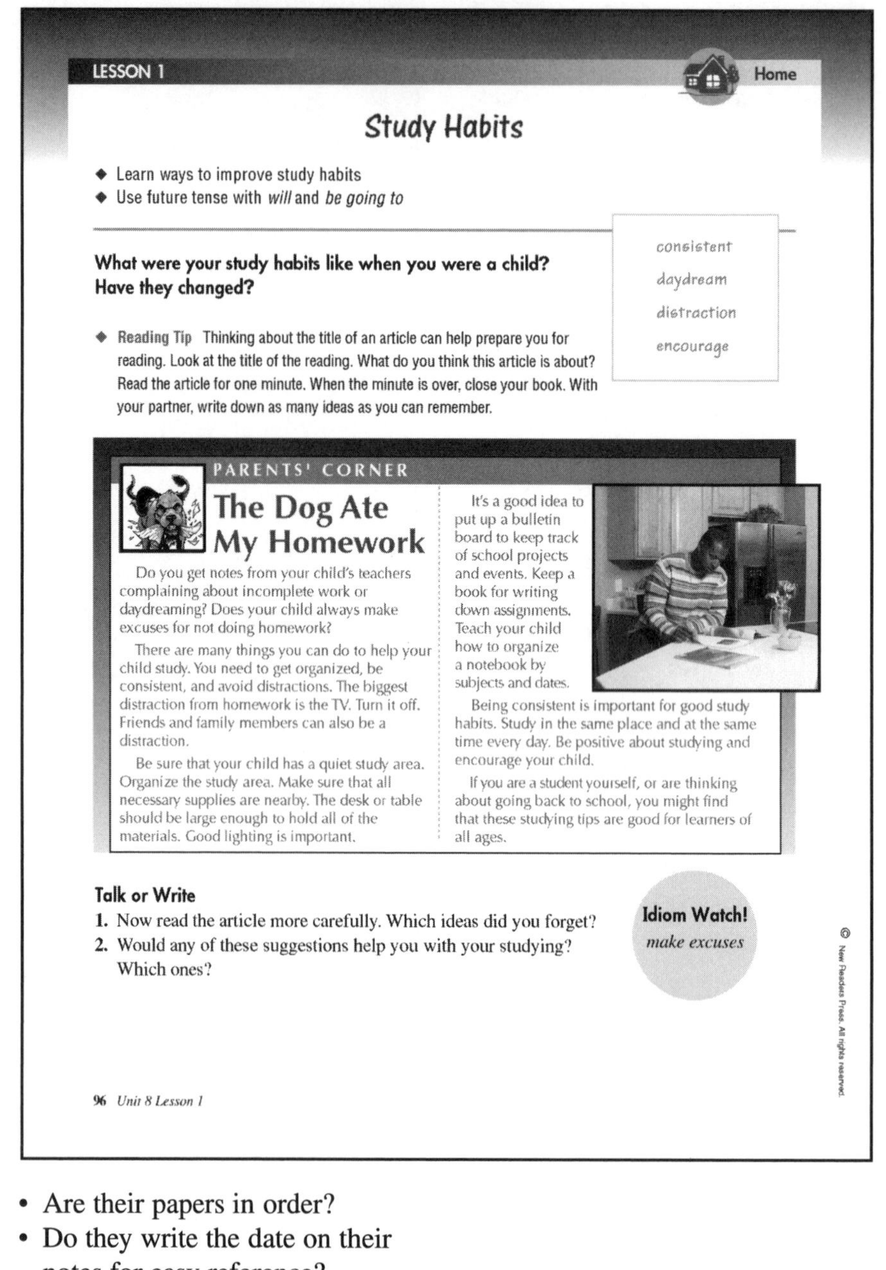

LESSON 1 Home

Study Habits

- Learn ways to improve study habits
- Use future tense with *will* and *be going to*

consistent
daydream
distraction
encourage

What were your study habits like when you were a child? Have they changed?

- **Reading Tip** Thinking about the title of an article can help prepare you for reading. Look at the title of the reading. What do you think this article is about? Read the article for one minute. When the minute is over, close your book. With your partner, write down as many ideas as you can remember.

PARENTS' CORNER

The Dog Ate My Homework

Do you get notes from your child's teachers complaining about incomplete work or daydreaming? Does your child always make excuses for not doing homework?

There are many things you can do to help your child study. You need to get organized, be consistent, and avoid distractions. The biggest distraction from homework is the TV. Turn it off. Friends and family members can also be a distraction.

Be sure that your child has a quiet study area. Organize the study area. Make sure that all necessary supplies are nearby. The desk or table should be large enough to hold all of the materials. Good lighting is important.

It's a good idea to put up a bulletin board to keep track of school projects and events. Keep a book for writing down assignments. Teach your child how to organize a notebook by subjects and dates.

Being consistent is important for good study habits. Study in the same place and at the same time every day. Be positive about studying and encourage your child.

If you are a student yourself, or are thinking about going back to school, you might find that these studying tips are good for learners of all ages.

Talk or Write

1. Now read the article more carefully. Which ideas did you forget?
2. Would any of these suggestions help you with your studying? Which ones?

Idiom Watch! *make excuses*

96 *Unit 8 Lesson 1*

- Are their papers in order?
- Do they write the date on their notes for easy reference?
- Do they use dividers between topics or units?
- Have they discarded papers that are no longer useful?

Help learners organize their binders by providing a three-hole punch and colored card stock (if they do not have dividers).

Check learners' binders, and provide feedback on their organization strategies.

Vocabulary

Follow the suggestions on p. 6 for introducing and reinforcing vocabulary words.

<u>One Step Up</u>

Follow the suggestions on p. 6 for categorizing the vocabulary words as nouns, verbs, and adjectives.

- Nouns: *distraction, priority, routine, schedule*
- Verbs: *distract, schedule*
- Adjectives: *consistent, inconsistent, routine*

<u>Pronunciation Tip</u>

Point out that when the words *consistent* and *inconsistent* are contrasted, the negative prefix is stressed in the word *<u>in</u>consistent.*

Group Chat

Use Customizable Master 1 (2-Column Chart). Follow the suggestions on p. 7 for customizing and duplicating the master and distributing the copies. Make a copy for each learner.

Grammar Talk

Follow the suggestions on p. 6 for introducing the grammar point.

- *Will* is usually expressed as a contraction when we use it to discuss planned activities: *I think I'll . . . ; Maybe I'll . . . ; I'll probably . . .* It is also used in more formal situations.
- Many learners answer a question like "What are you up to this weekend?" with "I will visit my brother," which sounds awkward or overly formal. Encourage learners to use *going to* when they are having an informal conversation describing planned activities.

Pronunciation Target

Play the audio or read the sentences in the student book.

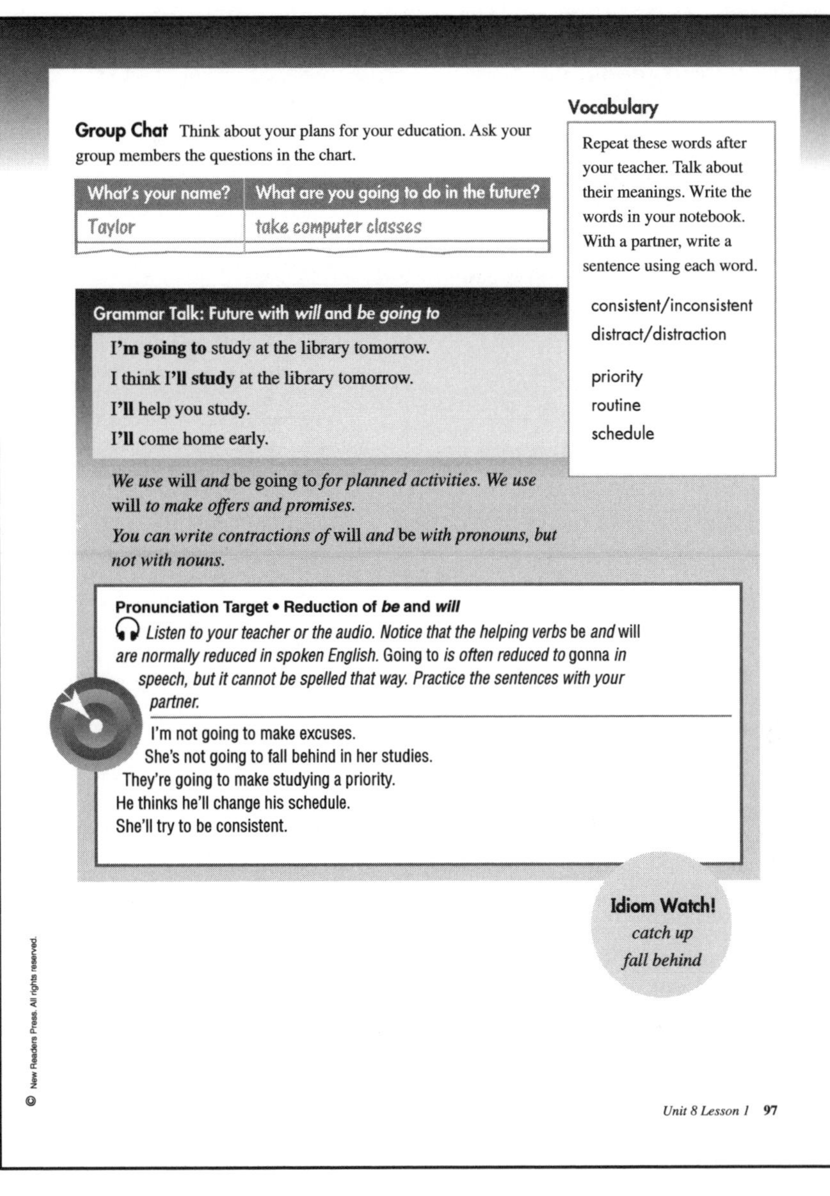

Group Chat Think about your plans for your education. Ask your group members the questions in the chart.

What's your name?	What are you going to do in the future?
Taylor	take computer classes

Vocabulary

Repeat these words after your teacher. Talk about their meanings. Write the words in your notebook. With a partner, write a sentence using each word.

consistent/inconsistent
distract/distraction
priority
routine
schedule

Grammar Talk: Future with *will* and *be going to*

I'm going to study at the library tomorrow.
I think **I'll study** at the library tomorrow.
I'll help you study.
I'll come home early.

We use will *and* be going to *for planned activities. We use* will *to make offers and promises.*

You can write contractions of will *and* be *with pronouns, but not with nouns.*

Pronunciation Target • Reduction of *be* and *will*

Listen to your teacher or the audio. Notice that the helping verbs be *and* will *are normally reduced in spoken English.* Going to *is often reduced to* gonna *in speech, but it cannot be spelled that way. Practice the sentences with your partner.*

I'm not going to make excuses.
She's not going to fall behind in her studies.
They're going to make studying a priority.
He thinks he'll change his schedule.
She'll try to be consistent.

Idiom Watch!
catch up
fall behind

Unit 8 Lesson 1 97

As learners practice the reduced forms, check that they are not saying *gonna to.* Emphasize that the reduced (spoken) form *gonna* includes both *going* and *to.*

Assign Workbook pp. 53–54.

Activity A

Play the audio or read the script below. Be sure that you and your learners reduce *will* and *going to* in the sentences.

- Repeat the sentences as necessary but, if you are reading them, pronounce them at normal speed, including the reduction.
- When learners finish writing, ask volunteers to put the sentences on the board or an overhead transparency. Correct the work together.
- Ask learners to read the sentences to their partners, practicing the reduced forms.

Listening Script/Answers

Listen to these sentences. You will hear each sentence twice.

1. Mary is going to *[gonna]* change her routine.
2. My son is going to *[gonna]* organize his notebook.
3. Anthony will *['ll]* go to the library to study.
4. Jim will *['ll]* study at the same time every day.
5. They are going to *[gonna]* catch up on their homework.

Listen again. Write the sentences.

1. Mary is going to *[gonna]* change her routine.
2. My son is going to *[gonna]* organize his notebook.
3. Anthony will *['ll]* go to the library to study.
4. Jim will *['ll]* study at the same time every day.
5. They are going to *[gonna]* catch up on their homework.

Activity B

Ask volunteers to read or perform their conversation for the class.

Activity C

Have learners use the information in their Group Chat charts to write sentences in their notebooks.

Activity A Listen to your teacher or the audio. Write the sentences that you hear. Your teacher will reduce *will* and *going to*. Don't write the reduced forms.

Activity B Read the conversation. Underline the future verbs.

Grant: What are you going to do tomorrow?
Garrett: I'm going to move my desk into the other room.
Grant: That's a good idea. I'll help you.

With your partner, write a conversation. Use *be going to* to tell about a plan and *will* to make an offer or a promise.

Activity C **Group Chat Follow-Up** Look at the chart from your Group Chat. Write sentences about your group members in your notebook.

Taylor is going to take computer classes.

Activity D Interview three classmates about their study habits. Take notes on their answers. Report back to your group to compare answers.

1. Are you consistent or inconsistent about studying English? Why?
2. Do you have a study routine? What is it?
3. Do you ever fall behind in your work? How do you catch up?
4. Describe your daily schedule.
5. Are there any distractions in your study area? What are they?
6. Do you ever make excuses for not studying? Give an example.
7. Is studying a priority for you? Explain your answer.

TASK 1: Make a Study Plan

Write a plan for improving your own study habits. List changes that you could make in your routine or study area that would help you with your English or with another subject that you study. Write each change in the correct place in a chart like this one.

Changes in Routine	Changes in Study Area
get up earlier	*clean my desk*

98 *Unit 8 Lesson 1*

Activity D

Extension

Ask learners to write sentences about their classmates based on the information from the interview. They should write about a different classmate for each question.

If learners are having difficulty forming the sentences, share this example:

Marco isn't consistent about studying English. Sometimes he has to work a lot of hours, and he doesn't have time to study.

Task 1

Use Customizable Master 1 (2-Column Chart). Follow the suggestions on p. 7 for customizing and duplicating the master and distributing the copies. Make one copy for each learner.

Use Unit Master 59 (Grammar: Plans and Promises) now or at any time during the rest of the unit.

Lesson 2: Get Informed

Follow the suggestions on p. 5 for talking about the title.

Questions

- Read the questions aloud.
- Ask learners to think of any experience they have had with libraries in their home countries or in the US.
- Find out whether they have library cards now.
- Ask what they know about obtaining a library card.

Photo

Follow the suggestions on p. 4 for talking about the photo.

Ask learners if they have heard of *ADHD* and find out what knowledge they have about the topic. Then share this information:

Attention Deficit/Hyperactivity Disorder (ADHD) is a condition characterized by impulsive behavior, difficulty paying attention, and sometimes an inability to sit still (hyperactivity).

Attention Box

This vocabulary should be understood, but learners should not be expected to produce the words at this point.

- Point out that *periodical* refers to both magazines and newspapers and is not a word used in everyday conversation.
- Use a real periodical to illustrate the words in the box.

Talk or Write

This exercise helps learners read for details.

Answers

1. "Study Tips for ADHD Children"
2. Market Press; New Jersey
3. Family Health
4. "Does Your Child Really Need Medication?"
5. p. 34; one page long
6. Answers will vary. Ask learners to explain their choices.

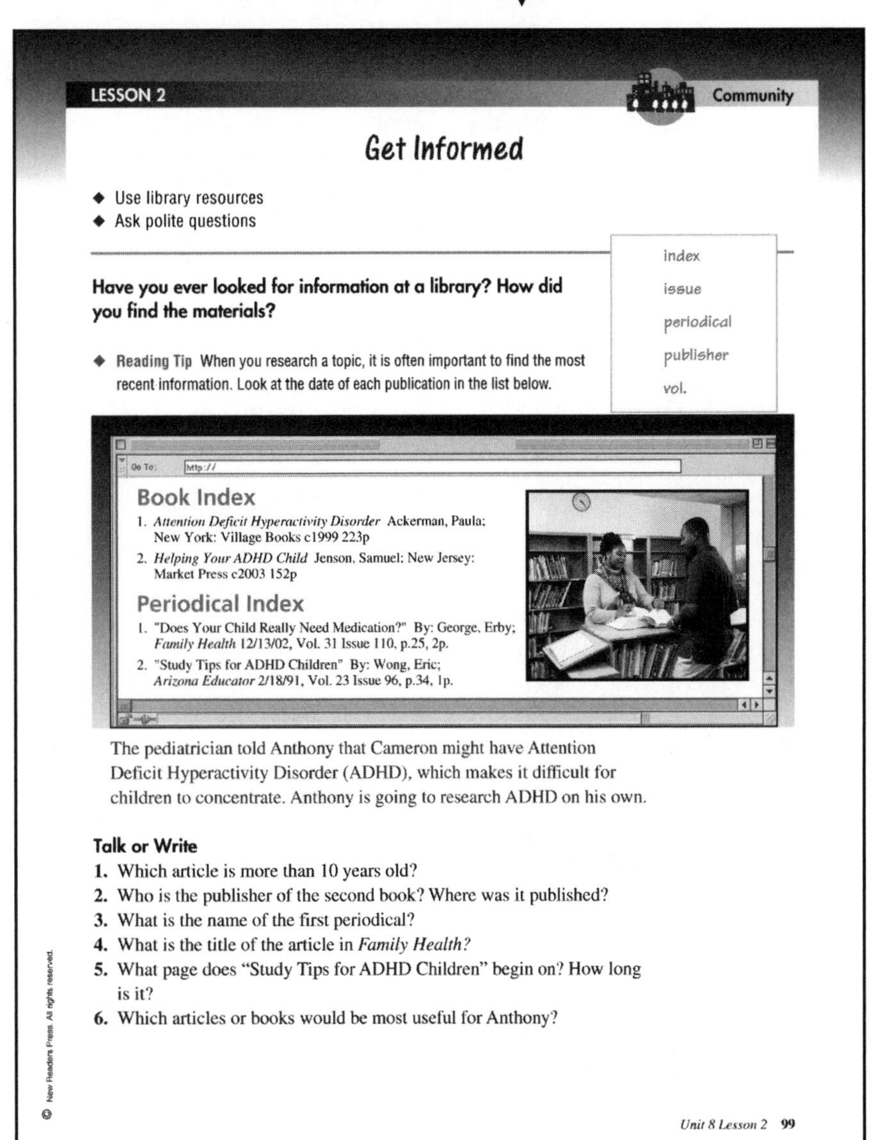

LESSON 2 Community

Get Informed

- ◆ Use library resources
- ◆ Ask polite questions

index
issue
periodical
publisher
vol.

Have you ever looked for information at a library? How did you find the materials?

◆ **Reading Tip** When you research a topic, it is often important to find the most recent information. Look at the date of each publication in the list below.

Go To: http://

Book Index

1. *Attention Deficit Hyperactivity Disorder* Ackerman, Paula; New York: Village Books c1999 223p
2. *Helping Your ADHD Child* Jenson, Samuel; New Jersey: Market Press c2003 152p

Periodical Index

1. "Does Your Child Really Need Medication?" By: George, Erby; *Family Health* 12/13/02, Vol. 31 Issue 110, p.25, 2p.
2. "Study Tips for ADHD Children" By: Wong, Eric; *Arizona Educator* 2/18/91, Vol. 23 Issue 96, p.34, 1p.

The pediatrician told Anthony that Cameron might have Attention Deficit Hyperactivity Disorder (ADHD), which makes it difficult for children to concentrate. Anthony is going to research ADHD on his own.

Talk or Write

1. Which article is more than 10 years old?
2. Who is the publisher of the second book? Where was it published?
3. What is the name of the first periodical?
4. What is the title of the article in *Family Health?*
5. What page does "Study Tips for ADHD Children" begin on? How long is it?
6. Which articles or books would be most useful for Anthony?

Unit 8 Lesson 2 99

Extension

- If you have access to the Internet in your classroom, show learners how to access an online library catalog and search for materials. The local library's catalog is best, but if it is not online, you can access the catalog of most major city libraries.
- Learners can practice looking for a book or an article by subject, title, or author. They can search for materials in their native languages, and they can check if items are currently available.

Vocabulary

Follow the suggestions on p. 6 for introducing and reinforcing vocabulary words.

One Step Up

Follow the suggestions on p. 6 for categorizing the vocabulary words as nouns, verbs, and adjectives.

- Nouns: *article, biography, documentary, nonfiction, periodical, reference, research*
- Verbs: *renew, research*
- Adjectives: *due, nonfiction, overdue*

Group Chat

Use Customizable Master 1 (2-Column Chart). Follow the suggestions on p. 7 for customizing and duplicating the master and distributing the copies. Make one copy for each group.

- After learners complete their group discussions, have them create a class chart to compile all the information.
- If you have more than one library in the area, make sure the chart includes information for each one.

Grammar Talk

Follow the suggestions on p. 6 for introducing the grammar point.

Possible Answer

The polite questions look more like statements, with the subject before the verb.

- Point out that if you cover up "Could you please" or "Would you please," the rest of the sentence reads like a statement, not a question.
- Questions with other introductory expressions, such as the one below, follow the same rule: *Do you know when the storytelling will begin?*

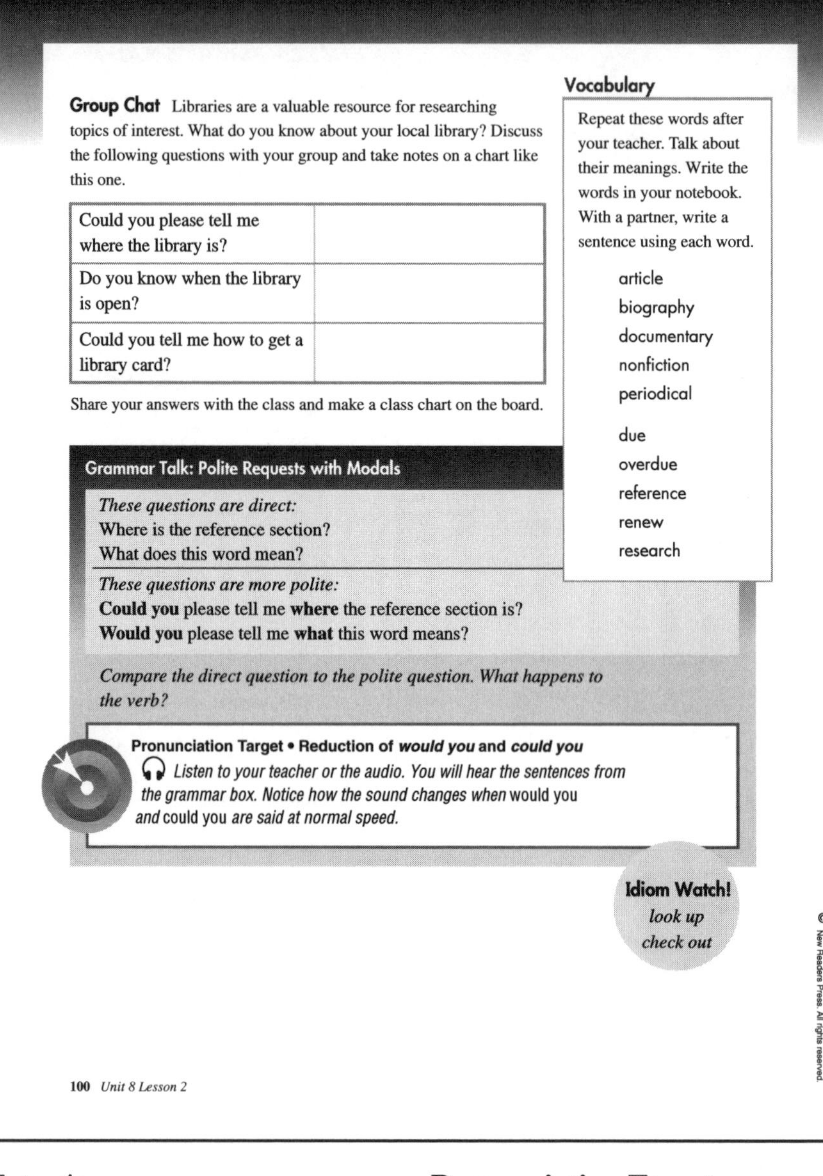

Group Chat Libraries are a valuable resource for researching topics of interest. What do you know about your local library? Discuss the following questions with your group and take notes on a chart like this one.

Could you please tell me where the library is?	
Do you know when the library is open?	
Could you tell me how to get a library card?	

Share your answers with the class and make a class chart on the board.

Vocabulary

Repeat these words after your teacher. Talk about their meanings. Write the words in your notebook. With a partner, write a sentence using each word.

article
biography
documentary
nonfiction
periodical

due
overdue
reference
renew
research

Grammar Talk: Polite Requests with Modals

These questions are direct:
Where is the reference section?
What does this word mean?

These questions are more polite:
Could you please tell me **where** the reference section is?
Would you please tell me **what** this word means?

Compare the direct question to the polite question. What happens to the verb?

Pronunciation Target • Reduction of *would you* and *could you*

Listen to your teacher or the audio. You will hear the sentences from the grammar box. Notice how the sound changes when would you *and* could you *are said at normal speed.*

Idiom Watch!
look up
check out

Extension

Write these questions on the board and ask learners to change them to polite questions.

1. When does the library open? *(Could you tell me when the library opens?)*
2. Where are the magazines? *(Would you tell me where the magazines are?)*
3. Why is the computer room closed? *(Could you tell me why the computer room is closed?)*
4. How can I get online? *(Would you tell me how I can get online?)*

Pronunciation Target

Play the audio or read the polite questions in the Grammar Talk box. Read the questions slowly and then again at normal speed.

Ask learners to practice saying the sentences with a reduced *would you* and *could you.*

 Assign Workbook pp. 55–56.

Idiom Watch!

Tell learners that these phrases are often used in libraries. Show meaning by using each phrase in a sentence.

Activity A

Encourage learners to do the following:

- Vary their questions.
- Ask as many people as possible.

Activity B

Have learners write sentences from the Class Chat in their notebooks.

Activity C

Answers

1. reference
2. due
3. renew
4. documentary
5. article
6. overdue
7. periodical
8. research

Task 2

Use Customizable Master 2 (3-Column Chart). Follow the suggestions on p. 7 for customizing and duplicating the master and distributing the copies. Make one copy for each learner.

One Step Down

If learners have difficulty thinking of examples for each topic, do the initial brainstorming as a class activity. Write learners' ideas on the board or an overhead transparency. Learners can then use the ideas to create their individual charts.

Extension

Arrange a field trip to a library. If this is not possible, have a local librarian come to class and discuss the services available.

Use Unit Master 60 (Grammar: Say Please) now or at any time during the rest of the unit.

Activity A Ask your classmates for help. Use "Would you/Could you please tell me" or "Would you/Could you please show me" in your questions.

Could you please show me where the pencil sharpener is?

Would you please tell me when the class ends?

Activity B **Group Chat Follow-Up** Look at the chart from your Group Chat. In your notebook, write what you learned.

There is a small library near the school. It is open on Sunday.

Activity C Fill in the blanks with words from the Vocabulary box on page 100. Compare your answers with your group.

1. I need to talk to the librarian. Could you tell me where the ________________ desk is?
2. Could you tell me when these books are ________________ ?
3. Can I ________________ these books over the phone?
4. I'd like to watch this ________________. Would you please show me how the VCR works?
5. Do you know if this magazine has an ________________ on ADHD?
6. These books are ________________ . Could you tell me how much I owe?
7. I'm looking for a magazine. Could you show me the ________________ index?
8. I'd like to do some ________________ on a medical problem. Could you please help me get started?

TASK 2: Narrow Down a Topic

Idiom Watch! *narrow down*

Talk to your group. Brainstorm three or more specific examples for each topic:

Biographies	Self-Help	Health	Politics
Personal Finance	History	Travel	Sports

Elvis Presley was a singer.

Choose three topics. In your notebook, make a chart like this. Under each topic, write three specific things within that topic that interest you. Tell your partner something you know about each example.

Topic: Biographies	Topic: Self-Help	Topic:
1. Elvis Presley	1. Losing weight	1.
2. Benjamin Franklin	2. Getting organized	2.
3. Nelson Mandela	3. Dealing with sorrow	3.

Lesson 3: Back to School

Follow the suggestions on p. 5 for talking about the title. Discuss the meaning of *go back* (return).

Question

- Ask learners about the enrollment process at your school.
- Find out how that process is different from other schools where they have enrolled.
- Discuss any problems with the process and ask learners to suggest improvements.

Attention Box

This vocabulary should be understood, but learners should not be expected to produce the words at this point.

Listening Tip

Ask learners about their experience with over-the-phone registration. Have they ever done it? Was their call answered by voice mail or a person in the registrar's office? Is over-the-phone registration common in their home countries? What other experiences have they had with automated telephone systems?

Read the tip aloud. Then play the audio or read the listening script on pp. 123–124.

Talk or Write

This exercise helps learners listen for sequencing.

Answers

4, 2, 1, 3, 6, 5

or

5, 2, 1, 3, 6, 4

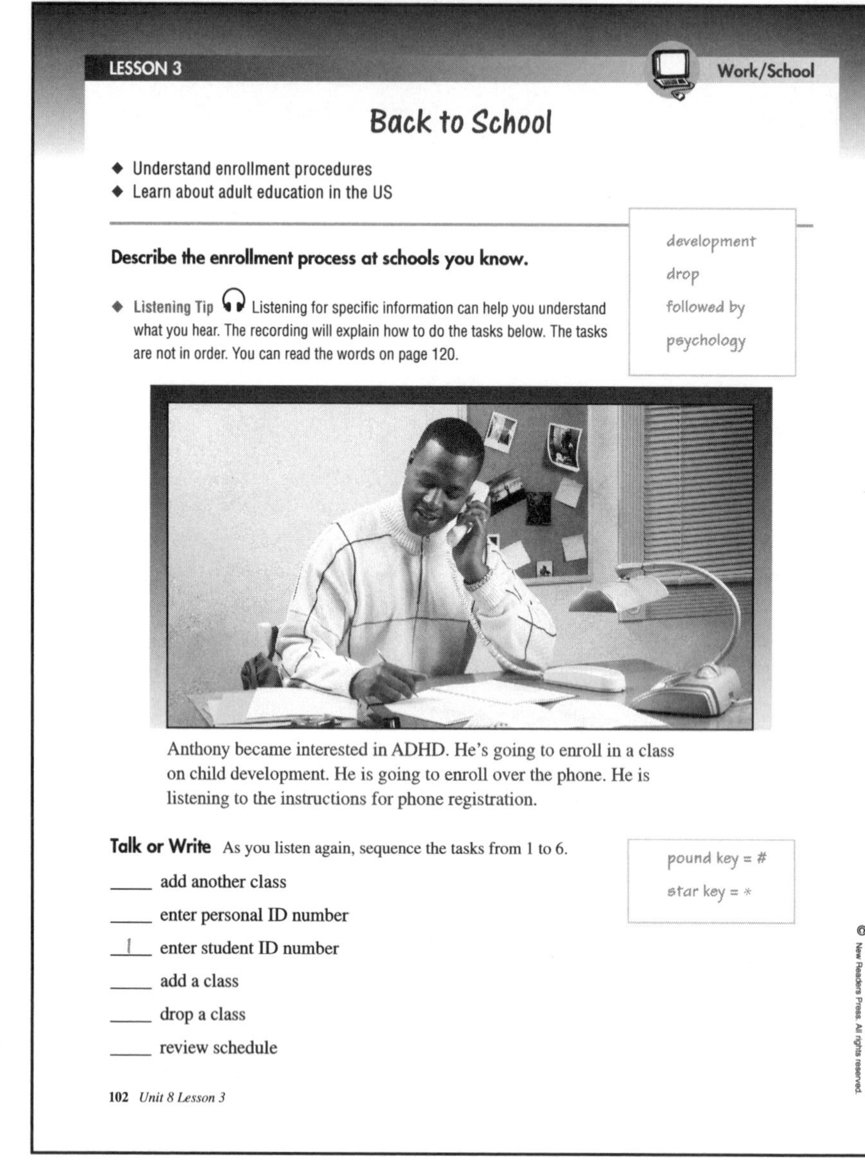

LESSON 3 Work/School

Back to School

- Understand enrollment procedures
- Learn about adult education in the US

development
drop
followed by
psychology

Describe the enrollment process at schools you know.

- Listening Tip Listening for specific information can help you understand what you hear. The recording will explain how to do the tasks below. The tasks are not in order. You can read the words on page 120.

Anthony became interested in ADHD. He's going to enroll in a class on child development. He is going to enroll over the phone. He is listening to the instructions for phone registration.

Talk or Write As you listen again, sequence the tasks from 1 to 6.

pound key = #
star key = *

____ add another class
____ enter personal ID number
__1__ enter student ID number
____ add a class
____ drop a class
____ review schedule

102 *Unit 8 Lesson 3*

© New Readers Press. All rights reserved.

Vocabulary

Follow the suggestions on p. 6 for introducing and reinforcing vocabulary words.

In the US

Before reading, discuss these questions to get learners thinking about the topic:

- What are some different kinds of schools for adults?
- Why do adults want to go back to school?

Compare Cultures

Use Customizable Master 1 (2-Column Chart). Follow the suggestions on p. 7 for customizing and duplicating the master and distributing the copies. Make a copy for each learner.

Alternatively, groups can discuss these questions without making the chart.

Activity A

Ask volunteers to tell about their future studying plans. Have learners give advice to the speakers about how they can achieve their goals.

Use Unit Masters 61 (Vocabulary: Mix and Match), 62 (Grammar: Review), and 63 (Game: Password) now or at any time during the rest of the unit.

 Assign Workbook pp. 57–58.

In the US Lifelong Learning

The United States offers many opportunities for lifelong learning. Many school districts have adult schools where adults can earn high-school diplomas or study computers and other work-related subjects. There are also many private schools where students can learn a particular skill, such as secretarial skills or electronics. There are community or city colleges in most areas. Students can get two-year degrees in many subjects or can take classes that prepare them for a college or university that offers four-year degrees and graduate degrees. These colleges and universities have higher tuition and more requirements for admission than other schools.

It is never too late for adults in the US to go back to school. Sometimes people are interested in learning about a specific subject. Sometimes people want more training so that they can earn more money on their job. Many people change careers and return to school to get a new degree. People who didn't go to college often decide later in life that they want to get a college degree. Sometimes retired people go back to school because they have always wanted to, but they've never had enough time or money before.

Vocabulary

Repeat these words after your teacher. Talk about their meanings. Write the words in your notebook. With a partner, write a sentence using each word.

- admission
- fee
- requirement
- tuition
- add
- drop
- earn

Compare Cultures Fill in a chart like this one with information about your home country. Then talk to your group about the educational system in your country.

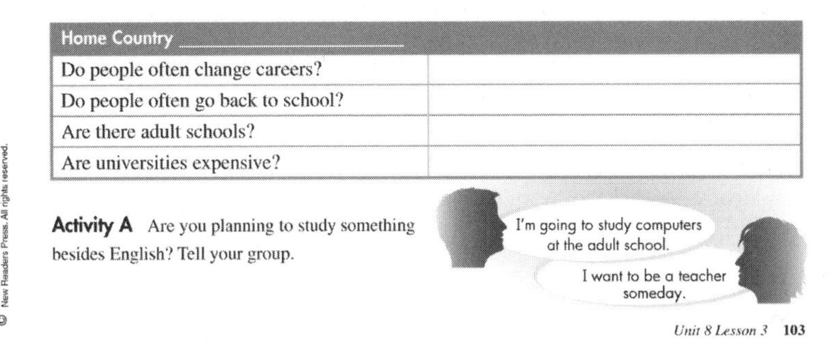

Home Country ______________	
Do people often change careers?	
Do people often go back to school?	
Are there adult schools?	
Are universities expensive?	

Activity A Are you planning to study something besides English? Tell your group.

Activity B

Ask learners to practice reducing *would you* and *could you* as they ask their questions.

Possible Questions

1. Could you please tell me how I can drop a class?
2. Could you please tell me how much the tuition is?
3. Could you please tell me what classes the adult school has?
4. Could you please tell me how much the fees are?
5. Could you please tell me what the requirements are for a diploma?
6. Could you please tell me what will happen if I drop a class late in the semester?
7. Could you please tell me what the admission requirements are?
8. Could you please tell me how I can enroll?

Extension

- Ask volunteers to write their questions on the board or an overhead transparency.
- Correct the questions together.
- Have learners suggest different possible answers for each question.

Task 3

To evaluate this task, use the Generic Assessment Master 9 (Written Communication Rubric).

Abbreviations and meanings:

PSY *psychology*
BUS *business*
ACCT *accounting*
HOME *home economics*
INDUS *industrial arts*
COMP *computers*
NURS *nursing*
DENT *dental technology*
MEDT *medical technology*
AUTO *automobile technology*
NUTR *nutrition*
HORT *horticulture*

Activity B Look at the following answers to questions someone might ask at a college admissions office. With your partner, practice asking the questions and giving the answers. Use the polite form for questions. If possible, use a word from the Vocabulary box on page 103 in each question.

1. During the first month, just tell the teacher you don't want to attend anymore.
2. It's $350 a semester.
3. You can learn computer repair and many other skills at the adult school.
4. You need to pay $25 with your application. You'll also need to pay for your books.
5. You can get your diploma by taking all of the units you need. It will take two years if you attend full-time.
6. You won't get a refund.
7. You need to have a high school diploma, and you need to live in the area.
8. Just turn in your application by May 10.

TASK 3: Write about a Topic of Interest

Look at the list of classes. Talk with your class about what the abbreviations mean. Choose which class is most interesting to you and explain why to your group. Tell which one you would least like to take and why.

Course No.	Course Name	Course No.	Course Name
PSY 321	Intro to Child Development	NURS 31	Intro to Nursing
BUS 101	Intro to Business	DENT 22	Intro to Dental Technology
ACCT 211	Intro to Accounting	MEDT 30	Intro to Medical Office
HOME 224	Intro to Fashion Design	AUTO 15	Intro to Auto Technology
INDUS 200	Intro to Carpentry	NUTR 12	Intro to Nutrition
COMP 102	Intro to Computers	HORT 50	Intro to Landscaping

Write a paragraph. In your topic sentence, tell which course is most interesting to you. Then explain why you think it's interesting. Think about these questions to help you get started. Are you interested in the subject for practical reasons? If so, how would learning about this subject be useful to you? Are you interested in the subject for personal reasons? If so, why would learning about this subject be meaningful to you?

Intro = the first course in the subject (introduction)

Ask learners what other classes might be offered in each subject area.

When learners are ready for final proofreading, refer them to the Writing Checklist on p. 125 of their books.

Review Unit Skills

See pp. 7–9 for suggestions on games and activities to review the vocabulary and grammar in this unit.

Unit 8 Project

Learners devise a research plan for an important topic.

Get Ready

- Have learners follow the example in their books for drawing a one-column chart. Divide the chart into four rows.
- Ask learners to copy the headings from the student book onto their charts.
- Suggest that learners refer to the work they did for Tasks 1, 2, and 3 to get ideas for their outline.

Do the Work

Encourage partners to help each other fill out their outlines.

- Ask learners to present their outlines to a partner from their group.
- Have partners share ideas about resources before they complete their outlines.

Present

Have the partners present their outlines to partners from a different group.

Writing Extension

For final proofreading, learners should refer to the Writing Checklist on p. 125 of their books.

Technology Extra

- Point out that most search engines have an "advanced search" link that explains how to narrow searches for that engine.
- Ask learners to share their "search term" experiences. Which search terms proved too broad? Which were too narrow?

Assign Workbook p. 59 (Check Your Progress).

Use Unit Master 64 (Unit 8 Checkup/Review) whenever you complete this unit.

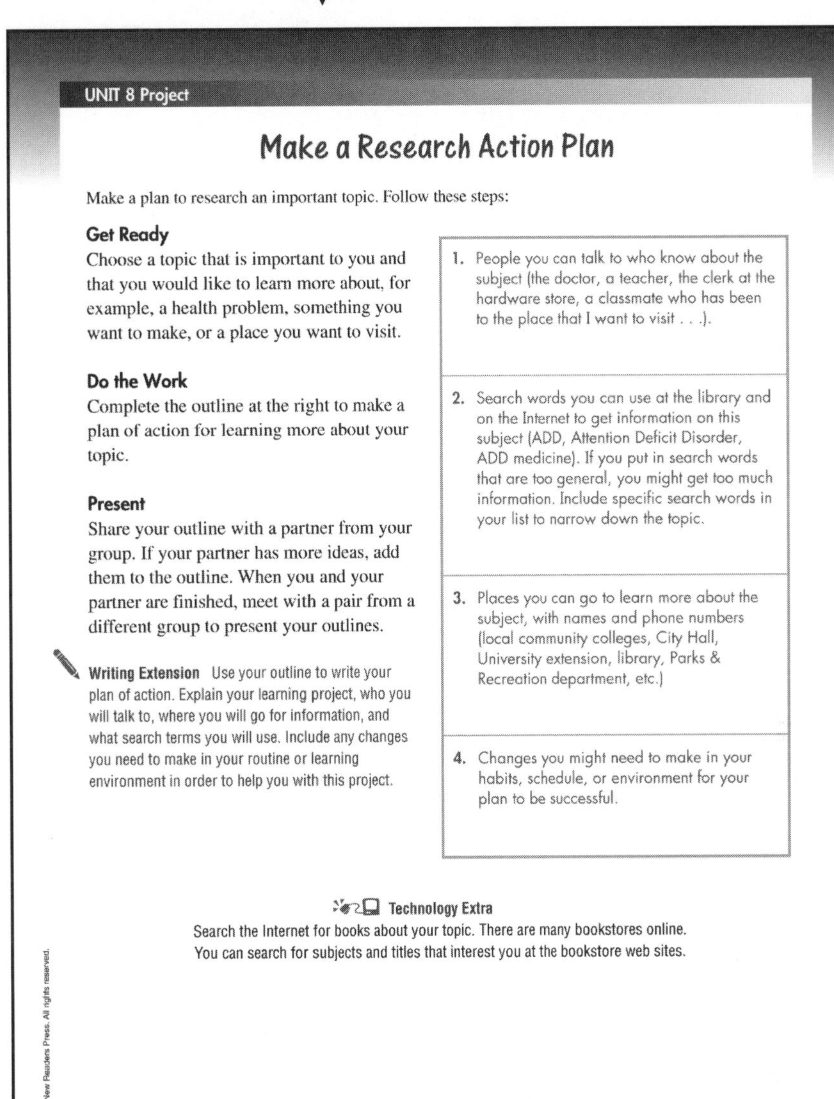

UNIT 8 Project

Make a Research Action Plan

Make a plan to research an important topic. Follow these steps:

Get Ready

Choose a topic that is important to you and that you would like to learn more about, for example, a health problem, something you want to make, or a place you want to visit.

Do the Work

Complete the outline at the right to make a plan of action for learning more about your topic.

Present

Share your outline with a partner from your group. If your partner has more ideas, add them to the outline. When you and your partner are finished, meet with a pair from a different group to present your outlines.

Writing Extension Use your outline to write your plan of action. Explain your learning project, who you will talk to, where you will go for information, and what search terms you will use. Include any changes you need to make in your routine or learning environment in order to help you with this project.

1. People you can talk to who know about the subject (the doctor, a teacher, the clerk at the hardware store, a classmate who has been to the place that I want to visit . . .).
2. Search words you can use at the library and on the Internet to get information on this subject (ADD, Attention Deficit Disorder, ADD medicine). If you put in search words that are too general, you might get too much information. Include specific search words in your list to narrow down the topic.
3. Places you can go to learn more about the subject, with names and phone numbers (local community colleges, City Hall, University extension, library, Parks & Recreation department, etc.)
4. Changes you might need to make in your habits, schedule, or environment for your plan to be successful.

Technology Extra

Search the Internet for books about your topic. There are many bookstores online. You can search for subjects and titles that interest you at the bookstore web sites.

Unit 9: Keeping Up with the Times

Materials for the Unit

- Poster paper
- Customizable Masters 1, 2, and 3
- Generic Assessment Masters 8, 10, and 11
- Unit Masters 65–69

Keeping Up with the Times

Follow the suggestions on p. 5 for talking about the title.

- Discuss the meaning of the word *times.* One meaning might be "modern life" or "now" (e.g., These are difficult *times.*).
- Discuss the meaning of the words *keep up with.* One meaning might be "stay equal with."
- Ask learners what they think the idiom *keep up with the times* might mean. One meaning might be to "stay current with modern life."
- Compare *keep up with the times* to *behind the times* (outdated; not up with the times). Ask learners when they might use this expression.

Photo

Follow the suggestions on p. 4 for talking about the photo. Then read the questions below the arrow.

Think and Talk

Write learners' answers on the board or an overhead transparency.

What's Your Opinion?

Consider these ideas in discussing responses to change:

- Changes that hurt you or the people you love are OK to avoid.
- People have no control over some changes, but they can decide whether to accept or reject those changes.
- Avoiding all change can make life very difficult.

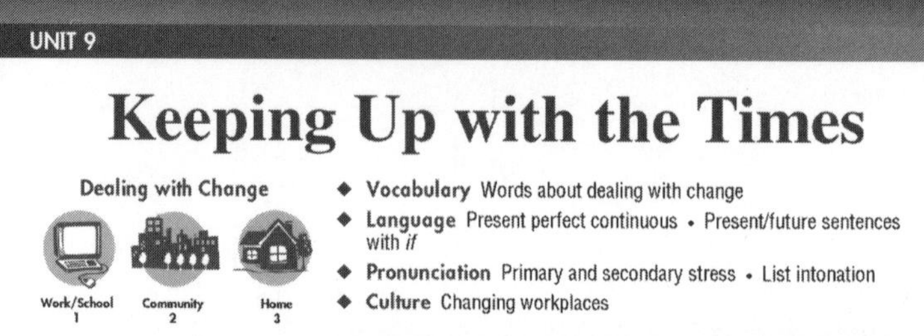

UNIT 9

Keeping Up with the Times

Dealing with Change

Work/School 1 · Community 2 · Home 3

- **Vocabulary** Words about dealing with change
- **Language** Present perfect continuous • Present/future sentences with *if*
- **Pronunciation** Primary and secondary stress • List intonation
- **Culture** Changing workplaces

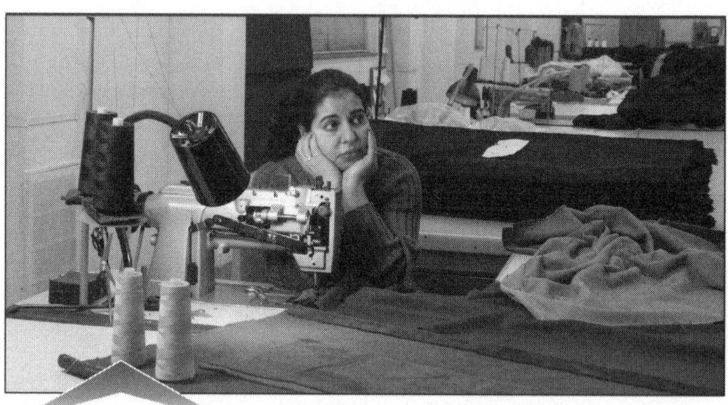

When was the last time you had to learn something new? How did you feel?

Rania has worked at the sewing factory for 10 years. Her company is going to make some changes. She is concerned about the changes at her workplace.

Think and Talk

1. What do you see in the photograph?
2. What changes at work do you think Rania is concerned about?
3. Why do you think she is concerned?
4. Are there changes happening in your life that you are concerned about or happy about? Explain your answer.

What's Your Opinion? Many people are afraid of or nervous about changes that happen in their lives. They'll do anything to avoid change. Give an example of when it's OK to avoid change and when it's important to accept change.

106 *Unit 9*

Extension

Discuss the following technology-related question with the learners:

Sometimes people are afraid of new technology. If employees have trouble learning a new skill, should they be fired? If so, how would you defend firing them? If not, what would you do about their lack of skill?

Vocabulary

Follow the suggestions on p. 6 for introducing and reinforcing the vocabulary words.

Extension

Many of these vocabulary words can be used to talk about change.

- Ask learners to think about some of the changes they talked about in What's Your Opinion.
- Have them use the vocabulary words to write sentences about the changes.

Idiom Watch!

- Discuss the meaning of the idiom *look forward to.* One meaning might be "to be eager or excited about something in the future" (e.g., "I'm *looking forward to* my daughter's graduation.") Note that *look forward to* refers to something that is actually going to happen; it is not the same as *hope for.*
- Discuss the meaning of the expression *deal with.* One meaning might be "to take action about"; another might be "to accept" (e.g., She is trying to *deal with* her husband's illness.).

Dictation

Play the audio or read the listening script below. Have learners write the sentences they hear. After they correct the sentences, they can discuss them with their partners.

Listening Script/Answers

Listen. Write the sentences that you hear.

1. I resist change when I'm afraid.
2. I need to confront my fear of speaking English.
3. I don't like to deal with my negative feelings.
4. I cope well with difficult changes.
5. I can adapt to most changes easily.
6. If we overcome our fear of change, we will be happier.
7. We need to discuss the pros and cons.
8. I'm looking forward to something that will happen soon.

Dictation Listen to your teacher or the audio. You will hear sentences about changes. Write the sentences. When you finish, correct them with the class. Talk about the sentences with your partner. Do you agree with them? Are they true for you?

Gather Your Thoughts In your group, brainstorm examples of changes that happen in people's lives. Categorize them in a chart like the one below. Decide which kind of change in each category would be the most difficult to deal with. Put a check by that example.

Personal/Home	School	Workplace	Community
get engaged	graduate	new boss	bank closes

Make a class list of changes from each group's chart. Copy the list in your notebook. You will use the ideas from *School* and *Workplace* for your Lesson 1 Group Chat.

What's the Problem? Look at the examples of life changes in the class chart. Why are these changes sometimes difficult? How can people deal with each change? Think or talk with a partner.

Setting Goals Think about how you deal with change in your life. Which goals are most important to you? Rank them from 1 (most important) to 6.

_____ **a.** discuss pros and cons
_____ **b.** explain how to use something
_____ **c.** describe the effects of technology
_____ **d.** discuss my feelings about different kinds of changes
_____ **e.** give a presentation
_____ **f.** another goal: ______________________________

Which was the most important goal for your class? Tally your answers. Talk about your most important goals.

Vocabulary

Repeat these words after your teacher. Talk about their meanings. Write the words in your notebook. With a partner, write a sentence using each word.

pros and cons
adapt
confront
cope
overcome
react/reaction
resist

Idiom Watch!
keep up with the times
look forward to
deal with

Gather Your Thoughts

Use Customizable Master 3 (4-Column Chart). Follow the suggestions on p. 7 for customizing and duplicating the master and distributing the copies.

Have learners work with their groups to brainstorm examples of change. Consider these ideas:

- Moving
- Getting married
- Breaking up or getting divorced
- Going away to college
- New job or work situation
- Having children
- Making new friends
- Death of a loved one

What's the Problem?

Follow the suggestions on p. 5 for identifying and analyzing problems.

Talk with learners about personality as a factor in how people deal with change.

Setting Goals

Follow the suggestions on p. 5 for setting goals.

Lesson 1: Go with the Flow

Follow the suggestions on p. 5 for talking about the title.

- Discuss the meaning of the word *flow* (a steady movement).
- Ask learners what they think the idiom *go with the flow* might mean. One definition might be to "not resist what is happening; to go along with what the majority of people are doing."

Question

Write the headings below next to each other on the board or an overhead transparency:

Think about Pros and Cons

Make Quick Decisions

- Separate the headings by drawing a vertical line.
- Ask learners what kinds of changes they would think carefully about and what kinds they would not. List a few examples under each heading.
- Ask learners to follow the example on the board to make their own lists.
- Have learners share their ideas with their groups and the class.

Attention Box

This vocabulary should be understood, but learners should not be expected to produce the words at this point.

- Note the prefix *out-* in *outdated* and *outweigh.* Explain that *outdated* means "no longer current" and that *outweigh* means "to be more important than something else."
- Point out that in English there are many verbs beginning with *out-* that suggest one thing is better than another (e.g., *outrun, outthink, outdo, outsmart*).

Reading Tip

- Have learners read the memo twice, first for comprehension, and then to look for the pros and cons.

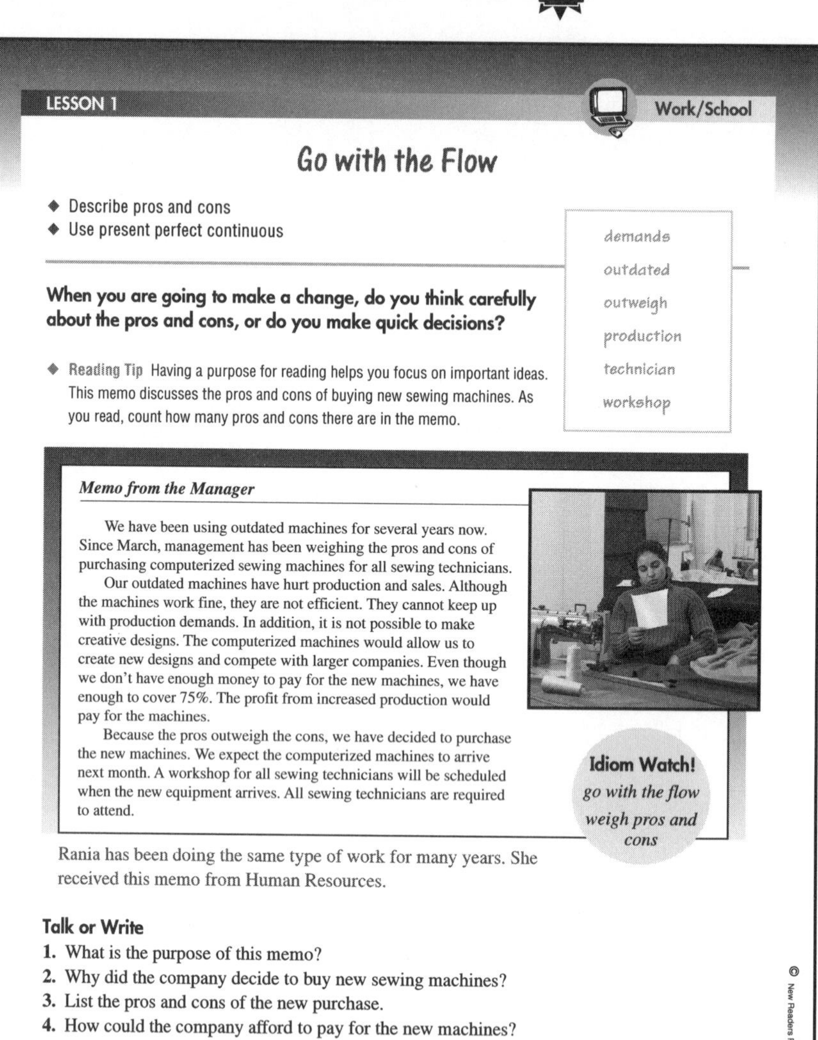

LESSON 1 Work/School

Go with the Flow

- Describe pros and cons
- Use present perfect continuous

demands
outdated
outweigh
production
technician
workshop

When you are going to make a change, do you think carefully about the pros and cons, or do you make quick decisions?

Reading Tip Having a purpose for reading helps you focus on important ideas. This memo discusses the pros and cons of buying new sewing machines. As you read, count how many pros and cons there are in the memo.

Memo from the Manager

We have been using outdated machines for several years now. Since March, management has been weighing the pros and cons of purchasing computerized sewing machines for all sewing technicians.

Our outdated machines have hurt production and sales. Although the machines work fine, they are not efficient. They cannot keep up with production demands. In addition, it is not possible to make creative designs. The computerized machines would allow us to create new designs and compete with larger companies. Even though we don't have enough money to pay for the new machines, we have enough to cover 75%. The profit from increased production would pay for the machines.

Because the pros outweigh the cons, we have decided to purchase the new machines. We expect the computerized machines to arrive next month. A workshop for all sewing technicians will be scheduled when the new equipment arrives. All sewing technicians are required to attend.

Idiom Watch!
go with the flow
weigh pros and cons

Rania has been doing the same type of work for many years. She received this memo from Human Resources.

Talk or Write

1. What is the purpose of this memo?
2. Why did the company decide to buy new sewing machines?
3. List the pros and cons of the new purchase.
4. How could the company afford to pay for the new machines?
5. Should the company ask employees to learn the new machines?

108 *Unit 9 Lesson 1*

- Ask them to underline the pros and cons in different colors.

Talk or Write

This exercise helps learners discover an author's purpose.

Answers

1. The purpose of this memo is to inform employees about the upcoming purchase of new sewing machines and to notify them about the training workshop.
2. The company decided to buy new sewing machines because they wanted updated equipment to increase production and sales.
3. *Pros:* replace outdated machines; increase production and sales; create new designs; produce better products faster; compete with large companies
   Cons: old machines still work; not enough money to pay for all machines
4. The company has enough funds to pay 75 percent and will use the profit from increased production to cover the remaining 25 percent.
5. Answers will vary.

Vocabulary

Follow the suggestions on p. 6 for introducing and reinforcing vocabulary words.

Point out that the noun *effect* and the verb *affect* are very similar in pronunciation and meaning:

- *effect:* an influence or an impact
- *affect:* to change or to influence

<u>One Step Up</u>

Write sample sentences like the ones below on the board or an overhead transparency. Have learners change each sentence that contains *effect* to a similar sentence using *affect,* and vice versa.

- The new machines had a positive effect on production this year.
  The new machines affected production in a positive way this year.
- Very hot weather affects how people feel.
  Very hot weather has an effect on how people feel.

Group Chat

Use Customizable Master 1 (2-Column Chart). Follow the suggestions on p. 7 for customizing and duplicating the master and distributing the copies. Make a copy for each group.

- After groups complete their charts, compile a class list of the effects the changes have had on learners.
- Ask learners to categorize the effects as positive or negative.

Grammar Talk

Follow the suggestions on p. 6 for introducing the grammar point.

Point out that the negative form of the verb indicates that the action has not been happening in the past and is not happening now.

<u>Answers</u>

- has been sewing
- have been using
- hasn't been updating
- has been feeling

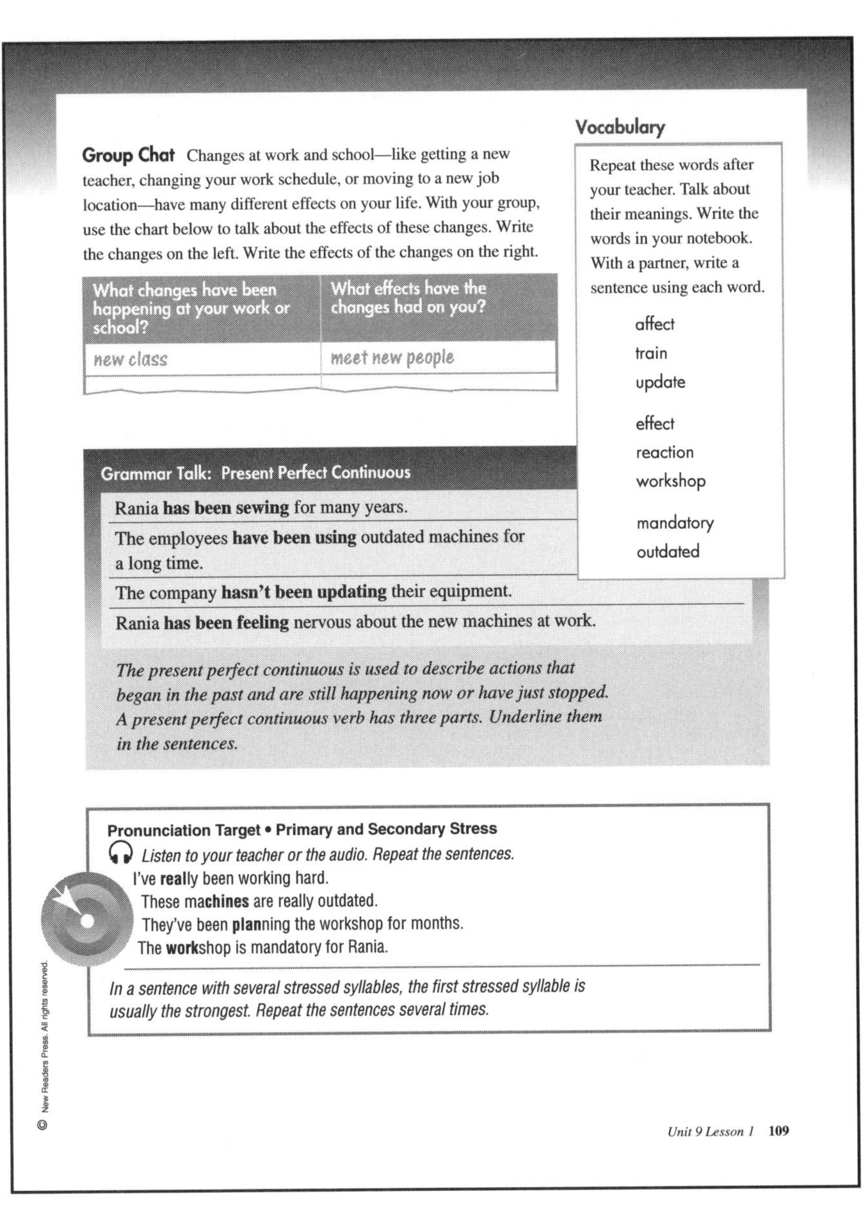

Group Chat Changes at work and school—like getting a new teacher, changing your work schedule, or moving to a new job location—have many different effects on your life. With your group, use the chart below to talk about the effects of these changes. Write the changes on the left. Write the effects of the changes on the right.

What changes have been happening at your work or school?	What effects have the changes had on you?
new class	meet new people

Vocabulary

Repeat these words after your teacher. Talk about their meanings. Write the words in your notebook. With a partner, write a sentence using each word.

affect
train
update

effect
reaction
workshop

mandatory
outdated

Grammar Talk: Present Perfect Continuous

Rania **has been sewing** for many years.
The employees **have been using** outdated machines for a long time.
The company **hasn't been updating** their equipment.
Rania **has been feeling** nervous about the new machines at work.

The present perfect continuous is used to describe actions that began in the past and are still happening now or have just stopped. A present perfect continuous verb has three parts. Underline them in the sentences.

Pronunciation Target • Primary and Secondary Stress

Listen to your teacher or the audio. Repeat the sentences.

I've **real**ly been working hard.
These ma**chines** are really outdated.
They've been **plan**ning the workshop for months.
The **work**shop is mandatory for Rania.

In a sentence with several stressed syllables, the first stressed syllable is usually the strongest. Repeat the sentences several times.

Pronunciation Target

Play the audio or read the listening script below.

- Have learners copy the sentences into their notebooks.
- Ask them to underline the primary stress and circle the secondary stress(es) in each sentence.

<u>Listening Script</u>

1. I've <u>re</u>ally been (work)ing hard.
2. These ma<u>chines</u> are (real)ly out(dat)ed.
3. They've been <u>plan</u>ning the (work)shop for (months).
4. The <u>work</u>shop is (man)datory for (Ran)ia.

Use Unit Master 65 (Song: I've Been Working on the Railroad) now or at any time during the rest of the unit.

Assign Workbook pp. 60–61.

Activity A

Remind learners to change the verb *have* to third person singular *(has)* when they talk about their partner.

Activity B

Play the audio or read the listening script below.

Listening Script/Answers

Listen. Write the sentences that you hear. Then, with a partner, write *true* or *false* after each sentence. Correct the false sentences with other learners.

1. Rania has been looking forward to the workshop. *(F)*
2. Rania has been working for the same company for many years. *(T)*
3. Rania's company is using outdated equipment. *(T)*
4. Rania's company has been training employees with new sewing machines. *(F)*
5. The training on the new machines is mandatory. *(T)*

Activity C

Possible Answers

1. *Pros:* be the leader; make the decisions; get higher pay

   Cons: more pressure; employees talk about you; lonely at the top
2. *Pros:* new people; new skills

   Cons: anxiety; unfamiliar with the job responsibilities
3. *Pros:* learn something new; might lead to a better job

   Cons: some schools expensive; takes time away from family
4. *Pros:* earn more money; save money toward a major purchase

   Cons: more time away from home; tired

Activity D

One Step Up

Have learners use their Activity D sentences to write more naturally. Ask them to write new sentences

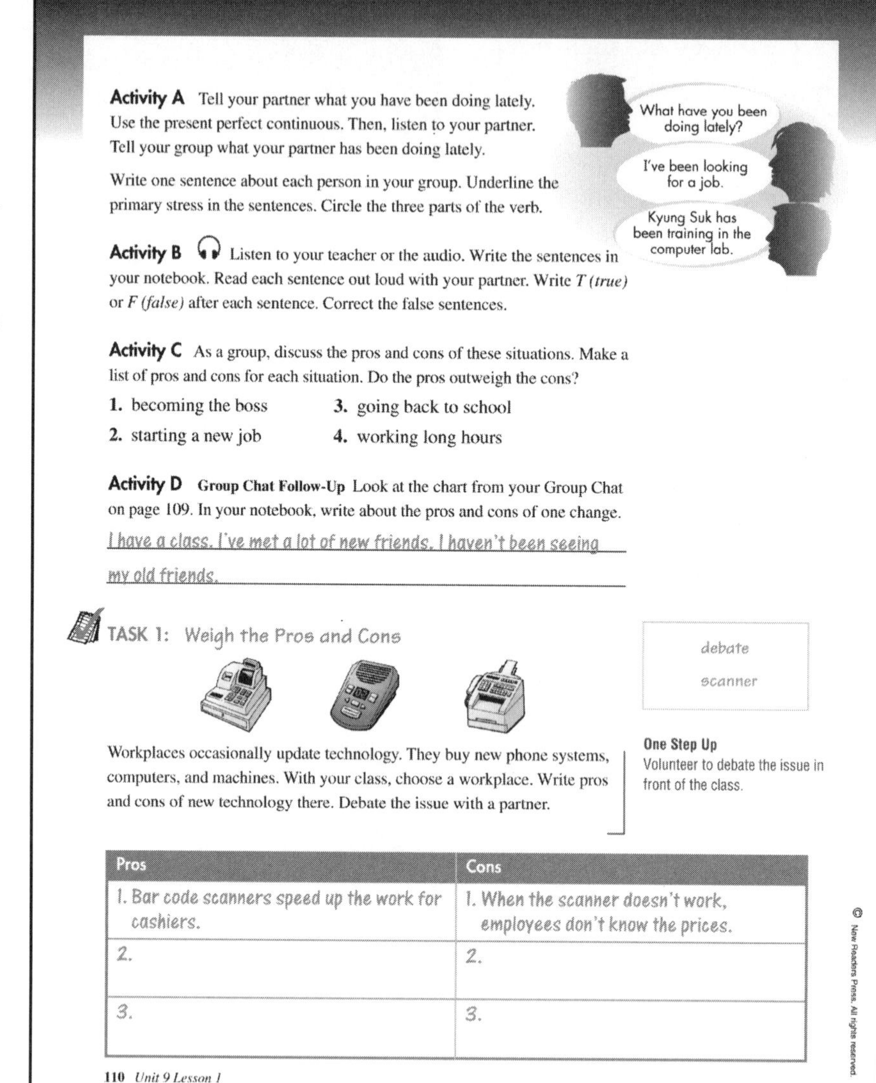

Activity A Tell your partner what you have been doing lately. Use the present perfect continuous. Then, listen to your partner. Tell your group what your partner has been doing lately.

Write one sentence about each person in your group. Underline the primary stress in the sentences. Circle the three parts of the verb.

Activity B Listen to your teacher or the audio. Write the sentences in your notebook. Read each sentence out loud with your partner. Write *T (true)* or *F (false)* after each sentence. Correct the false sentences.

Activity C As a group, discuss the pros and cons of these situations. Make a list of pros and cons for each situation. Do the pros outweigh the cons?

1. becoming the boss
2. starting a new job
3. going back to school
4. working long hours

Activity D **Group Chat Follow-Up** Look at the chart from your Group Chat on page 109. In your notebook, write about the pros and cons of one change.

I have a class. I've met a lot of new friends. I haven't been seeing my old friends.

TASK 1: Weigh the Pros and Cons

debate

scanner

Workplaces occasionally update technology. They buy new phone systems, computers, and machines. With your class, choose a workplace. Write pros and cons of new technology there. Debate the issue with a partner.

One Step Up
Volunteer to debate the issue in front of the class.

Pros	Cons
1. Bar code scanners speed up the work for cashiers.	1. When the scanner doesn't work, employees don't know the prices.
2.	2.
3.	3.

110 *Unit 9 Lesson 1*

modeled on the ones below, which build on the example in their book.

I'm really excited because I have a new class. I've met a lot of new friends. The only bad thing is that I haven't been seeing my old friends.

Attention Box

- To do Task 1, learners must understand the word *debate.* Explain that when two people *debate,* they present differing views on a topic or question.
- The *scanner* mentioned in the sample chart is used by a cashier. It reads the bar codes on labels and enters prices electronically into the cash register.

Task 1

Tell learners to copy the chart in the student book into their notebooks.

Assessment

To use this task as a formal evaluation, listen to each pair as they debate. Use Generic Assessment Master 8 (Oral Communication Rubric) to evaluate the debate.

One Step Up

Have learners write a few sentences telling who they think won each debate and why.

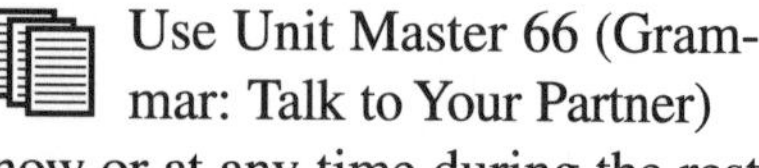

Use Unit Master 66 (Grammar: Talk to Your Partner) now or at any time during the rest of the unit.

Lesson 2: Learn New Technology

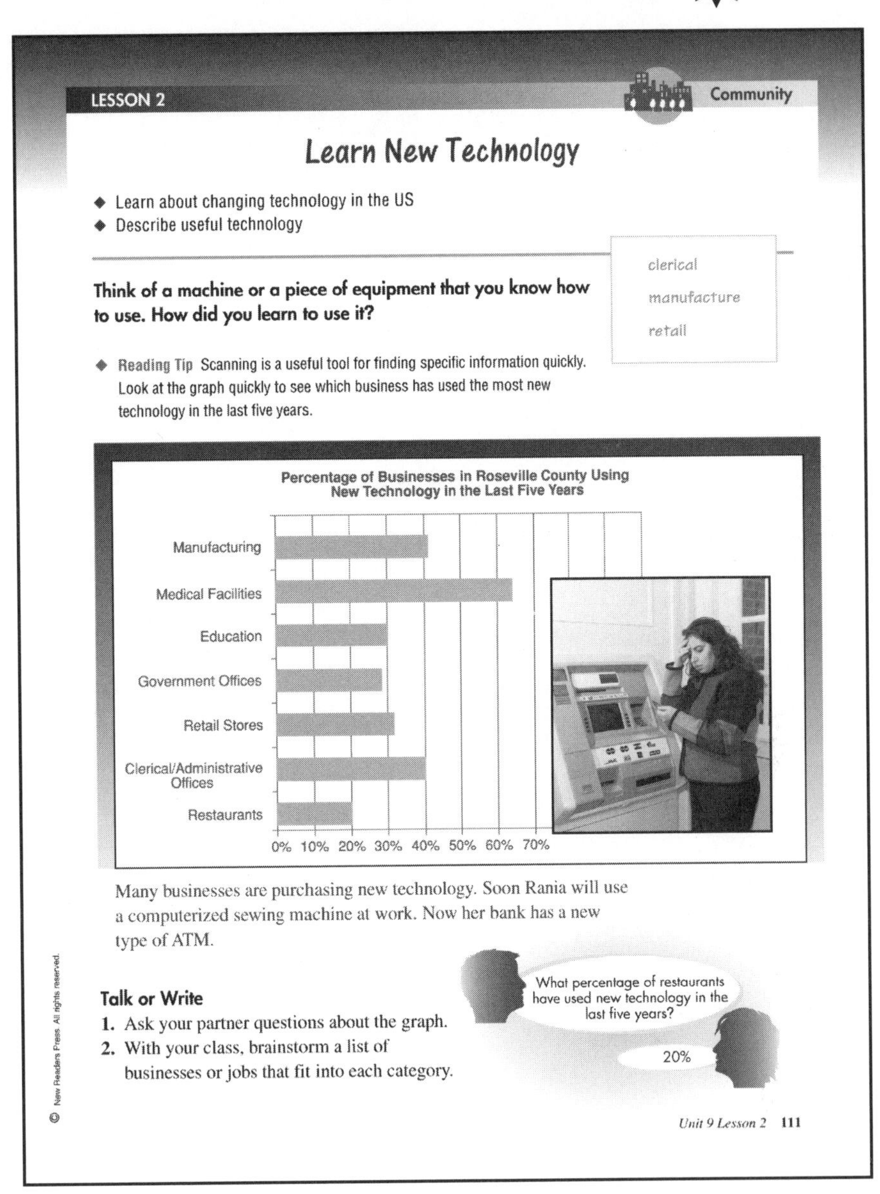
LESSON 2

Community

Learn New Technology

- Learn about changing technology in the US
- Describe useful technology

clerical
manufacture
retail

Think of a machine or a piece of equipment that you know how to use. How did you learn to use it?

- Reading Tip Scanning is a useful tool for finding specific information quickly. Look at the graph quickly to see which business has used the most new technology in the last five years.

Many businesses are purchasing new technology. Soon Rania will use a computerized sewing machine at work. Now her bank has a new type of ATM.

Talk or Write

1. Ask your partner questions about the graph.
2. With your class, brainstorm a list of businesses or jobs that fit into each category.

Follow the suggestions on p. 5 for talking about the title.

Question

Because many learners might have similar answers, have learners first answer this question in their groups. Then ask the groups to summarize their answers for the class.

Attention Box

This vocabulary should be understood, but learners should not be expected to produce the words at this point.

Reading Tip

Read the tip aloud. Then have learners complete the exercise.

Answer
medical facilities

Talk or Write

This exercise helps learners interpret a graph.

Possible Answers to Question 2

Restaurants: owner, manager, hostess, waiter/waitress or server, busboy or busgirl, cashier, cook, prep-cook, baker

Clerical/Administrative Offices: Chief Executive Officer (CEO), president, vice president, supervisor, manager, director, accountant, secretary, receptionist

Retail Stores: owner, manager, clerk, salesperson, cashier, stockperson, custodian

Government Offices:

USPS *US Postal Service*
DSS *Department of Social Services*
DOT *Department of Transportation*
FAA *Federal Aviation Administration*
FDA *Food and Drug Administration*
DEA *Drug Enforcement Agency*
ATF *Alcohol, Tobacco, and Firearms*
FBI *Federal Bureau of Investigation*
CIA *Central Intelligence Agency*
SSA *Social Security Administration*
IRS *Internal Revenue Service*
BLM *Bureau of Land Management*
EPA *Environmental Protection Agency*
HUD *Housing and Urban Development*

Education: superintendent, principal, vice principal or assistant principal, teacher, teacher's aide, counselor, secretary, nurse, computer technician, librarian

Medical Facilities: doctor, nurse, lab tech, physical therapist, receptionist, nurse practitioner, secretary, clerk, custodian, food server, cashier, administrative workers

Manufacturing: superintendent, supervisor, engineer, planner, manager, assembler, welder, machinist, mechanic, clerical worker

Vocabulary

Follow the suggestions on p. 6 for introducing and reinforcing vocabulary words.

Idiom Watch!

Introduce the business-related idioms *red tape* and *lay off:*

- Discuss the meaning of *red tape.* One meaning might be "official procedures and complex paperwork that often result in delay or inaction" (e.g., Her visa application has been delayed by *red tape.*). Note that the term *red tape* comes from the red tape once used to tie up legal documents to keep them together as they passed from one office to another.
- Discuss the meaning of *lay off.* One meaning might be "to dismiss workers from their jobs, sometimes temporarily" (e.g., Our factory is going to *lay off* 20 workers next week.).

In the US

Before reading, discuss these questions to get learners thinking about the topic:

- How do you respond to change?
- Have you ever had to move because of your job?
- Have changes in technology ever affected your job? What did you do?

Compare Cultures

Use Customizable Master 2 (3-Column Chart). Write in the headings *Discussion Questions, Home Country,* and *US* before copying the master for each learner.

- Ask learners to write the questions from the student book in the first column.
- Have learners individually fill in the answers for their home countries and then work with their groups to fill in the answers for the US.

In the US A Flexible Economy

Being flexible means being willing to accept change. Economic change is very common in the US, so people often say that the US has a flexible economy. One change that affects the economy is that people move a lot. In the US, most people move several times in their lives. People often move because they want to change jobs. They are willing to move where the work is. Even when people don't move to a new place, they often change jobs.

In a flexible economy, people can start new businesses easily. If you have money, you can start a small business in the US with very little red tape. A lot of small businesses fail, but people in the US are not ashamed of having a business that fails. Many people start several businesses before they are successful.

One result of all this flexibility is that employers expect employees to keep up with changes in technology. Most workers are not protected by *seniority,* the number of years on the job, and they must be willing to learn and change with the company if they want to keep their jobs. Even nontechnical employees have been learning how to use new technology. In many cases, it makes their jobs much easier. For example, more and more companies are using bar code scanning technology for shopping and identification. Office computers are connected to networks that make it easier for people to communicate with each other. Waiters and waitresses use touch-screen displays for turning in their orders to the kitchen. Because new technology is appearing in almost every workplace, it has become more and more important to keep up with the times.

Vocabulary

Repeat these words after your teacher. Talk about their meanings. Write the words in your notebook. With a partner, write a sentence using each word.

bar code
display
network
scanning
touch screen

Idiom Watch!
red tape
lay off

Compare Cultures Compare the economy of your home country with the economy of the US by discussing these questions with your group.

- How often do people move?
- Is it common to move far away from the family?
- Is it easy for employers to lay off or fire employees?
- Is it easy or difficult to start a new business?
- Is there a lot of new technology?

One Step Up
In groups, discuss the pros and cons of the flexibility in the US economy. Write as many pros and cons as you can.

- As a large group, compare answers from the different smaller groups.

One Step Up

Possible Answers

Pros: easy to start new business; workers protected by rules and regulations; good system of worker benefits; wide access to information; technological advancement makes work easier

Cons: business can easily fail; markets are very competitive; upgrading technology is expensive; workers can get laid off; workers leave jobs often to find better jobs; workers cannot always keep up with latest technology

Assign Workbook pp. 62–63.

Activity A

Possible Items for Class List

Microwave oven, blender, coffee maker, alarm clock, cell phone, calculator, personal digital assistant, typewriter, computer, Internet, adding machine, film camera, video camera, digital camera, overhead projector, cassette recorder, CD player, video game system, VCR, DVD, stereo system, sewing machine

Activity B

Use Customizable Master 1 (2-Column Chart) for this activity. Write in the headings shown in the student book before copying the master for each learner. Then do the following:

- Make sure learners understand the term *lately* (recently).
- During the class discussion, learners can copy sentences from the board into their charts.
- Practice reading the sentences as a class. Then ask learners to practice reading them in pairs.

Task 2

- After learners finish the group task, have them brainstorm new improvements they would like to see in technology.
- Write their ideas on the board or an overhead transparency under the heading *Future Technology.*
- As an enhancement, have learners use the Internet to research the latest technology.

One Step Up

- Draw a two-column chart on the board or an overhead transparency.
- Write the headings *Disappeared* and *Unaffected* at the top of the chart.
- Write the learners' ideas under the appropriate heading.

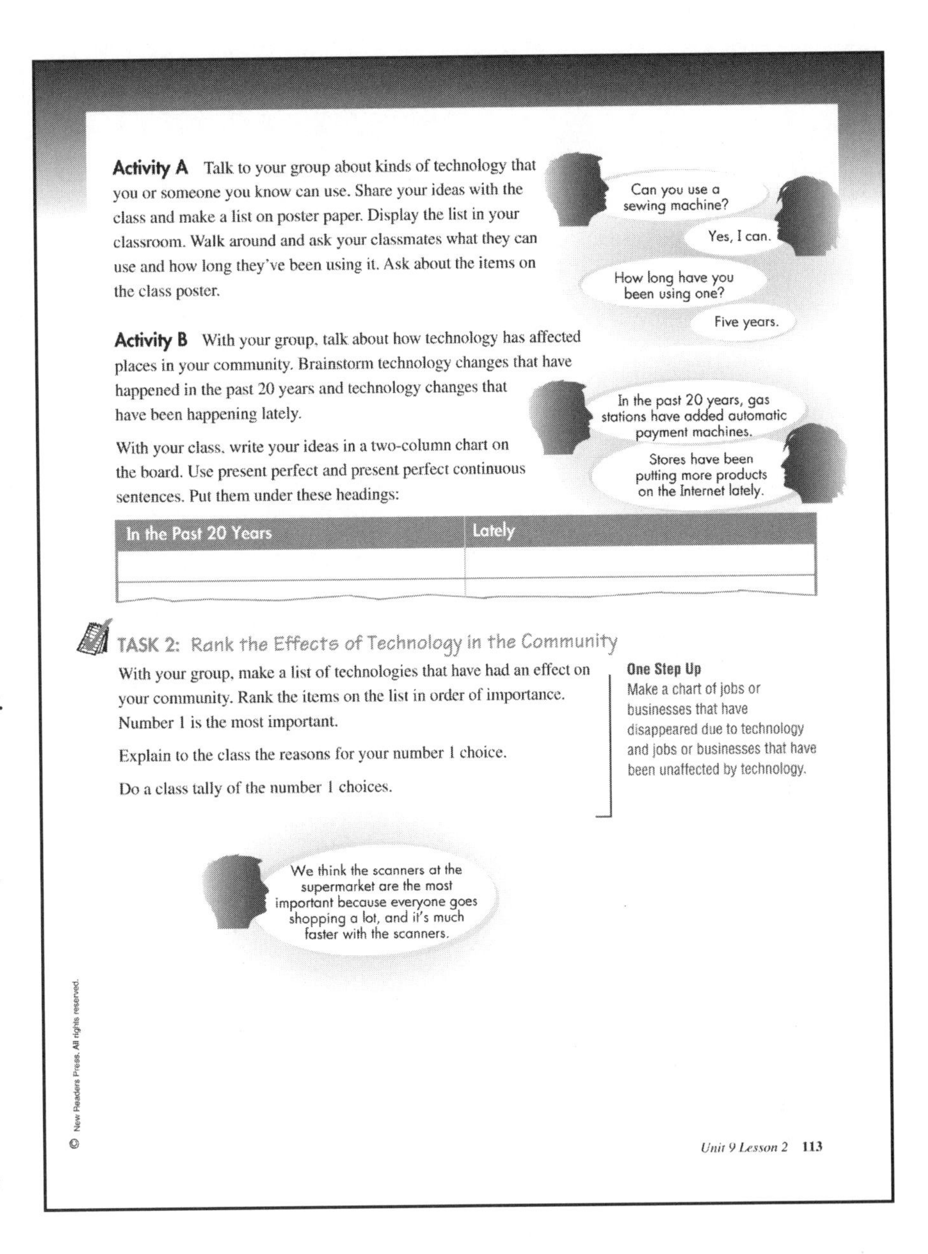

Activity A Talk to your group about kinds of technology that you or someone you know can use. Share your ideas with the class and make a list on poster paper. Display the list in your classroom. Walk around and ask your classmates what they can use and how long they've been using it. Ask about the items on the class poster.

Activity B With your group, talk about how technology has affected places in your community. Brainstorm technology changes that have happened in the past 20 years and technology changes that have been happening lately.

With your class, write your ideas in a two-column chart on the board. Use present perfect and present perfect continuous sentences. Put them under these headings:

In the Past 20 Years	Lately

TASK 2: Rank the Effects of Technology in the Community

With your group, make a list of technologies that have had an effect on your community. Rank the items on the list in order of importance. Number 1 is the most important.

Explain to the class the reasons for your number 1 choice.

Do a class tally of the number 1 choices.

One Step Up
Make a chart of jobs or businesses that have disappeared due to technology and jobs or businesses that have been unaffected by technology.

Unit 9 Lesson 2 113

Lesson 3: Three Cheers! WWW

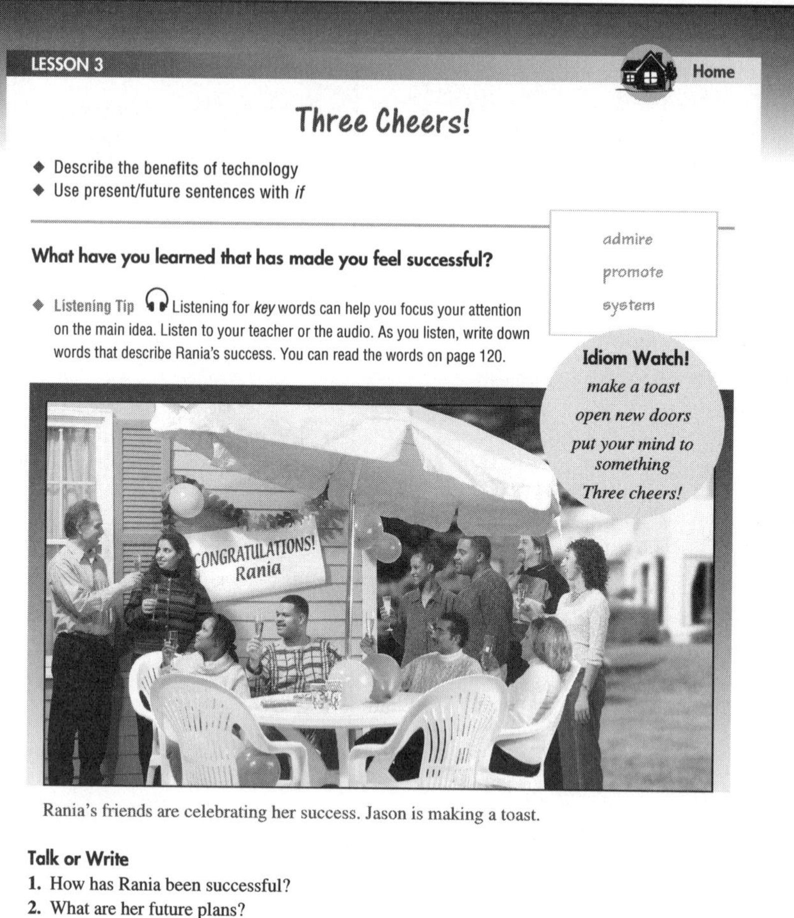
LESSON 3

Home

Three Cheers!

- Describe the benefits of technology
- Use present/future sentences with *if*

admire
promote
system

What have you learned that has made you feel successful?

- Listening Tip Listening for *key* words can help you focus your attention on the main idea. Listen to your teacher or the audio. As you listen, write down words that describe Rania's success. You can read the words on page 120.

Idiom Watch!
make a toast
open new doors
put your mind to something
Three cheers!

Rania's friends are celebrating her success. Jason is making a toast.

Talk or Write

1. How has Rania been successful?
2. What are her future plans?
3. Why does Jason admire Rania?
4. What doors were opened for Rania?
5. What kind of person is Rania? Think of three adjectives to describe her.

What's Your Opinion? Some people are jealous when other people succeed. Can you explain why? How can people avoid being jealous?

114 *Unit 9 Lesson 3*

Follow the suggestions on p. 5 for talking about the title.

- Explain that the expression *Cheers!* is usually a toast to good health. At special dinners when drinks are poured, people either raise their glasses or lightly touch them together and say, "Cheers!" If they are celebrating something in particular, they might say, "Here's to your job promotion!" or, "Three cheers for _______!"
- Ask learners to share the equivalent of "Cheers!" in their languages.

Question

Write learners' answers on the board or an overhead transparency.

Attention Box

This vocabulary should be understood, but learners should not be expected to produce the words at this point.

Idiom Watch!

Discuss the meaning of the following expressions:

- *Make a toast* (to call for someone's good health or honor, most commonly with a drink in hand). Point out that if the article *a* is not included, the meaning changes *(make toast).*
- *Open new doors* (create new opportunities)
- *Put your mind to something* (work hard at something)
- *Three cheers!* (Congratulations!)

Listening Tip

Read the tip aloud. Then play the audio or read the listening script on p. 124.

Possible Answers

accepting challenges, positive effect, learned, promoted, opportunities for growth and for discovering, accepted change, learning a new skill, opened new doors, manager, starting her own business, sell on the internet, wonderful job

Talk or Write

This exercise helps learners listen for main ideas.

Answers

1. Rania has been successful by accepting changes and challenges, dealing with her fears, learning a difficult computerized sewing system, and getting promoted to manager.
2. Rania's future plans are to start her own business making clothing and selling it on the Internet.
3. Jason admires Rania for overcoming her fears and showing people that anything is possible if you work hard.
4. The doors that were opened for Rania were becoming manager and the possibility of starting her own business.
5. Answers may vary. Rania is courageous, hard-working, and dedicated.

What's Your Opinion?

The words *jealous* and *envious* are sometimes synonymous (wanting to have what someone else has).

Vocabulary

Follow the suggestions on p. 6 for introducing and reinforcing vocabulary words.

Idiom Watch!

Discuss the meaning of the expression *figure out* (to solve a problem or to come to understand).

Group Chat

Use Customizable Master 2 (3-Column Chart). Follow the suggestions on p. 7 for customizing and duplicating the master and distributing the copies. Make one copy for each group.

- Have learners take turns asking each other the questions and writing the answers in the chart.
- Ask them to write each group member's name next to his or her answers in the left margin.
- Ask for a few examples from each group for a class discussion.

Grammar Talk

Follow the suggestions on p. 6 for introducing the grammar point.

Answers

- The present verb is in the part of the sentence with *if*.
- Sentences with *if* need a comma when an *if* clause begins the sentence.

Activity A

Ask learners to write the sentences using the information from the Group Chat. First, have them begin their sentences with the *if* clause. Then have learners write the sentences again, this time beginning with the main clause.

Demonstrate the activity by using the model sentence in the student book:

If I want to learn how to program the VCR, Don can teach me.

Don can teach me if I want to learn how to program the VCR.

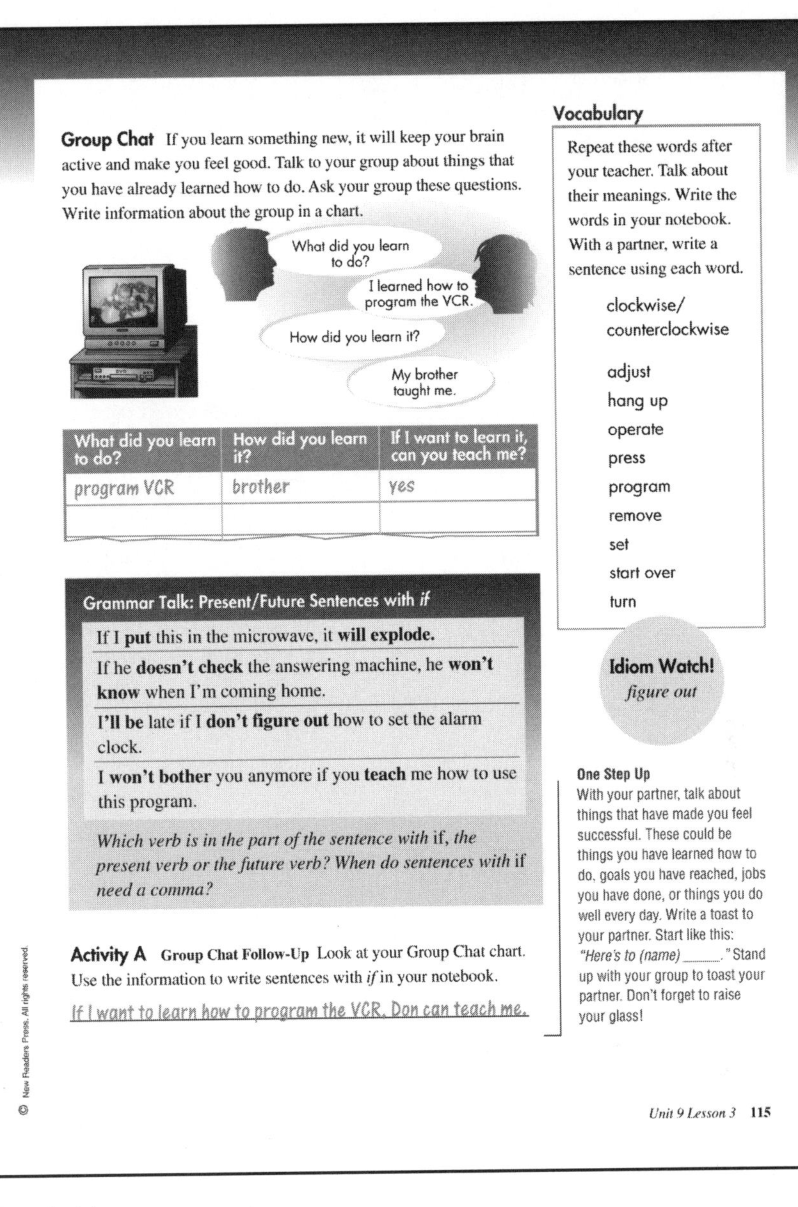

Group Chat If you learn something new, it will keep your brain active and make you feel good. Talk to your group about things that you have already learned how to do. Ask your group these questions. Write information about the group in a chart.

What did you learn to do?	How did you learn it?	If I want to learn it, can you teach me?
program VCR	brother	yes

Grammar Talk: Present/Future Sentences with *if*

If I **put** this in the microwave, it **will explode.**
If he **doesn't check** the answering machine, he **won't know** when I'm coming home.
I'll be late if I **don't figure out** how to set the alarm clock.
I **won't bother** you anymore if you **teach** me how to use this program.

Which verb is in the part of the sentence with if*, the present verb or the future verb? When do sentences with* if *need a comma?*

Activity A **Group Chat Follow-Up** Look at your Group Chat chart. Use the information to write sentences with *if* in your notebook.

If I want to learn how to program the VCR, Don can teach me.

Vocabulary

Repeat these words after your teacher. Talk about their meanings. Write the words in your notebook. With a partner, write a sentence using each word.

clockwise/
counterclockwise

adjust
hang up
operate
press
program
remove
set
start over
turn

Idiom Watch!
figure out

One Step Up
With your partner, talk about things that have made you feel successful. These could be things you have learned how to do, goals you have reached, jobs you have done, or things you do well every day. Write a toast to your partner. Start like this: *"Here's to (name)_____."* Stand up with your group to toast your partner. Don't forget to raise your glass!

Remind learners to put a comma after the *if* clause whenever a sentence begins with *if*.

One Step Up

Have learners discuss with a partner the things that make them feel successful. Then have them write toasts to one another's success.

 Assign Workbook pp. 64–65.

Activity B

Have learners follow the examples in the student book to play a game of round-robin in their groups.

Pronunciation Target

Play the audio or read the sentence in the student book aloud.

- Ask learners to listen for the rising intonation on the final syllable of *computer, cell phone,* and *microwave,* and the falling intonation on the last two syllables of *radio.*
  I have a computer, a cell phone, a microwave, and a radio.
- Remind learners that the normal syllable stress of words may change because when there are two or more words in a list, the intonation pattern takes precedence over the normal syllable stress of the words. For example, for the words above, the normal syllable stress would be as follows:
  computer
  cell phone
  microwave
  radio

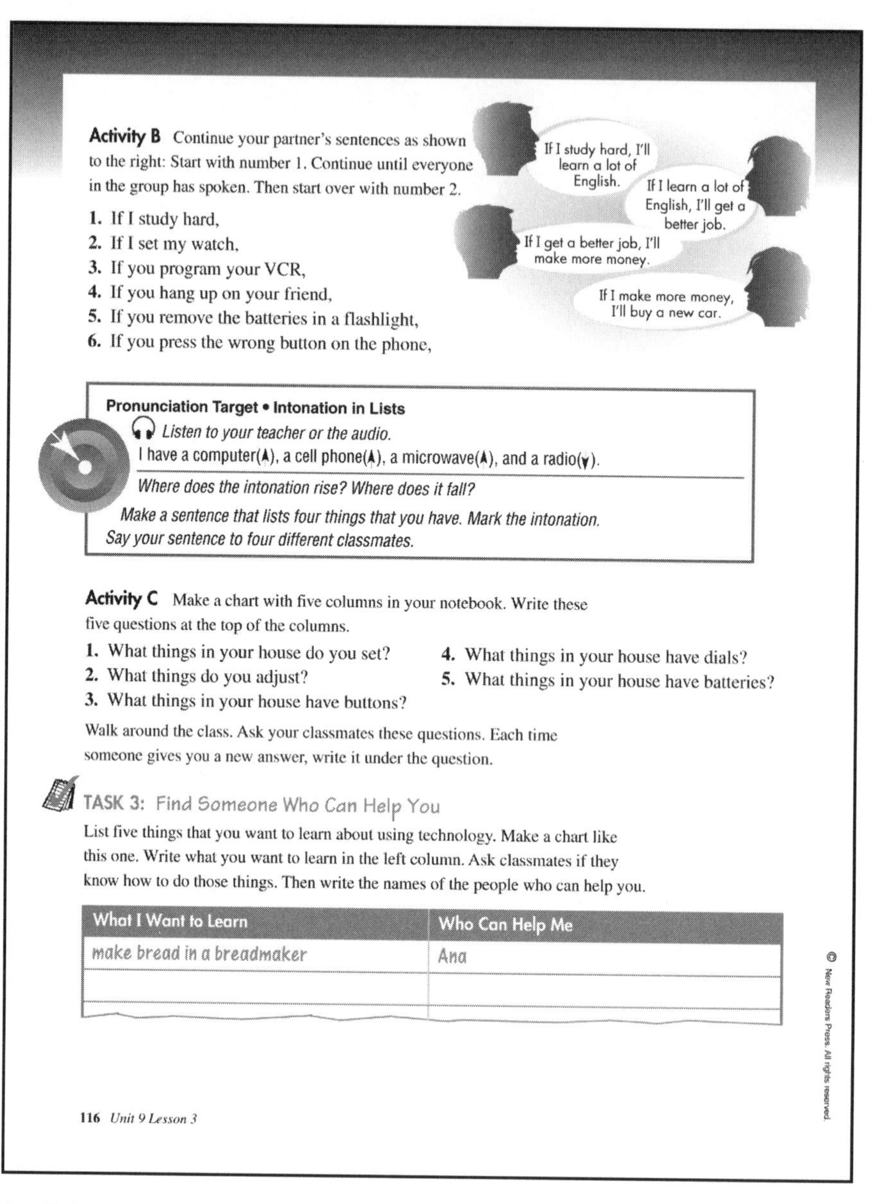

Activity B Continue your partner's sentences as shown to the right: Start with number 1. Continue until everyone in the group has spoken. Then start over with number 2.

1. If I study hard,
2. If I set my watch,
3. If you program your VCR,
4. If you hang up on your friend,
5. If you remove the batteries in a flashlight,
6. If you press the wrong button on the phone,

Pronunciation Target • Intonation in Lists

Listen to your teacher or the audio.

I have a computer(↗), a cell phone(↗), a microwave(↗), and a radio(↘).

Where does the intonation rise? Where does it fall?

Make a sentence that lists four things that you have. Mark the intonation. Say your sentence to four different classmates.

Activity C Make a chart with five columns in your notebook. Write these five questions at the top of the columns.

1. What things in your house do you set?
2. What things do you adjust?
3. What things in your house have buttons?
4. What things in your house have dials?
5. What things in your house have batteries?

Walk around the class. Ask your classmates these questions. Each time someone gives you a new answer, write it under the question.

TASK 3: Find Someone Who Can Help You

List five things that you want to learn about using technology. Make a chart like this one. Write what you want to learn in the left column. Ask classmates if they know how to do those things. Then write the names of the people who can help you.

What I Want to Learn	Who Can Help Me
make bread in a breadmaker	Ana

116 *Unit 9 Lesson 3*

Activity C

Explain that *adjust* in question 2 means "change or modify."

Possible Answers

1. timer, alarm clock, microwave or oven, watch, VCR, automatic coffee maker, lights, sprinklers
2. television picture, heater, air conditioner, stove, microwave or oven temperatures, computer features
3. computer keyboards, doorbell, blender, coffee maker, alarm clock, television, remote controls, home alarm, light controls, phone, recorders, stereo, VCR
4. dial phones, timers, alarm clock, watch, oven/range controls, stereo, CD player, radio, television
5. phone, cell phone, computer, radio, recorder, flashlight, games and toys

Task 3

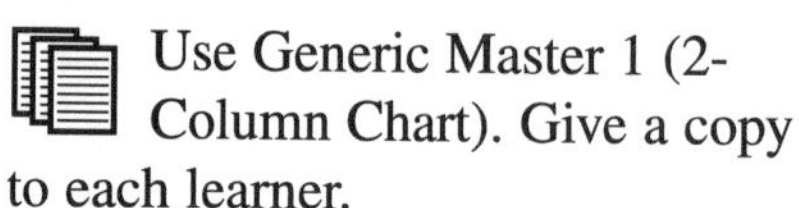

Use Generic Master 1 (2-Column Chart). Give a copy to each learner.

One Step Up

Ask students who actually carry out the task of learning to do something new to report back to the class about what they learned.

Use Unit Masters 67 (Grammar: Fortune Teller) and 68 (Thinking Skill: Possible Solutions) now or at any time during the rest of the unit.

Review Unit Skills

See p. 6 for suggestions on games and activities to review the vocabulary and grammar in this unit.

Unit 9 Project

Learners teach their groups how to use an item of technology.

Get Ready

- Have learners choose a form of technology that they like and know well enough to teach.
- If learners have difficulty finding a subject, suggest items like these: scanner, calculator, digital watch or clock, VCR, cell phone, fax machine, pager, CD player, digital camera, printer, tape recorder, answering machine.

Do the Work

Ongoing Assessment

While learners are completing this activity, circulate to listen to at least five different presentations. Make notes on how well learners perform on these features:

a. Quality of introduction (using four questions from the Unit Project page)
   - 0 = Three or more questions not clearly answered
   - 1 = Two or more questions not clearly answered
   - 2 = Three or more questions clearly answered

b. Quality of step-by-step instructions
   - 0 = steps out of order or hard to follow
   - 1 = steps mostly clear but somewhat hard to follow
   - 2 = steps clear and easy to follow, although language is not perfect

Present

Help learners organize their presentations by offering these opening lines:

- *I'd like to show you how to . . .*
- *Today, I'm going to demonstrate how to . . .*

One Step Down

Do a sample presentation before learners begin theirs.

UNIT 9 Project

Teach How to Use Something

Teach your group how to use an item of technology. Follow these steps:

Get Ready

1. Choose one form of technology from home, work, or community. This should be something that you like.
2. Look at the instructions one student wrote for using his clock radio.

1. To set the time, just press the hour button and the minute button until you get to the right time.
2. To set the alarm, hold down the alarm set button and press the hour button until you get to the right hour. Repeat with the minute button. If you are setting the alarm for the morning, be sure to check that the AM light is showing!
3. To turn up the sound, turn the volume dial clockwise.
4. If you want to sleep a little more after the alarm rings, press the snooze button.
5. Replace the batteries every year. If the power goes out or if you unplug the clock, the batteries will keep the right time on the clock.
6. Turn the tuning dial to get the radio station that you like.

Do the Work

1. Answer the following questions:
   - How long does it take to learn how to use this technology?
   - How often do you use it?
   - What are the costs?
   - Has it made your life easier?
2. Write out the steps for using the item.
3. Bring in the item or draw a picture of it.
4. Practice your presentation with your partner.

Present

First, introduce your topic. You can use the answers to the questions above as your introduction. Then teach your group how to use the item by showing them the parts and explaining the steps.

Be sure to congratulate your partners when they have successfully completed their presentations.

Writing Extension Choose one of these areas of technology: medical, household, or transportation. Write about what changes we might see in that area. Use your imagination. Do the possible changes frighten you? Are you excited about them?

Technology Extra
Find a picture of your item of technology on the Internet. Copy it into a document. Type the steps for using the item.

Writing Extension

Ask learners to refer to the Writing Checklist on p. 125 of their books for final proofreading.

Technology Extra

If possible, demonstrate how to find a picture on the Internet and copy it into a document. Be sure any images used are from "free art" sites and not copyrighted sources.

Assign Workbook p. 66 (Check Your Progress).

Use Unit Master 69 (Unit 9 Checkup/Review) whenever you complete this unit.

Self-Assessment

Give each learner a copy of the Speaking and Listening Self-Checks and the Writing and Reading Self-Checks (Generic Assessment Masters 10–11) when they complete Unit 9. Go over the items together. The completed forms will become part of each learner's portfolio. Have learners compare their responses to what they wrote on these forms at the beginning of the course.

Listening Scripts

This section contains scripts for the content of the audiotape and audio CD for *English—No Problem!* level 3. Pronunciation cues are indicated in square brackets.

Unit 1
Closing the Gap

Lesson 1, page 12
Activities for Young and Old

Mina *[Mee-nuh]* is calling the community center to get information about activities for seniors. Listen to the phone recording and the message that Mina leaves.

Recording: Thank you for calling the Springfield Community Center. If you would like information about our location and hours, press *one.* If you are interested in a schedule of youth activities, press *two.* For adult special-interest classes, press *three.* For a schedule of activities for seniors, press *four.* If you would like to speak to an operator, press *zero,* or stay on the line. To hear these options again, press *five. [beep]*

The Community Center offers activities for seniors, fifty and older, Monday through Saturday. Activities include exercise and craft classes, sports and games, travel opportunities, special-interest clubs, movies, and health lectures. To receive a brochure with a complete schedule of activities, please leave your name and address after the tone. *[beep]*

Mina: Could you please send me a brochure? My name is Mina Patel *[Puh-tell]*, that's P-A-T-E-L. My address is Twenty-four Thirty Ely Avenue, that's E-L-Y. Springfield, Washington, nine-eight-three-two-one. Thank you very much.

Lesson 1, page 13
Pronunciation Target: Linking

Listen to the sentences. Notice the linked sounds.
What time does the park open?
When does this class end?
Do you have activities for seniors?
The center offers aerobics.

Activity A

Listen. Write the sentences that you hear.
Number one. Is the pool open today?
Number two. The ceramics class meets in room 30.
Number three. When does the guitar class end?
Number four. The gymnastics class starts at 10 a.m.
Number five. They offer aerobics.

Listen again and check your writing for correct punctuation. Then underline the linking sounds.
[Repeat dictation of sentences above.]

Lesson 1, page 14
Activity C

Listen. You will hear questions about activities.
Number one. Do you think that aerobics is fun?
Number two. Does the community college offer aquatics?
Number three. Is cheerleading popular in your home country?
Number four. What do people make in a ceramics class?
Number five. Do you know how to play chess?
Number six. Do you like to do crafts?
Number seven. What kinds of lectures are interesting to you?
Number eight. Where can children learn gymnastics?
Number nine. Do many people practice martial arts in your home country?

Listen again and fill in the missing words.
[Repeat questions above.]

Lesson 2, page 17
Pronunciation Target: Contrasting Sounds

th/th [th *as in* thigh/th *as in* thy] ***and*** ch/sh [ch *as in* cherry/sh *as in* sherry]
Listen for the contrasting sounds. Then write the words in the correct column.

those, thin, thick, breathe, brother, tenth

chair, share, she's, cheese, teacher, T-shirt, watch, wash

Unit 2
Smoothing Things Over

Lesson 1, page 25
Pronunciation Target: Stress in Negative versus Affirmative Statements

Listen and repeat.
They were staring.
They weren't staring.
He was whistling.
He wasn't whistling.

Lesson 1, page 26
Activity A

Listen. Write the sentences that you hear. Listen carefully for negative and affirmative statements.
Number one. She was shrugging her shoulders.

Number two. The students weren't slouching in their chairs.
Number three. She was nudging her partner to get his attention.
Number four. He wasn't winking at you.
Number five. The children were staring out the window.

Lesson 2, page 28

Pronunciation Target: Syllable Stress

Listen. Repeat and emphasize the stressed syllables.
I'm sorry.
Excuse me.
Please forgive me.
I want to apologize.
I misunderstood you.

Lesson 3, page 30

In Public

Sarah is telling Koji *[Ko-jee]* and Jae Lee *[Jay Lee, equal accent on both syllables]* about something she did in Tae Kwon Do *[Tie-kwon-doe, equal accent on all syllables]* class that bothered her instructor. Listen to their conversation.

Jae Lee: How's it going, Sarah?
Sarah: Oh, I'm fine, except that I just made a fool of myself in Tae Kwon Do class.
Koji: What did you do?
Sarah: Well, I was just goofing around with my friend in back of the class, you know, talking and laughing. We used to be in the same aerobics class, and we had a lot of fun. But Tae Kwon Do is a martial art. Our teacher wants us to take it seriously.
Jae Lee: What did he do?
Sarah: He talked about appropriate behavior in a martial arts class, and I was so embarrassed! I'm an adult! I should know better.
Koji: You've never taken Tae Kwon Do before, Sarah, so you didn't know what they expected. Give yourself a break!
Jae Lee: Believe me, I know what it's like to make a mistake, too. I think that I offended my neighbor yesterday.
Koji: Oh yeah. Did you talk to her about that?
Jae Lee: Yes, I did. That was good advice. I went over to her house later that day and told her that I hoped I didn't offend her. I explained that it surprised me when she hugged me. She wasn't offended, and she was glad that I came over to talk about it. Maybe you should talk to your teacher, Sarah. It made me feel better!
Sarah: I think I will. And I'm going to apologize!

Unit 3
Better Safe Than Sorry

Page 35

Dictation

Listen. Write the sentences that you hear.
Number one. I want my children to be safe.
Number two. I want my children to learn about water safety.
Number three. I slipped on the floor.
Number four. The floor is slippery.
Number five. They were robbing the bank.
Number six. I saw a robbery.
Number seven. Be careful not to injure yourself.
Number eight. I'm sorry that you have an injury.
Number nine. Keep poisons away from children.
Number ten. Some cleaning substances are poisonous.
Number eleven. I was trying to prevent an accident.
Number twelve. The police help with crime prevention.
Number thirteen. What was the cause of the fire?
Number fourteen. A space heater caused the fire.
Number fifteen. The police arrested the suspect.
Number sixteen. He had a suspicious manner.

Lesson 1, page 37

Pronunciation Target: Endings of Regular Past-Tense Verbs

Listen. Each of these words ends in a different sound:
smashed
bruised
reported

Listen to these past-tense words. What sound does each one end in?
knocked over
smashed
treated
tripped over
bruised
fractured
shocked
spilled
sprained
wounded

Lesson 2, page 40

Pronunciation Target: Stress on Important Words

Listen for the stressed words.
I was scared when the smoke detector went off.
Do not place cords under rugs.

Lesson 2, page 40
Activity A

Listen. Write the sentences that you hear. Then write *T* for *true* or *F* for *false* after each sentence.
Number one. You should put away a ladder after you use it.
Number two. You should unplug the iron before you use it.
Number three. You should lock up medicines after you take them.
Number four. You should close the bedroom door before you go to sleep.
Number five. You should turn heaters off after you go to bed.

Lesson 3, page 42
At the Bus Stop

Officer Murphy asks Miguel questions about the purse-snatching. Listen to their conversation.
Officer Murphy: Can you tell me what happened?
Miguel: Well, two guys asked what time it was, and I said, "Sorry, I don't wear a watch." Then, they asked the same question to an older couple sitting next to me. All of a sudden, the woman was screaming to the man, "Don't give him your wallet! Don't give them anything!" Then, one guy grabbed the woman's purse and they both ran away.
Officer Murphy: Can you describe the suspects? What did they look like?
Miguel: They were young. They looked like teenagers. One was about my height. The other one was taller. I didn't really notice their faces.
Officer Murphy: What were they wearing?
Miguel: They were both wearing jeans. The taller one had a black T-shirt on, and I think the other one was wearing a green jacket.
Officer Murphy: The victims didn't get a good look at them. Were there any other witnesses?
Miguel: Some people were around, but they went inside after it happened.
Officer Murphy: Did anyone try to help?
Miguel: I tried to run after the two guys, but they got away. Then I came back to see if the people were OK.
Officer Murphy: Thank you for your information. You've been a lot of help.

Lesson 3, page 43
Pronunciation Target: Stress Changes in Verbs and Nouns

Listen for the stress.
I sus<u>pect</u> that man.
That man is a <u>sus</u>pect.

Lesson 3, page 44
Activity C

Listen to the 911 *[9-1-1]* emergency call.
Operator: 911 *[9-1-1]*. What is your emergency?
Man: My neighbor fell down our stairs, and he can't move.
Operator: Is he breathing?
Man: Yes, he's crying in pain.
Operator: Is he bleeding?
Man: No, I don't see any blood.
Operator: Okay, don't move him. Stay with him. Tell me your address and give me the major cross streets near your home.
Man: 445 *[four forty-five]* West Palmdale Avenue near Glendale Boulevard and Bell Avenue.
Operator: Stay calm. The ambulance will be right there.

Unit 4
Planning Ahead

Lesson 1, page 49
Pronunciation Target: Choice Intonation

Listen for the stressed words.
Is the deductible <u>five</u> hundred or <u>three</u> hundred?
Is this a <u>new</u> policy or an <u>old</u> policy?

Lesson 2, page 51
Protecting Your Home

An insurance agent is telling Olivia and Victor about the benefits of renters insurance. Listen to their conversation.
Agent: Thank you for meeting with me, Mr. and Mrs. Morales. I have a lot of information for you about insuring your home.
Victor: Oh, we don't have to get insurance. We don't own this house. We're renting.
Olivia: But I asked him to come talk to us about renters insurance, Victor. One of the women at work recommended him.
Victor: I've never heard of renters insurance. Doesn't the landlord have to cover everything?
Agent: Actually, no. Imagine you come home one day to find that someone broke into your apartment and damaged your belongings. Or what if you walked into your living room and found your furniture in several inches of water? Your landlord wouldn't pay for that.
Victor: But our things aren't worth very much.
Agent: Maybe, but would you be able to replace your valuables if they were stolen?
Olivia: No, we wouldn't. Which things are covered?

Agent: Your stereo, furniture, television, jewelry, computer, bicycles, and other belongings are all covered.
Victor: We haven't really had any problems with theft around here.
Agent: That's good. Your premiums are lower if you live in a safe neighborhood. But renters insurance doesn't only cover stolen items. It also covers damage from fire or smoke, lightning, explosions, windstorms, and water damage from plumbing.
Olivia: This is very interesting.
Victor: Yeah, well, we need to talk it over. We'll get back to you.

Lesson 2, page 52
Pronunciation Target: Schwa* [shwah] *in Unstressed Syllables
Listen to the sentences in the grammar box. Underline the *schwa* sounds.
If you want replacement insurance, you must pay more.
You must not forget to pay your premiums on time.
Insurance companies don't have to cover natural disasters.
If someone vandalizes your car, you have to report it immediately.
I've got to keep my valuables in a safe place.

Lesson 2, page 52
Activity A
Listen. Write the sentences that you hear.
Number one. Renters have to get renters insurance.
Number two. You don't have to insure your valuables.
Number three. Insurance companies must not cover flood damage.
Number four. You must not buy insurance if you have a lot of antiques.

Lesson 2, page 53
Activity C
Listen to the conversation. Write the missing words in the blanks.
Olivia: How much does renters insurance cost?
Agent: You've got to think about how much your belongings are worth. For example, if you want thirty thousand dollars' worth of coverage, you have to spend about two hundred dollars a year. For replacement insurance, you must pay a little more.
Olivia: What's replacement insurance?
Agent: The company will pay you enough money to buy new belongings. Without replacement insurance, the company only has to pay what your belongings are worth now. For example, your five-year-old TV may only be worth fifty dollars, but if you have to buy a new one, you'll spend a lot more.

Unit 5
Making Ends Meet

Lesson 1, page 61
Pronunciation Target: Stress on Superlative Adjectives
Listen to the sentences in the grammar box. Notice that the superlative adjectives are stressed.
I want the <u>high</u>est quality video camera that you sell.
I'm looking for the <u>most</u> compact cell phone that you have.
I want the remote control that is the <u>easi</u>est to use.
The tape recorder had the <u>best</u> warranty that I could find.
That store has the <u>worst</u> service in town.

Lesson 2, page 63
Second-Hand Rose
Gail can't afford to buy Tremaine a new dress. Listen to the radio announcement that Gail heard.

Why pay department store prices when you can have the same brand-name clothing at half the cost or less? At Second-Hand Rose, you'll find nearly-new clothing to satisfy all of your fashion needs. We take pride in choosing only the latest styles and top labels. Each item is carefully inspected for quality and appeal. Treat yourself to the coolest clothes, the hottest shoes, and the wildest accessories. You'll find us at the corner of Rose and Magnolia. We're open Wednesday through Sunday, nine to nine. Second-Hand Rose. Just for you, better than new!

Lesson 2, page 64
Pronunciation Target: Reductions
Listen to the sentences in the grammar box. Notice the reduced sound of *used to.*
Tremaine's dress used to *[yoos-tuh]* fit.
This sweater used to *[yoos-tuh]* be pretty, but now it's faded.
I used to *[yoos-tuh]* shop every weekend.
Did you use to *[yoos-tuh]* shop there?

Lesson 2, page 65
Activity C
Gail is returning some sunglasses. Listen.
Salesperson: May I help you?
Gail: Yes. I'd like to return these sunglasses.
Salesperson: What's the problem?

Gail: They're scratched!
Salesperson: Oh, I see. Would you like a refund or an exchange?
Gail: I'd like to exchange them.
Salesperson: No problem. I'll get you some new ones.

Unit 6
Facing Problems Head On

Lesson 1, page 73

Pronunciation Target: Reduction of –ing [ing]
Listen to the sentences in the grammar box. Notice the reduced sound of the I-N-G ending.
Smoking *[smo-ken]* at work is prohibited in some states.
She's worried about going *[go-en]* to jail.
You could receive a fine for smoking *[smo-ken]* marijuana.

Lesson 1, page 74

Activity C
Listen. Write the sentences that you hear.
Number one. They arrested him for drinking in his car.
Number two. Selling alcohol to teenagers is prohibited.
Number three. Bringing drugs across the border is illegal.
Number four. Drinking alcohol was not allowed in the 1930s.
Number five. He got a $300 *[three hundred dollar]* fine for carrying an illegal substance.

Lesson 3, page 78

A Helping Hand
When Leticia sees an ad for a treatment center on television, she realizes that the treatment center might be able to give her advice about helping her neighbor. Listen to the TV ad.

I'd like you to take a moment to think about these questions:

- Is drinking or drug use making your home life unhappy?
- Have you had financial problems as a result of drinking or drug use?
- Do you crave a drink or drugs at a certain time of the day?
- Has drinking or using drugs caused problems at your job or business?
- Do you drink or use drugs to escape from worries or troubles?
- Do you drink or use drugs alone?
- Have you ever had complete loss of memory from drinking or using drugs?

If you have answered YES to any of the above questions, you may need help. And the New Life Substance Abuse Center is here to help you.

We offer both residential and outpatient services to men and women who wish to recover from substance abuse and rebuild their lives. We respect your dignity and your privacy. Most insurance plans will cover the cost of treatment services. Your new life can begin today. Call now.

Lesson 3, page 80

***Pronunciation Target: Disappearing Initial* h**
Listen. Focus on the words that begin with *h.*
Where (h)ave you been all day?
He (h)as been aggressive lately.
They arrested (h)im for driving too fast.

Unit 7
Pitching In

Lesson 1, page 84

Get the Ball Rolling
Marlene is telling her daughter about the park near her house. Listen to their conversation.

Marlene: I can't believe what has happened to the park. It used to be so clean. But now I don't even like to walk there because there's so much trash everywhere. The graffiti in the bathrooms and on the buildings is horrible. It's an eyesore! I want to do something about it.
Jenny: OK Mom. I know what you're thinking. You already have a plan, don't you?
Marlene: Well, I've made a list of all the different jobs that need to be done to clean the park up.
Jenny: Isn't that the city's responsibility?
Marlene: Maybe it is. But I don't want to wait. I want to help clear the litter, get rid of the graffiti, and clean things up.
Jenny: How can we clean the whole park, Mom? It's so big!
Marlene: We need to get the neighbors involved. Maybe if they help us clean the park up, they'll be more interested in keeping it clean. Would you help me get this started?
Jenny: Well, I'm not really sure that we should do this, Mom. Don't we need permission?
Marlene: Yes. You could call Parks & Recreation. Or you could start talking to neighbors.

Jenny: I'll take Parks & Recreation. You visit the neighbors.
Marlene: OK. And maybe you could ask the kids to give us a hand.
Jenny: I can't even get them to clean their rooms!

Lesson 1, page 86

Pronunciation Target: Diphthongs [diff-thawngs]
Listen to the vowel sounds.
enjoy
avoid
now
about

Lesson 3, page 91

Pronunciation Target: Stress on Adjectives
Listen. Notice that the adjective after *for* is clearly stressed.
He has worked here for ten months.
I have known him for many years.

Unit 8
Into Your Own Hands

Page 95

Dictation
Listen. Write the sentences that you hear.
Number one. It is very fulfilling to get a college degree.
Number two. Learning about interesting topics is meaningful.
Number three. Using the Internet is a practical skill.
Number four. Many people change careers more than once.
Number five. I haven't had an opportunity to learn about computers.
Number six. Are you going to enroll next semester?

Lesson 1, page 97

***Pronunciation Target: Reduction of* Be *and* Will**
Listen. Focus on the helping verbs *be* and *will.*
I'm not going to *[gunna]* make excuses.
She's not going to *[gunna]* fall behind in her studies.
They're going to *[gunna]* make studying a priority.
He thinks he'll change his schedule.
She'll try to be consistent.

Lesson 1, page 98

Activity A
Listen to these sentences. You will hear each sentence twice.
Number one. Mary is going to *[gunna]* change her routine.
Number two. My son is going to *[gunna]* organize his notebook.
Number three. Anthony will *['ll]* go to the library to study.
Number four. Jim will *['ll]* study at the same time every day.
Number five. They are going to *[gunna]* catch up on their homework.

Listen again. Write the sentences. *[Repeat dictation of sentences above.]*

Lesson 2, page 100

***Pronunciation Target: Reduction of* Would You *and* Could You**
Listen to the sentences in the grammar box. Notice how the sound changes when *would you* and *could you* are said at normal speed.
[Say the first two sentences slowly and the second two at normal speed.]

Could you please tell me where the reference section is?
Would you please tell me what this word means?
Could you *[couldjoo]* please tell me where the reference section is?
Would you *[wouldjoo]* please tell me what this word means?

Lesson 3, page 102

Back to School
Anthony is enrolling in a class over the telephone. Listen to the instructions for phone registration.

Welcome to the Fredonia Community College Telephone Registration System. Before you register, you will need a copy of your class schedule, your student ID number, and your Personal Identification Number. If you make a mistake, press the star key followed by the pound key. If you are ready to begin, press *nine. [beep]*

Enter your student ID number, followed by the pound key. *[10 beeps]*

Now enter your personal identification number, followed by the pound key. *[5 beeps]*

If you want to add a class, press *two,* followed by the star key. Then press the class number, followed by the pound key. *[7 beeps]*

Do you want to add another class? For "yes," press *nine,* for "no," press *six. [beep]*

To review your schedule, press *five,* followed by the pound key. *[2 beeps]*

Introduction to Child Development, Psychology Three-twenty-one, Monday, seven to ten P.M., James Hall, Room Two-twenty-two, Dr. Powers.

If you want to add another class, press *two.* If you want to drop a class, press *three.*

If you are ready to exit the registration system, press *nine,* followed by the pound key. Do not hang up the phone without pressing the pound key or your registration will not be recorded. *[2 beeps]*

Thank you for using telephone registration.

Unit 9
Keeping Up with the Times

Page 107
Dictation

Listen. Write the sentences that you hear.
Number one. I resist change when I'm afraid.
Number two. I need to confront my fear of speaking English.
Number three. I don't like to deal with my negative feelings.
Number four. I cope well with difficult changes.
Number five. I can adapt to most changes easily.
Number six. If we overcome our fear of change, we will be happier.
Number seven. We need to discuss the pros and cons.
Number eight. I'm looking forward to something that will happen soon.

Lesson 1, page 109
Pronunciation Target: Primary and Secondary Stress

Listen to the sentences. Notice the stress.
I've <u>real</u>ly been working hard.
These ma<u>chines</u> are really outdated.
They've been <u>plan</u>ning the workshop for months.
The <u>work</u>shop is mandatory for Rania *[<u>Rah</u>-nee-yuh].*

Page 110
Activity B

Listen. Write the sentences that you hear. Then, with a partner, write *true* or *false* after each sentence. Correct the false sentences with other learners.

Number one. Rania *[<u>Rah</u>-nee-yuh]* has been looking forward to the workshop.
Number two. Rania has been working for the same company for many years.
Number three. Rania's company is using outdated equipment.
Number four. Rania's company has been training employees with new sewing machines.
Number five. The training on the new machines is mandatory.

Lesson 3, page 114
Three Cheers!

Rania's *[<u>Rah</u>-nee-yuh's]* friends are celebrating her success. Listen to Jason making a toast.

I'd like to make a toast to honor my dear friend, Rania. She has accepted challenges that have changed her life and have had a positive effect on the lives of others. She was able to deal with her fears of new technology at work. She learned a very difficult computerized sewing system. She learned it so well that she was promoted to manager of her department. We are here today to celebrate her success.

I remember when Rania first learned that her company was going to purchase computerized sewing machines. She said, "If I can't learn how to use the new machines, I'll get fired." She was so afraid that she would fail. She had worked on simple machines for so many years. Now, she loves the new machines.

Change is difficult for many of us. It can make us nervous and uncomfortable. It takes us away from what we know best. Yet, change brings opportunities for growth and for discovering new ways of doing things.

Rania is a perfect example of someone who accepted change by learning a new skill. That skill has opened new doors for her. Not only is she the manager, she is also thinking about starting her own business. She wants to make children's clothing and sell it on the Internet.

Rania, we really admire you. You have shown us that anything is possible if you put your mind to it. You've done a wonderful job, and I am proud to be your friend. Here's to your promotion and future business! Three cheers for Rania!

Page 116
Pronunciation Target: Intonation in Lists

Listen for the intonation.
I have a computer↑, a cell phone↑, a microwave↑, and a radio↓.

Working with Maps

Use the maps on pp. 126 and 127 for those opportunities when learners initiate topics about their home countries or about items in the news.

US Map

Use this US map to show learners where their state and city is located. Ask them what state they live in, what other states they know about, and in what states they have friends or relatives.

Here are some other activities you can do with the map:

- Use the map when appropriate to show where the characters in the student book live or where learners think they live.
- Addresses are referred to throughout the student book and workbook in the stories, forms, and elsewhere. Refer learners to the US map at each of these points. Ask them to find the city and/or state on the map.
- Have learners draw conclusions about life in different states based on the location of the state: e.g., north or south, near an ocean or not. Then have them write short, descriptive paragraphs about life in a certain state. Learners can write a paragraph about a state they think they might like to live in, giving reasons why, or a persuasive paragraph to convince someone to move to a certain state.
- Show learners what states are considered parts of a region (the West, the Southwest, the South, the East Coast, the Pacific Coast, etc.).
- Have learners estimate distances between major cities.
- Learners can ask questions or riddles about a city or state, such as the following: Which state is south of Georgia? (Florida) Which state is shaped like a hand? (Michigan) Which is the island state? (Hawaii or Rhode Island) Which states border Mexico? (California, Arizona, New Mexico, Texas)

World Map

Refer learners to the world map when presenting the "Compare Cultures" portion of each unit.

As a quick review of adjectives, quiz learners with these kinds of questions:

- What language do they speak in Russia? (Russian)
- What are people who live in Canada called? (Canadians)

Learners can make up riddles about their home country or other countries they are familiar with. Here are some examples:

- In what large country in South America is Spanish not the official language? (Brazil)
- What country is shaped like a rooster? (China)

Invite learners to draw conclusions about life in different countries based on location of the country. Then have them write short, descriptive paragraphs about life in a certain country. Learners can write a paragraph about a state they think they might like to live in, giving reasons why, or a persuasive paragraph to convince someone to move to a certain state. Other learners could add to the paragraph in a chaining exercise.

Invite learners to bring to class an object or a picture that represents a country and have classmates guess what that country could be.

The US

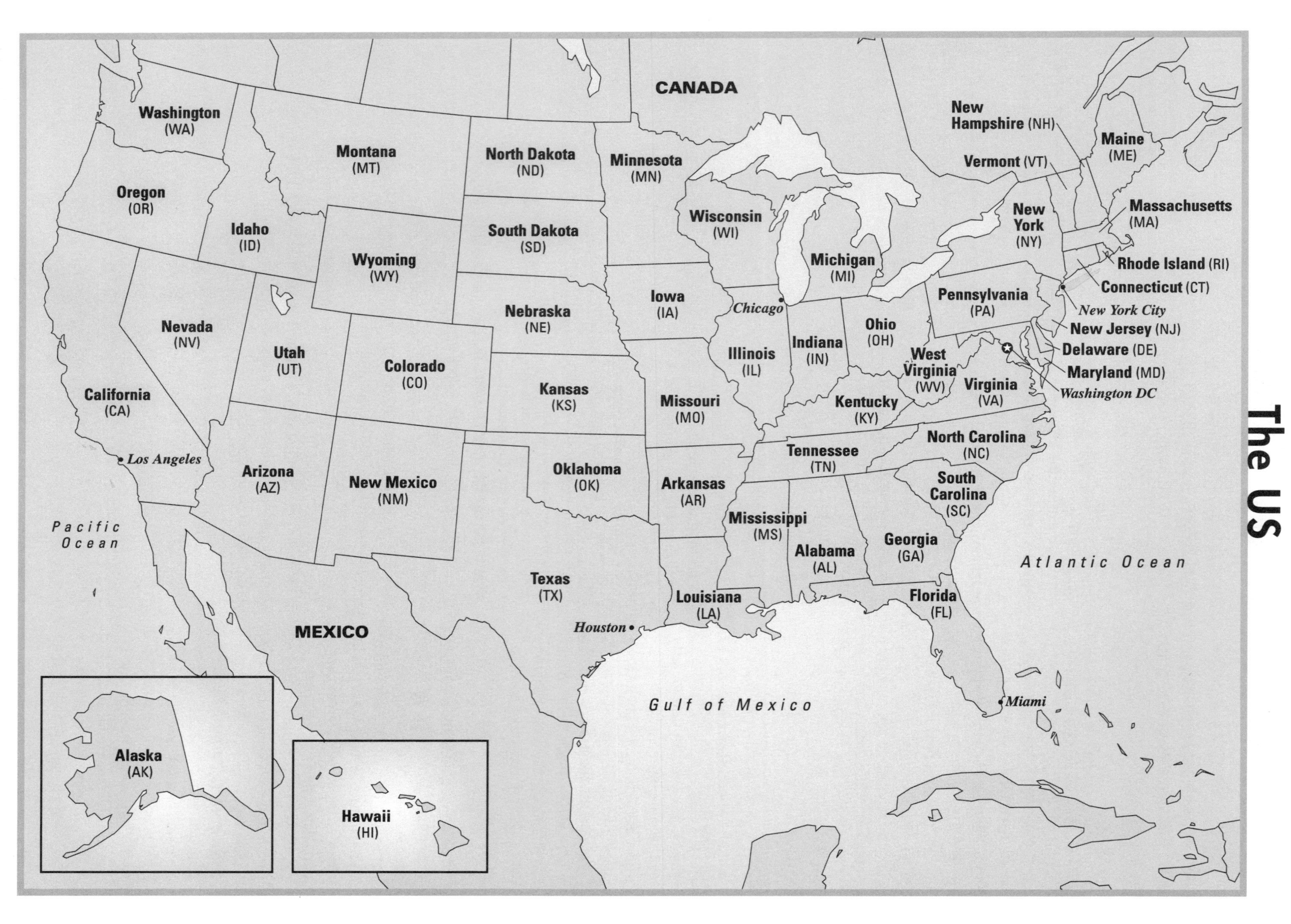

CANADA
Washington (WA)
Montana (MT)
North Dakota (ND)
Minnesota (MN)
New Hampshire (NH)
Maine (ME)
Vermont (VT)
Oregon (OR)
Idaho (ID)
South Dakota (SD)
Wisconsin (WI)
New York (NY)
Massachusetts (MA)
Wyoming (WY)
Michigan (MI)
Rhode Island (RI)
Iowa (IA)
Pennsylvania (PA)
Connecticut (CT)
Nebraska (NE)
Chicago
New York City
Nevada (NV)
Ohio (OH)
New Jersey (NJ)
Utah (UT)
Colorado (CO)
Illinois (IL)
Indiana (IN)
Delaware (DE)
West Virginia (WV)
Maryland (MD)
Kansas (KS)
Virginia (VA)
California (CA)
Missouri (MO)
Kentucky (KY)
Washington DC
North Carolina (NC)
Tennessee (TN)
Los Angeles
Oklahoma (OK)
Arizona (AZ)
New Mexico (NM)
Arkansas (AR)
South Carolina (SC)
Mississippi (MS)
Pacific Ocean
Georgia (GA)
Alabama (AL)
Atlantic Ocean
Texas (TX)
Louisiana (LA)
Florida (FL)
Houston
MEXICO
Miami
Gulf of Mexico
Alaska (AK)
Hawaii (HI)

The World

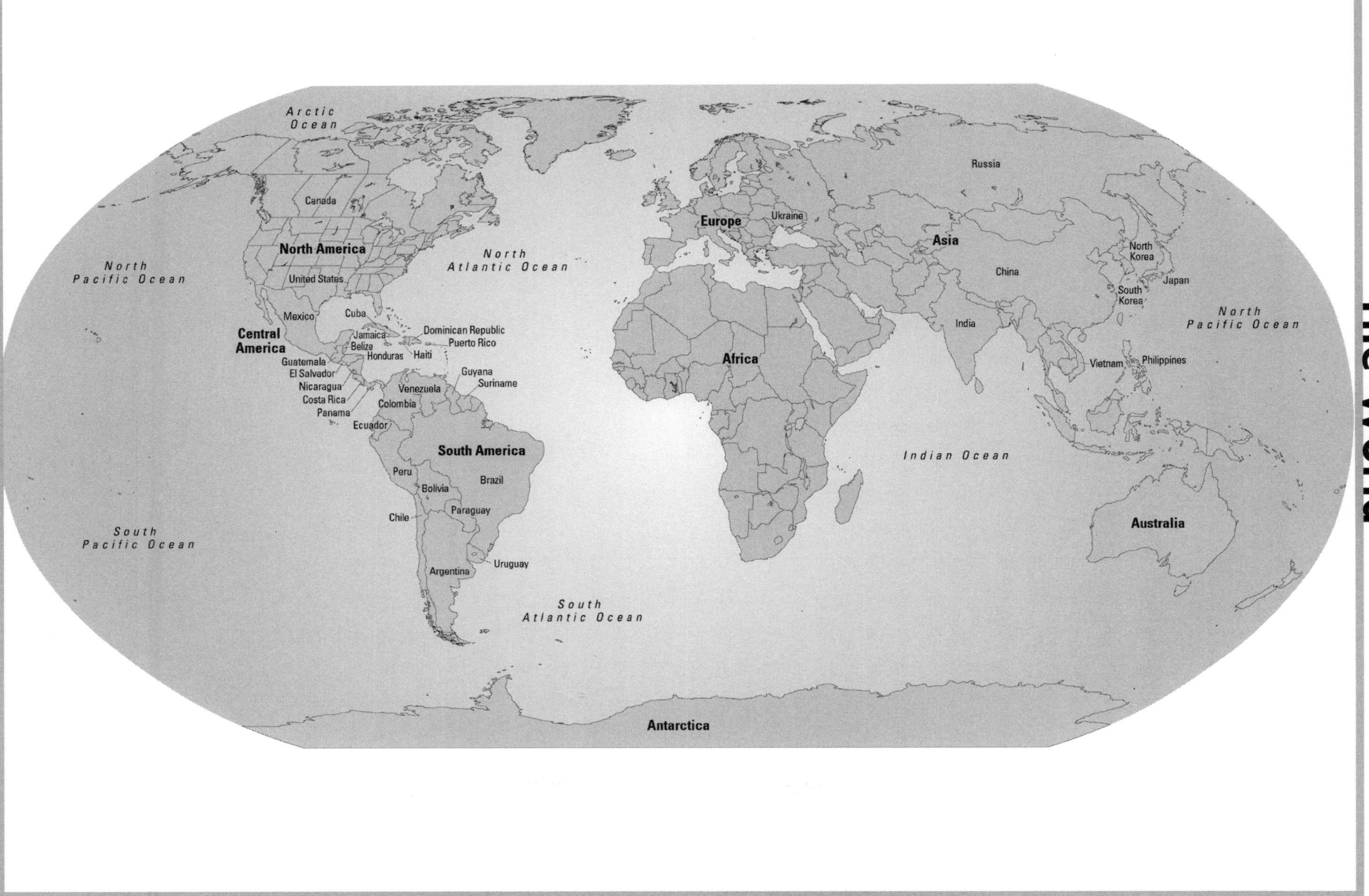

Arctic Ocean
Canada
North America
United States
North Pacific Ocean
Mexico
Cuba
Central America
Jamaica
Belize
Honduras
Haiti
Dominican Republic
Puerto Rico
Guatemala
El Salvador
Nicaragua
Costa Rica
Panama
Venezuela
Colombia
Ecuador
Guyana
Suriname
South America
Peru
Bolivia
Brazil
Paraguay
Chile
Argentina
Uruguay
South Pacific Ocean
North Atlantic Ocean
South Atlantic Ocean
Europe
Ukraine
Africa
Russia
Asia
China
India
North Korea
South Korea
Japan
North Pacific Ocean
Vietnam
Philippines
Indian Ocean
Australia
Antarctica

Irregular Verbs

Past-tense verbs are reviewed in Units 2 and 3. As learners work on the various activities using the past tense, remind them they can refer to this Appendix page for the irregular past forms.

Use flash cards to practice irregular past tense forms:

- Make flash cards for the verbs, with the present-tense form on the front and the irregular past-tense form on the back.
- If learners finish activities early, they can use the cards with their partners. One partner reads the verb, and the other has to give the past-tense form.

Practice using the irregular past-tense forms with this activity:

- Write this sentence on the board: *What did you ___ yesterday?*
- Ask learners to complete the question with one of the verbs in the list.
- Then have the learners' partners write responses. (e.g. *I bought food yesterday.*)
- Reverse the roles and repeat the activity.

Irregular Verbs

present	past	present	past
be	was	lay off	laid off
beat	beat	leave	left
break	broke	lose	lost
buy	bought	make	made
catch up	caught up	misunderstand	misunderstood
deal	dealt	overcome	overcame
do	did	pay	paid
drive	drove	put	put
eat	ate	ride	rode
fall	fell	run	ran
find	found	say	said
fit	fit	see	saw
forbid	forbade	send	sent
forgive	forgave	set	set
get	got	spend	spent
give	gave	steal	stole
go	went	take	took
hang up	hung up	teach	taught
have	had	tell	told
hurt	hurt	think	thought
keep	kept	wear	wore
know	knew	write	wrote

124 *Irregular Verbs*

Writing Checklist and Metric Chart

You may want to have learners use this checklist to review each piece of writing they do in the student book and workbook.

You can also have students do peer reviews in pairs, checking off points after reading a partner's writing.

Doing both of the above activities together is a good way to train learners to internalize a method for checking any piece of writing they do.

Those learners continuing on in their studies can benefit from frequent practice in writing simple paragraphs on a variety of topics. This will help them develop the skills needed to write a GED essay or develop the writing fluency needed to move into higher education. Descriptive paragraphs are the easiest type of writing for learners to do. You can provide a short list of topics related to the theme of a unit and have them choose one. Here are some examples:

- My oldest friendship
- Someone I admire
- A dream come true
- An exciting sports event
- A difficult decision

Writing Checklist and Metric Chart

- ❑ Did I take notes about my ideas before I started writing?
- ❑ Did I write a main idea at the beginning of the paragraph?
- ❑ Did I give details to explain my main idea?
- ❑ Do all my details relate to the main idea?
- ❑ Did I check my verbs for correct tense?
- ❑ Did I check for subject-verb agreement?
- ❑ Did I use complete sentences?
- ❑ Did I capitalize the first word of each sentence?
- ❑ Did I end every sentence with a period, question mark, or exclamation point?
- ❑ Did I check my spelling?
- ❑ Is my handwriting neat and easy to read?

METRIC CONVERSIONS

To Convert	To	Multiply by
LENGTH		
meters	feet	3.281
kilometers	miles	0.62
LIQUID		
liters	quarts	1.057
liters	gallons	.0264
WEIGHT		
grams	ounces	0.0353
kilograms	pounds	2.2046
TEMPERATURE		
Celsius	Fahrenheit	multiply by 1.8, then add 32

To Convert	To	Multiply by
LENGTH		
feet	meters	.03048
miles	kilometers	1.609
LIQUID		
quarts	liters	0.946
gallons	liters	3.785
WEIGHT		
ounces	grams	28.35
pounds	kilograms	0.4536
TEMPERATURE		
Fahrenheit	Celsius	subtract 32, then divide by 1.8

Metric Conversion Table

You may wish to create simple conversion problems using the characters and situations from each unit. For example, for Unit 1, you might provide the following problems:

Mina's daughter Annie weighs 51 kilos, or kilograms. Approximately how many pounds does she weigh?

Mina's father's home is 2 kilometers from the community center. If he goes there three times a week for a class, approximately how far will he drive altogether in miles?

Once learners show proficiency in converting measurements from one system to the other, you can give them problems in which they convert one US measure to another. Here is an example for Unit 3:

As part of his plan to make his home safe from fires, Miguel bought a ladder that measured 114 inches. How many feet high was his ladder?

While realistically speaking, learners will most often have an approximate understanding of the metric measure and want or need to express it in US measure, you may also want to provide problems that require the reverse conversion, since learners may read or hear a description in US measure and need to do a mental conversion in order to fully understand the meaning of this input.

You can make several of these problems part of your learners' study of every unit, or even every lesson.

After learners become accustomed to doing these conversions, you can ask them to create their own story problems to share with a partner, a group, or all learners.

Finally, learners can write problems for which the context is now an application of a story issue to their own lives.

List of Grammar Terms

adjective – a word that describes a noun or a pronoun: *a **tall** tree, he is **handsome**.*

adverb – a word that tells more about a verb, adjective, or another adverb: *I **often** go shopping, a **very** tall tree, he talks **extremely** fast.*

article – a word used to mark a noun: ***a** boy, **an** apple, **the** cat.*

base form – the simplest form of a verb: *think, go, play.* Also called simple form.

clause – a group of words that contains a subject and a verb, and that forms part of a sentence: *Before I go to bed, I turn the heater off.*

comparative adjective – an adjective with *-er* on the end or *more* in front of it: *faster, more compact.*

compound sentence – a sentence consisting of two main clauses connected by *and, or,* or *but: June thinks that all babies are pretty, and so do I.*

direct speech – the use of somebody's exact words. In writing, quotation marks indicate direct speech: *He said, "I hate saying goodbye!"*

future – a verb tense that expresses expected action or a condition in the future. Formed by combining *will* or *be* + *going to* + simple form of the verb. ***I'll study** tomorrow. **I'm going to study** tomorrow.*

gerund – a verb used as a noun; formed by adding *-ing* to the simple form of the verb: *She's worried about **leaving** home.*

infinitive – a base verb form that is preceded by *to: I would like **to invite** him to my party.*

modal – a helping verb that adds to the meaning of a main verb: *can, could, may, must, have to, will, would. You **must** be on time.*

noncount noun – a noun that represents a group or type of item, such as *coffee, juice, fruit.* These nouns do not take plural forms. They are also called uncountable or mass nouns.

noun – a word used to name a person, place, thing, or idea. *My **brother** is from **Portland.** He values **honesty.***

object – a noun, noun phrase, or noun clause that receives the action of a verb: *I hit **the ball.***

past continuous/past progressive – a verb tense that expresses an action that began and ended in the past. It's often used with the simple past to show that something was happening at the time another action occurred. *She **was working** when she got the news.*

plural – a noun form that indicates more than one of a kind; formed by adding *-s, -es,* or *-ies* to the noun: *sweaters, boxes, babies.* Some nouns have irregular plurals: *men, women, children;* and some do not take plural forms: *money, heat, furniture.*

preposition – a word that shows the relationship between a noun and another part of a sentence: *in, on, under, over, around, about, with, for, to. I'm looking **for** a job.*

present continuous/present progressive – a verb tense that expresses an action that is happening at the present time. *Sierra **is sleeping** right now.*

present perfect – *have* or *has* with a past participle: refers to an action or situation that has a strong connection to the present. Often used with *for* and *since. Grace **has played** tennis for three years* (she still plays).

present perfect continuous – *have been* or *has been* with a present participle, used to refer to past events that continue in the present: *Rania **has been sewing** for many years.*

pronoun – a word that takes the place of a noun, such as *he, her, myself, it.* Most pronouns have different forms, depending on their use.

simple past – a verb tense that expresses a single, completed action or situation in the past. Formed by adding *-ed* to a regular verb, or by using the irregular past form. *Last night, we **saw** a full moon. We **stared** at it for a long time.*

simple present – a verb tense that expresses an action or situation that is habitual, is true now, or is always true. *She **smokes** a lot. I **go** to school. Glass **is** breakable.*

singular – a noun form that indicates one of a kind; *computer, week, school.*

subject – a noun, pronoun, noun phrase, or noun clause that performs an action expressed by the main verb. In English, the subject almost always comes near the beginning of a sentence. ***James** plays basketball. **He** is good.*

subject-verb agreement – necessity for verbs to agree with their subjects within a sentence. Normally, a singular or noncount noun takes a singular verb: *Margaret always walks to work; Brown rice is healthy.* A plural noun takes a plural verb: *My shoes are dirty.*

superlative adjective – an adjective with *-est* on the end or *most* in front of it: *easiest, most compact.*

verb – a word that expresses action or existence. *Samuel **takes** long naps; Madison **is** my niece.*

Topics

Grammar and Pronunciation